Penguin Education

Decisions, Organizations and Society

Edited by F. G. Castles,
D. J. Murray and D. C. Potter

Decisions, Organizations and Society

Selected Readings

Edited by
F. G. Castles, D. J. Murray and D. C. Potter
at The Open University

Penguin Books in association with
The Open University Press

Penguin Books Ltd, Harmondsworth,
Middlesex, England
Penguin Books Inc, 7110 Ambassador Road,
Baltimore, Md 21207, USA
Penguin Books Australia Ltd,
Ringwood, Victoria, Australia

First published 1971
This selection copyright © The Open University, 1971
Introduction and notes copyright © The Open University, 1971

Made and printed in Great Britain by
Hazell, Watson & Viney Ltd, Aylesbury, Bucks
Set in Linotype Times

Contents

Editors' Note

This book is the result of a collective effort. For the three editors it has been a joint enterprise, but there are others to whom more is owed than is common in the preparation of a book. The book has grown out of the planning and development of a course at the Open University designed for second-level students of the social sciences, and though intended as a book that is valid and worthwhile independently of the course, nevertheless it owes a great deal to the united effort of those who have developed the course on Decision Making in Britain:

J. P. Barber	C. Haslam
A. T. Blowers	A. T. A. Learmonth
J. R. Blunden	J. Melling
D. Boswell	M. Philps
B. Connors	L. C. Power
D. Corcoran	J. Radcliffe
C. Cuthbertson	F. Sealey
C. Falkner	R. Thomas
R. Finnegan	L. Wagner

Without the ably executed secretarial work of Marie Hawley and Maureen Harriss the manuscript could not have been prepared, let alone been ready within the limited time available, and the editors wish to express their appreciation to them. They wish also to acknowledge the considerable contribution made by Leslie Lonsdale-Cooper and Roger Lubbock, Director of Publishing, and Coordinating Editor respectively in the Open University, to preparing the manuscript and handling arrangements for its publication.

Introduction

The focus of these Readings is the area of knowledge at which the concepts of decision and power intersect. A decision is a conscious choice between at least two possible courses of action. Power is an omnibus concept which refers generally to those social relations which control men and women. Therefore, these Readings are concerned primarily with the process by which the multiple possibilities of human activity are reduced by conscious choice to a single course of action with control consequences for persons in an arena of social relations.[1]

Countless arenas in which choice and power are involved can, in principle, be identified in modern society. Two ladies meet in a dark street, whereupon one lady deliberately stops, produces a pistol and demands money from the second lady. There is decision (the first lady could have chosen to walk on down the street), and there is power (the second lady's behaviour is controlled as a result of her relation with the first lady). This example falls, by definition, within our focus of interest. If, however, the same two ladies meet in the same dark street, whereupon the first lady deliberately chooses not to produce her pistol and instead walks on down the street, then there is decision, but there is no power because there is *no relationship of control*. Strictly speaking, then, this example falls outside our central concern. The example of the two ladies serves to clarify our definitions. However, examples of decisions more directly relevant to the focus of these Readings are those decisions, as defined, which have consequences for large numbers of people in organizations or in society generally. The British Government introduces

1. Two approaches to decision making need to be distinguished. Normative decision theory, as developed particularly in statistics, is concerned with the way a rational decision maker should analyze a problem and reach an optimum solution given a particular situation and specified information. Descriptive theory is concerned with how decisions are made in practice and also with what decision-making structures operate. These Readings are concerned with descriptive theory and do not seek to introduce normative decision theory.

legislation, subsequently enacted into law, to create the National Health Service. The arena is the entire country, in which there is decision (that particular scheme as opposed to others or none at all) and there is power (polity and society interact, with results binding on both). Shell Oil raises the price of petrol. There is decision (a choice is made between several alternative ways of increasing or maintaining profits) and there is power (the decision has control consequences for consumers despite manifest or latent opposition). Examples could be multiplied endlessly.

Decision making is so pervasive in society that it has attracted the attention of many academic disciplines, particularly in the social sciences. The concept is used, loosely or precisely as the case may be, in most social science literature, as well as in the press and everyday speech. We are required, therefore, to reduce this huge subject to manageable proportions, and this requires that a selection be made. The Readings we have selected are designed specifically to illustrate three distinct yet related perspectives on the subject, with emphasis on theory rather than concrete case studies.

The first is to look at the process by which individuals and a single collectivity make a decision. Considerable work has been done in recent years on these lines, notably by psychologists and economists on individual decision making, and on larger collectivities by organization theorists. A common point of departure is to chop the decision-making process into stages, and one then analyzes the features of each stage and their interconnection. A central interest is to identify the many constraints which bear upon, and influence, the behaviour of the decision makers. The major emphasis of our approach is on behaviour and process by individuals and within organizations.

The second perspective is to step outside, as it were, individuals and single organizations and to examine patterns of decision making involving several organizations or collectivities over a period of time. From this point of view, one organization's decision is another organization's constraint. Inter-organizational conflict becomes of central concern in this approach. There are similarities with the first approach, for conflict also occurs within single organizations. There are differences also; for example, conflict between organizations tends to be more public and there may be comparatively few formal rules governing the conflict. Characteristic of this approach is the examination of major issue areas in which pressure groups, political parties, labour unions, formal organizations and other collectivities interact continuously on behalf of their separate interests. Greater emphasis is placed in this approach, as compared with the first one, on decision content and objectives.

The third perspective singled out for attention in this book is perhaps unusual in the sense that it figures rarely in decision-making literature, at least in the form in which we present it. It is to step even further outside and ask: how are whole societies structured in consequence of the major patterns of decision making discernible within them? And are whole societies structured in such a way that certain groupings in them regularly benefit from the decision-making process more than others? This approach has to do with what men who have systematically analyzed whole societies believe to be the case about the distribution of power. Marx, for example, reached the conclusion after careful study that many societies in his time were structured so that a ruling class, in conflict with subject classes, consistently made the important decisions for its own benefit. Wright Mills looked carefully at the structure of American society in the 1950s and concluded that the decisions that matter were regularly made by a power elite. Dahl looked carefully at the same society and reached a different conclusion. Our ground for including several different models depicting the distribution of power is that since men and women are capable of the conscious reflection that makes decisional choice possible they are also capable of reflecting on the consequences of the decisions made for or by them, and deciding in terms of their own values whether or not they like what they see.

Part One
Individual and Organizational Decision Making

Decision making is a pervasive activity in society. As the introduction makes clear, this book directs attention to the point where decision and power meet; it concentrates therefore on particular decisions and structures of decision making. Yet, while it is orientated towards particular decisions, the basic processes by which decisions are made have common features, whether it is the British Prime Minister deciding to recommend a dissolution of Parliament or the man on Epsom Downs deciding to put his money on one horse rather than another, or alternatively, whether it is the decision-making process in the Department of Education and Science or in Unilever, and the purpose of this first part, therefore, is to introduce certain of the ideas and some of the understanding that have been developed about the common elements in decisions and decision making.

Making a decision may sound on the face of it like a single act but different stages in the basic process can be distinguished. Whatever the decision, it can be analyzed in terms of a series of subordinate activities, and one way of formulating these stages is that set out and explained by Scott, who characterizes them as the search process, formulation of objectives, selection of alternatives and evaluation of outcomes. All this, however, assumes two things: first that there is a problem recognized, and 'detecting the problem is as important as finding the answer' (Hilgard, 1959). Lindblom's brief extract states the difficulty succinctly. Problems are not self-evident, they have to be perceived, it involves a judgement to establish what a problem is, and in identifying a problem in particular terms, limitations are straightaway placed on the nature of the decisions taken about it. Secondly, an implicit assumption may be that only positive decisions are important, and this is to overlook the significance, which Barnard indicates, of avoiding a decision or taking a negative one.

A statement of the different stages in taking a decision serves simply to clear the ground for accounts of what occurs in practice when decisions are made. In investigating this, social scientists have, as Simon illustrates, started from the assumptions built into different branches of the social sciences about how decisions were made by individuals, groups, organizations and societies. In much of this writing there has been built in a model of man as a decision maker, who is not only wholly rational in his behaviour, but who is supplied with a complete range of information and has the computational capacity to exploit this information in order to discover the best possible course of action. Such a model of individual decision making both Simon and Audley, in their different ways, show to conflict with findings in psychology and sociology. Actual decision making by individuals is presented by them as being well removed from the ideal non-empirical one assumed in much theoretical writing.

While decision making takes place wherever choices are to be made, its characteristics differ according to the level at which it occurs. It is commonly represented that the general characteristics of decision making by individuals, groups, complex organizations and the state each have peculiarities that make it necessary to distinguish these four levels. The nature of certain of the differences between levels is discussed by Barnard and Downs, and is implicit in Brown. Each of these distinguishes decision making by individuals from that by complex organizations, and Downs and Brown in particular emphasize the extent to which decisions in large organizations belong to the organization as a whole, and are not attributable to any one individual.

The extent to which the decisions of an organization are made by the whole organization distinguishes decision making at this level from that of an individual, and provides the starting point for an investigation of organizational decision making. As Downs, Brown, and Strauss indicate, decisions are not made by a single individual – the boss, the minister, the adminstrator – they are made by the whole organization as a result of a complex process within the organization and surrounding it in the environment. The negotiations between individuals, the communication system, the formal rules – these and other factors interact to produce the decisions of the organization.

While certain points about decision making are common to all complex organizations, there is considerable discussion both about how far the consistency in decision-making processes stretches between different sorts of organizations, and about which approach is most helpful. The contributions by Downs, Brown and Strauss illustrate different positions on these issues. Downs starts from the standpoint that it is possible to generalize about decision making across all complex organizations; Brown, while drawing on research in a wide range of organizations, illustrates general processes and applies knowledge to understanding the British civil service, and in so doing draws attention to what is particular to this organization. Strauss, in contrast, treats the hospital as a distinct case though he raises the issue of whether the generalizations have a wider applicability.

Similarly, there are contrasts in the approaches used in these contributions. Both Downs and Brown employ an approach which concentrates on the flow of information and the way this affects the decisions of the organization : both use a communication model for understanding decision making in organizations. Strauss and his associates, on the other hand, focus on interactions between people in formulating their model of a negotiated order in the hospital. Approaching their organization in this way, they regard the nature of the order and the whole character of the institution as being fashioned by the interpersonal agreements that are, as they put it, 'continually being terminated or forgotten, but also as continually being established, renewed, reviewed, revoked, revised'. Downs and Brown have interpretations and emphases that differ, but they start from a common standpoint and adopt a similar approach, and these are distinct from those adopted by Strauss and his associates.

Decision making by individuals and organizations is an ongoing activity in society but only some decisions involve an exercise of power, and only some of these are important for society. Nevertheless, knowledge about decision making as a general process, whether undertaken by individuals or in organizations, is significant for an understanding of decision making in society, both because it helps to elucidate the processes involved in making those decisions that are important, and because it implicitly questions some of the assumptions about how decisions are made, which are inevitably built into theories about the decision-making process in society as a whole. An interpretation of decision making in society founded on the rational conception of the individual criticized by Simon will contrast with one founded on his conception of a satisficer, as will one which builds up from organizations regarded as goal-seeking institutions, and understood through the medium of a communication model, contrast with an organization understood in terms of Strauss's negotiated order.

References

HILGARD, E. R. (1959), 'Creativity and problem solving', in H. H. Anderson (ed.), *Creativity and its Cultivation*, Harper & Row.

1 W. G. Scott

Decision Concepts

Excerpts from 'Decision concepts', in W. G. Scott, *Organisation Theory*, Irwin, 1967, pp. 219–26.

Regardless of the level of decision making, the process involves certain common ingredients (see for example Archer, 1964, Thompson, 1965). They are as follows:

1. A search process to discover goals.
2. The formulation of objectives after search.
3. The selection of alternatives (strategies) to accomplish objectives.
4. The evaluation of outcomes.

The search process

In the search process, an individual or organization undertakes to find a new goal or goals because of dissatisfaction with outcomes within an existing goal structure. The present payoff structure growing out of the present set of goals is, in other words, less than an individual's (or organization's) level of aspiration.

The search process is evoked by a low level of satisfaction as Fig. 1 shows. The lower the level of satisfaction the more intensive is the search for new goals. The degree of satisfaction depends on the outcomes (expected value of reward) as does the level of aspiration. Satisfaction is achieved when payoffs correspond to the level of aspiration. However, since favourable experience with outcomes from goals often raises the level of aspiration, a new discrepancy might again appear between rewards and aspiration level setting the search process in motion again.

Formulation of objectives

Objectives, whether personal or organizational, are values which are desired by the decision maker. Usually, it is useful as a first approximation to view the decision maker as attempting to maximize or minimize values such as profits, losses, costs, salary, rate of advancement, or output. This approach, based largely on traditional economic theory of rationality, has been

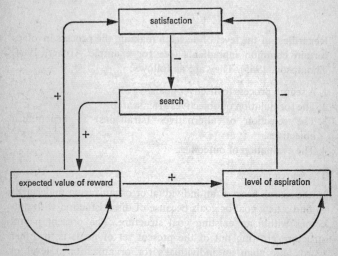

Figure 1 From March and Simon (1958, p. 49). Used with permission.

criticized. Simon (1959), for instance, introduces the concept of 'satisficing' which he offers as a substitute for the maximization concept [. . .]

We can conceive of goals, out of this framework, as 'states of tension' providing the motivation impetus to behavior (see Gore, 1964). There is little in psychological theory to suggest that outcomes have to be maximized in order to reduce or even eliminate the intensity of the drive. Indeed the theory of aspiration indicates adaptive flexibility whereby goals may be raised, lowered, or changed in the light of experience.[1]

1. The adaptation of organizational goals in the face of changing environment is developed by Dent (1959).

The theory of value maximization proposes an objective predictive model of behavior within a very narrow framework of adaptive modes. Most of the constraints of this model result from the rigid assumption regarding the relationships among economic variables. Satisficing, according to Simon, allows a richer model of adaptation which is closer to a more natural (realistic) explanation of decision behavior. For example, simply recognizing the lack of information necessary for rational decisions makes satisficing a more acceptable explanatory device.

Strategies

Once a goal, or hierarchy of goals, has been established, the decision maker prepares a repertory of alternatives for achieving his aims. For any given alternative, and there may be an infinite range of possibilities, is associated a decision system comprised of an outcome, a probability, and a value. With four alternatives, for example, there is:

$$A_1 \qquad O_1 \qquad P_1 \qquad V_1$$
$$A_2 \qquad O_2 \qquad P_2 \qquad V_2$$
$$A_3 \qquad O_3 \qquad P_3 \qquad V_3$$
$$A_4 \qquad O_4 \qquad P_4 \qquad V_4$$

In each case a payoff (outcome) is computed, a probability of payoff occurring arrived at, and the subjective value of the strategy decided.

As an illustration let us suppose a person, Mr X, is bitten by a dog and must make a decision to have rabies shots or not. The shots, as X knows, are painful, inconvenient, expensive, and even dangerous because of the remote chance that death might occur from them. The experience of having shots cast against the possibility of dying from rabies represents extremes on X's value scale.

Given these alternatives, X must have *information* on probabilities and outcomes in order to decide. Assume a dog is caught that X is fairly sure, but not positive, is the culprit. The presence of doubt about the dog is crucial. If there is certainty in this respect, and the dog is in custody, then the observation period will definitely establish the health of the animal. Based upon what we take as objective probability data, here X's decision tree is given in Fig. 2.

If X is optimistic he will not undergo shots because the ultimate outcome, the probability of death, is remote in either situation of right or wrong dog. X reasons that in nine chances out of ten the dog is the correct one, and since the dog under observation is a neighborhood pet the probability of its being rabid is very low. And even in the unlikely event the dog that actually did the biting got away the chance that it is rabid is

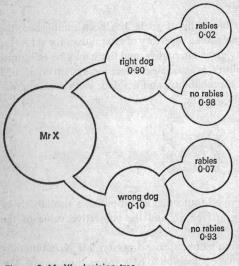

Figure 2 Mr X's decision tree

still quite low based on experience factors in the area. Thus according to X's value system incurring the small risk of rabies is more desirable than pain associated with the shots. Thus he chooses the no-shot alternative.

Instead of X, let us assume a Mr Y is in the identical situation, bitten one half hour later by the same dog. But Y is a pessimist. While the same probability information is available to Y, in his eyes a chance of one in ten error about the dog and the higher risk of rabies among strays leads him according to his value scale to take shots and endure the pain to secure positive protection. Several important concepts are derived from this simple example.

Risk

The nature of risk is such that the probability of an event occurring or not occurring can be assigned. Both X and Y we assume are confronted by the same objective probability data. But X thinks that since the chance of rabies is trifling he avoids the shots. Y perceives the same probability but he still does not want to run even this small chance and so he acts accordingly. This differential behavior does not stem from the probability data *per se*. Rather, it is a function of the value systems of X and Y respectively.

This case is analogous to another which has to do with the probability of being killed in an air crash on a commercial carrier. The objective probability data, which has been computed and is available to all, is very much against such a calamity happening. Yet there are people who refuse to fly for the very reason that they fear a crash. They choose other modes of transportation, like driving, even though the danger of accident with injury or death is higher. You might say this is not rational. But there is no claim, of course, that values are rational in any objective sense.

Some might argue that optimism or pessimism is reflected in probability data itself. That is, an optimistic person would say, 'I think it is a 90 per cent chance we got the right dog, *in the absence of any concrete probability data to the contrary*.' Whereas the pessimistic person would be more doubtful feeling the chances were only 50–50. Now while the resulting decisions of X and Y are likely to be identical to those postulated in the face of objective data, the line of reasoning is quite different. Under the conditions which we have just stated, X and Y are mixing value data and probability data. This is wholly erroneous in risk analysis, but is quite appropriate in the discussion of uncertainty.

Uncertainty

The nature of uncertainty is such that it is not possible to assign a probability to the occurrence of an event. This is because of either lack of information about the event, or the nonrepeatable character of the event, or both. Archer sums it up this way:

Uncertainty in decision theory describes all shades of knowledge of the probability distribution of the states of nature ranging from near accurate estimates based upon objective experience to an extreme case in which no knowledge exists. It is this type of model which most frequently applies to management decision. Uncertainty varies from the extreme of no information up to but excluding the condition of risk in which the probability of the states of nature is known. Short of risk conditions, exists uncertainty (1964).

Selection of strategies under uncertainty conditions requires the application of judgement, opinion, belief, subjective estimates of the situation, plus whatever objective data is available. The estimates of probability and payoff (P and O) become hopelessly dependent upon the values of the decision maker. The concept of 'subjective probability' is introduced into uncertainty situations as a shorthand notation that a strategy has been selected using decision criteria which are not entirely rational. Hence, subjective probabilities regarding strategies may vary among decision makers confronting the same situation. In short, under risk we can separate O and P from V. We cannot do this under uncertainty.

Uncertainty ranges between total ignorance at one end of an extreme to either, but not including, risk or certainty at the other. We dispel uncertainty with information.

Information

. . . Information, although imperfectly measured and qualitatively defined in an administrative setting similarly structures an uncertain environment for the decision maker. It permits him to make better decisions assuming effectiveness criteria are measured by the relationship between payoffs and goals. Therefore the decision maker wishes to reduce uncertainty or, if possible, to convert it to a state of either certainty or risk. That this is accomplished through the medium of information is highlighted in Fig. 3.

This figure requires several observations:

1. The nature of 'added information inputs' is data concerning outcomes and probabilities of given strategies. Suppose a de-

cision maker begins acquiring information at the point of 'total ignorance' or at some other point to the left of it. He may be unsure at this time whether added information will lead him to the risk state, the certainty state, or, for that matter, leave him at some advanced condition within the uncertainty state.

2. Of course it is clear, or should be, that a decision maker may never 'cross the dotted line' to either certainty or risk states regardless of how much information he acquires. More information may improve decisions within the uncertainty state. Beyond this the decision maker may never learn what the nature of a particular decision is. But he may avoid the error of using risk assumptions for a decision which more correctly lies in uncertainty.

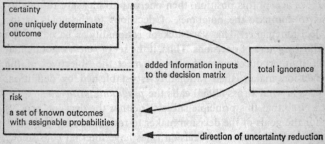

Figure 3 Information and uncertainty reduction

3. The amount of information the decision maker actually acquires depends on some marginal (or satisficing) calculus, in which he compares information cost to the value of uncertainty reduction. Naturally, we must think incrementally in terms of so many units of information for so many units of uncertainty reduction. It is unlikely that we can go from say total ignorance to some arbitrarily desirable point of uncertainty in a single leap [. . .]

The *need* for information may be as much *psychological*, in view of the qualitative character of most administrative decisions, as it is technical in some quantitative sense. This then would suggest that the need for information is *satisficed* at points other than where 'the cost of information equals the value of uncertainty reduction'. Most of the literature leads us to believe that these points are somewhere before the point of maximization.[2]

The evaluation of outcomes

The final element of the decision process, after the search has been made, goals set, and strategies determined, is the evaluation of outcomes. This process has been variously called the measurement of effectiveness or the rationality criteria. One of the problems with which we are confronted is that there are apparently no rationality criteria apart from decision rules.

Since there are many families of decision rules (or decision frameworks) there are also many criteria for effectiveness, which do not necessarily carry over from one set of rules to the next. If we accept this position, then one way to measure rationality is to compare the outcomes of decisions to the goals of the decision maker. This yardstick of rationality is based on the *consequences* of decisions. Thus, if the set of rules is 'good', that is, if it produces outcomes which meet the objectives of the decision maker, then rationality is established by definition. This is what Bross (1953) calls the *pragmatic principle*.

Note that this principle subjects neither the decision process nor the goals of the decision maker to rational scrutiny. It does not insist that a set of decision rules have internal consistency or that goals conform with some 'objective' standard of behavior. The presuppositions of conventional logic and conventional culture are *not* standards of rationality so far as the pragmatic principle is concerned.

The pragmatic principle is deceptively simple, since it does away with difficult problems by abolishing absolute standards. Goals become merely data of rationality measurement, not themselves subject to rationality analysis. So we must say that *given these goals,* such and such is a rational strategy to produce the sought-for outcomes. If it does not work out so well, then there is a more *rational strategy*. But how about a more rational goal? Since goals are relative, how can one talk about one goal being more rational than another? The pragmatic principle,

2. This is the implication in March and Simon (1958).

like positivism, is oriented in spirit toward conservatism. It is more compatible with what is, than with what ought to be [. . .]

References

ARCHER, S. H. (1964), 'The structure of management decision theory', *Acad. of Manag. J.*, December, pp. 269–73.

BROSS, I. D. J. (1953), *Design for Decision*, Macmillan Co.

DENT, J. K. (1959), 'Organizational correlates of the goals of business management', *Personnel Psychol.*, Autumn, pp. 365–9.

GORE, W. J. (1964), *Administrative Decision-Making*, Wiley.

MARCH, J. G., and SIMON, H. A. (1958), *Organizations*, Wiley.

SIMON, H. A. (1959), 'Theories of decision making in economics and behavioral science', *Amer. Econ. Rev.*, June, p. 263.

THOMPSON, H. E. (1965), 'Management decisions in perspective', in W. E. Schlender, W. G. Scott and A. C. Filley (eds), *Management in Perspective*, Houghton Mifflin, pp. 135–8.

2 C. E. Lindblom

Defining the Policy Problem

Excerpts from 'Limits on policy analysis', in C. E. Lindblom,
The Policy-Making Process, Prentice-Hall, 1968, ch. 3, pp. 12–14.

... How far can we go in reasoning out policy instead of fighting over it? A good way to find out is to specify what a man has to do to analyze a problem rationally, and see where he runs into difficulties. A 'classical' formulation runs something like this:

1. Faced with a given problem,

2. a rational man first clarifies his goals, values, or objectives, and then ranks or otherwise organizes them in his mind;

3. he then lists all important possible ways of – policies for – achieving his goals

4. and investigates all the important consequences that would follow from each of the alternative policies,

5. at which point he is in a position to compare consequences of each policy with goals

6. and so choose the policy with consequences most closely matching his goals.

Some people *define* a rational choice as one that meets these conditions. Others have merely claimed that these are the steps that any rational problem-solver should take. Either way, these steps constitute a classical model of rational decision. Let us examine them carefully.[1]

Policy makers are not faced with a *given* problem. Instead they have to identify and formulate their problem. Rioting breaks out in dozens of American cities. What is the problem? Maintaining law and order? Racial discrimination? Impatience of the Negroes with the pace of reform now that reform has gone

1. We shall follow the critique of the 'classical' model developed in Braybrooke and Lindblom (1963), part I.

far enough to give them hope? Incipient revolution? Black power? Low income? Lawlessness at the fringe of an otherwise relatively peaceful reform movement? Urban disorganization? Alienation?

To all these formulations, you may reply: The concrete observable problem is the riot itself. But perhaps the riots are merely symptomatic of 'real' problems to be solved. Then, the question arises again: What is the 'real' problem? During the summer riots of 1967, President Johnson appointed a commission not to solve the problem but first to find out what it was.

Even familiar problems require formulation. A problem like inequality in income distribution can be formulated as one big problem or as many relatively independent smaller problems such as:

1. Inadequate education for the children of low- and middle-income families, for whom we have developed free public education.

2. Inadequate retirement income, for which we have developed old-age assistance and insurance.

3. Inadequate income for broken families, for whom we have developed aid to dependent children and special benefits through social insurance.

4. Low earnings of the unskilled, for whom we have developed occupational training.

Moreover, there is a large class of problems that needs to be invented when new means or opportunities make new goals possible. Landing a man on the moon never used to be a problem for the US. We made it a problem when we began to develop a technology for space exploration that made such a problem possible. A problem is often a new opportunity, not an old sore.

For all these reasons, there is all kinds of room for controversy over what 'the problem' is, and no way to settle the controversy by analysis. Here already, then, is a limit on analytic policy making, and a necessary point of entry for 'politics' and other 'irrationalities' in policy making.[2]

2. For a detailed analysis of difficulties of defining a policy problem when 'there is no consensus on a definition of the problem', see Fesler (1964).

It is also generally recognized that not one of the steps 2 through 6 on p. 28 in 'classical' problem-solving can actually be completed for complex problems, even with the help of new techniques and electronic computation. A wise policy maker will not even try for completion. To clarify and organize all relevant values, to take an inventory of all important possible policy alternatives, to track down the endless possible consequences of each possible alternative, then to match the multi-fold consequences of each with the statement of goals – all this runs beyond the capacity of the human mind, beyond the time and energy that a decision maker can afford to devote to problem solving, and in fact beyond the information that he has available. A policy maker, whether an individual or an organization, will become exhausted long before the analysis is exhausted. Hence for complex policy problems, analysis can never be finished; it will always therefore fail to prove that the right policy has been found and will always be subject to challenge. And since it is inconclusive, men will have to fight over the issues remaining to be settled [. . .]

References

BRAYBROOKE, D., and LINDBLOM, C. E. (1963), *A Strategy of Decision*, Free Press.

FESLER, J. W. (1964), 'National water resources administration', in S. C. Smith, and E. N. Castle (eds), *Economics and Public Policy in Water Resource Development*, Iowa State University Press.

3 C. I. Barnard

Decisions in Organizations

Excerpts from 'The environment of decision', in C. I. Barnard,
The Functions of the Executive, Harvard University Press, 1938, ch. 13,
pp. 185–99.

The acts of individuals may be distinguished in principle as
those which are the result of deliberation, calculation, thought,
and those which are unconscious, automatic, responsive, the
results of internal or external conditions present or past. In
general, whatever processes precede the first class of acts culminate in what may be termed 'decision'. Involved in acts
which are ascribed to decision are many subsidiary acts which
are themselves automatic, the processes of which are usually
unknown to the actor.

When decision is involved there are consciously present two
terms – the end to be accomplished and the means to be used.
The end itself may be the result of logical processes in which
the end is in turn a means to some broader or more remote end;
or the immediate end, and generally the ultimate end, may not
be a result of logical processes, but 'given' – that is, unconsciously impressed – by conditions, including social conditions
past or present, including orders of organizations. But whenever
the end has been determined, by whatever process, the decision
as to means is itself a logical process of discrimination, analysis,
choice – however defective either the factual basis for choice
or the reasoning related to these facts.

The acts of organization are those of persons dominated by
organizational, not personal, ends. These ends, especially those
which are most general or remote, since they represent a consensus of opinion, may be arrived at by non-logical processes;
but since they must usually be formulated in some degree,
whereas individual ends more rarely need to be formulated, the
ends of organization to a relatively high degree involve logical
processes, not as rationalizations after decision but as processes

of decision. Moreover, when ends have been adopted, the co-ordination of acts as means to these ends is itself an essentially logical process. The discrimination of facts and the allocation of acts by specialization which coordination implies may quite appropriately be regarded as logical or deliberate thinking processes of organization, though not necessarily logical processes of thought of the individual participants. Generally, however, it will be observed that the more important *organization* acts of individuals are likely also to be logical – in that they require deliberate choice of means to accomplish ends which are not personal, and therefore cannot be directly automatic or responsive reactions.

This does not mean that unconscious, automatic, responsive, action is not involved in organization. On the contrary, non-logical organization processes are indispensable to formal organization. Moreover, much of the action of individuals as participating in organization is habitual, repetitive, and may be merely responsive by *organization design* – a result, for example, of specialization intended to enhance this non-logical process. What is important here, however, is the superlative degree to which logical processes must and can characterize organization action as contrasted with individual action, and the degree to which decision is specialized in organization. It is the deliberate adoption of means to ends which is the essence of formal organization. This is not only required in order to make cooperation superior to the biological powers and senses of individuals, but it is possibly the chief superiority of co-operative to individual action in most of the important cases of enduring organizations.

From this analysis it follows that acts of decision are characteristic of organization behavior as contrasted with individual behavior, and that the description of the processes of decision are relatively more important to the understanding of organization behavior than in the case of individuals. Moreover, whereas these processes in individuals are as yet matters of speculation rather than of science in the various psychologies, they are in organizations much more open to empirical observation. In fact they are themselves matters of deliberate attention and subject to intentional specialization, as will appear later.

The formulation of organization purposes or objectives and the more general decisions involved in this process and in those of action to carry them into effect are distributed in organizations, and are not, nor can they be, concentrated or specialized to individuals except in minor degree. The facts in this regard are obscured to many by the formal location of objective authority in various organization positions; but underlying the formal structure of authority and intraorganization communication are processes of interacting decisions distributed throughout the positions in the lines of communication. This may be regarded as the essential process of organization action which continually synthesizes the elements of cooperative systems into concrete systems.

Every effort that is a constituent of organization, that is, every coordinated cooperative effort, may involve two acts of decision. The first is the decision of the person affected as to whether or not he will contribute this effort as a matter of personal choice. It is a detail of the process of repeated personal decisions that determine whether or not the individual will be or will continue to be a contributor to the organization. This act of decision is *outside* the system of efforts constituting organization, although it is a subject for organized attention.

The second type of decisions has no direct or specific relation to personal results, but views the effort concerning which decision is to be made non-personally from the viewpoint of its organization effect and of its relation to organization purpose. This second act of decision is often made in a direct sense by individuals, but it is impersonal and organizational in its intent and effect. Very often it is also organizational in its process, as, for example, in legislatures, or when boards or committees determine action. The act of decision is a part of the organization itself.

This distinction between the two types of decision is frequently recognized in ordinary affairs. We very often say or hear sentences similar to this: 'If this were my business, I think I would decide the question this way – but it is not my personal affair'; 'I think the *situation* requires such and such an answer – but I am not in a position to determine what ought to be done'; or, 'The decision should be made by someone else'.

A sort of dual personality is required of individuals contributing to organization action – the private personality, and the organization personality.

These two kinds of decisions – organization decisions and personal decisions – are chiefly to be distinguished as to process by this fact: that personal decisions cannot ordinarily be delegated to others, whereas organization decisions can often if not always be delegated. For example, what may be called a major decision by an individual may require numerous subsidiary decisions (or judgements) which he also must make. A similar important decision by an organization may in its final form be enunciated by one person and the corresponding subsidiary decisions by several different persons, all acting organizationally, not personally. Similarly, the execution of a decision by one person may require subsequent detailed decision by him as to various steps, whereas the execution of a similar decision in an organization almost always requires subsequent detailed decision by several different persons. Indeed, it may be said that often the responsibility for an organization decision is not a personal responsibility until assigned. Responsibility for organization decision must be assigned positively and definitely in many cases because the aptness of decision depends upon knowledge of facts and of organization purpose, and is therefore bound up with organization communication. Thus central or general organization decisions are best made at centres of the communication system of the organization, so that such decisions must be assigned to those located at these central positions. Persons located at such positions are known as executives; so that the necessities of communication as an essential element in organization imposes the assignment of responsibility for some kinds of organization decision to executives. In short, a characteristic of the services of executives is that they represent a specialization of the process of making organization decisions – and this is the essence of their functions [. . .]

The evidences of decision

Not the least of the difficulties of appraising the executive functions or the relative merits of executives lies in the fact that there is little direct opportunity to observe the essential operations of decision. It is a perplexing fact that most executive decisions produce no direct evidence of themselves and that knowledge of them can only be derived from the cumulation of indirect evidence. They must largely be inferred from general results in which they are merely one factor, and from symptomatic indications of roundabout character.

Those decisions which are most directly known result in the emission of authoritative communications, that is, orders. Something is or is not to be done. Even in such cases the basic decision may not be evident; for the decision to attempt to achieve a certain result or condition may require several communications to different persons which appear to be complete in themselves but in which the controlling general decision may not be disclosed.

Again, a firm decision may be taken that does not result in any communication whatever for the time being. A decision properly timed must be made in advance of communicating it, either because the action involved must wait anticipated developments or because it cannot be authoritative without educational or persuasive preparation.

Finally, the decision may be not to decide. This is a most frequent decision, and from some points of view probably the most important. For every alert executive continually raises in his own mind questions for determination. As a result of his consideration he may determine that the question is not pertinent. He may determine that it is not now pertinent. He may determine that it is pertinent now, but that there are lacking adequate data upon which to base a final decision. He may determine that it is pertinent for decision now, but that it should or must be decided by someone else on the latter's initiative. He may determine that the question is pertinent, can be decided, will not be decided except by himself, and yet it would be better that it be not decided because his competence is insufficient.

The fine art of executive decision consists in not deciding questions that are not now pertinent, in not deciding prematurely, in not making decisions that cannot be made effective, and in not making decisions that others should make. Not to decide questions that are not pertinent at the time is uncommon good sense, though to raise them may be uncommon perspicacity.

Not to decide questions prematurely is to refuse commitment of attitude or the development of prejudice. Not to make decisions that cannot be made effective is to refrain from destroying authority. Not to make decisions that others should make is to preserve morale, to develop competence, to fix responsibility, and to preserve authority.

From this it may be seen that decisions fall into two major classes, positive decisions – to do something, to direct action, to cease action, to prevent action; and negative decisions, which are decisions not to decide. Both are inescapable; but the negative decisions are often largely unconscious, relatively non-logical, 'instinctive', 'good sense'. It is because of the rejections that the selection is good. The best of moves may be offset by a false move. This is why time is usually necessary to appraise the executive. There is no current evidence of the all-important negative decisions. The absence of effective moves indicates failure of initiative in decision, but error of action probably often means absence of good negative decisions. The success of action through a period of time denotes excellence of selection and of rejection of possible actions [. . .]

Within organizations, especially of complex types, there is a technique of decision, an organizational process of thinking, which may not be analogous to that of the individual. It would appear that such techniques differ widely among the various types of organization – for example, religious, political, industrial, commercial, etc. This is perhaps conveyed by the remark often made about the 'differences in approach' to similar questions. It may be suspected that more than differences in technological character or even of the ends or purposes are involved.

At any event, it is evidently important to consider the principles of the decisive process as it actually takes place from the organizational viewpoint rather than from that of either psychology or systems of logic.

4 H. A. Simon

Theories of Decision Making in Economics and Behavioral Science

Excerpts from H. A. Simon, 'Theories of decision-making in economics and behavioral science', *American Economic Review*, vol. 49, no. 3, June 1959, pp. 253–83.

Recent years have seen important new explorations along the boundaries between economics and psychology. For the economist, the immediate question about these developments is whether they include new advances in psychology that can fruitfully be applied to economics. But the psychologist will also raise the converse question – whether there are developments in economic theory and observation that have implications for the central core of psychology. If economics is able to find verifiable and verified generalizations about human economic behavior, then these generalizations must have a place in the more general theories of human behavior to which psychology and sociology aspire. Influence will run both ways.

How much psychology does economics need?

How have psychology and economics gotten along with little relation in the past? The explanation rests on an understanding of the goals toward which economics, viewed as a science and a discipline, has usually aimed.

Broadly speaking, economics can be defined as the science that describes and predicts the behavior of several kinds of economic man – notably the consumer and the entrepreneur. While perhaps literally correct, this definition does not reflect the principal focus in the literature of economics. We usually classify work in economics along two dimensions: (a) whether it is concerned with industries and the whole economy (macroeconomics) or with individual economic actors (microeconomics); and (b) whether it strives to describe and explain economic behavior (descriptive economics), or to guide decisions either at the level of public policy (normative macroeconomics) or at the level of the individual consumer or businessman (normative micro-economics).

The profession and literature of economics have been largely preoccupied with normative macroeconomics. Although descriptive macroeconomics provides the scientific base for policy prescription, research emphases have been determined in large part by relevance to policy (e.g., business cycle theory). Normative microeconomics, carried forward under such labels as 'management science', 'engineering economics', and 'operations research', is now a flourishing area of work having an uneasy and ill-defined relation with the profession of economics, traditionally defined. Much of the work is being done by mathematicians, statisticians, engineers, and physical scientists (although many mathematical economists have also been active in it).

This new area, like the old, is normative in orientation. Economists have been relatively uninterested in descriptive microeconomics – understanding the behavior of individual economic agents – except as this is necessary to provide a foundation for macroeconomics. The normative microeconomist 'obviously' doesn't need a theory of human behavior: he wants to know how people *ought* to behave, not how they *do* behave. On the other hand, the macroeconomist's lack of concern with individual behavior stems from different considerations. First, he assumes that the economic actor is rational, and hence he makes strong predictions about human behavior without performing the hard work of observing people. Second, he often assumes competition, which carries with it the implication that only the rational survive. Thus, the classical economic theory of markets with perfect competition and rational agents is deductive theory that requires almost no contact with empirical data once its assumptions are accepted.[1]

Undoubtedly there is an area of human behavior that fits these assumptions to a reasonable approximation, where the classical theory with its assumptions of rationality is a powerful and useful tool. Without denying the existence of this area, or

1. As an example of what passes for empirical 'evidence' in this literature, I cite pp. 22–3 of Friedman (1953), which will amaze anyone brought up in the empirical tradition of psychology and sociology, although it has apparently excited little adverse comment among economists.

its importance, I may observe that it fails to include some of the central problems of conflict and dynamics with which economics has become more and more concerned. A metaphor will help to show the reason for this failure.

Suppose we were pouring some viscous liquid – molasses – into a bowl of very irregular shape. What would we need in order to make a theory of the form the molasses would take in the bowl? How much would we have to know about the properties of molasses to predict its behavior under the circumstances? If the bowl were held motionless, and if we wanted only to predict behavior in equilibrium, we would have to know little, indeed, about molasses. The single essential assumption would be that the molasses, under the force of gravity, would minimize the height of its center of gravity. With this assumption, which would apply as well to any other liquid, and a complete knowledge of the environment – in this case the shape of the bowl – the equilibrium is completely determined. Just so, the equilibrium behavior of a perfectly adapting organism depends only on its goal and its environment; it is otherwise completely independent of the internal properties of the organism.

If the bowl into which we were pouring the molasses were jiggled rapidly, or if we wanted to know about the behavior before equilibrium was reached, prediction would require much more information. It would require, in particular, more information about the properties of molasses: its viscosity, the rapidity with which it 'adapted' itself to the containing vessel and moved towards its 'goal' of lowering its center of gravity. Likewise, to predict the short-run behavior of an adaptive organism, or its behavior in a complex and rapidly changing environment, it is not enough to know its goals. We must know also a great deal about its internal structure and particularly its mechanisms of adaptation.

If, to carry the metaphor a step farther, new forces, in addition to gravitational force, were brought to bear on the liquid, we would have to know still more about it even to predict behavior in equilibrium. Now its tendency to lower its center of gravity might be countered by a force to minimize an electrical or magnetic potential operating in some lateral direction. We would have to know its relative susceptibility to gravitational and electrical or magnetic force to determine its equilibrium position. Similarly, in an organism having a multiplicity of goals, or afflicted with some kind of internal goal conflict, behavior could be predicted only from information about the relative strengths of the several goals and the ways in which the adaptive processes responded to them.

Economics has been moving steadily into new areas where the power of the classical equilibrium model has never been demonstrated, and where its adequacy must be considered anew. Labor economics is such an area, oligopoly or imperfect competition theory another, decision making under uncertainty a third and the theory of economic development a fourth. In all of these areas the complexity and instability of his environment becomes a central feature of the choices that economic man faces. To explain his behavior in the face of this complexity, the theory must describe him as something more than a featureless, adaptive organism; it must incorporate at least some description of the processes and mechanisms through which the adaptation takes place. Let us list a little more concretely some specific problems of this kind:

1. The classical theory postulates that the consumer maximizes utility. Recent advances in the theory of rational consumer choice have shown that the existence of a utility function, and its characteristics, if it exists, can be studied empirically.

2. The growing separation between ownership and management has directed attention to the motivations of managers and the adequacy of the profit-maximization assumption for business firms. So-called human relations research has raised a variety of issues about the motivation of both executives and employees.

3. When, in extending the classical theory, the assumptions of perfect competition were removed, even the definition of rationality became ambiguous. New definitions had to be constructed, by no means as 'obvious' intuitively as simple maximization, to extend the theory of rational behavior to bilateral monopoly and to other bargaining and outguessing situations.

4. When the assumptions of perfect foresight were removed, to handle uncertainty about the environment, the definition of

rationality had to be extended in another direction to take into account prediction and the formation of expectations.

5. Broadening the definition of rationality to encompass goal conflict and uncertainty made it hard to ignore the distinction between the objective environment in which the economic actor 'really' lives and the subjective environment that he perceives and to which he responds. When this distinction is made, we can no longer predict his behavior – even if he behaves rationally – from the characteristics of the objective environment; we also need to know something about his perceptual and cognitive processes.

We shall use these five problem areas as a basis for sorting out some recent explorations in theory, model building, and empirical testing [. . .]

The utility function
The binary choice experiment

Much recent discussion about utility has centered around a particularly simple choice experiment. This experiment, in numerous variants, has been used by both economists and psychologists to test the most diverse kinds of hypotheses. We will describe it so that we can use it as a common standard of comparison for a whole range of theories and empirical studies.

We will call the situation we are about to describe the *binary choice* experiment. It is better known to most game theorists – particularly those located not far from Nevada – as a two-armed bandit; and to most psychologists as a partial reinforcement experiment. The subject is required, in each of a series of trials, to choose one or the other of two symbols – say, plus or minus. When he has chosen, he is told whether his choice was 'right' or 'wrong', and he may also receive a reward (in psychologist's language, a reinforcement) for 'right' choices. The experimenter can arrange the schedule of correct responses in a variety of ways. There may be a definite pattern, or they may be randomized. It is not essential that one and only one response be correct on a given trial: the experimenter may determine that both or neither will be correct. In the latter case the subject may or may not be informed whether the response he did not choose would have been correct.

How would a utility-maximizing subject behave in the binary choice experiment? Suppose that the experimenter rewarded 'plus' on one-third of the trials, determined at random, and 'minus' on the remaining two-thirds. Then a subject, provided that he believed the sequence was random and observed that minus was rewarded twice as often as plus, should always, rationally, choose minus. He would find the correct answer two-thirds of the time, and more often than with any other strategy.

Unfortunately for the classical theory of utility in its simplest form, few subjects behave in this way. The most commonly observed behavior is what is called *event matching*. The subject chooses the two alternatives (not necessarily at random) with relative frequencies roughly proportional to the relative frequencies with which they are rewarded. Thus, in the example given, two-thirds of the time he would choose minus, and as a result would make a correct response, on the average, in 5 trials out of 9 (on two-thirds of the trials in which he chooses minus, and one-third of those in which he chooses plus).

All sorts of explanations have been offered for the event-matching behavior. The simplest is that the subject just doesn't understand what strategy would maximize his expected utility; but with adult subjects in a situation as transparent as this one, this explanation seems far-fetched. The alternative explanations imply either that the subject regards himself as being engaged in a competitive game with the experimenter (or with 'nature' if he accepts the experimenter's explanation that the stimulus is random, or that his responses are the outcome of certain kinds of learning processes. We will examine these two types of explanation further [. . .] The important conclusion at this point is that, even in an extremely simple situation, subjects do not behave in the way predicted by a straightforward application of utility theory [. . .]

The goals of firms

Just as the central assumption in the theory of consumption is that the consumer strives to maximize his utility, so the crucial assumption in the theory of the firm is that the entrepreneur strives to maximize his residual share – his profit. Attacks on this hypothesis have been frequent.[2] We may classify the most important of these as follows:

1. The theory leaves ambiguous whether it is short-run or long-run profit that is to be maximized.

2. The entrepreneur may obtain all kinds of 'psychic income' from the firm, quite apart from monetary rewards. If he is to maximize his utility, then he will sometimes balance a loss of profits against an increase in psychic income. But if we allow 'psychic income', the criterion of profit maximization loses all of its definiteness.

3. The entrepreneur may not care to maximize, but may simply want to earn a return that he regards as satisfactory. By sophistry and an adept use of the concept of psychic income, the notion of seeking a satisfactory return can be translated into utility maximizing but not in any operational way. We shall see in a moment that 'satisfactory profits' is a concept more meaningfully related to the psychological notion of aspiration levels than to maximization.

4. It is often observed that under modern conditions the equity owners and the active managers of an enterprise are separate and distinct groups of people, so that the latter may not be motivated to maximize profits.

5. Where there is imperfect competition among firms, maximizing is an ambiguous goal, for what action is optimal for one firm depends on the actions of the other firms.

In the present section we shall deal only with the third of these five issues. The fifth will be treated in the following section; the first, second, and fourth are purely empirical questions that have been discussed at length in the literature; they will be considered here only for their bearing on the question of satisfactory profits.

2. For a survey of recent discussions see Papandreou (1952).

Satisficing versus maximizing

The notion of satiation plays no role in classical economic theory, while it enters rather prominently into the treatment of motivation in psychology. In most psychological theories the motive to act stems from *drives,* and action terminates when the drive is satisfied. Moreover, the conditions for satisfying a drive are not necessarily fixed, but may be specified by an aspiration level that itself adjusts upward or downward on the basis of experience.

If we seek to explain business behavior in the terms of this theory, we must expect the firm's goals to be not maximizing profit, but attaining a certain level or rate of profit, holding a certain share of the market or a certain level of sales. Firms would try to 'satisfice' rather than to maximize.

It has sometimes been argued that the distinction between satisficing and maximizing is not important to economic theory. For in the first place, the psychological evidence on individual behavior shows that aspirations tend to adjust to the attainable. Hence in the long run, the argument runs, the level of aspiration and the attainable maximum will be very close together. Second, even if some firms satisficed, they would gradually lose out to the maximizing firms, which would make larger profits and grow more rapidly than the others.

These are, of course, precisely the arguments of our molasses metaphor, and we may answer them in the same way that we answered them earlier. The economic environment of the firm is complex, and it changes rapidly; there is no a priori reason to assume the attainment of long-run equilibrium. Indeed, the empirical evidence on the distribution of firms by size suggests that the observed regularities in size distribution stem from the statistical equilibrium of a population of adaptive systems rather than the static equilibrium of a population of maximizers.

Models of satisficing behavior are richer than models of maximizing behavior, because they treat not only of equilibrium but of the method of reaching it as well. Psychological studies of the formation and change of aspiration levels support propositions of the following kinds.

1. When performance falls short of the level of aspiration,

search behavior (particularly search for new alternatives of action) is induced.

2. At the same time, the level of aspiration begins to adjust itself downward until goals reach levels that are practically attainable.

3. If the two mechanisms just listed operate too slowly to adapt aspirations to performance, emotional behavior – apathy or aggression, for example – will replace rational adaptive behavior.

The aspiration level defines a natural zero point in the scale of utility – whereas in most classical theories the zero point is arbitrary. When the firm has alternatives open to it that are at or above its aspiration level, the theory predicts that it will choose the best of those known to be available. When none of the available alternatives satisfies current aspirations, the theory predicts qualitatively different behavior : in the short run, search behavior and the revision of targets; in the longer run, what we have called above emotional behavior, and what the psychologist would be inclined to call neurosis.

Studies of business behavior

There is some empirical evidence that business goals are, in fact, stated in satisficing terms. First, there is the series of studies stemming from the pioneering work of Hall and Hitch that indicates that businessmen often set prices by applying a standard markup to costs. Some economists have sought to refute this fact, others to reconcile it – if it is a fact – with marginalist principles [. . .]

More recently, my colleagues Cyert and March (1955) have attempted to test the satisficing model in a more direct way. They found in one industry some evidence that firms with a declining share of market strove more vigorously to increase their sales than firms whose shares of the market were steady or increasing [. . .]

Economic implications

It has sometimes been argued that, however realistic the classical theory of the firm as a profit maximizer, it is an adequate theory for purposes of normative macroeconomics. Mason, for example, in commenting on Papandreou's essay (1952) says, 'The writer of this critique must confess a lack of confidence in the marked superiority, *for purposes of economic analysis*, of this newer concept of the firm over the older conception of the entrepreneur.' The italics are Mason's.

The theory of the firm is important for welfare economics – e.g., for determining under what circumstances the behavior of the firm will lead to efficient allocation of resources. The satisficing model vitiates all the conclusions about resource allocation that are derivable from the maximizing model when perfect competition is assumed. Similarly, a dynamic theory of firm sizes, like that mentioned above, has quite different implications for public policies dealing with concentration than a theory that assumes firms to be in static equilibrium. Hence, welfare economists are justified in adhering to the classical theory only if either the theory is empirically correct as a description of the decision-making process, or it is safe to assume that the system operates in the neighborhood of the static equilibrium. What evidence we have mostly contradicts both assumptions.

Conflict of interest

Leaving aside the problem of the motivations of hired managers, conflict of interest among economic actors creates no difficulty for classical economic theory – indeed, it lies at the very core of the theory – so long as each actor treats the other actors as parts of his 'given' environment, and doesn't try to predict their behavior and anticipate it. But when this restriction is removed, when it is assumed that a seller takes into account the reactions of buyers to his actions, or that each manufacturer predicts the behaviors of his competitors – all the familiar difficulties of imperfect competition and oligopoly arise.

The very assumptions of omniscient rationality that provide the basis for deductive prediction in economics when competition is present lead to ambiguity when they are applied to competition among the few. The central difficulty is that rationality requires one to outguess one's opponents, but not to be outguessed by them, and this is clearly not a consistent requirement if applied to all the actors [. . .]

The formation of expectations

While the future cannot enter into the determination of the present, expectations about the future can and do. In trying to gain an understanding of the saving, spending, and investment behavior of both consumers and firms, and to make short-term predictions of this behavior for purposes of policy-making, economists have done substantial empirical work as well as theorizing on the formation of expectations [. . .]

Expectations and probability

The classical way to incorporate expectations into economic theory is to assume that the decision maker estimates the joint probability distribution of future events.[3] He can then act so as to maximize the expected value of utility or profit, as the case may be. However satisfying this approach may be conceptually, it poses awkward problems when we ask how the decision maker actually estimates the parameters of the joint probability distribution. Common sense tells us that people don't make such estimates, nor can we find evidence that they do by examining actual business forecasting methods. The surveys of businessmen's expectations have never attempted to secure such estimates, but have contented themselves with asking for point predictions – which, at best, might be interpreted as predictions of the means of the distributions.

It has been shown that under certain special circumstances the mean of the probability distribution is the only parameter that is relevant for decision – that even if the variance and higher moments were known to the rational decision maker, he would have no use for them. In these cases, the arithmetic mean is actually a certainty equivalent, the optimal decision turns out to be the same as if the future were known with certainty. But the situations where the mean is a certainty equivalent are, as we have said, very special ones, and there is no indication that businessmen ever ask whether the necessary conditions for this equivalence are actually met in practice. They somehow make

3. A general survey of approaches to decision making under uncertainty will be found in Arrow (1951), and in Luce and Raiffa (1957, ch. 13).

forecasts in the form of point predictions and act upon them in one way or another.

The 'somehow' poses questions that are important for business cycle theory, and perhaps for other problems in economics. The way in which expectations are formed may affect the dynamic stability of the economy, and the extent to which cycles will be amplified or damped. Some light, both empirical and theoretical, has recently been cast on these questions. On the empirical side, attempts have been made: firstly to compare businessmen's forecasts with various 'naïve' models that assume the future will be some simple function of the recent past, and secondly to use such naïve models themselves as forecasting devices.

The simplest naïve model is one that assumes the next period will be exactly like the present. Another assumes that the change from present to next period will equal the change from last period to present; a third, somewhat more general, assumes that the next period will be a weighted average of recent past periods. The term 'naïve model' has been applied loosely to various forecasting formulae of these general kinds. There is some affirmative evidence that business forecasts fit such models. There is also evidence that elaboration of the models beyond the first few steps of refinement does not much improve prediction. Arrow and his colleagues (1951) have explored some of the conditions under which forecasting formulae will, and will not, introduce dynamic instability into an economic system that is otherwise stable. They have shown, for example, that if a system of multiple markets is stable and under static expectations, it is stable when expectations are based on a moving average of past values.

The work on the formation of expectations represents a significant extension of classical theory. For, instead of taking the environment as a 'given', known to the economic decision maker, it incorporates in the theory the processes of acquiring knowledge about that environment. In doing so, it forces us to include in our model of economic man some of his properties as a learning, estimating, searching, information-processing organism (Simon, 1958) [. . .]

Human cognition and economics

All the developments we have examined in the preceding four sections have a common theme: they all involve important modifications in the concept of economic man and, for the reasons we have stated, modifications in the direction of providing a fuller description of his characteristics. The classical theory is a theory of a man choosing among fixed and known alternatives, to each of which is attached known consequences. But when perception and cognition intervene between the decision maker and his objective environment, this model no longer proves adequate. We need a description of the choice process that recognizes that alternatives are not given but must be sought; and a description that takes into account the arduous task of determining what consequences will follow on each alternative (Simon, 1957a, ch. 3; 1957b, pt 4).

The decision maker's information about his environment is much less than an approximation to the real environment. The term 'approximation' implies that the subjective world of the decision maker resembles the external environment closely, but lacks, perhaps, some fineness of detail. In actual fact the perceived world is fantastically different from the 'real' world. The differences involve both omissions and distortions, and arise in both perception and inference. The sins of omission in perception are more important than the sins of commission. The decision maker's model of the world encompasses only a minute fraction of all the relevant characteristics of the real environment, and his inferences extract only a minute fraction of all the information that is present even in his model.

Perception is sometimes referred to as a 'filter'. This term is as misleading as 'approximation', and for the same reason: it implies that what comes through into the central nervous system is really quite a bit like what is 'out there'. In fact, the filtering is not merely a passive selection of some part of a presented whole, but an active process involving attention to a very small part of the whole and exclusion, from the outset, of almost all that is not within the scope of attention.

Every human organism lives in an environment that generates millions of bits of new information each second, but the bottleneck of the perceptual apparatus certainly does not admit more than 1000 bits per second, and probably much less. Equally significant omissions occur in the processing that takes place when information reaches the brain. As every mathematician knows, it is one thing to have a set of differential equations, and another thing to have their solutions. Yet the solutions are logically implied by the equations – they are 'all there', if we only knew how to get to them! By the same token, there are hosts of inferences that *might* be drawn from the information stored in the brain that are not in fact drawn. The consequences implied by information in the memory become known only through active information-processing, and hence through active selection of particular problem-solving paths from the myriad that might have been followed.

In this section we shall examine some theories of decision making that take the limitations of the decision maker and the complexity of the environment as central concerns. These theories incorporate some mechanisms we have already discussed – for example, aspiration levels and forecasting processes – but go beyond them in providing a detailed picture of the choice process.

A real-life decision involves some goals or values, some facts about the environment, and some inferences drawn from the values and facts. The goals and values may be simple or complex, consistent or contradictory; the facts may be real or supposed, based on observation or the reports of others; the inferences may be valid or spurious. The whole process may be viewed, metaphorically, as a process of 'reasoning', where the values and facts serve as premises, and the decision that is finally reached is inferred from these premises (Simon, 1957a). The resemblance of decision making to logical reasoning is only metaphorical, because there are quite different rules in the two cases to determine what constitute 'valid' premises and admissible modes of inference. The metaphor is useful because it leads us to take the individual *decision premise* as the unit of description, hence to deal with the whole interwoven fabric of influences that bear on a single decision – but without being bound by the assumptions of rationality that limit the classical theory of choice.

Rational behavior and role theory

We can find common ground to relate the economist's theory of decision making with that of the social psychologist. The latter is particularly interested, of course, in social influences on choice, which determine the *role* of the actor. In our present terms, a role is a social prescription of some, but not all, of the premises that enter into an individual's choices of behavior. Any particular concrete behavior is the result of a large number of premises, only some of which are prescribed by the role. In addition to role premises there will be premises about the state of the environment based directly on perception, premises representing beliefs and knowledge, and idiosyncratic premises that characterize the personality. Within this framework we can accommodate both the rational elements in choice, so much emphasized by economics, and the nonrational elements to which psychologists and sociologists often prefer to call attention [. . .]

Implications for economics

Apart from normative applications (e.g., substituting computers for humans in certain decision-making tasks) we are not interested so much in the detailed descriptions of roles as in broader questions:

1. What general characteristics do the roles of economic actors have?

2. How do roles come to be structured in the particular ways they do?

3. What bearing does this version of role theory have for macroeconomics and other large-scale social phenomena?

Characterizing role structure. Here we are concerned with generalizations about thought processes, particularly those generalizations that are relatively independent of the substantive content of the role [. . .] An example, of particular interest to economics, is the hypothesis we have already discussed [. . .] that economic man is a *satisficing* animal whose problem solving is based on search activity to meet certain aspiration levels rather than a *maximizing* animal whose problem solving involves finding the best alternatives in terms of specified criteria (Simon, 1957b). A third hypothesis is that operative goals (those associated with an observable criterion of success, and relatively definite means of attainment) play a much larger part in governing choice than nonoperative goals (those lacking a concrete measure of success or a program for attainment) (March and Simon, 1958).

Understanding how roles emerge. Within almost any single business firm, certain characteristic types of roles will be represented: selling roles, production roles, accounting roles, and so on (Dearborn and Simon, 1958). Partly, this consistency may be explained in functional terms – that a model that views the firm as producing a product, selling it, and accounting for its assets and liabilities is an effective simplification of the real world, and provides the members of the organization with a workable frame of reference. Imitation within the culture provides an alternative explanation. It is exceedingly difficult to test hypotheses as to the origins and causal conditions for roles as universal in the society as these, but the underlying mechanisms could probably be explored effectively by the study of less common roles – safety director, quality control inspector, or the like – that are to be found in some firms, but not in all.

With our present definition of role, we can also speak meaningfully of the role of an entire business firm – of decision premises that underlie its basic policies. In a particular industry we find some firms that specialize in adapting the product to individual customer's specifications; others that specialize in product innovation. The common interest of economics and psychology includes not only the study of individual roles, but also the explanation of organizational roles of these sorts.

Tracing the implications for macroeconomics. If basic professional goals remain as they are, the interest of the psychologist and the economist in role theory will stem from somewhat different ultimate aims. The former will use various economic and organizational phenomena as data for the study of the structure and determinants of roles; the latter will be primarily interested in the implications of role theory for the model of economic man, and indirectly, for macroeconomics.

The first applications will be to those topics in economics where the assumption of static equilibrium is least tenable. Innovation, technological change, and economic development are examples of areas to which a good empirically tested theory of the processes of human adaptation and problem solving could make a major contribution. For instance, we know very little at present about how the rate of innovation depends on the amounts of resources allocated to various kinds of research and development activity. Nor do we understand very well the nature of 'know how', the costs of transferring technology from one firm or economy to another, or the effects of various kinds and amounts of education upon national product. These are difficult questions to answer from aggregative data and gross observation, with the result that our views have been formed more by arm-chair theorizing than by testing hypotheses with solid facts.

Conclusion

In exploring the areas in which economics has common interests with the other behavioral sciences, we have been guided by the metaphor we elaborated at the beginning of this Reading. In simple, slow-moving situations, where the actor has a single, operational goal, the assumption of maximization relieves us of any need to construct a detailed picture of economic man or his processes of adaptation. As the complexity of the environment increases, or its speed of change, we need to know more and more about the mechanisms and processes that economic man uses to relate himself to that environment and achieve his goals.

How closely we wish to interweave economics with psychology depends, then, both on the range of questions we wish to answer and on our assessment of how far we may trust the assumptions of static equilibrium as approximations. In considerable part, the demand for a fuller picture of economic man has been coming from the profession of economics itself, as new areas of theory and application have emerged in which complexity and change are central facts. The revived interest in the theory of utility, and its application to choice under uncertainty, and to consumer saving and spending is one such area. The needs of normative macroeconomics and management science for a fuller theory of the firm have led to a number of attempts to understand the actual processes of making business decisions. In both these areas, notions of adaptive and satisficing behavior, drawn largely from psychology, are challenging sharply the classical picture of the maximizing entrepreneur.

The area of imperfect competition and oligopoly has been equally active, although the activity has thus far perhaps raised more problems than it has solved. On the positive side, it has revealed a community of interest among a variety of social scientists concerned with bargaining as a part of political and economic processes. Prediction of the future is another element common to many decision processes, and particularly important to explaining business cycle phenomena. Psychologists and economists have been applying a wide variety of approaches, empirical and theoretical, to the study of the formation of expectations. Surveys of consumer and business behavior, theories of statistical induction, stochastic learning theories, and theories of concept formation have all been converging on this problem area.

The very complexity that has made a theory of the decision-making process essential has made its construction exceedingly difficult. Most approaches have been piecemeal – now focused on the criteria of choice, now on conflict of interest, now on the formation of expectations. It seemed almost utopian to suppose that we could put together a model of adaptive man that would compare in completeness with the simple model of classical economic man. The sketchiness and incompleteness of the newer proposals have been urged as a compelling reason for clinging to the older theories, however inadequate they are admitted to be.

The modern digital computer has changed the situation radically. It provides us with a tool of research – for formulating and testing theories – whose power is commensurate with the complexity of the phenomena we seek to understand. Although the use of computers to build theories of human behavior is very recent, it has already led to concrete results in the simulation of higher mental processes. As economics finds it more and more necessary to understand and explain disequilibrium as well as equilibrium, it will find an increasing use for this new tool and for communication with its sister sciences of psychology and sociology.

References

ARROW, K. J. (1951), 'Alternative approaches to the theory of choice in risk-taking situations', *Econometrica*, vol. 19, October, pp. 404–37.

ARROW, K. J., and NERLOVE, M. (1951), 'A note on expectations and stability', *Econometrica*, vol. 26, April, pp. 250–72.

CYERT, R. M., and MARCH, J. G. (1955), 'Organizational structure and pricing behavior in an oligopolistic market', *Amer. Econ. Rev.*, vol. 45, March.

DEARBORN, D. C., and SIMON, H. A. (1958), 'Selective perception: a note on the departmental identification of executives', *Sociometry*, vol. 21, June, pp. 140–44.

FRIEDMAN, M. (1963), *Essays in Positive Economics*, University of Chicago Press.

LUCE, R. D., and RAIFFA, H. (1957), *Games and Decisions*, Wiley.

MARCH, J. G., and SIMON, H. A. (1958), *Organizations*, Wiley.

PAPANDREOU, A. G. (1952), 'Some basic problems in the theory of the firm', in B. F. Haley (ed.), *A Survey of Contemporary Economics*, vol. 2, Irwin.

SIMON, H. A. (1957a), *Administrative Behavior*, 2nd edition, Free Press.

SIMON, H. A. (1957b), *Models of Man*, Wiley.

SIMON, H. A. (1958), 'The role of expectations in an adaptive or behavioristic model', in M. J. Bowman (ed.), *Expectations, Uncertainty and Business Behavior*.

5 R. J. Audley

What Makes Up a Mind?

'What makes up a mind?', in R. J. Audley *et al*, *Decision Making*, BBC Publications, 1967, ch. 3, pp. 40–50.

Most real decisions involve a complex interplay of many factors and concern a highly specific set of circumstances. So a man's whole psychology converges upon any act of choice that he makes. From this it follows that, in one sense, what makes up his mind could be anything, or everything, from whether or not his mother believed in breast-feeding down to the shades of his political opinion. Understanding even a trivial everyday choice is as complicated and particular a problem as, for instance, determining the reasons behind the order to charge at Balaclava. Of course everyone, not forgetting the Light Brigade, tends to be more interested in hearing about the particular events controlling a famous decision such as this one. But here I must turn my back on the attractive special case and attempt instead to describe the more general properties of man as a decision maker.

A good case could be made out for characterizing man as a hierarchy of decision-making mechanisms; their complexity ranging from the selection of the route of impulses at successive synaptic junctions in the nervous system up to decisions of a highly intelligent kind which obviously demand a consideration of the function of the brain as a whole. Even in the explanation of seemingly simple sensory phenomena such as the detection by the eye of a weak flash of light – it is nowadays thought necessary to postulate the involvement of choice. This is because analysis of that task shows the sensory nervous system to be always active to some extent, whether a flash of light is actually there or not. Hence the brain must clearly select some level of activity which has to be exceeded before it accepts that any particular amount of excitation is due to the presence of the flash. Experimental evidence is in favour of this not being a fixed quantity, but a variable level dependent on experience and the relative pay-offs that the subject would receive for correct detections and false alarms. This kind of evidence strongly suggests the involvement of some process of choice. Decisions, then, in one form or another, are present in brain function at several levels.

Now most people only talk of decisions when there is cause for at least some rumination. In order, therefore, to show the relationship between the very simple choices which psychologists have usually studied and decisions which have some real human interest, I will start by considering aspects of men's decisions about wagers. After all, the wager is a fairly reasonable prototype of a wide range of decision situations; and in Britain is the occupation of kings, proles, and, for that matter, prime ministers. I am going first to consider what governs the making up of a mind in matters of chance and, in doing so, I shall simplify matters by talking of a decision as if it were a single process. Also, since the question of whether or not choosing is in whole or part a conscious process will not in any way affect anything I say about it, this issue can also be happily left aside.

It is only recently that psychologists have seriously begun to analyse choices of the complexity of even a simple wager, and consequently we have no established theory to provide an account of this kind of behaviour. But mathematicians and economists have long discussed what one ought to do when faced with a wager. It is now also fashionable in psychology to consider how far these logical notions could provide an account of actual behaviour, and normative theories have sometimes been adopted, lock, stock and barrel, as the basis for a descriptive theory. This means that a rational man – one who always makes the best decision in any given situation – is seen as a model for an ordinary mortal like you or me; and the justifications for this approach clearly need to be debated. But, starting from the rational man will provide a convenient basis for my examination of real decisions.

One difficulty in comparing the real man with his rational counterpart is that the latter is usually studied in situations in which all relevant information about a decision that could be available is laid out and ready for use. Now practical men are not usually in this happy state. However, in the case of wagers we are fairer in this respect to the ordinary mortal than is usual for most choices. In this context, any wealthy French gambler of the seventeenth century would provide an early prototype for the rational man. His approach to a wager, based on the advice of probability theorists, was to try to maximize his average earnings in the long run. He might, for example, (on a visit to London) choose a fifty-fifty bet on winning two pounds rather than take a nearly certain chance of winning, say, seventeen-and-six, because the first wager would fetch him in the long run the higher average gain of one pound.

A rational man is by no means an apt characterization of men away from the gaming table. This was seen from the armchair by several thinkers. For example, the contented survival of insurance companies suggests that the wagers we take with them would certainly not satisfy a rational chevalier. Simple experiments in which subjects are offered choices between alternative gambles, show that once the abacus is left at home and the calculus of probabilities is not in use, man deviates from the rational scheme even in this, its natural setting.

In 1738 Bernoulli proposed an ironic and classic modification to the concept of the rational man to make him resemble more closely the practical buyer of insurance who had hitherto been regarded as irrational. Bernoulli supposed that before we calculate the average value of a wager we should replace the monetary value of each of the possible outcomes by its subjective value to the gambler; what the economists call the utility of the outcome. He then showed that if the utility of an outcome – that is to say the satisfaction gained from it – grew at an ever decreasing rate in relation to its monetary value, then there would be many circumstances in which it would be rational to insure oneself against financial loss.

Modern experimental evidence demands even further modifications of the rational theory if it is to predict decisions made by real people in real-life choice situations. We have seen from the work of Bernoulli that utility or satisfaction gained is not directly related to monetary values. But it is also the case that there are subjective distortions in the evaluation of the probabilities themselves. We tend to over-estimate the likelihood of an event occurring which has a low objective probability of happening; and we tend to under-estimate how **often** events with a high probability are likely to occur. These subjective distortions follow no simple rules, and depend very much on the circumstances of a decision and the psychology of the individual. For example, it is even quite difficult to find a real event which, subjectively speaking, has a fifty-fifty chance of occurring. Experimental psychologists have had to resort to a die with one nonsense word on three faces and a different one on the other three, in order to achieve a bet which actually appears to give an even chance of win or loss.

So, if we are going to take in the broadest features of man's decisions in simplified situations of risk and still keep him in some sense rational, we have to allow him to assess both probabilities and values in a subjective way. Some recent laboratory studies of gambling suggest that this 'new, improved rational man', who maximizes his subjective expected utility, may on occasion mimic the real man quite well.

But even in the simplest gamble, mortal man possesses certain quirks which segregate him from his rational counterpart. He may, for no apparent reason, prefer some probabilities to others, and in gambling on the horses may always go for odds of five to two, completely ignoring any financial maximization principle. Other evidence may also be interpreted to mean that subjects attach some value to risk itself, and actually prefer a gamble to a certainty. Worse still for our attempt to make the mantle of the rational man fit ourselves, there is evidence that the subjective evaluation of the probability of an event is influenced by the utility this event has for the subject. That is, an event with a given odds against it, is treated as being more likely to occur if the gambler thereby stands to win a larger amount of money. Now this last finding could completely upset any attempt to describe choice in terms of the rational calculus. Of course, there are other species of normative or prescriptive decision makers which operate on other criteria of rationality. But the comparison I have made with the classical economic man, indicates that at best these logical schemes can provide only an approximate description of man's choices and it is quite likely that in certain instances the processes governing a real decision are entirely different in their form and basis from the rules of a rational calculus.

So far, I have considered human choices in an entirely static way; and for situations in which all the evidence is immediately available. But in most real-life decisions, it is usually first necessary to collect the relevant information which is needed before a decision can be made; and this takes time. So a static model is no longer appropriate. Again, we find that we may look at decisions in this way at many levels of brain function and have to infer that even the recognition of, say, simple shapes involves decision processes of some kind. The identification by eye of a shape which has many features in common with some other known shape will take a relatively long time, just as the business man will have to spend more time in collecting evidence before resolving a particularly difficult investment problem.

If we look for a rational norm with which to compare our performance in this more natural kind of decision situation, then it is to be found in certain recent forms of statistical decision procedures. When the classical statistician (who, as usual in this kind of discussion, must be represented only by a straw image) was required to determine which was the superior of two medical treatments, he would take two random samples of a fixed size from a group of appropriate patients and use some logically well-founded test to decide for or against one of the treatments. This could be a wasteful procedure. The difference in efficacy of the treatments may be so great that the experimenter need only have taken a small sample to show this. On the other hand, he might find indications that made him suspect the treatments did exert different effects but his samples were just not large enough to provide any conclusive evidence. With one of the newer approaches – the so-called sequential tests – the statistician will advise the experimenter to take observations one by one until the odds in favour of one treatment being superior reach some acceptable criterion value. We might therefore consider the possibility of formally representing real decision makers as collecting information until an adequate amount is available to justify one action or another.

In cases where man's assessment of the importance of a

sequence of evidence can be compared with its objective merit, there's little doubt that he tends to show conservative tendencies. He is much less swayed by the evidence than he ought to be. Professor Ward Edwards of Michigan, who has done a great deal to stimulate recent interest in the psychology of decision making, contrived a simple demonstration of this conservative employment of facts. Imagine two bags each containing a very large number of red and blue poker chips. In one of the bags 70 per cent of the chips are red and 30 per cent blue; call this bag R for red. In the other there is again a seventy/thirty split of the colours, but this time there are 70 per cent blue chips; call this bag B for blue. I now take one bag at random and ask you to say which it is. The evidence available is the following: I have drawn out a sample of only twelve chips and find that eight of these are red and four are blue. The question is: what are the odds that it was the bag R, with the majority of red chips, that I sampled from. (Try to give a rational answer, but don't resort to fancy computation.) The average answer given by a real man is that the odds are about three to one against the bag being the one with the majority of blue; that is, that there is a 75 per cent chance that it was bag R. That is very conservative. The true odds are thirty-three to one against its being the blue bag and there is in fact a ninety-seven per cent chance that it was bag R.

As you might expect, individual differences and experience also play a role in the quantitative appraisal of evidence. One rather frivolous example which I cannot resist describing is as follows. Subjects were presented with a 'find the lady' situation. Actually there was no lady, only a pea. This was hidden under one of three walnuts, and the subject had to indicate where it was hidden. The game was repeated until a correct choice was made. As there was not a pea either, this never happened. But at some point people in one way or another express doubts as to its presence. The subjects in this experiment were all psychology postgraduate students, but some specialized in clinical psychology and others in experimental psychology. The experimental group were very cautious and the number of games they watched was the same that would be required by a statistician who wanted to keep errors down to below one in a hundred.

The clinicians' average sample size corresponded to the higher error rate of one in twenty decisions. It may be reassuring to point out that there is no clear evidence that willingness to take a risk is a personality trait general to all of a man's choices.

In making use of evidence, the prior odds of an event must be taken into account. For example, in England, without even bothering to look out of the window first, it is pretty rational to take one's umbrella. But in this respect we now discover the other aspect of man's conservative use of evidence, for it is clear that we give far too much weight to our prior opinions. Even when these opinions are lightly held, about very simple and trivial choices, they affect the kinds and amounts of evidence we collect. One way of studying this and other phenomena of choice is to use a simple laboratory task called an expanded judgement. In this, subjects are presented with items of information, one by one, until they consider that they have gathered enough to decide in favour of one of the alternative actions open to them. An extremely simple version might have for each item of information, say, just a patch of red or green light and the task is to determine whether the sequence of lights is governed by a process which is biased in favour of green or in favour of red. In this situation, even a guess by the subject as to the true state of affairs prior to the arrival of any new evidence, will cause him to sample a longer sequence of evidence if his final decision is opposed to his guess than if the guess and the evidence incline him to the same view of the situation. Minds appear not to need making up; it is un-making them which takes time and evidence.

Biases may not always come from the person who is deciding, they are also induced by the particular sequence of evidence that is presented to him. In the expanded judgement task, a brief flurry of evidence in favour of one colour, even if this is soon neutralized objectively by later evidence, will operate much in the way of a prior prejudice.

Sequential effects of various kinds make themselves apparent in decisions which demand much more thought than the last example. If one dramatizes the legal evidence from a court case and presents it in different orders, then these orders will influence the opinion that is formed about the guilt of the defendant. In our undergraduate laboratory classes my colleague, Dr Legge, and I have composed in this way two particular orders of presentation of the testimony from a celebrated American bigamy case. The students are required to express on a simple scale, the degree of their belief in the defendant's guilt or innocence at every stage in the trial. We have always found consistent differences in the average beliefs in guilt resulting from the two orders when these are compared at the end of the evidence. Even more startling is the difference in the number of people actually considering the defendant guilty. Before retiring as a jury, the individual members are required to state whether they would vote for guilt or for innocence. Summarising the experimental results over four years' work we find that of fifty-six jurors receiving one order of evidence only three plump for 'guilty', for the other order eighteen out of fifty-six jurors regard the defendant as guilty. There is only one possibility in ten thousand that this difference could be due to chance. Sequential effects also find expression in the time that the two juries deliberate over their joint verdict. Of course, this is only an approximation, perhaps even a caricature of the law. But who knows without experiment what some aspects of the law may be a caricature of?

Experiments which have been conducted to find out what happens when people are interviewed for a job also reveal the operation of biases in important decisions. In a sample of employment interviews, each of which lasted fifteen minutes, a decision was found to be reached, on average, after only four minutes. In only one in twenty interviews was the early opinion reversed before the end of the quarter-hour. In another controlled experiment in the same kind of situation, the decision makers were experienced personnel selection officers and genuine employment interviews were studied. Three types of information were available to the interviewer: first, an application form; second, the initial face-to-face impressions of the applicant; and third, the interview proper. The order in which the interviewer was exposed to these data was systematically varied. It turns out that the result of such interviews can be predicted with eighty-five per cent accuracy if one knows the attitude of the employer after he has just studied the application form and looked at his man. If either of these two pieces of evidence create a negative impression, then the applicant will be rejected in eighty-eight per cent of cases. These and other results suggest that the interviewer assesses the applicant against a prior stereotype of the person suitable for the job. In short he starts out with hypotheses, or quickly forms them, often on irrational grounds; later evidence is just not given sufficient weight in his judgement.

In introducing the statistical model for making sequential decisions, I left out any consideration of the cost of making observations. But in practical matters information usually has to be bought. This question of costs complicates the whole issue of the rationality of man as a decision maker. If one considers logical decision in a broader context of the efficiency of a total system, such as an efficient business enterprise, then the logical device would have to balance the adequacy of the final decision on any one problem against the cost and effort required to reach a conclusion. This would lead to a sequential decision procedure in which, as time went on, the amount of information considered necessary for a decision diminished. It is even possible that just a guess would be made, if information was very expensive.

Metaphorically speaking, man is also faced with the cost of data in his own decisions. Time spent searching for a decision involves the expenditure of effort. Furthermore time spent choosing is time not spent in acting, and also subtracts from the time available to get on with other activities outside those depending on the particular choice in hand. The role of effort in choice has been insufficiently studied. Even in laboratory tasks with no apparent emotional content, the level of palmar-sweating, an index of effort, goes up when hard choices have to be made. It may be that the business of not doing anything while you make a choice in itself requires an effort. Even laboratory rats, when faced with a discrimination task, produce a more forceful response when they are in a difficult problem which forces them to delay their responses. Men exhibit similar effects for tasks no more important than determining which is the brighter of two lights.

The evidence from the expanded judgement task, which I

mentioned earlier, would seem to indicate that the human decision maker also trades the accuracy of his final decision against the human cost of his time and effort. If one artificially holds back a subject's decision, he requires less information to make up his mind.

If one speculates beyond the bounds of scientific respectability it would be possible to regard effort as having a wider determining role than its local influence upon any one decision. The seemingly irrational departures from a logical scheme may indeed have a logic of their own, by serving to reduce overall effort. Science itself tends to be resistant to evidence which would demand a drastic overhaul of a system of knowledge in which so much time and effort has been invested and which often possesses great beauty. An individual man's prejudices and biases may be looked on similarly as a fairly tightly interlocked complex. Looked at in this light our choices do not seem to be all that irrational. Even Hamlet breaks off his celebrated expanded judgement when Ophelia appears.

Still in speculative vein, I shall conclude by suggesting that in choosing between two actions A and B, man does not usually do as his modern logical or statistical counterpart would do, namely, ask whether A or B is the best action. Rather it is as if the processes governing our decisions first produced a statement like 'I think A is right', and then looked for evidence in the light of this prior hypothesis. This scheme would give at least a good preliminary description of simple laboratory decisions as well as really humanly important ones like the employment interviews I discussed earlier.

To give a categorical answer to the question of my title I would reply that what makes up a mind is its history, and evidence too – but only if that is in the right direction. Or to put it another way, minds quite often come already made up.

6 A. Downs

Decision Making in Bureaucracy

Excerpts from 'The basic dynamics of search and change',
and 'Search problems in bureaus', in A. Downs, *Inside Bureaucracy*,
Little, Brown, 1967, chs. 14–15, pp. 167–71, 178–90.

The depth of change

The behavior of both individuals and organizations changes
constantly. However, during any given period when some
elements are changing, others must remain stable, or there will
be a loss of identity. For example, the specific behavior of an
individual or bureau may be quite different on Tuesday from
what it was on Monday, but the rules governing that behavior
may be the same on both days. The first problem we encounter
is distinguishing the depth of change involved.

Each individual's goal structure contains different layers of
goals, varying from profound to shallow ones. Since the individual's behavior reflects his goals, we can identify the depth of
his actions by relating them to specific layers in his goal
structure. In this way, we can conceptually distinguish what
depths of actions or goals are involved when an individual
undergoes change.

Similarly, organizations have different structural depths. Our
analysis recognizes four 'organizational layers'. The shallowest
consists of the specific actions taken by the bureau, the second
of the decision-making rules it uses, the third of the institutional
structure it uses to make those rules, and the deepest of its
general purposes.

In both individuals and organizations, change can occur at
any depth without affecting layers of greater depth, though it
will normally affect all shallower layers. Thus, a bureau can
change its everyday actions without changing its rules; it can
change its rules without shifting its rule-making structure; and
it can alter its rule-making structure without adopting any

different fundamental purposes. But if it adopts new purposes, all the other layers will be significantly affected. This means that change is largely a matter of degree, ranging from trivial shifts in everyday actions to profound alterations in purpose. Our analysis of bureaus will focus upon major changes in rules, structure, and purposes, rather than minor shifts in any of these elements or in everyday behavior [. . .]

The basic model

In economic theory, there is a long-standing debate between theorists who believe that decisions are made (and hence change initiated) in a process of utility *maximizing* and those who believe they are made in a process of utility *satisficing* or *disjointed incrementalism*. Our own theory combines elements from all of these approaches.[1]

Our analysis of change is focused upon individual officials rather than upon the bureau as a whole, since individuals are the basic decision-units in our theory. Because they are utility maximizers, they are always willing to adopt a new course of action if it promises to make them better off, even if they are relatively happy at present. However, they cannot search for new courses of action without expending resources. Since the supply of these is limited, they tend to avoid further search whenever the likely rewards seem small *a priori* (that is, the expected marginal payoff seems smaller than the expected marginal cost). This is the case whenever their current behavior seems quite satisfactory in light of their recent experience.

Within this framework, our theory posits the following hypotheses:

1. All men are continuously engaged in scanning their immediate environment to some degree. They constantly receive a certain amount of information from newspaper articles, from radio and TV programs, from conversation with friends, and in the course of their jobs and domestic activities. This amounts to a

1. The leading proponents of 'satisficing' theory are Simon and March (see Simon, 1955), March and Simon (1958), pp. 47–52, 173–77. The term 'disjointed incrementalism' is from Braybrooke and Lindblom (1963). The latter work contains numerous references to earlier theorists who set forth the traditional 'maximizing' approach.

stream of free information, since it comes to them without specific effort on their part to obtain it.[2] In addition, many officials regularly scan certain data sources (such as the *Wall Street Journal* or *Aviation Week*) without any prior idea of exactly what type of information they are seeking or will find. They do this not because they are dissatisfied, but because past experience teaches them that new developments are constantly occurring that might affect their present level of satisfaction. This combination of unprogrammed free information streams and habitually programmed scanning provides a minimum degree of constant, 'automatic' search. Every official in every bureau undertakes such search regardless of how well satisfied he is with his own current behavior or that of his bureau.

2. Each official develops a level of satisfactory performance for his own behavior or that of other parts of the bureau relevant to him. He may or may not in fact attain this level. However, he is not aware of any alternative behavior pattern that would both yield more utility and could be attained at a cost smaller than the resulting gain in utility. In other words, when he is actually at the satisfactory level, he is maximizing his utility in the light of his existing knowledge.

Also, the satisfactory level of performance yields enough utility in relation to his recent experience so that when he attains it, he is not motivated to look for better alternatives. In short, he is not dissatisfied with his performance at this level. In this sense, the satisfactory level is a dynamic concept embodying not only his current, but also his past experiences.

3. Whenever the actual behavior of an official (or of a bureau section relevant to him) yields him less utility than the relevant level of satisfactory performance, he is motivated to undertake more intensive search for new forms of behavior that will provide him with more utility. He will designate the difference in utility he perceives between the actual and the satisfactory level of performance as the *performance gap*. The larger this gap, the greater his motivation to undertake more intensive search. He is already engaging in some search just by being alive; but in this

2. The concept of a stream of 'free information' providing at least minimal data to everyone was advanced in Downs (1957).

case, dissatisfaction leads him both to intensify his normal search and to direct it specifically at alternatives likely to reduce the causes of his dissatisfaction.

His first step is to consider alternatives involving those variables he can most easily control. If one or more of these alternatives will move him back to the satisfactory level, he ceases his search and adopts the best of these alternatives.[3] If none of the alternatives contained in this initial set is able to return him to the satisfactory level, he enlarges his search and considers other alternatives involving variables beyond his own control.

He continues broadening his search for alternatives in discrete steps, pausing to evaluate each incremental set as he compiles it. This process continues until he either finds an alternative that restores him to the satisfactory level (or puts him onto some even higher level), or the cost of further search exceeds the cost of accepting a level of performance below his satisfactory level.

In searching for alternatives, he starts with those he initially believes will yield him the highest net utility and works downward, evaluating them in relatively homogeneous sets in terms of their likely net utility as he sees it. He considers his own goals in this process as well as those of the organization. Hence he regards any personal benefits to him as plus factors in his utility evaluation, and considers personal costs, large organizational changes, or computational difficulties as minus factors. Therefore, he is more likely to include the following types of alternatives in each set he analyzes than he is their opposites, other things being equal:

(a) Those that provide ancillary 'side benefits' in terms of variables other than the ones whose drop from a satisfactory level caused him to initiate this intensive search.

(b) Those that are relatively simple and easy to comprehend.

(c) Those that involve marginal rather than major adjustments in the bureau's operations or structure.

(d) Those that do not depend upon estimations or consideration of highly uncertain variables, since such variables are difficult to use.

3. This sequence of search was suggested by March and Simon (1958).

4. If intensive search fails to reveal any ways he can return to the originally satisfactory level, he will eventually lower his conception of the satisfactory level down to the highest net level of utility income he can attain.

5. Whenever his constant search process reveals the possibility that a new course of action might yield more utility than offered by his present satisfactory level of performance, he undertakes intensive search of this new course of action and any close substitutes for it that also promise to yield net gains in utility. Thus chance encounters with possibilities for improving his situation create potential performance gaps without any change in his current utility income. If his intensified search reveals that he can indeed make a net gain in utility by shifting to a new behavior pattern, he will make the shift that yields the largest net gain he is aware of.

6. Once he has adopted the new course of action and his net utility income therefrom has risen, he regards the new higher utility income level as his satisfactory performance level.

7. After he has either moved to a new higher level (which he now regards as the satisfactory level) or discovered he cannot improve upon his prior performance (which therefore remains his satisfactory level), he reduces his search efforts back to their normal 'automatic' intensity. They remain at this intensity until he again falls below his satisfactory level, or encounters some specific reason to believe that particular alternatives might improve his position.

The above hypotheses form a theory of dynamic equilibrium involving firstly a tendency for the official to move toward a satisfactory position of equilibrium, secondly a constant stream of new inputs into the situation (both data and environmental obstacles to performance) displacing him from equilibrium and thereby initiating search, and thirdly a process by which he continually redefines the locus of his equilibrium position to reflect his recent experience regarding what is really possible [. . .]

How organizational decision making differs from individual decision making

Decision making within large organizations differs from that conducted by a single individual for the obvious reason that it involves many persons instead of one. As a result: the various steps in the decision and action cycle are carried out by different persons.

An organization must generate numerous conflict-controlling and consensus-creating mechanisms because its members have widely varying perception apparatuses, memories, images of the world, and goals.

Organizational decision making involves the following significant costs of internal communication that have no analogs within an individual:

1. Losses of utility due to errors of transmission.

2. Losses of utility (for the ultimate users of the data) due to distortion.

3. Resources (especially time) absorbed in internal communications.

4. Losses of utility due to overloading communications channels in the short run.

On the other hand, organizations have such advantages over individuals as much greater capacity to carry out all steps in the decision and action cycle, extensive internal specialization, and simultaneous maintenance of a diversity of viewpoints.

We have made explicit these rather obvious differences between organizations and individuals because we will also use our basic conceptual scheme for individual decision making in our analysis of organizational search.

Basic problems in organizational search

The basic problems of organizational search include some that are not relevant to individuals. These problems are generated by tensions arising from four factors:

1. *The unity of search, analysis, and evaluation.* Search, analysis, and evaluation cannot be separated from each other without

creating needs for almost continuous communications, irrational allocations of resources, or both.

2. *The need for consensus.* Bureaus operate on such a large scale that any significant decision almost invariably affects many bureau members and their activities. These intra-bureau repercussions are unlikely to be fully known to any one member (even the topmost official) unless he specifically seeks the advice of others. In essence, no one bureau member encompasses all the goals relevant to the bureau's whole operation. But evaluation requires measuring possible actions against one's goals (via the performance gap). Hence, evaluation is necessarily fragmentalized in every bureau.

3. *The economies of delegation.* Organizations can achieve huge economies of scale in search by assigning some of the steps involved to specialists. But this requires separating some of the steps in the search-analysis-evaluation cycle from others.

4. *Nontechnical divergence of goals.* Both delegation and the fragmentalizing of evaluation require giving certain powers of discretion regarding a given decision to many different officials. But officials always use some of whatever discretionary powers they have to benefit themselves and the bureau sections to which they are loyal rather than the bureau as a whole, thus introducing partly inconsistent goals into the theoretically unified search-analysis-evaluation cycle. This point is different from the need for consensus. The latter is required because a bureau is so large that no single member knows what all its relevant goals are. Hence consensus would be necessary even if all members had identical personal goals and ambitions. But nontechnical goal divergence arises from conflicts of interest that cannot be eliminated by knowledge alone.

We will now explore specific aspects of the search processes in bureaus arising from tensions among these four factors.

How the biases of individual officials affect the search process

As each official goes through the decision and action process, he behaves somewhat differently from the way he would if his goals were identical to the formal purposes of the organization. Among his biases relevant to search are the following:

1. His perception apparatus will partially screen out data adverse to his interests, and magnify those favoring his interests. (Festinger, 1957.) The probability that important data will not be screened out by such biases can be increased by assigning overlapping search responsibilities to persons with different and even conflicting interests and policy preferences, or assigning search tasks to persons who have no particular policy preferences and whose interests are not connected with the advancement of any bureau section.

2. In formulating alternative actions, each official will tend to give undue precedence to alternatives most favorable to his interests, and to those about which adequate consensus can most easily be established. The process of decision making within a bure~ involves significant costs. So... ⌐f these costs prob-⌐y rise more than proportionately with the number of alternatives considered. Hence it is often more rational for a bureau to choose from a set of alternatives it has already assembled than to expand that set, even if such expansion might provide it with additional choices markedly superior to those now facing it.

This implies that the order in which alternative actions are assembled and evaluated may have an extremely important impact on what an organization eventually does. If the first set of alternatives considered contains at least one that closes the performance gap, the bureau may never discover other alternatives that would not only close that gap, but also provide a new higher level of performance.

As a result, any biases among officials that cause certain types of alternatives to be systematically considered early in the game will cause those types of alternatives to be adopted more often than they would be if officials were unbiased. Among such biases are the following:

Since relatively simple proposals are much easier to discuss and obtain consensus about than complicated ones, officials will tend to consider such proposals first. This implies that over any given period, a bureau will tend to choose policies that are simpler than those it would choose if its members had perfect information about all possible proposals. Part of this simplification is a rational response to the costs of deliberation, but part results from officials' biases.

Officials will tend to consider those alternatives that benefit their own interests before those adverse to their interests. Thus, a bureau will tend to select alternatives that are unduly favorable to the particular officials who are in charge of proposing alternatives. Incumbents are usually favored by actions that do not radically alter the *status quo*. Staff members are more oriented toward change so long as it does not injure their own interests or those of their line superiors. Hence bureaus in which incumbent office holders design proposals will tend to make unduly conservative choices. Those in which staff members design proposals will not exhibit this bias unless the proposals concern their behavior or that of their line superiors.

The evaluation process in bureaus is fragmentalized; so officials proposing policies often need to obtain support from a number of others only marginally concerned. These officials usually bargain for a *quid pro quo* in return for their support. A common *quid pro quo* is including something in the alternatives that benefits them, even though it does not directly affect the performance gap concerned. Another is omitting from these alternatives anything damaging to their interests, even though it would benefit the bureau as a whole. The existence of such 'territorial bargaining' has the following implications:

(a) A bureau will choose actions that unduly favor continuance of the existing allocation of resources and power among its subsections.

(b) Officials shaping alternatives will try to exclude marginal effects from their proposals so as to reduce the amount of consensus they need to achieve. This will unduly narrow the impact of actions taken by the bureau.

(c) The alternatives formulated will be irrationally affected by the particular organization of the bureau.

(d) If the initial set of alternatives assembled by an official has been rejected, he can either abandon the project, search for wholly new alternatives, or try to reformulate the rejected ones. If the latter include proposals strongly supported by powerful officials, he will tend to devote too much effort to reformulating those proposals.

(e) Officials will tend to propose alternatives involving as little uncertainty as possible in order to avoid complicated and conflict-engendering negotiations. Thus, over any given period, a bureau will tend to adopt actions that do not take sufficient account of future uncertainties.

The above analysis indicates that the need to establish consensus before making decisions has a tremendous influence upon the processes of search within a bureau. The more officials involved in a decision, and the greater the diversity of their views and interests, the more factors must be taken into account, the more alternatives must be explored, and the harder it is to get a consensus on any alternative.

This creates a dilemma for bureaus regarding search. On one hand, those who formulate alternatives often try to restrict the choices they consider to those that affect as few other officials as possible. This renders decision making both faster and easier. But bureaus will systematically tend to consider narrower alternatives than they would if officials were unbiased.

On the other hand, if officials extend their range of search to encompass alternatives affecting a great many others, they will generate both extremely high costs of reaching a decision and a strong probability that the decision will support the *status quo* to an excessive degree. Thus it appears extraordinarily difficult to create incentives for the officials involved so that firstly they will extend their search for alternatives far enough to encompass all significant interdependencies, secondly they will make decisions relatively quickly and easily, and thirdly those decisions will incorporate really significant changes in the *status quo* when warranted.

This situation results partly from a correct perception of the costs of change. If each part of a bureau merely had to consider changing its behavior every time an official anywhere else was making a decision that might affect it, the bureau would lose a great deal of its operating efficiency. Furthermore, it would become almost chaotic if it actually made changes in a high percentage of such cases. Hence resistance to suggestions of change is partly a rational behavior pattern for officials. But the biases of officials make this resistance excessive in terms of efficiently achieving the bureau's social functions.

There may be a partial escape from this dilemma for more significant decisions if the bureau's top officials can create some outside agency that will be free from direct operational responsibilities within the bureau, but quite familiar with its goals, rules, behavior, and routines. Such an agency can be used as an aid in searching for alternative courses of action, and for information useful in analyzing and evaluating alternatives. Ideally, its members should be familiar enough with the bureau to understand the inter-dependencies therein, but detached enough to propose changes involving major departures from the *status quo*. Such detachment normally results only when men have no direct operational responsibilities. The payoffs from such an arrangement can be very large.

The impact of time pressure upon search

Search is greatly affected by the time pressure associated with a given decision. The cost of delay – that is, procuring additional information – rises sharply with pressure to act quickly. Under such pressure, a rational decision maker will decide on the basis of less knowledge than he would if time pressure were lower. Conversely, when there is little pressure to decide quickly, he can acquire a great deal of information before reaching any conclusions. Thus there is an inverse relationship between the extension of search and the time pressure on the decision. Whenever time pressure is high, the following will occur:

A minimal number of alternatives will be considered. The more complex the decision, the smaller the number.

Whenever only a few alternatives are considered, all the biases influencing the order in which possible alternatives are formulated become accentuated. Moreover, officials will tend to give primary consideration to 'ready made' alternatives that have been thought out in advance. Since zealots will offer the pet policies they have been promoting for a long time, their ideas will have a much greater chance of being implemented than usual.

The decision makers involved will try to restrict the number of persons participating in the decision and the diversity of views among them. Hence secrecy may be used simply to prevent knowledge of the decision from reaching persons who might want to be included in the deliberations if they knew the decision was being made. Furthermore, secrecy may enable more complex decisions to be made. If a great many people must be consulted in making a decision, it becomes difficult to communicate to each person the issues involved, the possible alternatives, and the responses and views of other consultants. But if secrecy restricts the number of persons consulted, those persons can consider much more complicated possibilities.

Clearly, the degree of time pressure has critical impacts upon decision making. High time pressures usually spring from either crises or deadlines. The former are normally of exogenous origin, but deadlines are usually deliberate, hence they can be manipulated to exploit the effects of time pressure. For example, if a high-ranking official wants to restrict the number of people his subordinates consult on a given decision, he can place a very short deadline on it. Conversely, if he wants wide-ranging deliberations, he can give it a long time horizon.

'Gresham's Law of Planning' may nullify this strategy if subordinates are assigned both short deadline and long deadline tasks (see March and Simon, 1958). In order to complete their short deadline tasks, they may keep on postponing work on longer-run problems until once-distant deadlines loom in the near future. Therefore, extending search across a really wide and deep spectrum of possibilities normally requires assignment of long deadline tasks to officials or organizations separate from those responsible for short deadline tasks.

Search extension and organizational policies

The foregoing analysis suggests a number of policies organizations can use to influence the degree of search extension in making a decision. These policies are set forth briefly in Table 1.

Our analysis also implies that the optimal degree of search extension depends both upon the nature of the problem and the time pressure for solving it. Other things being equal, the bigger

Table 1 Organizational Policies that Extend or Contract Search

Policies that tend to extend degree of search and increase diversity of alternatives considered	Policies that tend to contract degree of search and narrow diversity of alternatives considered
Allow a long time before conclusions must be reached	Enforce a very short deadline
Bring many people into decision making	Restrict decision making to a small number
Insure that those involved have a wide variety of views and interests – even conflicting	Insure that those involved have similar views and interests
Reduce number of persons to whom final decision must be justified or intelligibly communicated	Increase number of persons to whom final decision must be justified or intelligibly communicated
Increase proportion of analytically skillful or highly trained persons participating, or to whom it must be justified or communicated	Decrease proportion of analytically skillful or highly trained persons participating, or to whom it must be justified or communicated
Isolate those making decision from pressures of responsibility for other decisions, especially short deadline ones	Assign the decision to those immersed in making other decisions, especially short deadline ones
Reduce proportion of extremely busy persons to whom decision must be intelligibly communicated	Increase proportion of extremely busy persons to whom decision must be intelligibly communicated

the problem, the more likely that extension of search will be valuable, since potential savings from finding better alternatives are much greater.

The effects of separating search, analysis, and evaluation
When separation is rational

Because of the inherent unity of search, analysis, and evaluation, there is strong pressure to keep the specialists carrying out these steps for any particular decision relatively close together in 'organizational space'. In many cases, each department has its own specialists in search and analysis assisting the people actually making decisions. Then the decision makers can advise the searchers about how much and what kinds of data they need. Moreover, there can be frequent communications between the producers and consumers of these data during the decision-making process.

Even more important, the consumers of information must pay the costs of search. Hence such an arrangement minimizes misallocations of resources to search.

However, in certain situations, the economies of scale in search become enormous. Then nearly complete separation of the producers and consumers of data is almost mandatory. Such economies occur when three conditions exist simultaneously.

First, the sources of relevant information are remote from the decision makers. By remote we mean relatively inaccessible in terms of space, technically specialized knowledge, cultural unfamiliarity, secrecy, or extreme fragmentalization in diverse locations. Second, the data required by persons working on one type of decision are also useful for persons working on other types. Third, the means of access to remote information can be used to procure data useful for different kinds of decisions.

The remoteness of data sources means that a large, indivisible capital investment of some type must be created in order to gain access to them. This investment can be a network of scattered foreign observers; the education of certain technical specialists; creation of linguistic, sociological, or political expertise; or a group of clandestine agents. The need for this large initial investment constitutes a forbidding 'entry fee' which forces small-scale users to eschew such data altogether, or else to band together and establish joint search facilities [. . .]

The impact of separation upon policy formation

What types of problems does an agency face in deciding firstly what to search for with its existing facilities, secondly how many resources to expend searching for each item or type of item, and finally what investments to make in creating additional access facilities?

Some of its major problems occur because it cannot judge the relative importance of acquiring any given piece of information. It is not the ultimate consumer of such information, nor can it charge the ultimate consumers money prices. No profit-making firm is the ultimate consumer of its products either, but such a firm can rationally allocate resources because it charges its consumers money for whatever it gives them. We will assume that the central search agency cannot use this mechanism. Instead, it asks the bureaus it serves to describe the relative urgency of their data needs.

Each bureau has no way of estimating how urgent its requests are in comparison with those of other bureaus, and the natural advocacy of each bureau's officials leads them to exaggerate the importance of their own needs. Hence the central agency is forced to make its own judgements about the relative importance of the needs of different bureaus. This it cannot do accurately unless its own personnel start becoming involved in the policy decision making of its bureau clients. Since many officials within the search agency seek to increase their own power and that of their agency, such involvement is quite likely.

In this involvement, members of the central search agency may exhibit the following viewpoints regarding policy making in other bureaus.

1. In many matters they may act like statesmen. There is no *a priori* reason why the central search agency should have any particular substantive policy biases. Furthermore, the agency's members are encouraged to develop a broad viewpoint in order to choose among competing demands for information made by the various bureaus they serve.

True, insofar as this agency is attached to a particular political entity (such as the chief executive), it will be influenced by the political perspective of that entity. Even so, the search agency is partly prevented from becoming an advocate of any particular policy by its need to serve many different advocates of a wide variety of conflicting policies.

2. Members of the central search agency will inevitably seek to augment their own and the agency's power, income, and prestige. As a result:

The agency will attempt to establish a monopoly over as many remote data sources as possible, partly by advocating 'eliminating unnecessary duplication' of search facilities.

It will exaggerate the need for secrecy in its operations to conceal discovery of how efficiently it operates.

Its reporting will exaggerate those types of information likely to contribute to its significance. This significance derives from its usefulness to other bureaus, which will consider information most useful that both justifies existing policies and indicates enough change and instability to make larger appropriations desirable. The existence of external threats often performs the latter function. On the other hand, the governing party wishes to present a public image of competence and control of the situation. Hence the central search agency will tend to supply excessively alarming data to individual bureaus and excessively soothing data to the public in general.

It will exaggerate the importance of expensive forms of search and analysis, and underplay that of inexpensive ones.

It will overemphasize forms of search involving a great deal of analysis and evaluation by its own specialists.

3. Members of the central search agency may act as advocates for bureaus within the search agency. This will probably occur only if promotion of these liaison officials is controlled by the agencies in which they are working.

The impact of separation upon resource allocation

The bureau 'customers' of the central search agency will have an ambivalent attitude toward it. They will ask it to furnish all information of any positive value, regardless of cost, since they do not have to pay for it. This conclusion has the following implications. First, no matter how large a data gathering and handling capacity the central search agency possesses, its facilities will always be overloaded. This results from the Law of Free Goods: Requests for free services always rise to meet the capacity of the producing agency.

Second, officials of the central search agency will develop non-pecuniary prices for their services. These are devices for imposing costs upon members of other bureaus who request information. They will be designed both to discourage requests and to provide rewards to central search agency members. Such 'quasi-prices' will include demands for reciprocal favors, long delays, and frustrating barriers of red tape. This illustrates the Law of Non-Money Pricing: Organizations that cannot charge money for their services must develop non-monetary costs to impose on their clients as a means of rationing their outputs. Hence much of the irritating behavior of bureaucrats often represents necessary means of rationing their limited resources so they will be available to those truly anxious to use them.

Third, such rationing systems may result in irrational allocations from the viewpoint of society in general. Information seekers persistent enough to penetrate 'quasi-price' barriers may not have needs that would be considered most urgent if all concerned had perfect information.

The other part of each information-using bureau's ambivalent attitude is its desire to 'capture' some of the search agency's activities and incorporate them into its own program. This would bring its decision makers closer to their data sources as well as add to its total resources.

'Spreading the word' and the noise problem
The fragmentalized perception of large organizations

Since an organization has no personality, only individual members can perceive or search. Therefore, organizational perception and search are inherently fragmentalized. Information is first perceived by one or several members, who must then pass it on to others.

Thanks to the ubiquity and speed of modern communications some information is perceived almost simultaneously by all members of even very large organizations. For example, over 90 per cent of the entire population in the United States knew of President Kennedy's assassination within four hours of his death. Similarly, if members of a bureau all read the same newspapers or watch the same TV programs, they may learn about a wide range of events almost simultaneously. Nevertheless, such high-exposure sources transmit only a small part of the information important to any bureau. A large proportion of the data it needs is initially perceived by only one or a few low-level members, who then transmit it upwards through channels.

Yet it is not clear just when the organization has perceived any particular item of information, for a statistical majority does not by any means comprise the substantive decision makers. We can say that the organization has been informed when the given information has become known to all those members who need to know it, so that the organization can carry out the appropriate response.

The problem of assessing the significance of data

There is a great difference between knowing a fact and grasping its true significance. The radar superviser in Hawaii whose subordinate picked up returns from unidentified aircraft on the morning of 7 December 1941 knew that fact, but he did not grasp its significance. The number of facts gleaned every day by any large organization is immense. In theory, the screening process transmits only the most significant facts to the men at the top, and places them in their proper context along the way. But, as we have seen, considerable distortion occurs in this process. Each part of the organization tends to exaggerate the importance of some events and to minimize that of others. This naturally produces a healthy skepticism among officials at the top of the hierarchy.

An inescapable result of this situation is a rational insensitivity to signals of alarm at high levels. This may have disastrous consequences when those signals are accurate. It is the responsibility of each low-level official to report on events he believes could be dangerous. However, the real danger of the supposed threat is not always clear, and his messages must therefore contain suppositions of his own making.

In organizations always surrounded by potentially threatening situations (eg the Department of Defense), officials at each level continually receive signals of alarm from their subordinates.

But they are virtually compelled to adopt a wait and see attitude toward these outcries for three reasons. First, they do not have enough resources to respond to all alleged threats simultaneously. Second, experience has taught them that most potential threats fail to materialize. Third, by the time a potential threat does develop significantly, either the threat itself or the organization's understanding of it has changed greatly. Hence it becomes clear that what initially appeared to be the proper response would really have been ineffective. Therefore, initial signals concerning potential threats usually focus the attention of intermediate-level officials on a given problem area, but do not move them to transmit the alarm upward.

Only if further events begin to confirm the dire predictions of 'alarmists' do their superiors become alarmed too, and send distress signals upward. But higher-level officials also have a wait and see attitude for the same reasons, and it takes even further deterioration of the situation to convince them to transmit the alarm still higher. Therefore, a given situation may have to become very threatening indeed before its significance is grasped at the top levels of the organization.

This is one of the reasons why top-level officials tend to become involved in only the most difficult and ominous situations faced by the organization. Easy problems are solved by lower-level officials, and difficult situations may deteriorate badly by the time they come to the attention of the top level.

As Wohlstetter (1962) argued in her study of the Pearl Harbor attack, fragmentalization of perception inevitably produces an enormous amount of 'noise' in the organization's communications networks. The officials at the bottom must be instructed to report all potentially dangerous situations immediately so the organization can have as much advanced warning as possible. Their preoccupation with their specialties and their desire to insure against the worst possible outcomes, plus other biases, all cause them to transmit signals with a degree of urgency that in most cases proves exaggerated after the fact. These overly urgent signals make it extremely difficult to tell in advance which alarms will prove warranted and which will not.

There are no easy solutions to this problem. With so many 'Chicken Lickens' running around claiming the sky is about to fall, the men at the top normally cannot do much until 'Henney Penney' and 'Foxy Loxy' have also started screaming for help, or there is a convergence of alarm signals from a number of unrelated sources within the organization. Even the use of high-speed, automatic data networks cannot eliminate it. The basic difficulty is not in procuring information, but in assessing its significance in terms of future events – from which no human being can eliminate all uncertainty.

References

BRAYBROOKE, D. and LINDBLOM, C. E., and (1963), *A Strategy of Decision*, Free Press.

DOWNS, A. (1957), *An Economic Theory of Democracy*, Harper & Row.

FESTINGER, L. (1957), *A Theory of Cognitive Dissonance*, Harper & Row.

MARCH, J. G. and SIMON, H. A. (1958), *Organizations*, Wiley.

SIMON, H. A. (1955), 'A behavioral model of rational choice', *Q. J. Econ.*, vol. 69, pp. 129–38.

WOHLSTETTER, R. (1962), *Pearl Harbor: Warning and Decision*, Stanford University Press.

7 R. G. S. Brown

The Administrative Process in Britain: Decisions

Excerpts from 'Decisions', in R. G. S. Brown, *The Administrative Process in Britain*, Methuen, 1970, ch. 7, pp. 137–54.

The most characteristic activity of a government department is reaching decisions; at senior levels, there may be no other output. 'Decisions' in the sense of grand strategic determinations of policy are, of course, infrequent and elusive. But decisions of another sort are being made all the time – whether to consult a committee, how to time a memorandum, what advice to give the Minister, how to deal with a particular case. There are equivalents to these at managerial levels in most organizations. Administration, indeed, is sometimes defined as a problem-solving and enabling process.

Theories about decisions can be divided into two groups. One is concerned with the way decisions ought to be made, the other with the way they are in fact made [. . .]

If we are looking for a more generally helpful approach to decisions, it is fruitful to turn from normative theories to theories which try to explain how decisions are actually reached in real-life situations:

The role of decision making in behavioral science is to describe how people make decisions under conditions of imperfect information – that is, where complete information as to the present state of affairs, possible courses of action, and consequences is not available. Decisions are influenced by individual differences, social pressures, leadership differences, communication structures, etc. Social scientists are interested in how individuals and groups reach a decision; how much information is necessary, who influences the outcome the most, how disagreements are resolved, what procedures are used and how choices are made (Applewhite, 1965, p. 54).

Unfortunately, it is difficult to study the normal processes of decision making. There are practical difficulties, including confidentiality, about observing senior people in their normal settings at all. It is also difficult to isolate a 'decision' from the incessant stream of consultations, committee discussions, authorizations and initialling of papers that makes up the normal day. Many experiments, therefore, have been made with college students – or with administrators when they are on courses, away from their normal work – and can be criticized as artificial. This in itself is not a ground for dismissing theories which appeal to common sense and experience, which provide insight into the way administrators' minds work, and which are not apparently contradicted by any research findings so far.

The main framework concept behind most of these studies is the assumption that any decision is reached in stages, each of which can be analysed and examined separately. First there must be an awareness that the problem exists. A signal must be received which suggests that some change in policy is neede? In a government department, the signal may come through political channels, or through the formal and informal machinery that links the department to the outside world, or perhaps from some internal source in the department, like a research and intelligence section which receives information suggesting that an existing policy is not working as well as it might. However the signal originates, it needs to be interpreted and related to other information so that the nature of the problem can be seen. When it has been structured in this way, there is an exploration stage. Possible courses of action or inaction are listed and a rough estimate is made of the probable consequences, desired and undesired, of each. This is followed by evaluation and by a provisional decision that one policy is preferable to the others. (In Whitehall terms, this is the point at which a 'departmental line' is taken.) There may follow a process of consultation in which the proposals are tested for acceptability (to interested parties and political groups) and feasibility (in the eyes of various sorts of expert), and finally, perhaps after modifications, brought to a higher level for authorization. This might be followed by communication of the decision reached, its implication and, ultimately, review to check whether the consequences are as expected.

Bounded rationality

If the problem is at all complex (as are most problems in public administration) the range of considerations which this process entails is beyond the scope of a single human mind. The only way it can be tackled at all is by factorization. Different aspects are handled by different people, each of whom is forced, by and large, to take the work of the others on trust. To take a crude example, civil servants who are considering the merits of a proposed increase in a service do not personally have to work out the 'opportunity costs' that would be incurred through spending money on it rather than in an infinity of other ways. They assume, if they think about it at all, that opportunity costs are somehow reflected in the amount of Treasury opposition that has to be overcome. It would be unreasonable to expect them to do more. Similarly, if a proposal entails the use of scarce manpower, they would seek advice about its availability from the appropriate department, which they would not question.

Responsibility for a decision can be divided horizontally and vertically. In a hierarchical system different contributions will be made at different levels. Typically, junior members will not question their seniors' definition of the ends to be served, while the latter will assume that the factual information reported by their juniors is correct. Typically, too, the most senior levels will be concerned with authorization – with the final check that a proposed course of action is consistent with a general system of values – rather than with working out detailed proposals. But they may also take the initiative by setting a broad agenda, or specifying general rules to which their subordinates have to work.

But the factors have to be brought together again. An administrative organization can be regarded as a system of communication which exists in order to link decision makers and to reassemble information about aspects of a problem that have been settled separately. Its coherence is maintained by specifying rules to guide its members in their partial decisions and by setting limits to the range of acceptable solutions that they may adopt. The limits appropriate to different levels in the hierarchy may be laid down precisely in so many words in terms of the financial or other commitments that an official has authority to incur. More often there is merely an understanding, to which the inexperienced officer may find it difficult to attach a precise meaning, that he ought to 'take his superiors with him' on questions of a certain character. The decision rules say what criteria should influence the decision, what consultations should be undertaken and so on. Again, the rules may be unwritten but this does not necessarily make them less compelling or less rigid.

So far, this is simply a spelling-out, using different language, of the structure of a Weberian bureaucracy. Duties and responsibilities are allocated in order to allow finite human beings to contribute collectively to the rational solution of infinitely complex problems. Marshak, indeed, suggests that the student of an organization should ask, not for an organization chart, but for a rough description of 'who does what in response to what information' (Marshak, 1959). But while the system tries to be rational, it can never quite succeed. Its rationality is ultimately limited by the capacity of its human members.

In a typical decision situation, an official looks at a number of pieces of information, rejects some and selects others to be rearranged and passed on in the form of information, a recommendation or an instruction to somebody else. Both in what he takes into account and in what he does with it there is an unavoidable element of uncertainty. Even in the most routine cases, when his choice of action is supposed to be completely determined by circumstances, he may not react as expected. He may be insufficiently trained to understand what he has to do or he may mistakenly believe that there is some room for the exercise of his own judgement; this is a frequent cause of misunderstanding. In non-routine matters, where there is room for discretion, the number of factors an official thinks of and the weight he gives to them will significantly affect his performance as a decision maker. They are influenced – and meant to be influenced – by his personal qualities and by his position within the organization. Rarely will he exercise choice over the complete range of possibilities that is logically open to him. The real situation, even after some aspects of it have been dealt with by others, is nearly always too complicated to be grasped. It cannot be tackled unless some of the detail is removed. 'Rational behaviour involves substituting for the complex reality a model of reality that is sufficiently simple to be handled by problem-solving processes' (March and Simon, 1958).

Selective perception

The first element of uncertainty is whether the existence of a problem will be recognized at all. If the problem is one that the organization is accustomed to handling there will be programmes for bringing it to the notice of the appropriate people – government departments have well-developed procedures for dealing with the Minister's correspondence, questions in Parliament, and so on. In other cases a good deal depends on the ability of someone in the organization to recognize it as a problem.

Different people will identify a problem in different ways. In an experiment at the Carnegie Institute of Technology some middle-management executives were asked to read a long factual account of a company and its current position and to say what aspect of it they thought should be attended to first. 83 per cent of the sales executives saw the main problem as sales. But only 29 per cent of the executives from other divisions saw it as sales, although both groups were working from identical material (Dearborn and Simon, 1958). Training and experience help people to structure a problem situation by focusing on one or two main features of it. But the focus will be different for different people.

In administration it is sometimes a sign of immaturity and inexperience to accept complaints and suggestions at their face value. It is not difficult to imagine a penetrating parliamentary question which evokes quite different responses from three officials, one of whom has for some time been advocating a review of the policy under attack, while another is an expert at the political game and knows that the questioner is unlikely to know how well-aimed his question is and a third is mainly anxious to keep the peace until he retires and hands over a tidy block of work to his successor. Each reaction might be predicted from social and psychological information about the official concerned.

People 'rationalize'. They try to structure their experience in ways that are consistent with their previous background, beliefs, prejudices and values. Features that do not fit in tend to be rejected. In an organizational setting an official's approach to a problem will be governed by his experience. He will have developed a repertory of programmes for handling different situations. If the problem looks superficially like ones he has already solved successfully he will be inclined to look for a solution along the same lines. In a large-scale organization experience takes on an extra dimension, since the collective experience of the whole organization over a period of time is, in theory, available to the individual decision maker. Relevant facts may be ascertainable from the filing system or from colleagues working on similar problems. Problem-solving techniques may be available and some of these may have been elevated into decision-rules. Methods that have been developed for one purpose tend to be used for another. For example, consultative procedures in government departments tend to follow a set pattern, regardless of the subject matter. Once an organization has settled down and developed a memory, precedents are available for many situations and much has to be treated as given that would be left to discretion in a more open situation. All this makes for economy of effort and is fairly commonplace. But there is inevitably a biasing effect on the way problems are perceived and structured. The policies that result may be less than optimal.

Moreover, if collective experience is to be useful, it must be accessible. In large organizations the arrangements for pooling information tend to become very complex. The staff may be unable to use them without special training. We can say that a person's potential contribution depends on: (1) his personal qualities and experience; and/or (2) the total relevant experience that is available in the organization as a whole combined with (3) procedures, channels of communication and filing systems (with the staff to operate them) to make the experience accessible and (4) his own knowledge of the procedures and readiness to use them. Characteristically, a professional will tend to be most at home with (1); a general adminstrator will tend to rely on (2) to (4). In both cases there is likely to be some distortion.

A different type of distortion appears when decisions are taken collectively by groups or committees. Groups do not necessarily use all the experience that their members possess. It has to be communicated and accepted by a majority as relevant. If most members of the group share certain attitudes, these are reinforced by 'resonance' and are difficult to dislodge. A group that has been successful in the past is particularly inclined to reject unfamiliar suggestions from new members. Even in a 'brainstorming' session, when the group is actively seeking new ideas, it is psychologically difficult for members to produce ideas that deviate markedly from the general consensus. Fewer creative ideas emerge in a homogeneous group, in spite of the ease of communication. Face-to-face groups are inclined to accept the ideas of more senior members, if there are differences in status, or from the most talkative, regardless of their merit. In tackling constructive problems groups seldom surpass the performance of their best individual members: a greater range of creative solutions is likely to be produced by the members working independently for an equivalent number of man-hours. Groups can be more effective than individuals at analytic problems of an arithmetical or 'twenty questions' type, when effort can be saved by division of labour and through the mutual correction of errors. But even this is not true if much time is needed for intercommunication and co-ordination. The utility of group work as a device for achieving consensus, is, of course, another matter.

Search activity

The individual decision maker has different types of considerations at his disposal. There are 'facts', or at least statements supplied by others which appear to describe a real situation. There are 'value-premises' indicating the objectives, sometimes conflicting and sometimes ambiguous, at which he should aim. And there are problem-solving techniques and 'decision-rules' to guide him in integrating and relating these other premises. Some of these will be in the front of his mind, immediately within his span of attention. Normally they will be a small sample, far short of what he needs to make anything approaching an objectively 'rational' decision. If he feels unable to reach an 'adequate' decision on this basis, he will have to search for additional material, in his own memory for personal experience, in his set of office instructions or regulations for decision rules and procedures, in files and consultation with colleagues for information and advice. The search may be intensive or it may be superficial. The more it is extended, the more complete will be the decision maker's model of the situation, and the closer will his actual decision approximate to a theoretically ideal one (always assuming that he structures his material logically when he has it, since there is a point beyond which additional information does not assist effective decision making but is merely confusing). The question of how widely search is likely to range is a motivational one, conditioned partly by the prevailing 'ethos' of the organization. It has been illuminated in laboratory investigations at Carnegie.

An individual will not search beyond the point at which he is enabled to make a decision that appears satisfactory to him. If such a solution occurs to him right away, he will not spend time and energy looking for an 'ideal' one. In Simon's phrase, the administrator does not 'maximize', he 'satisfices'. If he does not feel that any of the obvious solutions is satisfactory, he will search for a better one, by calling more and more factors into his span of attention. The search will be sequential; only a few additional factors will be considered at a time and the search will be abandoned when he feels that he has found a reasonably satisfactory answer. His standard of 'satisfactoriness' will vary. If he does not find a satisfactory answer fairly quickly, he may continue searching, or he may lower his standards. Sometimes circumstances may compel him to decide on what he feels to be unsatisfactory evidence. In any case he is likely to stop long before all possible alternatives have been examined. This may be partly because of the way human beings reason. The character of a situation is quickly inferred from a few tentative observations and perhaps only the scientist feels a need to test exhaustively for the unexpected; for others, 'subjective rationality' is enough.

Search-activity may be cut short by time pressure. The number of other problems clamouring for attention is a major factor influencing the quality of decisions. It is also affected by increasing difficulty. As the inquiry extends from familiar territory to more distant parts of the organization it is pursued with decreasing vigour unless it is known from experience that information of a given sort is normally available at a certain point. A participant in a highly complex system tends to be uncertain about how to deal with more remote parts of it and therefore to concentrate on the factors within his immediate range of vision. It is no disparagement of civil servants to say that they are often unaware of information that is relevant to their problems even when it is being collected as a matter of routine in another department. A study of the possible applications of census data or material from the Household Expenditure Survey might reveal many instances of this.

Perhaps this can be summed up by saying that the depth to which it is felt 'reasonable' to take a problem will vary with its importance, the accessibility and adequacy of relevant data, the training and experience of the official dealing with it, and the number of other problems requiring his attention in the time available. These factors may not seem to apply in, say, a research and planning division since such divisions 'are deliberately constructed to enable the organization to continue search activity even when most of the organizations' members are quite satisfied' (Etzioni, 1964). But this is simply to say that different conditions may be made to apply in different parts of the same organization.

Uncertainty absorption

Much of the information reaching an official will already have passed through a similar process at the hands of colleagues. In an organization of any size information may be used as a basis for decision many removes away from the point at which it enters the system. As it is transmitted it is progressively structured and simplified. One consequence may be that material which was initially highly ambiguous tends to become more and more precise. Decision making is impeded if there are inconsistencies in the information relating to the same situation. 'Official' figures are developed so that conflicting information can be ignored. 'The greater the need for coordination in the organization, the greater the use of legitimized facts' (March and Simon, 1958). This is how interest groups become committed to policies that may have originated in marginal choices by a bare majority of their members. To selective perception and rationalization, we have to add uncertainty absorption as the third main source of distortion in the simplified picture of reality with which decision makers work.

This is one reason why it is so difficult to say who 'makes' a decision; filtering at each stage successively reduces the range of possibilities that is available to be considered. Once proposals have been formulated the range begins to decline quite sharply. Ultimately, only one possibility may be presented for approval. There is also an important difference between formulating proposals and considering them. Experiments have confirmed the common-sense observation that once concrete suggestions have been put on paper (for example to a Minister or a committee) it is less likely that fresh ideas, independent of the set framework, will come to mind (Applewhite, 1965). This means that great power is wielded by those at the point where the greatest amount of uncertainty is absorbed, since they can considerably influence the decisions that will finally be made by others. Such a position may be filled by an 'expert' who is nominally quite junior in the hierarchy or by an 'adviser' who can be appealed to on matters of difficulty that cannot be resolved by rational analysis.

Structural influences

The decision maker emerges from this analysis as a sort of human computer, with limited storage capacity and a partially random input. Up to a point, he can be programmed. Organizations influence their members by structuring their environment, that is, by controlling the information supplied to them and, through training and other means, conditioning the way they react to it. The extreme case of a fully programmed decision, in which all the ingredients are supplied and also rules for dealing with them, is a clerk dealing with routine cases according to the rule-book. Programmes allow central but recurring problems to be handled as routine. Hence the paradox noted by Mackenzie and Grove that 'on the whole the least qualified members of the service must do one of the most difficult parts of the business, that of meeting the public as individuals' (Mackenzie and Grove, 1957).

Organizations also try to control the framework of experience which their members bring to problems. The main instruments are recruitment, training and career policies.

It is not always easy to predict what sort of personal experience will be most appropriate. One factor is the amount of experience that is already available in the organization's memory. Many problems which face civil servants involve the application of general administrative principles to a concrete situation. What bodies should be consulted? Should Treasury be brought in? Should the matter be cleared with the Cabinet? How should any decision be made public? A great deal of experience has been accumulated on such matters, so that new problems can often be handled effectively and economically as examples of a familiar type. Internal experience of precedents and procedures over a wide field may then be most useful. Hence the case for recruiting people of general ability and transferring them frequently from one post to another, assimilating 'organizational wisdom' and learning how to use it as they go.

No amount of mutual laundering, however, will create expertise that does not already exist. If the problem contains substantial new elements, additional experience may have to be imported by recruiting staff with special qualifications.

The relative emphasis on personal or 'organizational' experience implies different types of career structure. Personal experience can be kept at a high level by avoiding frequent changes of post. But long periods in specialized posts may not help officials to accumulate the general knowledge of the system that they need in order to exploit its resources of information. Specialist knowledge of a professional type is less relevant to problems which are too complex for the individual specialist to grasp.

Training has a number of functions. Training courses can supply a repertory of programmes for solving problems. By making people familiar with the organization's resources and its communication system, training can develop self-confidence and make them more ready to search fairly widely for relevant information. Sometimes training courses have a 'staff college' function. They provide an opportunity for colleagues to meet and develop a common outlook. This helps communication, since the usage of communication channels is affected by the ease with which they can be used and this in turn is influenced by the compatibility of the users. Channels that are socially rewarding tend to be used while others are neglected: one effect of the long courses at the Centre for Administrative Studies has been easier communication between departments, since at any one time their private offices are staffed by a cohort of Assistant Principals who got to know one another at the Centre. Generally speaking, decision making becomes more predictable if participants share a common culture of beliefs, norms and aspirations. Training courses, therefore, often focus on certain values and beliefs about the system and its objectives in the hope that the trainee will make them part of his own frame of reference. One aim of this sort of training is to sensitize the official to certain aspects of problems and to guide his choice of priorities.

Perhaps the most effective instrument of orientation is departmentalization. If officials are grouped so that over their careers they are constantly exposed to the same kind of information and value systems, and interact with others in the same position, all the findings about selective perception, role-concept and group resonance point to the emergence of a characteristic departmental philosophy.

Priorities

Administrators have finite spans of attention. They also have finite amounts of time at their disposal. Can we say anything about the way they allocate their priorities? How do they decide to which problem, or to which aspect of a particular problem, they should pay most attention?

The administrator tends to give his attention first to tasks for which a programme exists ready to hand. In another laboratory experiment at Carnegie subjects were made responsible for managing an inventory control system. They had to pass on to clerical staff some routine information about inventory levels in various warehouses; at the same time they were responsible for adjusting the allocation of clerks to warehouses so that each group of clerks had a comparable work-load; finally, they were to suggest changes in procedures. They were told that all three jobs were equally important and should receive equal attention. All the subjects spent considerably more than a third of their time on the routine part of their job even when the flow of information was kept light. As the amount of information was increased, the time they spent on planning was consistently reduced until virtually no planning was done at peak loads (March, 1959). This is 'Gresham's Law' of planning – that daily routine drives out planning. Staff at all levels tend to get the easy jobs out of the way first and there is a risk that long-term ones never get done at all. Many observers have commented on the perfectionism which higher civil servants in Britain bring to matters of detail, especially the niceties of drafting. Penmanship comes easily to the British type of generalist. Stylistic weaknesses, when they occur, are an easy target for criticism in Parliament and the press, and there is every temptation to spend a disproportionate amount of time trying to eliminate them. This means, of course, that difficult questions of substance are, perhaps unconsciously, pushed into the background.

When activities are not programmed there is an apparently random element about the way priorities are determined among them. Similarly, if no technique for analysing a problem is ready to hand, decision time tends to be short and the outcome is likely to be influenced more by the order in which alternatives are presented than by any serious attempt to find a common yardstick. This seems to apply particularly to problems of allocating uncommitted resources. If some additional money suddenly becomes available, it will go to those who are quick off the mark. The beneficiaries are likely to be those whose strategic position in the communication system enables them to time their bids rather than those who have a good case on merit.

An important part may be played by external cues. Fire precautions will receive more attention than normal if there has been a fire recently. Safety precautions will be tightened up after an air crash. There is likely to be a spate of instructions on even minor aspects of security (to an extent that may seriously interfere with normal performance until it is felt safe to ignore them) after a prominent espionage trial. Sometimes it is impossible to restore the previous balance because a system of priorities becomes institutionalized, for example by appointing a security inspector to report breaches of regulations. Similarly, an active training department may succeed in making a whole department training-minded, even if this entails a loss in productive time.

There are various ways in which the organization can influence the individual's choice of priorities. Through training and programming some kinds of jobs can be made easier to tackle. A common device is to provide a formula which enables easy computational problems to be substituted for difficult qualitative ones. This may entail giving excessive attention to aspects of a problem that can be measured. Eckstein thought that the use of formulas significantly reduced the rationality of decision making in the Ministry of Health (1958).

Priorities can be attracted for some questions by the use of deadlines: a letter from a Member of Parliament has to be answered within a given number of days; a parliamentary question is given top priority because of the tight timetable for preparing a reply. Considerations thought to be important can be 'cued-in' to the administrator's frame of reference by constant reminders (like the annual reference to economy in the Treasury's letter inviting departmental estimates – although this particular line has perhaps lost its punch!). They can be institutionalized by building pressures into the structure – for example in an advisory committee – and instituting procedures to ensure that they are brought into play. The tendency to give priority to the short-term can be counter-balanced by creating a special unit which is concerned solely with long-term planning and innovation.

The problem of priorities is no less acute for the organization as a whole. It is seldom possible to attend to all its objectives simultaneously. They may be inconsistent – fresh commitments are acquired over time without always being related to existing ones. Separate units develop their own goals, which may be mutually incompatible. The goal of the training branch is to develop training schemes; the finance officer is concerned with economy; the establishment officer is interested in the efficient use of personnel; administrators in executive divisions are at various times concerned with all of these, as well as with carrying out the wishes of Parliament, placating pressure groups, sponsoring new legislation and furthering their own careers. In normal times an organization manages to survive with inconsistent goals by the simple expedient of failing to attend to more than a few of them at any one time. Lord (then Sir Edward) Bridges unwittingly emphasized this point in an address which he gave to the Royal Institute of Public Administration at Exeter in November 1954:

However complicated the facts may be – however much your junior may try to persuade you that there are seventeen arguments in favour of one course and fifteen in favour of the exact opposite, believe me, in four cases out of five there is *one* point and one only which is cardinal to the whole situation. When you have isolated that one point, and found the answer to it, all the other things will fall into place. And until you have done that, you have done nothing.

Lord Bridges would no doubt agree that the 'one essential point' may differ from time to time.

But sometimes inconsistencies cannot be ignored and an apparatus is needed for resolving disputes. One of the functions of a hierarchy is to provide a court of appeal.

The important difference between the formulation and the authorization of policy has already been mentioned. There is a stage at which the various components of a decision can be brought together and integrated in a workable set of proposals. The proposals may have to be referred to higher authority for approval but this is often a formality. Usually, the 'level of integration' is kept as low as possible to ease the burden at the top and to increase the speed of decision making. Occasionally a deliberate attempt is made to keep the options open by making it impossible for the various strands to be woven together except at the top. Senior members of the hierarchy may also be forced to review matters of detail if they have to resolve conflicts among their subordinates. This is one of the ways in which they keep in touch.

But those at the top have value-systems of their own which they apply in giving judgement. Consequently a centralized system of authority is one means of securing priority for these values. Junior staff learn what considerations will rank as most important if their work is reviewed. If, for example, the formal structure allows conflicts to be resolved only at 'political' level (perhaps because two departments have strong opposing interests in a question which neither of them can settle independently) officials try to anticipate their Minister's (or the Cabinet's) frame of reference when they are deciding whether a particular point of view is worth pursuing to the limit. In the late 1960s, when responsibility for economic policy was divided between the Treasury and the Department of Economic Affairs, some journalists alleged that the object was to ensure that the Prime Minister's view prevailed on certain issues. This would have been achieved even if no disputes were in fact referred to him, so long as those involved kept in mind how he would decide if he had to.

Concluding comments

The theories discussed are concerned with the supply of information, including information about other people's ideas, to the decision maker, and the use he makes of it. The model of the organization as a communication system makes it possible to judge a procedure, an arrangement of functions, a recruitment policy or a training scheme by its contribution to good decision making. If these are well devised, they will make it more likely that the 'relevant' considerations will be taken into account by the right people at the right time. Decision making is not the whole of organizational life, but it is a very important part of the life of government departments. It is worth taking some trouble to see how it can be improved [. . .]

There are no universal prescriptions. If the head of a department knows what kinds of decisions he wants, he can be shown how to design an organization to increase the chances of getting them. Often he will not know too clearly what he does want. He may be persuaded to say in broad terms what relative weights he places on particular elements in decision making, like accuracy, speed, economy, flexibility, good coordination and various sorts of expertise. It is certain that he will not be able to get an organization in which all these elements are maximized. Compromises are unavoidable, because there are limits to what human minds can assimilate and because there are limits to what a communication system can handle. Moreover, there is no absolute standard of 'relevance'. The requirements change with time. What is relevant to 'good' Treasury decisions today may be relatively unimportant next year. But it is some help to see what is involved.

It is especially useful to have a model which interprets . . . general theories . . . in terms of individual performance at decision making. What emerges is the now familiar point that every conceivable arrangement carries costs as well as advantages. If decision makers are trained and equipped to focus sharply on A, their vision of B inevitably becomes a little bit distorted. The cumulative distortions that result can to some extent be balanced within the overall organizational structure, but never completely, because of communication and coordination problems.

In aiming at the best available balance the organization cannot control the perceptions of its participants. But it can influence them through training, recruitment, the structure of authority, communication links and so forth. The mechanisms at work are largely cognitive. In a bureaucracy ignorance is usually a structural problem – the official does not know what he has not been told, or had a chance to learn, nor can he remember everything all the time. But motivational factors are important too. The bureaucrat can sometimes be induced to try a little harder, given reasonable conditions and a modicum of encouragement.

References

APPLEWHITE, P. B. (1965), *Organizational Behavior*, Prentice-Hall.

DEARBORN, D. C., and SIMON, H. A. (1958), 'Selective perception: a note on the departmental identification of executives', *Sociometry*, vol. 21, pp. 140–44.

ECKSTEIN, H. (1958), *The English Health Service*, Oxford University Press.

ETZIONI, A. (1964) *Modern Organizations*, Prentice-Hall.

MACKENZIE, W. J. M., and GROVE, J. W. (1957), *Central Administration in Britain*, Longmans.

MARCH, J. G. (1959), 'Business decision making', *Indust. Res.*, Spring.

MARCH, J. G., and SIMON, H. A. (1958), *Organizations*, Wiley.

MARSHAK, J. (1959), 'Efficient and viable organizational forms', in M. Haire (ed.), *Modern Organization Theory*, Wiley.

8 A. Strauss, L. Schatzman, D. Ehrlich, R. Bucher, M. Sabshin

The Hospital and its Negotiated Order

A. Strauss *et al*, 'The hospital and its negotiated order',
in E. Friedson (ed.), *The Hospital in Modern Society*, Macmillan Co.,
1963, pp. 147–69.

Introduction

In the pages to follow, a model for studying hospitals will be sketched, along with some suggested virtues of the model. It grew out of the authors' research, which was done on the premises of two psychiatric hospitals. The reader must judge for himself whether a model possibly suited to studying psychiatric hospitals might equally well guide the study of other kinds of hospitals. We believe that it can, and shall indicate why at the close of our presentation; indeed, we shall argue its usefulness for investigating other organizations besides hospitals.

Our model bears upon that most central of sociological problems, namely, how a measure of order is maintained in the face of inevitable changes (derivable from sources both external and internal to the organization). Students of formal organization tend to underplay the processes of internal change as well as overestimate the more stable features of organizations – including its rules and its hierarchical statuses. We ourselves take our cue from Mead, who some years ago, when arguing for orderly and directed social change, remarked that the task turns about relationships between change and order:

How can you bring those changes about in an orderly fashion and yet preserve order? To bring about change is seemingly to destroy the given order, and yet society does and must change. That is the problem, to incorporate the method of change into the order of society itself (1936).

Without Mead's melioristic concerns, one can yet assume that order is something at which members of any society, any organization must work. For the shared agreements, the binding contracts – which constitute the grounds for an expectable, non-surprising, taken-for-granted, even ruled orderliness – are not binding and shared for all time. Contracts, understandings, agreements, rules – all have appended to them a temporal clause. That clause may or may not be explicitly discussed by the contracting parties, and the terminal date of the agreement may or may not be made specific, but none can be binding forever – even if the parties believe it so, unforeseen consequences of acting on the agreements would force eventual confrontation. Review is called for, whether the outcome of review be rejection or renewal or revision, or what not. In short, the bases of concerted action (social order) must be reconstituted continually; or, as remarked above, 'worked at'.

Such considerations have led us to emphasize the importance of negotiation – the processes of give-and-take, of diplomacy, of bargaining – which characterizes organizational life. In the pages to follow, we shall note first the relationship of rules to negotiation, then discuss the grounds for negotiation. Then, since both the clients and much of the personnel of hospitals are laymen, we wish also to underscore the participation of those laymen in the hospital's negotiative processes. Thereafter we shall note certain patterned and temporal features of negotiation; then we shall draw together some implications for viewing social order. A general summary of the argument and its implications will round out the paper.

A psychiatric hospital

Before discussing negotiation in hospitals, it will help to indicate two things: first, what was engaging our attention when research was initiated; and, second, the general characteristics of the hospital that was studied.[1] At the outset of our investigation, three foci were especially pertinent. The first was an explicit concern with the professional careers of the personnel: Who was there? Where did they come from? Where did they think they were going in work and career? What were they doing at this particular hospital? What was happening to them at this

1. Two psychiatric hospitals were studied, but only one will be discussed here, namely, the psychiatric wing of Michael Reese Hospital in Chicago.

place? A second concern was with psychiatric ideology: Were different ideologies represented on the floors of this hospital? What were these ideologies? Did people clearly recognize their existence as well as did their more articulate advocates? And anyway, what difference did these philosophies make in the lives and work of various personnel? A third focus consisted of the realization that a hospital is par excellence an institution captained and maintained principally by professionals. This fact implied that the nonprofessionals who worked there, as well as those nonprofessionals there as patients, must manage to make their respective ways within this professionalized establishment. How, then, do they do this – and vice versa, how do the professionals incorporate the nonprofessionals into their own schemes of work and aspiration? These directions of interest, and the questions raised in consequence, quickly led us to perceive hospitals in terms to be depicted below.

A professionalized locale

A hospital can be visualized as a professionalized locale – a geographical site where persons drawn from different professions come together to carry out their respective purposes. At our specific hospital, the professionals consisted of numerous practising psychiatrists and psychiatric residents, nurses and nursing students, psychologists, occupational therapists, and one lone social worker. Each professional echelon has received noticeably different kinds of training and, speaking conventionally, each occupies some differential hierarchical position at the hospital while playing a different part in its total division of labor.

But that last sentence requires elaboration and amendment. The persons within each professional group may be, and probably are, at different stages in their respective careers. Furthermore, the career lines of some may be quite different from those of their colleagues: thus some of our psychiatrists were just entering upon psychoanalytic training, but some had entered the medical specialty by way of neurology, and had dual neurological-psychiatric practices. Implicit in the preceding statement is that those who belong to the same profession also may differ quite measurably in the training they have received, as well as in the theoretical (or ideological) positions they take toward important issues like etiology and treatment. Finally, the hospital itself may possess differential significance for colleagues: for instance, some psychiatrists were engaged in hospital practice only until such time as their office practices had been sufficiently well established; while other, usually older, psychiatrists were committed wholeheartedly to working with hospitalized patients.

Looking next at the division of labor shared by the professionals: never do all persons of each echelon work closely with all others from other echelons. At our hospital it was notable that considerable variability characterized who worked closely with whom – and how – depending upon such matters as ideological and hierarchical position. Thus the services of the social worker were used not at all by some psychiatrists, while each man who utilized her services did so somewhat differently. Similarly some men utilized 'psychologicals' more than did others. Similarly, some psychiatrists were successful in housing their patients almost exclusively in certain wards, which meant that, wittingly or not, they worked only with certain nurses. As in other institutions, the various echelons possessed differential status and power, but again there were marked internal differences concerning status and power, as well as knowledgeability about 'getting things done'. Nor must it be overlooked that not only did the different professions hold measurably different views – derived both from professional and status positions – about the proper division of labor; but different views also obtained within each echelon. (The views were most discrepant among the psychiatrists.) All in all, the division of labor is a complex concept, and at hospitals must be seen in relation to the professionalized milieu.

Ruled and unruled behavior

The rules that govern the actions of various professionals, as they perform their tasks, are far from extensive, or clearly stated or clearly binding. This fact leads to necessary and continual negotiation. It will be worth deferring discussion of negotiation per se until we have explored some relationships between rules and negotiation, at least as found in our hospital; for the topic of rules is a complicated one.

In Michael Reese, as unquestionably in most sizeable establishments, hardly anyone knows all the extant rules, much less exactly what situations they apply to, for whom, and with what sanctions. If this would not otherwise be so in our hospital, it would be true anyway because of the considerable turnover of nursing staff. Also noticeable – to us as observers – was that some rules once promulgated would fall into disuse, or would periodically receive administrative reiteration after the staff had either ignored those rules or forgotten them. As one head nurse said, 'I wish they would write them all down sometimes' – but said so smilingly. The plain fact is that staff kept forgetting not only the rules received from above but also some rules that they themselves had agreed upon 'for this ward'. Hence we would observe that periodically the same informal ward rules would be agreed upon, enforced for a short time, and then be forgotten until another ward crisis would elicit their innovation all over again.

As in other establishments, personnel called upon certain rules to obtain what they themselves wished. Thus the nurses frequently acted as virtual guardians of the hospital against some demands of certain attending physicians, calling upon the resources of 'the rules of the hospital' in countering the physicians' demands. As in other hospital settings, the physicians were only too aware of this game, and accused the nurses from time to time of more interest in their own welfare than in that of the patients. (The only difference, we suspect, between the accusatory language of psychiatrists and that of internists or surgeons is that the psychiatrists have a trained capacity to utilize specialized terms like 'rigid' and 'overcompulsive'.) In so dredging up the rules at convenient moments, the staff of course is acting identically with personnel in other kinds of institutions.

As elsewhere, too, all categories of personnel are adept at breaking the rules when it suits convenience or when warrantable exigencies arise. Stretching the rules is only a further variant of this tactic, which itself it less attributable to human nature than to an honest desire to get things accomplished as they ought, properly, to get done.[2] Of course, respective parties must strike bargains for these actions to occur.

In addition, at the very top of the administrative structure, a tolerant stance is taken both toward extensiveness of rules and laxity of rules. The point can be illustrated by a conversation with the administrative head, who recounted with amusement how some members of his original house staff wished to have all rules set down in a house rule book, but he had staved off this codification. As will be noted more fully later, the administrative attitude is affected also by a profound belief that care of patients calls for a minimum of hard and fast rules and a maximum of innovation and improvisation. In addition, in this hospital, as certainly in most others, the multiplicity of medical purpose and theory, as well as of personal investment, are openly recognized: too rigid a set of rules would only cause turmoil and affect the hospital's over-all efficiency.

Finally, it is notable that the hospital must confront the realities of the attending staff's negotiations with patients and their families – negotiations carried out beyond the physical confines of the hospital itself. Too many or too rigid rules would restrict the medical entrepreneurs' negotiation. To some degree any hospital with attending men has to give this kind of leeway (indeed, the precise degree is a source of tension in these kinds of hospitals).

Hence, the area of action covered directly by clearly enunciated rules is really very small. As observers, we began to become aware of this when, within a few days, we discovered that only a few very general rules obtained for the placement of new patients within the hospital. Those rules, which are clearly enunciated and generally followed, can, for our purposes, be regarded as long-standing shared understandings among the personnel. Except for a few legal rules, which stem from state and professional prescription, and for some rulings pertaining to all of Michael Reese Hospital, almost all these house rules are much less like commands, and much more like general understandings: not even their punishments are spelled out; and mostly they can be stretched, negotiated, argued, as

2. Dalton's book (1959) is crammed with such instances. See especially pp. 104–7.

well as ignored or applied at convenient moments. Hospital rules seem to us frequently less explicit than tacit, probably as much breached and stretched as honored, and administrative effort is made to keep their number small. In addition, rules here as elsewhere fail to be universal prescriptions: they always require judgement concerning their applicability to the specific case. Does it apply here? To whom? In what degree? For how long? With what sanctions? The personnel cannot give universal answers; they can only point to past analogous instances when confronted with situations or give 'for instance' answers, when queried about a rule's future application.

The grounds for negotiation

Negotiation and the division of labor are rendered all the more complex because personnel in our hospital – we assume that the generalization, with some modification, holds elsewhere – share only a single, vaguely ambiguous goal. The goal is to return patients to the outside world in better shape. This goal is the symbolic cement that, metaphorically speaking, holds the organization together: the symbol to which all personnel can comfortably and frequently point – with the assurance that *at least* about this matter everyone can agree! Although this symbol, as will be seen later, masks a considerable measure of disagreement and discrepant purpose, it represents a generalized mandate under which the hospital can be run – the public flag under which all may work in concert. Let us term it the institution's constitutional grounds or basic compact. These grounds, this compact, are never openly challenged; nor are any other goals given explicit verbal precedence. (This is so when a hospital, such as ours, also is a training institution.) In addition, these constitutional grounds can be used by any and all personnel as a justificatory rationale for actions that are under attack. In short, although personnel may disagree to the point of apoplexy about how to implement patients' getting better, they do share the common institutional value.

The problem, of course, is that when the personnel confront a specific patient and attempt to make him recover, then the disagreements flare up – the generalized mandate helps not at all to handle the specific issues – and a complicated process of negotiation, of bargaining, of give-and-take necessarily begins. The disagreements that necessitate negotiation do not occur by chance, but are patterned. Here are several illustrations of the grounds that lead to negotiation. Thus, the personnel may disagree over what is the proper placement within the hospital for some patient: believing that, at any given time, he is more likely to improve when placed in one ward rather than in another. This issue is the source of considerable tension between physicians and ward personnel. Again, what is meant by 'getting better' is itself open to differential judgement when applied to the progress – or retrogression – of a particular patient. This judgement is influenced not only by professional experience and acquaintance with the patient but is also influenced by the very concept of getting better as held by the different echelons. Thus the aides – who are laymen – have quite different notions about these matters than do the physicians, and on the whole those notions are not quite equivalent to those held by nurses. But both the nurses and the aides see patients getting better according to signs visible from the patient's daily behavior, while the psychiatrist tends to relate these signs, if apprehended at all, to deeper layers of personality; with the consequence that frequently the staff thinks one way about the patient's 'movement' while the physician thinks quite otherwise, and must argue his case, set them right, or even keep his peace.

To turn now to another set of conditions for negotiation: the very mode of treatment selected by the physician is profoundly related to his own psychiatric ideology. For instance, it makes a difference whether the physician is neurologically trained, thus somatically oriented, or whether he is psychotherapeutically trained and oriented. The former type of physician will prescribe more drugs, engage in far more electric shock therapy, and spend much less time with each patient. On occasion the diagnosis and treatment of a given patient runs against the judgement of the nurses and aides, who may not go along with the physician's directives, who may or may not disagree openly. They may subvert his therapeutic program by one of their own. They may choose to argue the matter. They may go over his head to an administrative officer. Indeed, they have many choices of action – each requiring negotiative behavior. In truth, while physicians are able to command considerable obedience to their directives at this particular hospital, frequently they must work hard at obtaining cooperation in their programing. The task is rendered all the more difficult because they, as professionals, see matters in certain lights, while the aides, as laymen, may judge matters quite differently – on moral rather than on strictly psychiatric grounds, for instance.

If negotiation is called for because a generalized mandate requires implementation, it is also called for because of the multiplicity of purpose found in the hospital. It is incontestable that each professional group has a different set of reasons for working at this hospital (to begin with, most nurses are women, most physicians are men); and of course colleagues inevitably differ among themselves on certain of their purposes for working there. In addition, each professional develops there his own specific and temporally limited ends that he wishes to attain. All this diversity of purpose affects the institution's division of labor, including not only what tasks each person is expected to accomplish but also how he maneuvers to get them accomplished. Since very little of this can possibly be prefigured by the administrative rule-makers, the attainment of one's purposes requires inevitably the cooperation of fellow workers. This point, once made, scarcely needs illustration.

However, yet another ground of negotiation needs emphasizing: namely, that in this hospital, as doubtless elsewhere, the patient as an 'individual case' is taken as a virtual article of faith. By this we mean that the element of medical uncertainty is so great, and each patient is taken as – in some sense – so unique, that action round and about him must be tailor-made, must be suited to his precise therapeutic requirements. This kind of assumption abets what would occur anyhow: that only a minimum of rules can be laid down for running a hospital, since a huge area of contingency necessarily lies outside those rules. The rules can provide guidance and command for only a small amount of the total concerted action that must go on around the patient. It follows, as already noted that where action is not ruled it must be agreed upon.

One important further condition for negotiation should be mentioned. Changes are forced upon the hospital and its staff not only by forces external to the hospital but also by unforeseen consequences of internal policies and negotiations carried on within the hospital. In short, negotiations breed further negotiations.

Lay personnel and negotiated order

Before turning to certain important features of negotiation, we shall first discuss the impact of laymen – both personnel and patients – upon the hospital's negotiated order. A special feature of most hospitals is that, although administered and controlled by professionals, they also include among their personnel considerable numbers of nonprofessionals. This they must, for only in the most affluent establishments could floors be staffed wholly with professionals. The nonprofessionals set special problems for the establishment and maintenance of orderly medical process.

To suggest how subtle and profound may be the lay influence, we give the following illustration as it bears upon negotiated order. The illustration pertains to the central value of our hospital: returning patients to the outside world in better shape than when they entered. Like everyone else, the aides subscribe to this institutional goal. A host of communications, directed at them, inform them that they too are important in 'helping patients get better'. Yet none of the professionals ascribe an unduly important role to the aides: in the main, aides are considered quite secondary to the therapeutic process. The aides do not agree. They do not contest the point, because in fact the point does not arise explicitly: yet our own inquiry left no doubt that most aides conceive of themselves as the principal agent for bringing about improvement in most patients. The grounds of their belief, in capsule form, are as follows.

Working extensively with or near the patients, they are more likely than other personnel to see patients acting in a variety of situations and ways. The aides reason, with some truth, that they themselves are more likely to be the recipients of patients' conversations and even confidences, because of frequent and intimate contact. They reason, with common sense, that no one else can know most of the patients as well as do the aides. ('I always know more than the nurses and the doctors. We are with the patients almost eight hours, whereas the nurses and doctors don't come in. The nurse reads the charts and passes the medicine.') With due respect to the best nurses – and some are greatly admired – nurses are too busy with their administrative work; and lazy ones just never leave the office! As for the physicians: not only do they make evident mistakes with their patients, and spend scarcely any time with them, but they must even call upon the nurses and aides for information about their patients.

Actually, aides have no difficulty in comprehending that they themselves cannot give shock treatment – only the physicians know how to do that – but we found that our aides could not, with few exceptions, make a clear distinction between what the doctor does when he helps the patient 'by talking' and what they themselves do when they talk with him. Even the aides who have worked most closely with head nurses do not really comprehend that a substantial difference exists between talking and psychotherapy. Hence aides believe that everyone may contribute toward patients' improvement, by acting right toward them and talking properly with them. The most that aides will admit is: 'Sometimes the patients will really talk more about their problems with the doctor than they will with us. Sometimes it's vice versa.' But on the whole those who talk most with patients are the aides.

It does not take much imagination to anticipate what this view of the division of labor implies for the aides' handling of patients. However frequently the aides may attend staff meetings, however frequently they listen to psychiatrists talk about the problems of patients and how to handle patients, they end by perceiving patients in nonpsychiatric (nontechnical) terms and use their own kinds of tactics with patients. Aides guide themselves by many common-sense maxims, and are articulate about these when questioned about how they work with patients. The professional staff generally regards good aides as being very 'intuitive' with patients; but aides are probably no more intuitive than anyone else; it is that their reasoning is less professionalized. Lest this seem to be a characterization of psychiatric aides alone, we hasten to add that aides on medical services seem to us to think and operate in similar ways.

Turning briefly now to how these nonprofessionals affect the processes of negotiation, one may begin by stating that, like anyone else, they wish to control the conditions of their work as much as possible. Of course, they must negotiate to make that possible: they must stake claims and counterdemands; they must engage in games of give-and-take. Among the prizes are: where one will work, the colleagues with whom one will share tasks, the superiors under whom one will work, and the kinds of patients with whom one will deal. Illustrating from one area only, that of controlling superiors: aides have various means of such control. These include withholding information and displaying varying degrees of cooperativeness in charting or in attending meetings. Aides also are implicated, as are the nurses, in negotiations with the physicians – except that the head nurse tends to carry on the necessary face-to-face bargaining. Since aides have their own notions about how specific patients should be handled and helped, they may negotiate also with the nurses in order to implement those notions. Nurses and physicians, in their turn, need to transact negotiations with the aides: while the physicians usually work through the head nurse, on occasion they may deal directly with an aide. In any event, professionals and nonprofessionals are implicated together in a great web of negotiation. It does not take much imagination to see that this world, and its negotiated order, would be different without nonprofessionals. More important: unless one focuses upon the negotiated character of order, he is most unlikely to note the above kinds of consequential actions and relations.

The patients and negotiated order

The patients are also engaged in bargaining, in negotiative processes. (As some public-administration theorists have put it, clients are also part of the organizational structure.) Again, a significant aspect of hospital organization is missing unless the clients' negotiation is included. They negotiate, of course, as laymen, unless they themselves are nurses or physicians. Most visibly they can be seen bargaining, with the nurses and with their psychiatrists, for more extensive privileges (such as more freedom to roam the grounds); but they may also seek to affect the course and kind of treatment – including placement on given wards, amounts of drugs, and even choice of psychiatrist, along with the length of stay in the hospital itself. Intermittently, but fairly continually, they are concerned with their ward's orderliness, and make demands upon the personnel – as well as upon other patients – to keep the volume of noise down, to keep potential violence at a minimum, to rid the ward of a trouble-making patient. Sometimes the patients are as much guardians of ward order as are the nurses, who are notorious for this concern in our hospital. (Conversely, the nursing personnel must also seek to reach understandings and agreements with specific patients; but sometimes these are even collective, as when patients pitch in to help with a needy patient, or as when an adolescent clique has to be dealt with 'as a bunch'.)

An unexpected dividend awaits anyone who focuses upon the patients' negotiations. An enriched understanding of their individual sick careers – to the hospital, inside it, and out of it – occurs. In the absence of a focus upon negotiation, ordinarily these careers tend to appear overly regularized (as in Parsons and Fox, 1952) or destructive (as in Goffman, 1959). When patients are closely observed 'operating around' the hospital, they will be seen negotiating not only for privileges but also for precious information relevant to their own understandings of their illness. We need only add that necessarily their negotiations will differ at various stages of their sick careers.

What Caudill (1952) and Goffman (1957) have written of as patient culture is roughly equivalent to the demands and expectations of the patients; but their accounts require much supplementation by a conception of patients entering, like everyone else, into the over-all negotiative process. How demands and claims will be made and met, by whom, and in what manner – as well as who will make given demands and claims upon them, how, and in what manner – are of utmost importance for understanding the hospital's structure. When patients are long-term or chronic, then their impact upon structure is more obvious to everyone concerned; but even in establishments with speedy turnover, patients are relevant to the social order.

Patterned and temporal features of negotiation

To do justice to the complexity of negotiative processes would require far more space than can be allowed here. For present purposes, it should be sufficient to note only a few aspects. In our hospital, as elsewhere, the various physicians institute programs of treatment and care for their patients. Programming involves a mobilization and organization of action around the patient (and usually involves the patient's cooperation, even in the psychiatric milieu). Some physicians in our hospital had reached long-standing understandings with certain head nurses, so that only a small amount of communication was necessary to effectuate their treatment programs. Thus a somatically oriented psychiatrist typically would attempt to get his patients to those two wards where most electric-shock treatment was carried out; and the nurse administrators there understood quite well what was expected in handling 'their type of patients'. It was as if the physician were to say 'do the usual things' (they sometimes did) – little additional instruction being needed. We ourselves coined the term 'house special' (as opposed to '*à la carte*') treatment, to indicate that a patient could be assigned to these wards and handled by the ward staff without the physician either giving special instructions or asking for special favors. However, an original period of coaching the nurses and of reaching understandings was necessary. Consequently when personnel leave, for vacations or permanently, then arrangements must be instituted anew. Even with house-special treatment, some discussion will be required, since not every step of the patient's treatment can be imagined ahead of time. The nurses are adept (as in nonpsychiatric hospitals) at eliciting information from the physician about his patient; they are also adept both in forcing and fostering agreements about action vis-à-vis his patient. We have watched many a scene where the nurse negotiates for such understandings, as well as many staff meetings that the nurses and aides consciously convert into agencies for bringing recalcitrant physicians to terms. When physicians choose, they can be equally concerned with reaching firm agreements and understandings.

It is important that one realize that these agreements do not occur by chance, nor are they established between random parties. They are, in the literal sense of the word, patterned. Thus, the somatically oriented physicians have long-standing arrangements with a secretary who is attached to the two wards upon which their patients tend to be housed; this secretary does a variety of jobs necessitated by these physicians' rather medical orientation. The more psychotherapeutically minded physicians scarcely utilize her services. Similarly, the head nurses and the administrative residents attached to each ward reach certain kinds of understandings and agreements, which neither tends to establish with any other type of personnel. These latter agreements are less in evidence when the resident is new; then the nurse in some helplessness turns to the next highest administrative officer, making yet other contracts. Again, when an attending physician is especially recalcitrant, both resident and nurse's aide seek to draw higher administrators into the act, negotiating for support and increased power. This kind of negotiation occurs with great predictability: for instance, certain physicians because of their particular philosophies of treatment use the hospital in certain ways; consequently, their programs are frequently troublesome for the house staff, who must then seek to spin a network of negotiation around the troublesome situation. When the ward is in high furor, then negotiative activity of course is at its most visible!

In sum: there is a patterned variability of negotiation in the hospital pertaining to who contracts with whom, about what, as well as when these agreements are made. Influencing this variability are hierarchical position and ideological commitments, as well as periodicities in the structure of ward relationships (for instance, because of a rotational system that moves personnel periodically on and off given wards).

It is especially worth emphasizing that negotiation – whether characterized as 'agreement', 'understanding', 'contract', 'compact', 'pact' or by some other term – has a temporal aspect, whether that aspect is stated specifically or not by the contracting parties. As one listens to agreements being made in the hospital, or watches understandings being established, he becomes aware that a specific termination period, or date line, is often written into the agreement. Thus a physician after being accosted by the head nurse – who may in turn also be responding to her own personnel – may agree to move his patient to another ward after this specific ward has agreed 'to try for two more days'. What he is doing is issuing to its personnel a promissory note that if things don't work out satisfactorily, he will move his patient. Sometimes the staff breaks the contract, if the patient is especially obstreperous or if tempers are running especially high, and transfers the patient to another ward behind the back of the physician. However, if the patient does sufficiently better, the ward's demands may subside. Or, interestingly, it often happens that later both sides will negotiate further, seeking some compromise: the staff, for instance, wishing to restrict the patient's privileges or to give him stronger drug prescriptions, and the physician giving in on these issues to gain some ends of his own. On less tender and less specific grounds, the physician and the head nurse may reach nodding agreement that a new patient should be handled in certain ways 'until we see how he responds'. Thus there exists a continuum running from specific to quite nonspecific termination dates. But even those explicit and long-term permissions that physicians give to nurses in all hospitals – such as to administer certain drugs at night without bothering to call upon the physicians – are subject to review and withdrawal along with later qualified assent.

It should be added that the very terms 'agreements' and 'understandings' and 'arrangements' – all used by hospital personnel – point up that some negotiations may be made with full explicitness, while others may be established by parties who have scarcely talked. The more implicit or tacit kinds of contracts tend to be called 'understandings'. The difference can be high-lighted by the following contrasting situations: when a resident suggests to a nurse that an established house rule temporarily be ignored, for the good of a given patient, it may be left implicit in their arrangement that he must bear the punishment if administration discovers their common infraction. But the nurse may make this clause more explicit by demanding that he bear the possible public guilt, otherwise she will not agree to the matter. It follows that some agreements can be both explicit and specific as to termination, while others are explicit but nonspecific as to termination, and so on. What might be referred to as 'tacit understandings' are likely to be those that are neither very specific nor very explicitly discussed. When a physician is not trusted, the staff is likely to push him for explicit directives with specific termination clauses.

Negotiation, appraisal, and organizational change

We come now to the full import of the above discussion, for it raises knotty problems about the relationships that exist between the current negotiated order and genuine organizational change. Since agreements are patterned and temporal, today's sum total of agreements can be visualized as different from tomorrow's – and surely as quite different from next week's. The hospital can be visualized as a place where numerous agreements are continually being terminated or forgotten, but also as continually being established, renewed, reviewed, revoked, revised. Hence at any moment those that are in effect are considerably different from those that were or will be.

Now a skeptic, thinking in terms of relatively permanent or slowly changing structure, might remark that from week to week the hospital remains the same – that only the working arrangements change. This contention only raises the further question of what relationship exists between today's working agreements and the more stable structure (of rules, statuses, and so on).

With an eye on practicality, one might maintain that no one knows what the hospital 'is' on any given day unless he has a comprehensive grasp of what combination of rules and policies, along with agreements, understandings, pacts, contracts, and other working arrangements, currently obtains. In any pragmatic sense, this is the hospital at the moment: this is its social order. Any changes that impinge upon this order – whether something ordinary like a new staff member, a disrupting event, a betrayed contract; or whether unusual, like the introduction of a new technology or a new theory – will call for renegotiation or reappraisal, with consequent changes in the organizational order. Mark the last phrase – a new order, not the re-establishment of an old, a reinstituting of a previous equilibrium. This is what we remarked upon earlier as the necessity for continually reconstituting the bases of concerted action, or social order.

That reconstituting of social order, we would hazard, can be fruitfully conceived in terms of a complex *relationship between the daily negotiative process and a periodic appraisal process*. The former not only allows the daily work to get done; it also reacts back upon the more formalized – and permanent – rules and policies. Further elaboration of this point will follow, but first the following illustration taken from our field notes should be helpful. For some time the hospital had been admitting an increased number of nonpaying adolescent patients, principally because they made good supervisory subjects for the residents. As a consequence, the hospital began to get the reputation of becoming more interested in adolescents than previously; also, some attending physicians were encouraged to bring adolescents for treatment to the hospital. Their presence on the wards raised many new problems, and led to feverish negotiative activity among the various actors implicated in the daily drama. Finally, after some months of high saturation with an adolescent population, a middle-level administrative committee formally recognized what was happening to the institution. The committee recognized it primarily because the adolescents, in the mass, were much harder to handle than an equal number of adults. Yet the situation had its compensatory aspects, since adolescents remained longer and could be given more interesting types of therapy. After some debate, the committee decided that no more adolescent patients would be admitted after an additional stated number had been reached. The decision constituted a formal proclamation, with the proviso that if the situation continued, the policy should be reviewed at high administrative levels in light of 'where the institution was going'. The decision was never enforced, for shortly thereafter the adolescent census dropped and never rose again to such dangerous heights. The decision has long since been forgotten, and if the census were again to rise dangerously, doubtless a new discussion would take place rather than an evocation of the old rule.

But this is precisely how more long-standing policy and many rules become established in what conventionally is called 'hospital structure'. In turn, of course, the policies and rules serve to set the limits and some of the directions of negotiation. (This latter proposition is implicit in much of our foregoing discussion on rules and negotiation as well as the patterning of negotiation.) We suggest that future studies of complex relationships existing between the more stable elements of organizational order and the more fleeting working arrangements may profit by examining the former as if they were sometimes a background against which the latter were being evolved in the foreground – and sometimes as if the reverse obtained. What is needed is both a concentrated focus upon, and the development of a terminology adequate to handle, this kind of metaphor. But whether this metaphor or another, the question of how negotiation and appraisal play into each other, and into the rules or policies, remains central.

Summary and implications

As remarked at the outset of this paper, the reader must judge for himself whether a model possibly suited to studying psychiatric hospitals might equally guide study and understanding of other types of hospitals. The model presented has pictured the hospital as a locale where personnel, mostly but not exclusively professionals, are enmeshed in a complex negotiative process in order both to accomplish their individual purposes and to work – in an established division of labor – toward clearly as well as vaguely phrased institutional objectives. We have sought to show how differential professional training, ideology, career, and hierarchical position all affect the negotiation; but we have also attempted to show how nonprofessionals may affect the total process. We have outlined important relationships between daily working arrangements and the more permanent structure.

We would argue that this mode of viewing hospitals can be very useful. One reason is that it directs attention to the interplay of professionals and nonprofessionals – *as* professionals and nonprofessionals rather than just in terms of hierarchical position. It forces attention also upon the transactions of professionals, among echelons and within echelons. Properly carried out, the approach will not permit, as in many studies, a focus upon the hospital without cognizance of how the outside world impinges upon what is going on within the hospital: a single hospital, after all, is only a point through which multiple careers stream – including the patients' careers. As suggested in the opening page, the approach also pins one's gaze upon processes of change, and of stability also, providing one assumes that 'no change' must be worked at within the organization. Among other considerations, it allows focus upon important internal occurences under the impact of external pressures as well as of internal changes within the establishment. Whatever the purely specific characteristics of psychiatric hospitals as compared with nonpsychiatric ones, it is evident that most of the latter share certain features that make them amenable to our approach. Hospitals are evolving as institutions – and rapidly. They are locales where many different kinds of professionals work – and more are joining the ranks. The very heterogeneity of personnel and of professional purpose, along with the impact of a changing medical technology, bespeaks the kind of world sketched above.[3]

But what of other organizations, especially if sizable or complex – is this kind of interactional model also relevant to them? The answer, we suggest, is strongly in the affirmative. Current preoccupation with formal organization tends to underplay – or leave implicit – the interactional features underscored in the foregoing pages. Yet one would expect interactional features to jump into visibility once looked for systematically. We urge that whenever an organization possesses one or more of the following characteristics, such a search be instituted : if the organization firstly utilizes personnel trained in several different occupations, or secondly, if each contains an occupational group including individuals trained in different traditions, then they

3. Without drawing the same conclusions, Sayre (1956), a professor of public administration, has suggested similar features of modern hospitals: 'In the health and medical professions together in a hospital these stresses between *organization* and *profession* are made the more complex by a multiplicity of professions, a multiplicity of values and perspectives not easily reconciled into a harmonious organization. ... The hospital would seem to be an organizational setting where many semi-autonomous cooperators meet for the purpose of using common services and facilities and to provide services to each other, but in a loosely integrated organizational system.'
4. Dalton (1959) has made the same criticism of this literature.

are likely to possess somewhat different occupational philosophies, emphasizing somewhat different values; then also if at least some personnel are professionals, the latter are likely to be pursuing careers that render them mobile – that is, carrying them into and out of the organization. The reader should readily appreciate why those particular characteristics have been singled out. They are, of course, attributes of universities, corporations, and government agencies, as well as of hospitals. If an organization is marked by one or more of those characteristics, then the concept of 'negotiated order' should be an appropriate way to view it.

References

CAUDILL, W. *et al* (1952), 'Social structure and interaction processes on a psychiatric ward', *American Journal of Orthopsychiatry*, no. 22, pp. 314–34.

DALTON, M. (1959), *Men Who Manage*, Wiley.

GOFFMAN, E. (1957), 'On the characteristics of total institutions', *Proceedings of the Symposium on Preventive and Social Psychiatry*, Walter Reed Army Institute of Research.

GOFFMAN, E. (1959), 'The moral career of the mental patient', *Psychiatry*, no. 22, pp. 123–42.

MEAD, G. H. (1936), 'The problem of society – how we become selves', *Movements of Thought in the Nineteenth Century*, University of Chicago Press.

PARSONS, T., and FOX, R. (1952), 'Illness, therapy and the modern urban American family', *Journal of Social Issues*, no. 7, pp. 31–44.

SAYRE, W. S. (1956), 'Principles of administration', *Hospitals*, 16 January, 1 February.

Part Two
Influencing Decisions

Part One has concentrated on those processes internal to individuals, groups and organizations which help to shape the nature of the decisions which emerge from each. This is essential for an understanding of how decisions are made but it only provides a partial explanation of the decision-making process. Quite apart from the high level of abstraction required in a consideration of processes that are common to decision making as a whole, individuals, groups and organizations operate in a wider social environment. The environment affects them, and they frequently seek to have an effect on it.

In fact, if we wish to understand how decisions are made, we must look beyond the internal processes of decision making and take into account the interrelations between different decision-making bodies and the character of social and political attitudes. The decisions made by one body are virtually certain to affect others, and these others are likely to exert influence to ensure, at a minimum, that the results for themselves are not disadvantageous. The first selection in this section, Gamson's 'Influence in use', shows the various ways in which the use of influence may be identified. It also illustrates the variety of strategies open to the individual or group who wishes to influence a decision; constraint, inducement and persuasion may all be used, and the success of one rather than another is dependent on the resources available to those involved.

One resource that is important to groups and organizations is the support of members, and thus one of the important factors operating to affect them is their concern to provide incentives or compulsion of a kind which will keep their membership faithful to group purposes. Those who have studied politics have often assumed that the formation of groups is voluntary, and that adherence to group aims is consequently guaranteed by the spontaneous enthusiasm of the membership, but, as Olson points out, there are very good reasons for believing that individual enthusiasm is a very poor guardian against the danger of decisions being of a kind which damage one's interests.

Irrespective of the degree to which groups are voluntary, there can be no doubt that group influence is vital in shaping all categories of decisions at all levels of society. Only some of these relationships are significant because only some decisions intersect with power in a way that is important for society, thus the extracts in this part concentrate on political relationships and attitudes. The usual emphasis of those who talk of pressure groups or interest groups is on the influence they exert on governmental policy. This approach is exemplified by the extract from Eckstein's book, *Pressure Group Politics*, which, among other things, points out that the form of pressure group activity, that is, the channels of action on which groups concentrate, is largely a function of the decision-making processes they attempt to influence, and the nature of the actual decisions which affect them. Although the focus of pressure group activity is on government for the most part, the degree to which they are successful or unsuccessful in exerting influence in their chosen direction affects decision making at all levels. Where a law-reforming group is successful, the individual's freedom to make certain types of decision is altered; where the business lobby is successful, the trade unions' freedom to make certain types of decision may be circumscribed.

Pressure groups are by no means the only source of influence on decision makers. This point is made clear in the piece by Jones, which shows how an important decision maker, the Prime Minister, is limited in the decisions he can take by influences from a variety of sources. Because of the need to maintain the loyalty of senior party members, he is constrained in his choice of Cabinet, and where the policy of the Opposition has gained some favour with the electorate, even Opposition influence may have some weight with him. For the purposes of this Reader the Prime Minister is only chosen as an example for dramatic effect. If it is true that someone so reputedly powerful is only as strong as his colleagues will let him be, if his decisions are so greatly influenced by external constraints, then a similar situation is likely to pertain in respect of other more humble makers of decisions.

The influence exerted by pressure groups is quite explicit, and so often are the pressures exerted in a more informal way on powerful individuals like the Prime Minister. But frequently decision makers are influenced in their choices by beliefs and attitudes taken for granted in the society in which they operate. As Eckstein notes, the exercise of overt group pressure is more likely to be favoured in a country such as Britain, where corporatist ideas have persisted, than in the United States, where the Lockean view, that decisions should stem from the interaction of individual and state, has prevailed. The excerpts from Almond and Verba show a further instance of the way in which beliefs and attitudes held in different societies affects the nature of the decision-making process, in this case, by pointing to empirical evidence that attitudes may determine differentially the individual's willingness to participate in political decision making, whether acting alone, through an informal grouping, a political party or an organized pressure group.

Nettl's piece on 'Consensus or Elite Domination: The Case of Business' takes this same point about attitudes, and tries to illustrate its peculiar relevance to British political activity. He suggests, in fact, that the ethos of decision making in Britain, whether in private or public life, is one which is set by the attitudes, values and procedures current in the civil service. Indeed, he argues that the importance of this influence is such that much of the overt posturing and conflict of pressure groups may in reality be little more than shadow-boxing. Whether or not this view can be fully sustained, Nettl's article certainly points to the way in which civil service practice has become an unconscious influence and constraint on decision-making procedures.

The final selection in this section on influencing decisions is intended to perform two functions. First, in discussing 'The collective organization of industry', Grove offers a most useful summary of the types of organization which influence the process of decision making in this important area. Second, this factual analysis of group pressures operating in the industrial field offers an opportunity for a re-examination in a concrete context of some of the points made previously in the section. For instance, Grove reiterates Eckstein's point about the executive focus of group influence in Britain, and goes on to explore the factors conditioning the amount of interaction between government departments and sectional groups. Moreover, he suggests, as did Gamson, that the type of influence a group exerts is likely to influence decision makers in the sense that administrators are more likely to be persuaded by inducements than reasoned arguments or threats. It may also be noted that Grove's closing remarks suggest that it may be worthwhile subjecting Nettl's argument to critical scrutiny, for the danger of what Grove calls 'clientalism' is seemingly the very opposite of Nettl's thesis of an institutional consensus dominated by civil service values. In other words, one of the major reasons for including 'The collective organization of industry' in this Reader is that it provides very useful material in the light of which some of the more analytical points about decision making may be viewed.

Taken together, the selections in Part Two are intended conclusively to make the case that it is impossible to study any group of decision makers in isolation. The content of their decisions is, of course, very largely a function of their aims and interests and of the procedures whereby those decisions are reached, but it is also a function of the influences exerted upon them by others and of the attitudes and values current in their society. Together all these factors create a pattern of decision making, which it is the object of Part Three to examine.

9 W. A. Gamson

Influence in Use

Excerpts from 'Influence in use', in W. A. Gamson, *Power and Discontent*, Dorsey Press, 1968, ch. 4, pp. 59–85.

Any discussion of power and influence is hampered by the fact that no established consensus on terminology exists. Some writers, for example, distinguish the terms power and influence while others use them interchangeably. As used here, power refers both to authorities operating on potential partisans and to the reverse operation. I will use the term social control when I wish to speak of what authorities do to potential partisans, and influence to cover the reverse. Influence is the family name for an array of connected concepts and this chapter identifies the members and tries to clarify their kinship relations.

The task has already begun through specifying the agents and targets of influence: potential partisans and authorities. This hardly reduces the number of people involved since authorities are more than simply government officials. Almost everyone makes binding decisions at some level of social organization, be it community, voluntary association, work organization, family, or some other. But while defining authorities as the target of influence does not reduce who is involved, it does circumscribe the behavior being influenced. Many kinds of influence are beyond the scope of this discussion: influences on attitudes and values and on various actions are of concern only when they affect the binding choices of people acting in an authority role.

The nature of influence

What is the nature of this influence that partisans attempt to exercise over authorities? It is a special case of behavioral effects. Simon (1957, p. 5) puts it in terms of causality. 'The statement "A has power over B" is equivalent to the statement "A causes B's behavior".' This is an extremely broad concept of influence, omitting as it does any idea of A's intention. But it underlines the fact that A must be at least partially determining B's behavior, altering it from what it would have been in A's absence.

There is a story about a man, who, early each morning, enthusiastically threw bits of newspaper in the street. One morning, a woman who had watched this performance for several months approached him and asked him what he was doing. 'I'm throwing this paper down to keep the elephants out of the streets', he replied. 'But there are no elephants in the streets', she reproached him. 'That's right!' he said triumphantly, 'Effective, isn't it?'

Fundamental to the idea of influence then, is the requirement that the decision-making behavior of authorities has been altered from what it would have been in the absence of the influencer. To conceive of influence as a shift in the probability of an outcome is one of Dahl's (1957) several outstanding contributions to this area. Assume that a particular potential partisan group does nothing to influence the outcome of a given decision and that the authorities do not know the group's preferred outcome. Let us use a term to cover this situation: P_b or the probability that the political system will produce preferred outcomes without the group doing anything to bring them about. This may be thought of as the probability before or without influence. But assume that our group becomes active and does various things which alter P_b. The new probability of obtaining the preferred outcome after influence attempts have occurred will be called P_a. A partisan group can be said to have exercised influence *if and only if* there is a difference between P_a and P_b.

Operationalizing influence

This simple and appealing definition has an array of operational and conceptual problems. There are three approaches to the operational difficulties.

1. *The relative frequency approach.* Since there is no meaningful way of talking about the 'objective' probability of a single event, one can restrict statements about the exercise of power

to classes of similar decisions. An operational index of influence is then provided by subtracting the frequency of obtaining a particular outcome when a partisan group works against it from the frequency when it works in favor of it. For example, one can examine the relative frequency of (say) a foreign policy bill passing when Senator X works in favor of it and the relative frequency of it passing when he works against it. If the first probability is substantially higher, then Senator X can be said to exercise substantial influence on foreign policy decisions.

Such an index of influence runs into serious difficulties if one must use, as a matter of convenience, the senator's recorded vote as a measure of his activities prior to the vote. As Dahl emphasizes in using such a measure, it becomes impossible to distinguish the genuine influencer from the 'chameleon'. 'Suppose' Dahl asks (1957, pp. 212–13) 'a Senator takes no prior position on any bill and always decides how to vote by guessing how the Senate majority will vote; then, if he is a perfect guesser [he will appear to be exercising maximum possible influence when he is, in fact, exercising none].' A close relative of the chameleon is the 'satellite', the senator who religiously follows the dictates of a powerful colleague but exercises no independent influence of his own. He would appear to be exercising the same influence as his colleague when, in fact, he was only reflecting such influence. MacRae and Price suggest still another source of spurious influence.

It results from the fact that legislators often cast roll-call votes so as to locate themselves along a one-dimensional continuum in a given subject matter area (e.g., foreign policy or taxation). . . . Insofar as this is true, those legislators nearest the median of the distribution of legislators along this continuum will necessarily have the highest indices [of influence by the operational definition being discussed] (1959, p. 213).

In this case, the more 'representative' the senator is of senatorial sentiment, the more influence he will appear to have even when he is exercising none.

Such criticisms of a particular index may lead to undue pessimism about operational difficulties. The problems above are far from insoluble; they require only that one have some measure of actual partisan activity prior to a vote rather than relying on the vote itself as a measure of this. Dahl suggests that 'observations of this kind are available only with great difficulty' (1957, p. 214) but the difficulties seem no greater than for myriad other research situations in which information must be painfully gathered through interviews and observations rather than simply plucked from the pages of *Congressional Quarterly* or from some other volume in the reference room of the nearest library [. . .]

2. *The subjective probability approach.* Frequently we want to make statements about the exercise of influence on a single issue. For example, we may want to say whether President Johnson's skill in handling Congress increased the probability that the Civil Rights Act of 1964 would pass over the probability that it would have passed if President Kennedy had lived. Or, to take another example, we may want to know whether the opposition of various groups in the United States to the administration's conduct of the war in Vietnam 'had any influence' over the probability of various policy decisions. One cannot conclude that no influence has occurred simply by a failure to achieve a preferred outcome. A partisan group may start with little chance of a policy being accepted but by waging a vigorous fight, it may reach a point where acceptance of the policy is touch and go. Perhaps in the end the group loses, but the change from almost certain failure to a near-miss is a mark of its influence.

The theoretical definition of influence as the difference between P_a and P_b is still useful in talking about influence on a single event. However, we must abandon *objective* probability as a way of operationalizing influence on a single event, and substitute *subjective* probability. What odds would a set of informed observers give on the outcome of the decision before and after the relevant acts of influence occurred? If the preferred alternative is now a 'better bet', then we can say that influence has occurred. For example, if a bill is given one chance in four of passing the Senate by experienced and informed observers before Senator X takes a stand and is given two chances in three of passing after Senator X has waged a vigorous campaign on its behalf, we can say that Senator X has influenced the decision. The actual outcome is irrelevant to this operational definition which measures influence by a shift in subjective probability. Of course, one must deal with the reliability and validity of the observers' judgements but there are standard techniques for dealing with such problems.[1]

3. *The influence attempt approach.* The final approach to operationalizing influence involves an end run. Instead of examining influence, one examines two other related concepts: influence attempts and capability of influence. Influence attempts are considerably easier to measure than is influence since one only needs to look at the behavior of partisans without worrying about the response of authorities. Rosenau (1961) takes this approach in his examination of public opinion and foreign policy. He substitutes for the difficult concept of influence a more manageable one: 'the transmission of opinion'. 'Thus, by distinguishing and classifying the various participants in the opinion-policy relationship according to the form which their communicative behavior takes, it should be possible to avoid the difficulties of measuring influence . . .' (p. 16).

If we can understand the process of influence attempts and can then combine it with some measure of capability, we may move far toward inferring influence without measuring it. Capability is handled by the concept of *resources*, and is discussed at length below. The influence attempt approach involves making one central assumption: the possession of resources plus the existence of influence attempts implies influence. This assumption cannot be tested without using one of the direct measures of influence suggested above. However, if it is accepted as reasonable or established by evidence, one can then proceed to study influence by measuring influence attempts and the distribution of resources without ever attempting to assess influence directly.

Each of these approaches to an operational definition of influence is viable and appropriate for particular situations. When MacRae and Price (1959, p. 218) conclude that 'Although the

1. See, for example, Guilford (1954), for an extended discussion of such techniques.

conceptualization of [influence] has been advanced [by Dahl], the operational definition of it has not yet been accomplished,' they react too much to the faults of one particular operational definition. In fact, the operational problems seem manageable enough.

Theoretical problems in defining influence

A major theoretical problem is created by the fact that when one group attempts influence, it frequently stimulates similar action from other, opposing groups. Suppose, for example, that a civil rights group wishes a city council to pass an Open Housing Ordinance and that a group of citizens on the north side of town fear such an ordinance. The northsiders regard the ordinance as unlikely to pass and, therefore, plan little activity against it. If and only if the civil rights group becomes active will the northsiders become active on the other side. For the sake of argument, assume that the activity of the northsiders always is exactly enough to neutralize the actions of the civil rights group. Thus P_a is the same as P_b in spite of a vigorous campaign by the civil rights group. Must we say that they have had no influence on this decision?

One might be tempted to see this as a measurement difficulty rather than a conceptual one. A theoretical solution might be found by assigning the effects to the immediate actions of the civil rights group regardless of any future action by the north-siders. This would then be a case in which the council was influenced in one direction by the civil rights group and then later influenced back to the starting point by their opponents. Unfortunately, this will not suffice. First, the northsiders' action was not *independent*; it was contingent on the first group's action. Second, the civil rights group may have exercised influence by galvanizing other supporting groups – for example, the Ministerial Alliance which would have remained quiet had they not been prodded. If future actions that are conditional on the group's activity are to be included, then we must include both the ministers' wanted action and the northsiders' un-wanted action.

It seems necessary, then, to define influence in terms of *net effects*. If the civil rights group produced reactions which offset its influence attempts, then it exercised no influence. One must be able to attribute the effect to the group in question. We cannot conclude that the civil rights group exercised no influence over the city council unless we know that the actions of the northsiders were contingent on those of the civil rights group. It may be that they would have launched a campaign against the Open Housing Ordinance in any event. If their actions are not conditional, if they represent no 'backlash', their impact cannot be considered part of the net effect of the actions of the civil rights group. The net effect of a group's presence and its actions includes only the *contingent* actions of other groups.

Influence can occur without any current action on the part of the potential partisan group. If a federal civil rights bill is changed or not introduced in the first place because of fears of a Southern filibuster in the Senate, then it is not unreasonable to say that the Southern senators have affected the probability of the passage of the civil rights bill *even if no filibuster has occurred*. Nor need a Southern spokesman warn the Justice Department that a filibuster will occur or even make a veiled and implicit threat to this effect. The very existence of a rule allowing unlimited debate in the Senate and a group that has used it on certain specified occasions in the past and can do so again, is enough to create the influence.

To restate the definition of P_b and P_a in a form that incorporates these points, P_b is the probability that a preferred alternative will be passed if the potential partisan group can or will take *no action* contingent on what the authorities propose to do. P_a is the net result of the addition of the potential partisan group to the situation. Influence has occurred if there is a difference between P_a and P_b regardless of whether the potential partisan group has taken some action. Of course, the amount of influence may vary if the group acts in one way rather than another. In many cases, there may be no difference between P_a and P_b *unless* the group takes some action.

It is worth noting that this definition of influence which is drawn so heavily from Dahl, violates one of the two *necessary* conditions which he suggests must be present before influence can be said to exist.

A necessary condition for the power relation is that there exists a time lag, however small, from the actions of the actor who is said to exert power to the responses of the respondent. This requirement merely accords with one's intuitive belief that A can hardly be said to have power over a unless A's power attempts precede a's responses. . . . Who runs the XYZ Corporation? Whenever the president announces a new policy, he immediately secures the compliance of the top officials. But upon investigation it turns out that every new policy he announces has first been put to him by the head of the sales department (Dahl, 1957, p. 204).

It is possible, however, that the head of the sales department is careful to suggest only those alternatives that he believes will be supported by the chairman of the board of directors. In the absence of this gentleman, he would not propose a particular alternative and the president would not accept it if he did. The probability of its adoption would be greatly altered. Are we then correct in attributing all the influence to the head of the sales department who has taken some action rather than allocating some to the chairman of the board whose presence has changed the probability of the policy being adopted perhaps even more?

Dahl suggests a second necessary condition which can be more fully accepted.

Unless there is some 'connection' between A and a, then no power relation can be said to exist. . . . In looking for a flow of influence . . . from A to a, one must always find out whether there is a connection, or an opportunity for a connection, and if there is not, then one need proceed no further (1957, p. 204).

If the head of the sales department asked himself how Jomo Kenyatta or the Queen of England would feel about the policy, no influence would be attributed to them. No matter how important they are as figures of identification, they are not present in the situation in the same sense that the chairman of the board is. While there need not necessarily *be* an action by the influencer, there must be the possibility for action. The influencer must be able and likely to know how the authorities will act and be able to respond to their actions. Interaction is a necessary condition of influence.

Some concepts in the influence family
Negative influence

Intentionality is imbedded in the definition of influence through the concept of a preferred outcome. Groups may also do various things which affect outcomes inadvertently. Such effects constitute influence only when they involve *preferred* outcomes. 'Any reciprocal contact between human beings leads to the modification of the actions of the participants', Easton argues.

If [influence] is so broadly conceived, then every relation is an illustration of [an influence] situation. . . . To give [influence] any differentiated meaning we must view it as a relationship in which one person or group is able to determine the actions of another in the direction of the former's own ends (1953, p. 143).

Actions must affect preferred outcomes to be considered influence but what if they affect them in an unintended direction? Is it influence if the actions of a group make P_a lower than P_b instead of higher as the group intended? Dahl (1957, p. 205) suggests that we might call this 'negative' influence. 'If whenever I ask my son to stay home on Saturday morning to mow the lawn, my request has the inevitable effect of inducing him to go swimming, when he would otherwise have stayed home, I do have a curious kind of negative [influence] over him.'

This negative influence may be produced in two basic ways. First, a group may, by its actions, create resistance on the part of authorities. Cartwright (1959) and French and Raven (1959) have pointed to a distinction between 'opposition to an influence attempt' and 'resistance generated by an influence attempt'. Opposition is based on the content of the proposed policy. 'In resistance the content is quite secondary and may even be irrelevant' (Cartwright, 1965, p. 34). Resistance may lead authorities to 'punish' a group by withholding preferred outcomes and to protect and reward the group's adversaries. It is in this sense that civil rights groups frequently have regarded some of their cruder enemies as assets for their cause. A clumsy influence attempt will produce negative influence when the resistance it generates makes P_a lower than P_b.

The second way in which negative influence occurs is through activating other potential partisan groups with opposing objectives. 'White backlash', for example, seems to mean anti-Negro and anticivil rights activity, stimulated by the influence attempts of Negroes and their allies. To give the term a more general meaning, *backlash* is the counterinfluence of opposing groups which is *conditional* on the influence activity of a given partisan group. It should not be confused with the influence activities of opposing groups when such activities are partly or wholly *independent* of what the partisan group is doing and would have gone on in any event. The backlash portion of such activity is that part which is contingent. A group has exercised negative influence if the impact of backlash activity outweighs the impact of the group's own activity.

Amount of influence

The amount of influence exercised is simply the degree of probability of change in the desired direction. It is worth emphasizing again that defeat does not necessarily imply lack of influence. This point is typically forgotten in the postmortem that accompanies a political defeat. The losers will take themselves to task for various failures, assuming that their a priori probability of winning was 0.5. The other side is seen as having spent more resources or as having used its resources more efficiently. While this may be the case, not infrequently the losing side exercises a large amount of influence while the winning side does little or nothing to further their cause.

Basis of influence

The basis of influence refers to *what* is used and the means to *how* it is used. What is it that a group uses to exercise influence? In any decision, there exists some 'thing' or 'weight' such that if enough of this weight is applied to the authorities, P_b will be altered. Lasswell and Kaplan (1950, p. 83), define a 'base value' as follows: 'Whenever X has influence over Y, there is some value with regard to which X enjoys a favorable position, and because of which he can exercise influence over Y. This is the base value of the influence relation. . . .' A more natural term, and one which I shall use here, is *resource*. Thus, Dahl (1957, p. 203) writes that the 'base of an actor's power consists of all the *resources* – opportunities, acts, objects, etc. – that he can exploit in order to affect the behavior of another.'

Two important conditions must be satisfied before something can be called a resource. First, the thing must be possessed by, or more accurately, *controlled* by the influencer. He must be able to determine its use. Second, he must be able to bring it to bear on authorities in interaction with them. Something which is a resource with respect to one social system and one group of authorities will not necessarily be a resource for all systems and all authorities.

The concept of resources is elaborated in the discussions of potential influence and cost of influence below. At this point, a few examples are sufficient, but their justification is deferred. All of the following are resources in some situations: the ability to hire, promote and fire people; the ability to allocate corporation money to civic projects; the authority to make decisions on a variety of issues; the ability to influence large numbers of voters to withdraw their political support from an individual or project; the ability to enhance or damage reputation through control of some communication medium; the possession of a generalized reputation for wisdom on public affairs.

Means of influence

Knowing what resources a group controls does not tell us how it uses them. For example, a person with money might use it to bribe officials, to employ a private army which threatens them, or to publish and distribute a pamphlet setting forth the reasons why they should act in the desired fashion. A typology of means of influence tells us the different ways in which resources are used to influence authorities.

It is clear that there are many ways of classifying influence. Where one author carefully distinguishes between three or four means, another will ignore their differences and casually treat them as a piece. The particular distinctions employed are dictated by one's objectives and there are many valid typologies, each useful for specific purposes.

The classification of means used here is dictated by a desire to relate means of influence to political trust. It is based on two underlying dimensions:

1. *Situational versus orientational influence*. This distinction is made in a number of discussions, most explicitly by Parsons.

There is a very simple paradigm of means by which one acting unit . . . can attempt to get results by bringing influence to bear on another unit. . . . The first variable is whether ego attempts to work through potential control over the *situation* in which alter is placed and must act, or through an attempt to have an effect on alter's *intentions* independently of changes in his situation (1963, pp. 42–43).

2. *Adding advantages versus adding disadvantages*. This distinction is a further breakdown of situational influence. It is important whether changes or promised changes in the situation are advantageous or disadvantageous to the authorities. As Thibaut and Kelley (1959, p. 105) point out, if the target of influence is 'controlled solely by augmentation (say he is offered rewards for compliance), he will monitor himself. . . . In contrast, when reduction [e.g., punishment] . . . is threatened for noncompliance [the target's compliance must be kept] under surveillance.' Lasswell and Kaplan (1950, p. 97) recognize the distinction in defining 'constraint' and 'inducement'. '*Constraint*', they write, 'is the exercise of influence by threat of deprivation; *inducement*, by promise of indulgence.'

These two dimensions, then, yield three means of influence. They are outlined in Table 1 with the labels used here: constraints, inducements, and persuasion.

Table 1 Typology of Means of Influence

Underlying dimensions	Addition of disadvantages	Addition of advantages
Changes in the situation of the authorities	Constraints	Inducements
Changes in the orientation of the authorities	Persuasion	

1. *Constraints*. Constraints are the addition of new disadvantages to the situation or the threat to do so, regardless of the

Approval and disapproval as a means of influence are very interesting in this regard. Approval may be influential for two reasons; firstly it may be regarded by the recipient as an implicit promise of future rewards. Thus, he may vote to please his boss on the expectation that this pleasure will be translated into more tangible rewards when promotions and salary raises are being considered; or secondly the influencer's approval may be intrinsically rewarding. He may be a friend whose pleasure in the outcome of the decision is its own reward. In this case, there is no expectation of getting future benefits except those that stem from the relationship itself. The first of these examples represents inducement influence while the second involves persuasion. Similarly, disapproval may be either an implicit threat of future disadvantages or it may be psychologically punishing. If it is the latter, it is persuasion rather than constraint.

Since the word persuasion usually has a more limited meaning than the variegated one given here, it is worth underlining this category with a number of examples. If the brother of a member of a city council asks him to vote against a proposed fluoridation ordinance because he finds it objectionable, the councilman may do so even if he, personally, has nothing against fluoridation. The brother *may* give no reasons why he considers it objectionable and make no effort to convince the councilman of its undesirable characteristics. Or, the health officer may come to the council meeting and give arguments in favor of fluoridation which are not understood by the councilmen but which, on the basis of their faith in his expertness, convince the council to pass fluoridation. Finally, the health officer may present the council with a detailed description of the experiments conducted and the exhaustive checks made by scientists on possible dangers in such a way that the councilmen are left with a deep conviction of the desirability of fluoridation. Each of these is an example of persuasion.

Persuasion influence is not always distinguished from constraint and inducement influence by the degree of coerciveness involved. Any means of influence may vary in (a) the amount of restriction it places on the behavior of the targets and (b) on the degree of bindingness it carries for them.

(a) On the amount of restriction, imagine that a school board is threatened with punishment if they pick site X for a school, but are left free to pick any other site. Alternatively, by an overwhelming propaganda campaign replete with lies, the school board might be manipulated into seeing compelling and over-riding advantages in site X which do not exist. They may be less 'free' to consider alternative sites in such circumstances than they are under the influence of threats.

(b) A similar point can be made for degree of bindingness. If by completely binding influence, we mean a change in probability such that $P_a = 1 \cdot 0$, force or the threat of force is not necessarily more binding than persuasion. The prospect of a possible punch in the nose may not completely deter someone from choosing an undesired alternative when the 'persuasive' orders of a hypnotist leave him no choice. Manipulation, lying, hypnosis, 'hidden' persuasion, 'brainwashing', advertising, propaganda, are all names for particular kinds of persuasion influence, as long as they involve the manipulation of the target's orientation rather than the addition of sanctions to the situation. There is no implicit hierarchy of morality involved in the classification of means of influence.

Scope and site of influence

There has been a healthy emphasis among students of power on the necessity of specifying the areas over which influence extends. This emphasis comes from a reaction against a view of power relations as one of dominance-submission. Clearly, the influence relation being discussed here is not a general relation of dominance and subordination. Yesterday's partisan is today's authority and vice versa. Influence has already been narrowed in scope by making it refer only to certain specified actions of authorities, those which affect the probability of accepting preferred alternatives.

There is, however, a sense in which influence can be regarded as 'content free' or independent of the subject matter of the decision. If a set of would-be influencers unequivocally control some resource, then they have a basis of influence which is not altered when the decision shifts from urban renewal to schools to fluoridation. A resource is still a resource and is unaltered by changes in the content of the decisions as long as the authorities remain constant.

However, a resource for one set of authorities may not hold for another set. This suggests that the crucial aspect of the scope of influence is not the content of the decision but the *arenas* or *sites* in which resources are relevant. 'The *arena* of power,' write Lasswell and Kaplan (1950, p. 78) 'is the situation comprised by those who demand power or who are within the domain of power.' Similarly, Dahl (1966, p. 338) suggests that the 'situation or circumstances in which an opposition employs its resources to bring about a change might be called a *site* for encounters between opposition and government.' The site of an influence attempt can be identified with the target of influence; each set of authorities represents a different site.

Scope of influence, I am suggesting, should refer to the sites of influence rather than the content of issues. Thus, a given partisan group might be capable of exercising great influence over the President's decision to introduce a bill into Congress. On the very same issue, it might have little capability of exercising influence over a congressional committee which is considering the bill.

The assertion that resources are content-free with respect to any given site needs an important qualification. It is true only if the *control* of these resources is unaffected by the content of the decision. Many resources depend on the ability of the influencer to control the actions of other people. A union leader, for example, who holds the threat of a strike as a major resource in bargaining cannot call a strike on any issue at any time. The existence of this resource is very much dependent on the content of the issue. If it concerns a matter of fundamental union concern, then his ability to add the disadvantage of a strike is unquestionable; if he attempts to apply this resource in areas that are peripheral or irrelevant to his followers, his resource may be quite questionable. At the very least, to institute a strike in the latter case will require that he use additional resources to influence his membership that would not be required in the first case. If one cannot assume a constancy of control over resources regardless of the issue, then it is necessary to specify the scope of resources not only by indicating the applicable authorities but also by indicating the range of applicable decisions. Note, however, that the designation of scope would not consist of an *ad hoc* classification of content such as 'economic' issues, 'education' issues, and 'political' issues, but would clearly focus on the relation of the issue to the influencer's control of resources.

Cost of influence

There are a number of possible concepts of the 'cost' of influence. A very important one considers the sacrifices that a would-be influencer must make in exercising influence and, in particular, the alternative use of his resources which he foregoes. However, this concept of 'opportunity costs' is different from the one used here which focuses on the resources consumed in the influence transaction. These transactional costs include the resources involved in communicating and completing an act of influence and in maintaining an organization for such purposes.

There are a wide variety of specific resources which can be used to bring about influence. It is helpful to think of costs as involving the generalized inducement resources described above as *obligations*. Carrying out influence involves making commitments which place a future call on one's resources. The transactional cost of influence is the cost of fulfilling obligations contracted.

Fixed costs and variable costs. Partisan groups which participate regularly in the arena of politics generally find it necessary to maintain their resources in a state of high liquidity or readiness. To be able to influence when the occasion arises, one must spend resources to maintain readiness. Such costs transcend any particular act of influence; they represent an overhead cost which can be distributed over a series of acts. The cost of maintaining a defense establishment to be used as a constraint in international politics is an example of such fixed costs. The cost of employing a public relations firm to enhance reputation is another example. The expenses of a legislative representative or lobbyist by an organization interested in influencing Congress is still another example of a cost of influence which, while not specific to any single influence attempt, may be an important part of the total cost of influence for a partisan group.

Besides such relatively fixed costs, the sheer act of bringing influence to bear on the authorities will involve some cost. If we are concerned with persuasion influence, then the costs involved are the resources consumed in changing the orientation of the authorities. Included in such campaign costs are any which were preparatory to the act of attempted persuasion. For example, the costs to a group of professors who wished to encourage Congress to support a disarmament treaty would include not only the resources used to wire congressmen and the expense of a full page advertisement presenting their views in the *New York Times* but those used to solicit signatures for the advertisement and to establish contact with supporters around the country and enlist their participation.

Research costs are included here as well. A local group which wishes to have the community approve money for a new high school might have to spend considerable resources acquiring information which would enable them to answer arguments which are or might be raised. Having acquired such information, they might then have additional expenditures in getting this information to the voters. Both types of expenditure would be included as part of the cost of influence.

In some instances, a group which was involved in an effort at persuasion might solicit funds from supporters at the same time they were attempting influence. For example, an organization might mail a message which presents an argument for the need for a new high school while in the same message they ask for donations to cover the expenses of such a campaign. Suppose that the organization succeeds in raising sufficient money to offset the costs of the campaign. Would we then wish to say that the campaign had been costless? No, because the fact that money was raised at the same time that an influence attempt was taking place rather than before or after is fortuitous. The costs are there even if as a result of the influence attempt the solvency of the organization is greatly increased. An advertisement which costs a manufacturer $5000 still has cost him $5000 even if he shows a subsequent profit through the additional sales which his advertisement produces.

Inducements and constraints also must be communicated if the advantage or disadvantage being added is conditional on the behavior of the authorities. The costs of such communication may be trivial, as in the situation in which an influencer simply informs an official whom he has encountered what he will do if the official acts in the desired fashion. On the other hand, bargaining may be a long drawn-out process in which both parties must maintain a staff for the purpose of communicating promises or threats to the other side [. . .]

References

BLAU, P. M. (1964), *Exchange and Power in Social Life*, Wiley.

CARTWRIGHT, D. (ed.) (1959), '*Studies in Social Power*', Institute of Social Research, Ann Arbor.

CARTWRIGHT, D. (1965), 'Influence, leadership, control', in J. G. March, (ed.), *Handbook of Organizations*, Rand McNally.

DAHL, R. A. (1957), 'The concept of power', *Behavioral Science*, vol. 2, pp. 201–18.

DAHL, R. A. (1966), *Political Oppositions in Western Democracies*, Yale University Press.

EASTON, D. (1953), *The Political System*, Knopf.

FRENCH, J. R. P., and RAVEN, B. (1959), 'The basis of social power', in D. CARTWRIGHT.

GUILFORD, J. P. (1954), *Psychometric Models*, McGraw-Hill.

LASSWELL, H. D., and KAPLAN, A. (1950), *Power and Society*, Routledge & Kegan Paul.

MACRAE, D., and PRICE, H. D. (1959), 'Scale positions and "power" in the Senate', *Behavioral Science*, vol. 4, p. 213.

MITCHELL, W. C. (1962), *The American Polity*, Free Press.

PARSONS, T. (1963), 'On the concept of influence', *Public Opinion Quarterly*, vol. 27, pp. 37–62.

ROSENAU, J. N. (1961), *Public Opinion and Foreign Policy*, Random House.

SIMON, H. A. (1957), *Models of Man*, Wiley.

THIBAUT, J. W. and KELLEY, H. H. (1959), *The Social Psychology of Groups*, Wiley.

10 M. Olson

Groups and Organizations and their Basis of Support

Excerpts from 'A theory of groups and organizations', and 'The by-product and special interest theories', in M. Olson, *The Logic of Collective Action*, Harvard University Press, 1965, chs. 1 and 6, pp. 5–16 and 132–7.

The purpose of organization

Since most (though by no means all) of the action taken by or on behalf of groups of individuals is taken through organizations, it will be helpful to consider organizations in a general or theoretical way. The logical place to begin any systematic study of organizations is with their purpose. But there are all types and shapes and sizes of organizations, even of economic organizations, and there is then some question whether there is any single purpose that would be characteristic of organizations generally. One purpose that is nonetheless characteristic of most organizations, and surely of practically all organizations with an important economic aspect, is the furtherance of the interests of their members. That would seem obvious, at least from the economist's perspective. To be sure, some organizations may out of ignorance fail to further their members' interests, and others may be enticed into serving only the ends of the leadership. But organizations often perish if they do nothing to further the interests of their members, and this factor must severely limit the number of organizations that fail to serve their members.

The idea that organizations or associations exist to further the interests of their members is hardly novel, nor peculiar to economics; it goes back at least to Aristotle, who wrote,

Men journey together with a view to particular advantage, and by way of providing some particular thing needed for the purposes of life, and similarly the political association seems to have come together originally, and to continue in existence, for the sake of the general advantage it brings (*Ethics* viii, 9, 1160a).

More recently Festinger (1953, p. 93), a social psychologist, pointed out that 'the attraction of group membership is not so much in sheer belonging, but rather in attaining something by means of this membership.' The late Harold Laski, a political scientist, took it for granted that 'associations exist to fulfil purposes which a group of men have in common' (1939, p. 67).

The kinds of organizations that are the focus of this study are *expected* to further the interests of their members. Labor unions are expected to strive for higher wages and better working conditions for their members; farm organizations are expected to strive for favorable legislation for their members; cartels are expected to strive for higher prices for participating firms; the corporation is expected to further the interests of its stockholders; and the state is expected to further the common interests of its citizens (though in this nationalistic age the state often has interests and ambitions apart from those of its citizens).

Notice that the interests that all of these diverse types of organizations are expected to further are for the most part *common* interests: the union members' common interest in higher wages, the farmers' common interest in favorable legislation, the cartel members' common interest in higher prices, the stockholders' common interest in higher dividends and stock prices, the citizens' common interest in good government. It is not an accident that the diverse types of organizations listed are all supposed to work primarily for the *common* interests of their members. Purely personal or individual interests can be advanced, and usually advanced most efficiently, by individual, unorganized action. There is obviously no purpose in having an organization when individual, unorganized action can serve the interests of the individual as well as or better than an organization; there would, for example, be no point in forming an organization simply to play solitaire. But when a number of individuals have a common or collective interest – when they share a single purpose or objective – individual, unorganized action (as we shall soon see) will either not be able to advance that common interest at all, or will not be able to advance that interest adequately. Organizations can therefore perform a function when there are common or group interests, and though organizations often also serve purely personal, individual interests, their characteristic and primary function is to advance the common interests of groups of individuals.

The assumption that organizations typically exist to further the common interests of groups of people is implicit in most of the literature about organizations, and two of the writers already cited make this assumption explicit: Laski emphasized that organizations exist to achieve purposes or interests which 'a group of men have in common', and Aristotle apparently had a similar notion in mind when he argued that political associations are created and maintained because of the 'general advantages' they bring. MacIver (1932) also made this point explicitly when he said that 'every organization presupposes an interest which its members all share.'

Even when unorganized groups are discussed, at least in treatments of 'pressure groups' and 'group theory', the word 'group' is used in such a way that it means 'a number of individuals with a common interest'. It would of course be reasonable to label even a number of people selected at random (and thus without any common interest or unifying characteristic) as a 'group'; but most discussions of group behavior seem to deal mainly with groups that do have common interests. As Bentley (1949, p. 211), the founder of the 'group theory' of modern political science, put it, 'there is no group without its interest.'[1] The social psychologist Cattell (1955, p. 115) was equally explicit, and stated that 'every group has its interest'. This is also the way the word 'group' will be used here.

Just as those who belong to an organization or a group can be presumed to have a common interest, so they obviously also have purely individual interests, different from those of the others in the organization or group. All of the members of a labor union, for example, have a common interest in higher wages, but at the same time each worker has a unique interest in his personal income, which depends not only on the rate of wages but also on the length of time that he works.

1. Truman (1958) takes a similar approach, see pp. 33–5. See also Verba, (1961), pp. 12–13.

Public goods and large groups

The combination of individual interests and common interests in an organization suggests an analogy with a competitive market. The firms in a perfectly competitive industry, for example, have a common interest in a higher price for the industry's produce. Since a uniform price must prevail in such a market, a firm cannot expect a higher price for itself unless all of the other firms in the industry also have this higher price. But a firm in a competitive market also has an interest in selling as much as it can, until the cost of producing another unit exceeds the price of that unit. In this, there is no common interest; each firm's interest is directly opposed to that of every other firm, for the more other firms sell, the lower the price and income for any given firm. In short, while all firms have a common interest in a higher price, they have antagonistic interests where output is concerned. This can be illustrated with a simple supply-and-demand model. For the sake of a simple argument, assume that a perfectly competitive industry is momentarily in a disequilibrium position, with price exceeding marginal cost for all firms at their present output. Suppose, too, that all of the adjustments will be made by the firms already in the industry rather than by new entrants, and that the industry is on an inelastic portion of its demand curve. Since price exceeds marginal cost for all firms, output will increase. But as all firms increase production, the price falls; indeed, since the industry demand curve is by assumption inelastic, the total revenue of the industry will decline. Apparently each firm finds that with price exceeding marginal cost, it pays to increase its output, but the result is that each firm gets a smaller profit. Some economists in an earlier day may have questioned this result (see Clark, 1923, p. 417, Knight, 1921, p. 193), but the fact that profit-maximizing firms in a perfectly competitive industry can act contrary to their interests as a group is now widely understood and accepted (Chamberlin, 1950, p. 4). A group of profit-maximizing firms can act to reduce their aggregate profits because in perfect competition each firm is, by definition, so small that it can ignore the effect of its output on price. Each firm finds it to its advantage to increase output to the point where marginal cost equals price and to ignore the effects of its extra output on the position of the industry. It is true that the net result is that all firms are worse off, but this does not mean that every firm has not maximized its profits. If a firm, foreseeing the fall in price resulting from the increase in industry output, were to restrict its own output, it would lose more than ever, for its price would fall quite as much in any case and it would have a smaller output as well. A firm in a perfectly competitive market gets only a small part of the benefit (or a small share of the industry's extra revenue) resulting from a reduction in that firm's output.

For these reasons it is now generally understood that if the firms in an industry are maximizing profits, the profits for the industry as a whole will be less than they might otherwise be.[2] And almost everyone would agree that this theoretical conclusion fits the facts for markets characterized by pure competition. The important point is that this is true because, though all the firms have a common interest in a higher price for the industry's product, it is in the interest of each firm that the other firms pay the cost – in terms of the necessary reduction in output – needed to obtain a higher price.

About the only thing that keeps prices from falling in accordance with the process just described in perfectly competitive markets is outside intervention. Government price supports, tariffs, cartel agreements, and the like may keep the firms in a competitive market from acting contrary to their interests. Such aid or intervention is quite common. It is then important to ask how it comes about. How does a competitive industry obtain government assistance in maintaining the price of its product?

Consider a hypothetical, competitive industry, and suppose that most of the producers in that industry desire a tariff, a price-support program, or some other government intervention to increase the price for their product. To obtain any such assistance from the government, the producers in this industry will presumably have to organize a lobbying organization; they will have to become an active pressure group. This lobbying organization may have to conduct a considerable campaign. If significant resistance is encountered, a great amount of money will

2. For a fuller discussion of this question see Olson and McFarland (1962).

be required.[3] Public relations experts will be needed to influence the newspapers, and some advertising may be necessary. Professional organizers will probably be needed to organize 'spontaneous grass roots' meetings among the distressed producers in the industry, and to get those in the industry to write letters to their congressmen.[4] The campaign for the government assistance will take the time of some of the producers in the industry, as well as their money.

There is a striking parallel between the problem the perfectly competitive industry faces as it strives to obtain government assistance, and the problem it faces in the market place when the firms increase output and bring about a fall in price. Just as it was not rational for a particular producer to restrict his output in order that there might be a higher price for the product of his industry, so it would not be rational for him to sacrifice his time and money to support a lobbying organization to obtain government assistance for the industry. In neither case would it be in the interest of the individual producer to assume any of the costs himself. A lobbying organization, or indeed a labor union or any other organization, working in the interest of a large group of firms or workers in some industry, would get no assistance from the rational, self-interested individuals in that industry. This would be true even if everyone in the industry were absolutely convinced that the proposed program was in their interest (though in fact some might think otherwise and make the organization's task yet more difficult).

Although the lobbying organization is only one example of the logical analogy between the organization and the market, it is of some practical importance. There are many powerful and well-financed lobbies with mass support in existence now, but these lobbying organizations do not get that support because of their legislative achievements. The most powerful lobbying

3. See Heard (1960), especially note 1, pp. 95–6. For example, in 1947 the National Association of Manufacturers spent over $4·6 million, and over a somewhat longer period the American Medical Association spent as much on a campaign against compulsory health insurance.

4. 'If the full truth were ever known . . . lobbying, in all its ramifications, would prove to be a billion dollar industry.' US Congress Select Committee on Lobbying Activities (1950).

organizations now obtain their funds and their following for other reasons, as later parts of this study will show.

Some critics may argue that the rational person will, indeed, support a large organization, like a lobbying organization, that works in his interest, because he knows that if he does not, others will not do so either, and then the organization will fail, and he will be without the benefit that the organization could have provided. This argument shows the need for the analogy with the perfectly competitive market. For it would be quite as reasonable to argue that prices will never fall below the levels a monopoly would have charged in a perfectly competitive market, because if one firm increased its output, other firms would also, and the price would fall; but each firm could foresee this, so it would not start a chain of price-destroying increases in output. In fact, it does not work out this way in a competitive market; nor in a large organization. When the number of firms involved is large, no one will notice the effect on price if one firm increases its output, and so no one will change his plans because of it. Similarly, in a large organization, the loss of one dues payer will not noticeably increase the burden for any other one dues payer, and so a rational person would not believe that if he were to withdraw from an organization he would drive others to do so.

The foregoing argument must at the least have some relevance to economic organizations that are mainly means through which individuals attempt to obtain the same things they obtain through their activities in the market. Labor unions, for example, are organizations through which workers strive to get the same things they get with their individual efforts in the market—higher wages, better working conditions, and the like. It would be strange indeed if the workers did not confront some of the same problems in the union that they meet in the market, since their efforts in both places have some of the same purposes.

However similar the purposes may be, critics may object that attitudes in organizations are not at all like those in markets. In organizations, an emotional or ideological element is often also involved. Does this make the argument offered here practically irrelevant?

A most important type of organization – the national state – will serve to test this objection. Patriotism is probably the strongest non-economic motive for organizational allegiance in modern times. This age is sometimes called the age of nationalism. Many nations draw additional strength and unity from some powerful ideology, such as democracy or communism, as well as from a common religion, language, or cultural inheritance. The state not only has many such powerful sources of support; it also is very important economically. Almost any government is economically beneficial to its citizens, in that the law and order it provides is a prerequisite of all civilized economic activity. But despite the force of patriotism, the appeal of the national ideology, the bond of a common culture, and the indispensability of the system of law and order, no major state in modern history has been able to support itself through voluntary dues or contributions. Philanthropic contributions are not even a significant source of revenue for most countries. Taxes, *compulsory* payments by definition, are needed. Indeed, as the old saying indicates, their necessity is as certain as death itself.

If the state, with all of the emotional resources at its command, cannot finance its most basic and vital activities without resort to compulsion, it would seem that large private organizations might also have difficulty in getting the individuals in the groups whose interests they attempt to advance to make the necessary contributions voluntarily.

The reason the state cannot survive on voluntary dues or payments, but must rely on taxation, is that the most fundamental services a nation-state provides are, in one important respect, like the higher price in a competitive market: they must be available to everyone if they are available to anyone. The basic and most elementary goods or services provided by government, like defense and police protection, and the system of law and order generally, are such that they go to everyone or practically everyone in the nation. It would obviously not be feasible, if indeed it were possible, to deny the protection provided by the military services, the police, and the courts to those who did not voluntarily pay their share of the costs of government, and taxation is accordingly necessary. The common or collective benefits provided by governments are usually called 'public goods' by economists, and the concept of public goods is one of the oldest and most important ideas in the study of public finance. A common, collective, or public good is here defined as any good such that, if any person X_i in a group $X_1, \ldots, X_i, \ldots, X_n$ consumes it, it cannot feasibly be withheld from the others in that group. In other words, those who do not purchase or pay for any of the public or collective good cannot be excluded or kept from sharing in the consumption of the good, as they can where noncollective goods are concerned.

Students of public finance have, however, neglected the fact that the achievement of any common goal or the satisfaction of any common interest means that a public or collective good has been provided for that group. The very fact that a goal or purpose is common to a group means that no one in the group is excluded from the benefit or satisfaction brought about by its achievement. As the opening paragraphs of this discussion indicated, almost all groups and organizations have the purpose of serving the common interests of their members. As MacIver puts it, 'Persons . . . have common interests in the degree to which they participate in a cause . . . which indivisibly embraces them all' (1932). It is of the essence of an organization that it provides an inseparable, generalized benefit. It follows that the provision of public or collective goods is the fundamental function of organizations generally. A state is first of all an organization that provides public goods for its members, the citizens; and other types of organizations similarly provide collective goods for their members.

And just as a state cannot support itself by voluntary contributions, or by selling its basic services on the market, neither can other large organizations support themselves without providing some sanction, or some attraction distinct from the public good itself, that will lead individuals to help bear the burdens of maintaining the organization. The individual member of the typical large organization is in a position analogous to that of the firm in a perfectly competitive market, or the taxpayer in the state: his own efforts will not have a noticeable effect on the situation of his organization, and he can enjoy any improvements brought about by others whether or not he has worked in support of his organization.

There is no suggestion here that states or other organizations provide *only* public or collective goods. Governments often provide noncollective goods like electric power, for example, and they usually sell such goods on the market much as private firms would do.

Moreover, large organizations that are not able to make membership compulsory *must also* provide some noncollective goods in order to give potential members an incentive to join. Still, collective goods are the characteristic organizational goods, for ordinary noncollective goods can always be provided by individual action, and only where common purposes or collective goods are concerned is organization or group action ever indispensable [...]

The 'by-product' theory of large pressure groups

If the individuals in a large group have no incentive to organize a lobby to obtain a collective benefit, how can the fact that some large groups are organized be explained? Though many groups [in the USA] with common interests, like the consumers, the white-collar workers, and the migrant agricultural workers, are not organized, other large groups, like the union laborers, the farmers, and the doctors have at least some degree of organization. The fact that there are many groups which, despite their needs, are not organized would seem to contradict the 'group theory' of the analytical pluralists; but on the other hand the fact that other large groups have been organized would seem to contradict the theory of 'latent groups' offered in this study.

But the large economic groups that are organized do have one common characteristic which distinguishes them from those large economic groups that are not, and which at the same time tends to support the theory of latent groups offered in this work. This common characteristic will, however, require an elaboration or addition to the theory of groups developed in this study.

The common characteristic which distinguishes all of the large economic groups with significant lobbying organizations is that these groups are also organized for some *other* purpose. The large and powerful economic lobbies are in fact the by-products of organizations that obtain their strength and support because they perform some function in addition to lobbying for collective goods.

The lobbies of the large economic groups are the by-products of organizations that have the capacity to 'mobilize' a latent group with 'selective incentives'. The only organizations that have the 'selective incentives' available are those that either have the authority and capacity to be coercive, or have a source of positive inducements that they can offer the individuals in a latent group.

A purely political organization – an organization that has no function apart from its lobbying function – obviously cannot legally coerce individuals into becoming members. A political party, or any purely political organization, with a captive or compulsory membership would be quite unusual in a democratic political system. But if for some nonpolitical reason, if because of some other function it performs, an organization has a justification for having a compulsory membership, or if through this other function it has obtained the power needed to make membership in it compulsory, that organization may then be able to get the resources needed to support a lobby. The lobby is then a by-product of whatever function this organization performs that enables it to have a captive membership.

An organization that did nothing except lobby to obtain a collective good for some large group would not have a source of rewards or positive selective incentives it could offer potential members. Only an organization that also sold private or noncollective products, or provided social or recreational benefits to individual members, would have a source of these positive inducements. Only such an organization could make a joint offering or 'tied sale' of a collective and a noncollective good that could stimulate a rational individual in a large group to bear part of the cost of obtaining a collective good. There are for this reason many organizations that have both lobbying functions and economic functions, or lobbying functions and social functions, or even all three of these types of functions at once. Therefore, in addition to the large group lobbies that depend on coercion, there are those that are associated with organizations that provide noncollective or private benefits which can be offered to any potential supporter who will bear his share of the cost of the lobbying for the collective good.

The by-product theory of pressure groups need apply only to the large or latent group. It *need not* apply to the privileged or intermediate groups, because these smaller groups can often provide a lobby, or any other collective benefit, without any *selective* incentives, as has already been shown. It applies to latent groups because the individual in a latent group has no incentive voluntarily to sacrifice his time or money to help an organization obtain a collective good; he alone cannot be decisive in determining whether or not this collective good will be obtained, but if it is obtained because of the efforts of others he will inevitably be able to enjoy it in any case. Thus he would support the organization with a lobby working for collective goods only if he is either coerced into paying dues to the lobbying organization, or has to support this group in order to obtain some other noncollective benefit. Only if one or both of these conditions hold will the potential political power of a latent group be mobilized.

The following pages will attempt to show how the largest economic pressure groups in the US are in fact explained by the by-product theory. It will argue that the main types of large economic lobbies – the labor unions, the farm organizations, and the professional organizations – obtain their support mainly because they perform some function besides lobbying [. . .] and that labor unions are a dominant political force because they also deal with employers, who can be forced to employ only union members; that farm organizations obtain their members mainly through farm cooperatives and government agencies; and that professional associations rely in part on subtle forms of coercion and in part on the provision of noncollective services to get their membership.

Labor lobbies

The labor union is probably the most important single type of pressure-group organization and accordingly deserves first place in any discussion of large lobbying organizations. Though the opponents of the labor unions are exaggerating when they claim that the Democratic candidates in industrial states are merely puppets of labor leaders, it is quite clear that the Democrats in these states are normally very friendly to labor, and that the Republicans usually treat the labor unions as the major source of enemy strength. The membership of the AFL-CIO is *several times larger* than the membership of any other lobbying organization. The labor unions have, moreover, an impressive organizational network to match their numbers: there are about 60,000 to 70,000 union locals in the USA (Key, 1958, p. 62). Labor leaders have claimed that they could influence about 25 million voters (McKean, 1949, p. 464). Their purely political expenditures are measured in the millions (ibid., pp. 475-6). In 1958 some candidates may have been elected as a result of the large labor vote brought out by 'right-to-work' proposals on the ballot in some industrial states. In Michigan the Democratic party came out of the doldrums as labor organizations grew (Key, 1958, p. 73). There were about 200 unionists who were either delegates or alternate delegates to the 1952 Democratic national convention (Slichter, 1950, p. 7). The late Sumner Slichter argued that 'the American economy is a laboristic economy, or at least is rapidly becoming one.' By this he meant 'that employees are the most influential group in the community and that the economy is run in their interest more than in the interest of any other economic group.' Slichter may have been mistaken, but if so only because many business, professional, and agricultural organizations unite in intense opposition to what they regard as the excessive claims of labor.

Just as there can be little doubt that labor unions are a significant political force, neither can there be much question that this political force is a by-product of the purely industrial activities that unions regard as their major function. It was only when labor unions began to concentrate on collective bargaining with employers and abandoned the mainly political orientation of the earlier American unions, that they came to have any stability or power. It was only when the labor unions started to deal with the employers, who alone had the power to *force* the workers to join the union, that they began to prosper. It is, moreover, hard to see how the labor unions could have obtained and maintained the 'union shop' in a democratic country like the USA if they had been solely political organizations. Labor unions came to play an important part in the political struggle only long after they had forsaken political action as a major goal. It is worth noting that the Wagner Act, which made organizing a union with compulsory membership much easier, and which led to the greatest increase in union membership, was passed *before* labor unions came to play a really important role in politics. The experience of Great Britain also shows that a democratic nation is often happy to overlook compulsory membership in organizations that engage in collective bargaining, but hesitant to make membership in a political organization in any degree automatic. Although . . . it has long been taken for granted in Britain that unionists will often not work with non-union men, there has been a great deal of bitter controversy over whether union men should 'contract in' or 'contract out' of a contribution to the Labour party. (The vast majority of the members of that party, incidentally, are a by-product of the trade unions' activities; all except a small minority belong through the trade unions.) If, then, it is true that a democratic nation would not normally want to make membership in a purely political union compulsory, and that compulsion is essential to a stable labor movement of any size, then it follows that the political power of unions is a by-product of their non-political activities [. . .]

References

BENTLEY, A. (1949), *The Process of Government*, Principia Press.

CATTELL, R. (1955), 'Concepts and methods in the measurement of group syntality', in A. P. Hare, E. F. Borgatta, and R. F. Balos (eds), *Small Groups*, Knopf.

CHAMBERLIN, E. H. (1950), *Monopolistic Competition*, 6th edn, Harvard University Press.

CLARK, J. M. (1923), *The Economics of Overhead Costs*, University of Chicago Press.

FESTINGER, L. (1953), 'Group attraction and membership', in D. Cartwright and A. Zander (eds), *Group Dynamics*, Harper and Row.

HEARD, A. (1960), *The Costs of Democracy*, University of North Carolina Press.

KEY, V. O. Jr (1958), *Politics, Parties and Pressure Groups*, 4th edn, Crowell.

KNIGHT, F. H. (1921), *Risk, Uncertainty and Profit*, Houghton Mifflin.

LASKI, H. (1939), *A Grammar of Politics*, Allen & Unwin.

MacIver, R. M. (1932), 'Interests', in *Encyclopedia of the Social Sciences*, vol. 7, Macmillan Co.

McKean, D. D. (1949), *Party and Pressure Politics*, Houghton Mifflin.

Olson, M. Jr, and McFarland, D. (1962), 'The restoration of pure monopoly and the concept of the industry', *Quarterly Journal of Economics*, vol. 76, November, pp. 613–63.

Slichter, S. H. (1950), *The American Economy*, Knopf.

Truman, D. B. (1958), *The Governmental Process*, Knopf.

US Congress Select Committee on Lobbying Activities (1950), *Report*, 81st Congress, 2nd session, quoted in *Congressional Quarterly Almanac*, vol. 6, pp. 764–5.

Verba, S. (1961), *Small Groups and Political Behavior*, Princeton University Press.

11 H. Eckstein

The Determinants of Pressure Group Politics

Excerpts from 'Theoretical framework: the determinants of pressure group politics', in H. Eckstein, *Pressure Group Politics: The Case of the British Medical Association*, Allen & Unwin, 1960, ch. 1, pp. 15–39. Originally published by Stanford University Press.

Problems

Case studies never 'prove' anything; their purpose is to illustrate generalizations which are established otherwise, or to direct attention towards such generalizations. Since this is a case study of the political activities of the British Medical Association it may be well to state at the outset the broad principles it illustrates. These principles are formulated in answer to three questions:

1. What are the determinants of the *form* of pressure group politics in various political systems? What factors determine the principal channels and means through which pressure groups act on government and the character of the relations between the groups and organs of government?

2. What are the determinants of the *intensity* and *scope* of pressure group politics? 'Intensity' here refers to the fervour and persistence with which groups pursue their political objectives as well as to the relative importance of political activities in their affairs; scope, to the number and variety of groups engaged in politics.

3. What determines the *effectiveness* of pressure groups? From what principal sources do they derive their power *vis-à-vis* other pressure groups and the more formal elements of the decision-making structure, such as parties, legislature and bureaucracy? [. . .]

Determinants of the form of pressure group politics
Channels

By the 'form' of pressure group activities I mean, first, the channels of action on which such groups concentrate. The most important, and the most obvious, determinant of the selection of channels for pressure group activity, in any political system, is the *structure* of the decision-making processes which pressure groups seek to influence. Interest groups (or any other groups) become pressure groups because they want to obtain favourable policy decisions or administrative dispositions; hence, obviously, they must adjust their activities to the processes by which decisions and dispositions are made. To cite a very simple example: in Great Britain the National Union of Teachers is one of the larger and more active pressure groups on the national level, while in the United States teachers' groups play only a very minor role, if any, in national politics,[1] the reason is simply that British educational policies are made and administered by the national government, while in the American federal system this is not the case, except only in the most indirect sense. But this is perhaps too simple an example. Pressure groups tend to adjust the form of their activities not so much to the formal (constitutional) structure of governments as to the distribution of effective power within a governmental apparatus, and this is often something very different from formal structure; in the competition for influence they cannot afford to be deceived by political myths. Hence their activities are themselves one of the more reliable guides to the loci of effective power in any political system, whenever the 'political formula' of the system – as Lasswell and Kaplan call it (1950) – does not indicate these loci correctly.

Not only the structure of the decision-making process but also the decisions which emerge from it – the *activities* of government – influence the predominant channels of pressure group politics, and this just because decisions have a reciprocal effect on the structures that make them. The most obvious example is the devolution of decision-making powers from legislatures to

1. Key (1947) does not even mention them. Truman's encyclopaedic *The Governmental Process* (1958), mentions the National Education Association, but does not bother to describe its activities.

bureaucracies in this age of the social service state, both through the direct delegation of legislative powers and the indirect influence which bureaucrats enjoy over decisions still formally taken by legislatures.

Finally, the dominant channels of pressure group politics may be determined by certain *attitudes*, the most obviously important being attitudes toward pressure groups themselves. Where, for example, the pursuit of corporate interests by political means is normatively reproved – where 'liberal' individualist assumptions are deeply ingrained – pressure groups are likely to work through more inconspicuous channels and with more unobtrusive means than where corporate politics are normatively tolerated. But even attitudes not directly concerned with pressure groups may, indirectly, affect the form of their activities, at any rate if the attitudes have a bearing on the distribution of effective decision-making power. For example, a broad consensus on major policies – the sort of policies usually made by cabinets and legislatures – will tend to shift the major arena of political conflict, hence the major efforts of pressure groups, toward the administrative departments.

Basically, it is always the interplay of governmental structure, activities and attitudes which determines the form of pressure group politics (in the sense of channels of participation) in a given society. These factors may, of course, pull in different directions. Usually, however, they do not – chiefly because firstly the attitudes which bear directly upon a society's structure of decision making (constitutional myths) and the attitudes which bear upon it indirectly (e.g. attitudes underlying governmental activities) tend to be integrated, and secondly because the activities of government and non-'constitutional' attitudes (such as attitudes on policy) generally have an important bearing on the decision-making structure itself. In Great Britain, at any rate, all three factors pull in a single direction: toward the concentration of pressure group activities on the administrative departments.

Pressure is concentrated upon the executive in Britain, first, because of the logic of cabinet government in a political system having two highly disciplined parties; such a system simply precludes any consistently successful exertion of influence through members of Parliament, or, less obviously perhaps, through the political parties. Secondly, pressure is focused on the executive because the broad scope and technical character of contemporary social and economic policies has led to a considerable shift of functions to the bureaucracy; not only that, but the decision-making powers usually exercised by administrative departments are, generally speaking, of much more immediate and greater interest to British interest groups than the kinds of decisions made in Cabinet and Parliament. Attitudes, finally, lead in the same direction. There does not exist in Britain any profound prejudice against corporate politics, against the organization of opinion by 'interested' groups; this makes possible extraordinarily free, easy, open and intimate relations between public officials and lobbyists (using that term in a purely descriptive sense). Attitudes in Britain also tend to shift pressure toward the executive in more direct and obvious ways: for example, because the lack of inhibitions upon delegating legislation gives to the administrative departments powers which legislatures more jealous of their functions than the British Parliament are likely to exercise themselves, and because there has in fact existed in Britain a consensus on general policy, shifting political conflict to matters of technique and detail, that is, matters generally dealt with by administrative departments.

All this, of course, applies to pressure groups only in a general sense – to predominant and characteristic modes of pressure group activity rather than the activities of every particular pressure group. Whether any particular pressure group will concentrate on the executive or some other part of the governmental machinery and political apparatus of a society depends on certain factors additional to the broad variables I have sketched. For example, the power base of the group certainly plays a role in the matter. A group which commands a large number of votes will tend, other things being equal, to exert pressure on elected members of the decision-making structure; a wealthy group on party organizations; a group in command of specialized knowledge on the specialists in the governmental structure, chiefly the bureaucrats. But, to repeat, this is so *ceteris paribus*, not under all circumstances. It is very likely to be the case, for example, where there exists a relatively even distribution of power among representatives, party oligarchy and bureaucracy; or it may be the case where the group has only one power base which can be effectively brought to bear only in one direction. Both these cases, however, are unusual. In the ordinary instance, speaking metaphorically, the power base of the group will do little more than deflect the momentum of its pressure off the idealized path prescribed by governmental structure, activity and relevant attitudes. The ultimate aim of pressure groups is always to bring power to bear where it will produce intended consequences, and this makes the power structure of government a more decisive desideratum than the power base of the group – granted that in unitary political systems like the British fewer alternatives for exerting effective pressure tend to present themselves than in polycentric systems like the American, and that in the latter, consequently, the power base of the group plays a more significant role in determining pressure group behaviour. Even in a system like the British, however, the direction of pressure may be seriously deflected, in special cases, from the executive departments. A group which simply does not have ready access to an executive department – which has no close clientele relationship with such a department – may be driven willy-nilly to seek its aims through other channels; so may a group which stands in a close relationship with a very weak department, when it wants a policy involving the interests of stronger departments; so also may a group pressing for a decision on some very controversial issue involving intense public opinion or high party politics, the sort of issues decided only at the very highest levels. These factors also work in the other direction. Where groups tend to press mainly on the legislature, the existence of close clientele relations with an executive department, or the fact that a group's business is not politically significant, may induce it to steer clear of parliamentary channels. But all these exceptions and modifications are just that, exceptions and modifications; they do not affect the general validity of the main point.

One should add that the main factors which induce pressure groups to use certain channels of influence also have effects upon their internal organization and the means they use to exert political pressure. Pressure groups tend somehow to resemble the organizations they seek to influence. Take two examples, one American, the other British. Not only does the American federal system guide political pressure into certain channels, as in the case of teachers' organizations, but it impedes the formation of national associations as such. The American Bar Association, for instance, has a very small membership and was relatively late in getting under way compared to state and local legal associations. Why? Simply because training and admission to the profession – the two political concerns which most often lead to the formation and growth of professional associations – are controlled by state governments, not the federal government (Truman, 1958, p. 95). In broader terms, the formal dispersion of authority in government inhibits the concentration of membership in voluntary organizations, a fact with far-reaching consequences, because the 'density' of members affects many aspects of a pressure group's activities (such as its political effectiveness and the extent to which it can participate in genuine negotiations with public authorities). In Britain we can see equally clearly the effect of informal governmental power relations on the organization and tactics of pressure groups. As long as Parliament held the centre of the political stage – as long, that is to say, as political conflicts centred on parliamentary policies – interest groups tended not only to act chiefly through 'interested' MPs but to be ephemeral, one-purpose organizations, chiefly concerned with raising a large volume of public support for important legislative changes. Nowadays, however, they possess much greater continuity and engage in a much wider variety of political activities, for their interests are being constantly affected by governmental actions. The public campaign has been replaced largely by informal and unostentatious contacts between officials, and interest groups themselves have become increasingly bureaucratized (in short, more and more like the government departments with which they deal), for only bureaucratic structure is appropriate to the kinds of negotiations groups nowadays must carry on to realize their interests. The changing pattern of policy is not alone responsible for this. The shift of power from Parliament to the Cabinet and from the Cabinet to the administrative departments is equally important. These shifts have not been simple adjustments to new policies but are the results of many other factors, such as the professionalization of the civil service and the development of large, disciplined, national parties (paralleled by the development of large, national interest group organizations in place of the much greater decentralization of vested interest organizations in the nineteenth century). The striking correspondence of governmental organization and the internal organizations of pressure groups in most countries may of course be the result of a still more basic factor: deeply established 'constitutional' attitudes (an aspect of what Bentley called the 'habit background' of societies) which dictate forms of organization and power relations (structures of authority) not only in government but also in voluntary associations. For the present purpose, however, it is sufficient to point out the similarity and to suggest that it is a product both of social norms and calculations as to where and how group pressure can be exerted most effectively.

There is then a two-fold relation between the channels of pressure group activity on one hand and structure of government, pattern of policy and political attitudes on the other: structure, policy and attitudes decide the channels pressure groups will use predominantly to exert influence, and the nature of these channels in turn affects pressure group organization and tactics.

Consultations and negotiations

By 'form' of pressure group politics, I do not mean channels of influence only but also the kinds of relations which predominate among groups and governmental bodies. Leaving aside the intimacy and easiness of these relations (which has already been touched upon), we may distinguish here between two polar extremes, consultations and negotiations, granting that most concrete relations involve both to some extent. Negotiations take place when a governmental body makes a decision hinge upon the actual approval of organizations interested in it, giving the organizations a veto over the decision; consultations occur when the views of the organizations are solicited and taken into account but not considered to be in any sense decisive. What decides whether one relationship or the other plays a significant role in government-group relations? The determining factors again are structure, policies and attitudes.

Structure is important because genuine negotiations can take place only if governmental decision-making processes and patterns of action within pressure groups are of a certain kind. Above all, those who speak for the public authority and those who speak for the interest group must be able to commit those whom they represent; otherwise their deliberations will have only a kind of consultative value, whatever their intentions. Negotiations, then, demand the concentration of authority on both sides, as well as the vesting of considerable discretionary authority in the negotiators. Indeed, the latter presupposes the former. Genuine negotiations between governmental bodies and pressure groups are not likely to take place when a decision must be obtained from a large number of bodies before it has force – as in the American separation-of-powers system – so that decisions are made in effect by negotiations among governmental bodies themselves; and how can there be any negotiations when the negotiators have no discretion, no room to manoeuvre, to make concessions, to meet unexpected gambits and pressures? From both standpoints, an effective cabinet system like the British clearly permits negotiations more easily than a balance-of-power system like the American. It is also necessary, of course, that there should be on the side of the group a formal organization that can speak for most of the members, rather than many competing organizations, or organizations unable to mobilize a sizeable majority of group members. This also is the case in Britain more often than in America.

Policies and attitudes in Britain reinforce the tendency of governmental and group structure to produce negotiations as the dominant form of pressure group politics. The policies of the social service state, for example, demand technical knowledge which, frequently, the members of some interest groups (doctors, for example) are best able to supply. In any case, they often require the positive cooperation of interest groups if they are to be effectively carried out, and what is more natural than to give the groups a direct voice of some sort both in the formulation and administration of policies which cannot be administered without their support?

Among attitudes making for negotiations between government and pressure groups in Britain three are of particular significance. One is the widespread belief (in this case both in Britain and America) that technical experts (practitioners) have some singular competence even in regard to the social policies and administrative forms that touch upon their fields of practice, competence which politicians and bureaucrats do not possess. The second (certainly without an American counterpart) is the persistent 'corporatism' in British social attitudes, the still lingering anti-individualist bias which Beer (1957, p. 614) has labelled the 'Old Whig Theory of Representation'; by this is meant a conception of society as consisting primarily not of individuals but of sub-societies, groups having traditions, occupational and other characteristics in common. Where Lockean liberalism is the dominant political myth, decisions of government are supposed to be the result of conversations, as it were, between individuals (electorate) and sovereign (state); the intervention of groups is considered inherently pernicious or at best something merely to be tolerated. Where corporatistic attitudes persist, on the other hand, functional representation – that is, the representation of corporations (in the sociological, not legal, sense of the term) rather than individuals – is not only tolerated but insisted upon; governments tend to be regarded not as sovereigns in the Austinian sense but, in the pluralistic sense, as corporations among many other kinds of corporations. Hence the frequent normative insistence on negotiations between government and 'voluntary' associations on matters of policy; in Britain, at any rate, a policy regulating, say, farmers, embarked upon without close conversations between government and farm organizations, would be considered to be only on the margins of legitimacy, whether highly technical in character or not. Indeed, close conversations are not enough. Note, for example, that in the debate on the second reading of the National Health Service Bill of 1946 – the stage at which the most general policy considerations raised by a bill are discussed – the Opposition hinged its case upon a motion alleging the failure of the Ministry of Health to *negotiate* the proposed Service with the medical profession; this despite the fact that plenty of talks (consultations) between the Ministry and the profession had taken place and that technical details were not at issue. And to the survival of the Old Whig Theory of Representation we may add the concomitant survival of what might be called the Old Tory Theory of Authority: the tendency both in British government and British voluntary associations to delegate inordinately wide powers to leaders and spokesmen, to ratify decisions taken by leaders almost as a matter of form, which affords such leaders a wide range of manoeuvre when they come face to face in negotiations.

Consultations and negotiations are not, of course, the only 'practices' through which pressure groups act upon government. In fact, these two concepts may be useful for characterizing pressure group activities only in political systems which have two, not in the least universal, characteristics: a high degree of differentiation between pressure groups, parties and formal decision-making offices, and relatively great ease of access by pressure groups to the formal decision-making offices. Where these conditions do not exist, pressure group activity will inevitably assume other forms. In multi-party systems, where parties and pressure groups are not sharply differentiated (that is to say, where many parties are pressure groups that merely call themselves parties and sometimes behave like parties) decisions will often be made, not by negotiations between pressure groups and formal decision-making officers, but by negotiations among the pressure groups themselves. In such countries, the basic assertion on which contemporary 'group theorists' in political science have built their model – that politics is 'the allocation of social values through group conflict' – comes much closer to a full description of political decision making than it does in countries where political parties perform their integrating function effectively and where the formal structure of decision making represents something more than the myths of the dominant groups in institutionalized form. At the other extreme, where groups are effectively segregated out of the formal political process – prevented from having access to formal offices – the chief form of pressure group politics will be intrigue, or violence; perhaps, however, it would be better in this case to speak of the cessation of politics rather than of a particular form of it.

Determinants of scope and intensity

To discover the factors on which depends the scope and intensity of pressure group activity, it is necessary to bear in mind just what sort of political activity pressure group politics is. As I define it pressure group politics has certain peculiar characteristics which are very important. On one hand, it involves the *political* promotion of interests and values, that is, the attempt to realize aspirations through governmental decision making; on the other, it involves something less than an attempt by the group to become itself the government, or even to seize for itself certain political offices which are vitally concerned with its goals. That, at any rate, is how we generally differentiate pressure groups from parties, or political movements, or purely political 'associations' (like the parliamentary associations which antedate the advent of mass parties in Great Britain). Moreover, pressure groups, normally, are not solely engaged in political activities; even in the case of 'promotional' groups (groups seeking to achieve not their own interests but what they conceive to be broader social values) political activities rarely exhaust the full range of activities of the group. Pressure group politics, then, represents something less than the full 'politicalization' of groups and something more than utter 'depoliticalization'; it constitutes an intermediate level of activity between the political and the apolitical. In accounting for the growth and development of pressure group activity, therefore, we must simultaneously account for two things which are, at first sight, nearly paradoxical: how groups come to seek the political promotion of certain of their goals, yet are kept from attempting to promote them by the capture of authoritative offices or from pursuing politically all their objectives. I shall concentrate on the first of these problems, the political mobilization of groups; the second is of less immediate concern to the present case-study, although I shall touch upon it at the end of the section.

The political mobilization of groups: policy

As governmental structure is the most obvious determinant of the form of pressure group activities, so the activities of governments are the most obvious determinants of their entrance into politics. British pressure groups have been so much discussed recently for the simple reason that welfare state policies have, so to speak, generated such groups in large number (that is, transformed groups into 'pressure groups'), or, where they already existed, intensified the pressures they exert. This is clearly due to the fact that private associations now have much more to gain or lose from governmental decisions than in the past: farmers their incomes, doctors the conditions in which they practise, businessmen a host of matters, from capital issues to raw materials. The state in Britain today disposes directly of 40 per cent of the national income; and that fact speaks for itself. We may regard political systems as amalgams of potential and actual pressure groups: groups which from a political standpoint are merely 'categoric' groups and groups which have actually been drawn into politics, chiefly through the impact of public policies, either policies actually adopted or policies which are 'threatened'. In short, we can usefully stand Bentley on his head to supplement Bentley right side up: if interaction among politically active groups produces policy, policy in turn creates politically active groups.

There is also, however, a connection between the mobilization of pressure groups and governmental structure, and a further connection between the former and political attitudes, though neither may be quite so manifest as the influence of policy.

Attitudes

Attitudes influence the scope and intensity of pressure group politics not only because they determine policy but also because pressure groups generally require some sort of legitimation before they come into play in the political process. The obstacle to legitimacy may be internal or external, so to speak; it may arise either from the convictions of group members or that of non-members, particularly if the latter occupy positions of power, that the political promotion of the group's collective interests is somehow illegitimate. Trade unions, for example, play a more significant political role today than in the nineteenth century, both in Britain and the United States, not only because they are larger and better managed, but also because they are more widely accepted and because they themselves are more reconciled to action within the operative political system. To consult with trade union leaders is no longer tantamount to conspiracy; nor do trade union leaders any longer regard political participation in democratic government as a kind of class treason, or as a trespass upon alien domain. Of course, the legitimacy of a group is not absolutely decisive in determining whether it will play a political role or not. Conspiracies do occur where negotiations are prohibited, but the difficulties in such cases are so great that 'illegitimate' groups may find it desirable to leave politics alone, or impossible to find channels through which to act. The attitudes which legitimate pressure groups or deny them legitimacy usually constitute the fundamental political ethos of a society, such as the long prevalent liberal belief that economic actors should act upon each other through the spontaneously adjusting mechanics of the market rather than through the political process.

Legitimacy in this case need not mean legitimacy in regard to political action only; a group may be prevented from taking an intense part in politics by much more general attitudes: for example, a prejudice against corporate organization as such. Beer (1958) has pointed out that the major occupational interests – business, labour, and agriculture – are far more thoroughly and monolithically organized in Britain than in the United States, and related this fact to the profound influence of liberal 'atomism' in America and the survival of the older corporatistic theory of society in Britain. These differences in organization are marked by differences in the groups' involvement in politics and administration. The sub-groups of larger societies may, however, have significantly different attitudes toward organization as well as political action itself. Thus, while it is true, broadly speaking, that British attitudes are more corporatistic than American attitudes – and that, as a result, British pressure groups 'even if compared with American examples . . . are numerous, massive, well-organized and highly effective' (Beer, 1956, p. 1) – it is also true that British professional groups resist corporatization as much as, if not more than, their American counterparts. The British Medical Association, for example, has not until very recently (when special factors compelling corporatization have been at work) managed to outstrip the American Medical Association in proportion of doctors enrolled in it. This is just one facet of a much broader behaviour pattern; another facet of this pattern is the resistance of the British medical profession to all corporate forms of practice, in partnerships, group practices and especially health centres. Both reflect a profound bias against association which, in the American case, is much stronger in the realm of economic affairs, the area in which the liberal atomistic model of society was most rigidly applied in the United States. But such inhibitions against corporatization may be overcome. In medicine, for example, contemporary scientific development has made isolated practice almost obsolete, and this undoubtedly has had an effect on the willingness of British doctors to participate in corporate activities, both strictly professional and not strictly professional, however much some of the old biases may linger.

Attitudes may determine the intensity of group politics in still another way. Even when they permit intense political activity by a group, they may keep that activity from assuming certain forms, i.e. limit the group's range of political activities. Some groups which play a legitimate role in government may be prevented, by normative attitudes no less than considerations of expediency, from openly associating themselves with a political party or taking a part in electoral campaigns; again, certain groups such as professional associations may have deep inhibitions against anything that smacks of trade unionism (any sort of bargaining, for example); still others may be prevented by their internal ethics from using certain instruments of pressure, such as strikes and boycotts, or certain kinds of publicity – although changes in the situation of the group may also change such attitudes, as they may change attitudes toward corporatization and political action themselves.

Structure

Of the three basic determinants of pressure group behaviour which I have stressed, perhaps the least manifest determinant of their political mobilization is governmental structure; nevertheless, it also plays a role. Key, for example, argues (1947, p. 177) that a two-party system stimulates the formation of pressure groups because special interests cannot find consistent champions in any party which must continuously appeal to a great many interests. That, however, strikes me as an over-simplification. The parties in a two-party system may themselves be composed of wings and sub-groups which consistently espouse certain interests, making them, as Key himself has pointed out, more like multi-party systems in fact than they seem in form (ch. 10). This is certainly true of American parties. It may also apply to British parties, for both Labour and the Tories include certain enduring sub-groups which stand for special, chiefly economic interests. The point that should be made surely is that two-party systems do not encourage all interest groups to seek political channels outside of the parties but only groups having certain characteristics (Truman, 1958, p. 87) and rather than maintaining that multi-party systems discourage the formation of organized pressure groups because the parties themselves are freely available to special interests, one should argue that (just because of this) many 'parties' in such systems are themselves pressure groups in disguise, but pressure groups more fully politicalized than those we find in two-party systems.

Somewhat more persuasive is Truman's argument that certain groups are likely to pursue their goals through politics when the structure of government gives them important advantages over others and when they are in a relatively weak position on the 'market', that is, in spontaneous adjustment to other groups. His chief case in point is that of American farmers who have a relatively weak bargaining position on the market but are over-represented in both state and national legislature (p. 107). Rural areas in many other countries tend to be over-represented too, which may help to explain the relatively great readiness of farm groups everywhere to seek out government interference in their market relations.

This argument may, however, be stated much more broadly: governmental structure affects the scope and intensity of pressure group activity chiefly because expectations of success govern the political mobilization of groups, and whether or not a group can be successfully influential is determined at least partly by the structure of the government on which it acts. Undoubtedly there are factors which enhance a group's chances of political success under any circumstances, but the weight of these factors tends to vary according to the structure of decision making in which they are brought to bear. This point will be discussed further below, in connection with a more general analysis of the conditions which determine the effectiveness of pressure groups. It ought to be noted here, however, that governmental structure may determine not only the influence of particular pressure groups (and therefore whether or not they will actually organize for politics) but also whether pressure groups in general can effectively translate their demands into policies (and therefore whether or not large numbers of them will be active, or whether political activity will play a large role in their affairs). I have in mind here the difference between systems like British cabinet government, which are highly effective in making decisions, and systems like the American or highly fragmented parliamentary systems, which seem more effective in frustrating them. The first kind of system is more likely to induce the political mobilization of groups than the second, if only because government offers them a reasonable chance of action – any sort of action; although, of course, everything depends in this case on whether groups actually want decisions to be made or to keep them from being taken. In the latter case, systems like the American clearly offer the greater chances, so that the distinction between active and inactive governments ought not perhaps to be made in terms of their effects on the political mobilization of groups as such, but in terms of the kinds of groups and aspirations they tend to involve in political affairs. In terms of sheer quantity of political activity one would certainly be hard put to find a significant difference between British and American pressure groups, but this does not preclude significant differences of other sorts.

Inhibitions on political mobilization

If certain attitudes, elements of governmental structure, and the impact of governmental policy, adopted and threatened, account for the political mobilization of groups, what inhibits them from mobilizing on a full scale once they decide to become politically involved? Clearly, the relevant factors are the ways in which groups define their goals and evaluate their chances in the political area, and the extent to which an existing governmental apparatus appears capable of satisfying their demands without being changed or captured. Each of these considerations, however, requires some elaboration.

There are conditions when government itself, not the detailed products of government, is the primary concern of politics, most clearly of all when new states are in the building or old forms of government widely discredited. Such conditions are obviously inhospitable to pressure group politics, for they awaken much more profound political concerns. Intensive pressure group politics then presupposes as its most fundamental condition a stable and widely accepted political apparatus – political consensus. To 'press' upon a government is itself, in a way, a form of commitment to it; profoundly disaffected groups will rarely stoop to sully themselves by dealing with an abominated system. This accounts for the curious impression one gets in societies widely committed to their governments both of intense politics and political apathy; intense politics, because the society seems split into a myriad groupings, loosely, if at all, associated, all busily seeking to exert influence, to capture opinion, to enlist decision makers; political apathy, because no fundamental issues are ever raised and people seem remarkably uninterested in what looms, in other societies, as decisive political activity: elections, for example. The simple reason for this apparent paradox is, of course, that political activities do not possess decisiveness intrinsically but only in terms of what people want to be decided: if the chief political question is one of the very location of formal power, then elections (or violence) become decisive; if political questions involve less fundamental issues – the detailed uses to which formal power is to be put – then influence-wielding, i.e. pressure group politics, becomes decisive. Consensus does not imply the cessation of politics, but it does imply a shift of political concerns to issues best dealt with through the unobtrusive interplay of semi-politicalized groups; in 'consensual' systems, therefore, fully politicalized groups will perform certain routine functions but only rarely absorb primary allegiances. Lack of consensus is a society will make almost every group join fully politicalized organizations, or try to become themselves such organizations, or wash their hands of politics altogether. Politics will become no concern of theirs, or all of their concern. Whether it will be the first or the second depends on contingent characteristics of the group and the situation under which it has to operate: its size, the extent to which an existing political state of affairs threatens it, the repressive power of existing governments, and the extent to which its aims can be achieved outside of politics.

Whether groups will define their goals as being fully political or, as do pressure groups, only partially political may depend also on still more fundamental characteristics of a society. A high degree of pressure group activity presupposes logically a high degree of social differentiation. It is difficult to envisage intensive pressure group politics in relatively primitive societies, not only because basic political questions loom relatively large in them these days, but also because the vast multiplicity of criss-crossing groups existing in more advanced societies does not exist (at least to the same extent) in the less advanced. Group politics in such societies tend therefore to define goals of very wide concern, and associations tend to absorb wide segments of society; in such a situation group politics becomes almost by definition social politics. The communications system of a society also plays a fundamental role, at any rate in deciding the very possibility of association as a preliminary to political mobilization. But apart from such absolutely fundamental and obvious (perhaps tautological) conditions, the extent of politicalization of groups is primarily a reflection of the degree of consensus among them. In that sense, the existence of a multiplicity of pressure groups is a sign of health in the political organism, not, as the muckrakers thought, a symptom of disease.

Within consensual systems, however, different groups have different propensities to act in politics, depending on contingencies like those operating in non-consensual systems. Very large groups and very wealthy groups may be encouraged to play a direct role in party-political conflict, as do British trade unions although one gets the impression nowadays that their identification with Labour is a cultural lag from days of more profound political disagreements, and that they yearn (many at any rate) for looser forms of political engagement. Stable two-party systems also discourage full political involvement, although such party systems may themselves be, at bottom, products of consensus. Finally, groups may become disenchanted in the process of pressure politics if the resolution of group conflicts is consistently against their interests – if, in the political market, their power to compete is small, due to their objective characteristics or the structure of government on which they act. In that case, however, they are more likely to become fully alienated from the political system rather than fully involved in it. In any case, the market of political competition tends to become so widely disjointed in highly consensual systems that almost any groups can get 'satisfactions' out of it; that is to say, groups which are relatively weak in absolute terms (in size, wealth, prestige, etc.) may, due to wide agreement, simply not have to confront significant opposition in their political affairs. Despite that, however, calculations of the chances of a group's effectiveness help to decide not only whether the group becomes politically active at all, but also the extent to which it carries its political activity. What then determines the effectiveness of pressure groups?

Determinants of effectiveness

Factors determining the effectiveness of pressure groups may be classified under three headings:

1. Attributes of the pressure groups themselves.
2. Attributes of the activities of government.
3. Attributes of the governmental decision-making structure.

Perhaps operative attitudes constitute a fourth category, since the ability of a group to mobilize opinion certainly enhances its chances of success in any political system in which opinion matters; but that is obvious and needs no elaboration.

Group characteristics

Certain characteristics of groups are likely to determine decisively their effectiveness under almost any pattern of policies or structure of government (popular government, of course): for example, physical resources, size, organizational cohesiveness, and political skills. Physical resources means wealth, first and foremost: wealth to contribute to party treasuries, wealth for 'buying' the goodwill of influential persons, wealth with which to advertise and circularize, and so forth. Other resources, of course, are useful too; for example, the possession by a group of a journal or newspaper, especially a popular newspaper, or (in a rather different sense of the term 'resource') the fact that it has members in influential positions. Among useful resources must be included also the prestige of the group: the capital of public support, so to speak, which it can command regardless of the substantive policies it espouses. Certain groups possess not merely legitimacy to participate in decision-making processes, but also a sort of special privilege to determine the outcome of these processes; this is true especially of groups possessing technical competence in fields where there is a wide gulf between the professional and the layman, although any high status and prestige can usually be converted into political profit, if only through the day-to-day influence of 'opinion leaders'.

The size of the group may itself be reckoned among its resources, although brute size is never likely to be of crucial account. Rather we should speak of the politically effective size of a group: its ability to make its quantitative weight felt. This is partly a matter of the other resources it commands – its wealth, prestige, whether it has easy access to public opinion and to influential persons – but still other considerations enter the equation as well. One of these is organizational cohesiveness, and this is a function of a great many variables. Does the group possess any formal organization at all? Is the membership split among a large number of such organizations or concentrated in an omnibus organization? Is membership perfunctory or the result of genuine commitment to the formal organization? Do members in fact participate in organizational affairs? Are their personal interactions frequent and persistent? Do they have important conflicting loyalties outside the group? Are their interests really compatible? Can the leaders mobilize disciplined and loyal legions in times of crisis? The answers to these questions will determine whether membership statistics can in fact be translated into influence.

Among the skills which enable groups to achieve their political objectives we must therefore reckon the internal political and administrative skills of their leaders. Some groups, to be sure, are more cohesive than others in their very nature: if, for example, they have no cultural or ideological inhibitions against close association (unlike businessmen in a truly 'liberal' society, or doctors in a country having a deep tradition of individual practice, as in Britain); if their members do have largely identical, at any rate easily comparable, interests; if they are concentrated in small areas; if status considerations or the nature of the members' work lead to social as well as occupational identification among the members. But here, as in everything else, art can guide and support nature.

The nature of the objectives sought by a group may also be a determinant of effectiveness, but chiefly because this factor affects the other internal group characteristics mentioned. I have in mind here primarily the difference between groups agitating for their own corporate interests and groups dedicated to social causes not necessarily arising out of their members' self-interest – 'interest groups' as against 'promotional groups', as S. E. Finer calls them. The former generally have a more disciplined membership, more affluent treasuries, tighter bureaucratic organization, a more permanent and indeed also more active clientele. Their officers tend to acquire great skill in propaganda and negotiations, and they frequently have their own private channels of propaganda – journals and press departments, for example.

Policy

As there are many kinds of resources which constitute political capital, so there are many kinds of organizational forms and political skills which may be turned to account in the decision-making process; *which* is likely to exercise a decisive influence depends largely on the setting in which the group functions. Generals cut a wider swath in war or cold war than in peace; groups that want money spent have a relatively hard task in times of inflation and retrenchment. The pattern of policies enforced in a political system is an important determinant of the effectiveness of pressure groups simply because it is one of the situational elements which selects among the objective attributes of groups those which are of special political account. Take two examples. A policy may demand, in its formulation or administration, some skill or knowledge over which members of a special group have, or are believed to have, a monopoly; this is increasingly the case in the age of the social service state. Again, it may be impossible to carry out a policy without some sort of active support by the group; what use, for instance, is an agricultural policy without cooperative farmers? In either case, the pressure group concerned may not get exactly what it wants, but the need for knowledge and cooperation at least acts as a limit on what can be imposed upon it; usually, of course, the group's influence is much more positive than that.

Policy may also impinge upon the effectiveness of groups in another way: by affecting their size and the resources they command. When a group is subjected to public regulation and control its members are more likely to join organizations which press the group's interests. They are more likely to contribute to group treasuries; to tolerate specialization of leadership and administration in their organizations; to sublimate differences of interest and attitude for the sake of common ends, and to respond in a disciplined way to group decisions. Policy, in short, may make it easier to mobilize the potential power of groups by accelerating tendencies toward corporatization and by making for greater cohesiveness within the organized groups.

Governmental structure

Finally, the effectiveness of pressure groups is also determined to some extent by governmental structure. There is, for example, a great difference between systems in which power is concentrated and those in which it is dispersed. In American government, groups can ordinarily get what they want, at any rate if they want something important, only by obtaining favourable decisions from a large number of bodies: legislatures, legislative committees, executive officers; this, as has been repeatedly pointed out, favours defensive pressure groups, those that want to maintain the *status quo*, by promoting delay and inaction as such. But while under effective cabinet government it is much easier to obtain positive decisions at all levels, from Parliament to the lowliest interdepartmental committee, such systems inhibit many manipulative activities familiar in systems where power is widely dispersed (senatorial courtesy, for example) which give minor groups useful entrées into politics and means for getting 'positive' decisions.

On a somewhat lower level of generalization, the influence of pressure groups may also be affected by electoral systems. Under proportional representation sheer weight of numbers is likely to be a matter of importance, while under the single-member system the distribution of members will be an important factor determining the 'effective size' of a group; a group the members of which are strategically posted in a large number of doubtful constituencies will be able to exercise influence disproportionate to its size in simple quantitative terms. So also will a group which derives special advantages from distributive anomalies in an electoral system; a case in point are American farmers, who are benefited not only by the over-representation of agricultural districts in the House of Representatives, but even more by the peculiar system used to elect the Senate. The National Farmers Union of England and Wales failed in its original aim to play a role like that of the American farm bloc in British politics, partly because of the existence of two highly disciplined parties in Great Britain, but partly also because the British electoral system never favoured farmers as much as the American system.

Third, there is a relationship between the effectiveness of pressure groups and the character of the administrative structure upon which they act. A close 'clientele relationship' between group and administrative department always tends to give the group important advantages over others, if only by obtaining for it a permanent spokesman within the structure of government; it has been argued, for example, that in America the air lines have important political advantages over other public carriers because they have a public regulatory agency all to themselves (the Civil Aeronautics Board) while the other carriers all come under the jurisdiction of the Interstate Commerce Commission, within which there is consequently a stiff, often self-defeating, struggle for power. Much depends also on the power which a given administrative department can exert on behalf of its clients within the executive structure. Administrative systems are not merely tools for executing policy, but are themselves structures of power; they influence (often make) policy, and within them different departments carry different degrees of weight, depending on the political positions of their heads, the broadness and significance of their functions, and their traditions. In British government, there certainly is a world of difference between important departments like the Treasury, Supply, and the Board of Trade on one hand and Education and Pensions on the other. Whether a pressure group can carry great weight in government obviously depends on the power of the agency through which its weight is exerted, as indeed do also certain aspects of the form of its activities – for example, the extent to which its relations with government have the character of genuine negotiations; normally a President of the Board of Trade can negotiate far more easily than a Minister of Education, if to negotiate means to take decisions by bargaining with pressure groups. Finally, we should add to clientele relations between groups and departments, clientele relations between groups and legislative committees. Similar considerations apply, although the absence of specializing standing legislative committees make this point inapplicable to the country with which this case-study deals.

Summary

To sum up the argument in very general terms, pressure group politics in its various aspects is a function of three main variables: the pattern of policy, the structure of decision making both in government and voluntary associations, and the attitudes – broadly speaking, the 'political culture' – of the society concerned. Each affects the form, the intensity and scope, and the effectiveness of pressure group politics, although in each case the significance of the variables differs – structure, for example, being especially important in determining the form of pressure group politics, policy especially important in determining its scope and intensity.

References

BEER, S. H. (1956), 'Pressure groups and parties in Britain', *Amer. Polit. Sci. Rev.*, March.

BEER, S. H. (1957), 'Representation of interests in British government', *Amer. Polit. Sci. Rev.*, September.

H. Eckstein 189

BEER, S. H. (1958), 'Group representation in British and American democracy', *The Annals*, September.

KEY, V. O. Jr (1947), 4th edn, *Politics, Parties and Pressure Groups*, Crowell.

LASSWELL, H. D., and KAPLAN, A. (1950), *Power and Society*, Routledge & Kegan Paul.

TRUMAN, D. B. (1958), *The Governmental Process*, Knopf.

12 G. W. Jones

The Prime Minister's Power

Excerpts from G. W. Jones, 'The Prime Minister's power', *Parliamentary Affairs*, vol. 18, no. 2. 1965, pp. 167–85.

It has become part of the conventional wisdom expressed by some academics and journalists that the position of the Prime Minister in the British system of government has altered significantly in recent years. No longer, they assert, is he merely *primus inter pares* or just the leading member of the Cabinet, but he has been transformed into something quite new, perhaps a quasi-President, or an elected monarch or even an autocrat. The Prime Minister's predominance, attained by Churchill during the Second World War, is said to have persisted in peace-time during the administrations of Attlee, Churchill again, Eden, Macmillan, Douglas-Home and Wilson. If this view is correct then Cabinet Government is a dignified façade behind which lurks the efficient secret of Prime Ministerial power.[1]

It may not be possible to test the validity of these suppositions until the Cabinet papers are made available, fifty years after the events they refer to have taken place, and until the politicians and civil servants involved in the process have published their memoirs. But even with the scanty evidence at present before us, there are grounds to argue that the Prime Minister's power has been exaggerated and that the restraints on his ascendancy are as strong as ever, and in some ways even stronger [. . .]

His actual position is not as predominant as has been presented.

1. For literature on this topic, see Hinton (1960), Heasman (1962), Crossman (1964, pp 51–7), Crick (1964, pp 34–9), Sampson (1962, pp 330–33), Johnson (1964). Mackintosh (1962) is often quoted as supporting this argument, but [his] book contains serious inconsistencies, noted in Chester (1962). However, Mackintosh clearly supports this argument in an ITV broadcast 10 January 1965, 'Power in Britain'.

Election studies and opinion poll data present no firm evidence for a categorical statement that people vote for or against party leaders (Blondel, 1963, pp. 81-4). What can be said is that voters are greatly influenced by the images they have in their minds of the parties, and the image is not composed just of the leader but it is a compound, whose main component is the record and achievement of the party when it was in government. The overall performance of the government and not the activity of the leader shapes the image of the party. Other less significant elements of the image consist of the main figures of the party, their views and attitudes, the ways they behave to each other, the history of the party, its traditional and present associations, its past and present policies and its broad ideals. These, however, are not as decisive as the conduct of the party when in office. This creates the impression of the party in the minds of most electors. Elections then are won or lost by governments not by oppositions, and not just by the leaders. If the role of the leaders were as important as some suggest, then it might be expected that the electoral swings in the constituencies where they stand would show significant variations from the regional and national swings. In fact no such divergencies can be shown. The leader is as much the prisoner of the image of his party as the other candidates. Although much of the propaganda of the parties concentrates on the leaders, there is no evidence that it is effective. Studies of the effects of television show that most people display a sturdy resistance to the blandishments of the manipulators. They seem to absorb from a programme only what fits in with their preconceived notions. Their previous attitudes are reinforced not overturned. The claims that advertisers and public relations men make for their techniques are exaggerated in the face of the dogged obstinacy of the public (Trenaman and McQuail, 1961; Birch, 1964, pp. 171–88).

If the leader is not the individual whom the electors vote for or against, then there is no mandate on the MPs to support their leaders.[2] Their obedience to their leader is not based on the wishes of the electorate, nor does it arise because of his ability to call for a dissolution when he likes. The cost of an election

2. On the mandate see Birch (1964, pp. 114–30).

campaign is no burden to an MP, since his expenses are paid by his party. The campaign is not very arduous; for most MPs, a three weeks irritation at worst, while it is more arduous for the leader who is the leading campaigner, having to travel over the whole country. Since the bulk of parliamentary seats, over two-thirds, are safe, few MPs worry that they will lose (Jones 1964). Thus dissolution is not a very realistic threat against potential or actual rebels. Indeed, the individual who has most to lose from a dissolution is the Prime Minister himself, who may lose his government office, his prestige, power and high salary. Further, since he wants to win, he is hardly likely to enter an election campaign wielding the weapon of dissolution against his own party, for the opposition will make much capital out of the splits within his party. If dissolution is the potent device some suggest, then there should be a tendency for rebels to sit for safe seats, immune from the changes of electoral fortune. But there is no correlation between the tendency to rebel against the party leadership and the size of the MP's majority. Thus neither the actual use of nor the threat to use the power of dissolution are the means of enforcing discipline on MPs.[3] They are kept in line by their constituency parties who may not readopt them. But local parties do not penalise their members for all acts of rebellion. MPs can expect trouble from their local parties if they go against their Parliamentary party over a period of time by taking up a position close to that of the opposition party. A revolt to the centre will arouse the anger of the local parties far more than a revolt to the extreme wing, farthest from the position of the opposition (Epstein, 1960). A revolt therefore is not completely out of the question.

Parties are not the monoliths as depicted by some commentators. Neither inside nor outside Parliament are the parties tamely subservient to the will of the Prime Minister. They are riven with factions, divided over both short and long term policy objectives, the claims of various interests and local and regional issues (Rose, 1964). More commonly in the Labour than in the Conservative Party the alignment over one topic persists for a whole range of others, so that more permanent cleavages exist in the Labour Party than in the Conservative

3. On the power of dissolution see Andrews (1960).

(Finer, Berrington and Bartholomew, 1961). The most important factions in both parties are those which coalesce around the main figures in the party. Each of the chief colleagues of the Prime Minister has a personal following which would prefer to see their man leader rather than the actual leader. There is no loyalty at the top because the Prime Minister's colleagues are his rivals, eager to replace him, and he is engaged in a constant battle to fend them off. Many attempts were made to displace Attlee, but they collapsed because his prima donna rivals failed to unite around a successor (Hunter, 1959; Dalton, 1962). Churchill, it seems, had to retire earlier than he wanted in order to please Sir Anthony Eden and his following (McKenzie, 1963, p. 581, Churchill, 1959, p. 192).[4] Even before the Suez venture there were serious rumblings against Eden, and if he had not retired through ill-health after the Suez affair, it is most likely that he would have been forced out (McKenzie, 1963, pp. 582–6; Churchill, 1959, p. 309).[5] Macmillan had to fight hard to remain leader, and but for his operation he too might have been forced out. Sir Alec Douglas-Home became Prime Minister not because Macmillan or the Queen chose him but because his chief rivals tolerated him and led no revolt against him. It is significant that the Queen asked him at first only to try to form an administration. He kissed hands as Prime Minister twenty-four hours later. These were the crucial hours when he sought to win over Butler, Maudling and Hogg; it was during those hours that he was chosen as Prime Minister by his colleagues. Today Harold Wilson is not secure; George Brown's reputation has risen considerably. Some commentators detect opposition to Wilson from within his own party. He has been described, in *The Spectator*, as tending 'to look more and more like a Labour Foreign Secretary, with Mr Brown as Prime Minister'.[6] The Prime Minister is only as strong as his colleagues let him be. Without their support he falls. To become and remain Prime Minister a man must work hard to retain the

4. Lord Dalton in an obituary of Sir Winston Churchill said that 'his younger colleagues pushed him overboard' (1965).

5. Hill said that Eden was made a scapegoat for Suez (1964, p. 179).

6. A *Times* leader (1965) noted that 'the word is going round that he [Mr Wilson] has not got a good backbone'.

support of his main colleagues and not present them with an opportunity to remove him.

Television has enhanced the stature of the Prime Minister's rivals far more than his own standing. Gladstone and Disraeli, Asquith and Balfour, MacDonald and Baldwin were at the centre of the stage because of the office they held; their colleagues did not have the opportunities to display themselves to their party members and public which the colleagues of a post-war Prime Minister have. Today television brings into almost every home not just the Prime Minister, who cannot be on the screen all the time, but also the major ministers, his chief colleagues. They have the chance to win, consolidate and encourage a personal following, which their pre-war counterparts never had. They have been strengthened in their relations *vis-à-vis* the Prime Minister. Thus the significance of the development of television is not that it has elevated the Prime Minister but that it has contributed to undermining his position. Maudling, Heath, Macleod, Brown and Callaghan are the men who have been helped by television. Even if the Prime Minister does receive considerable attention from television, it is not necessarily a one-sided blessing. Much depends on his telegenic qualities. Sir Alec Douglas-Home seemed to think that exposure together with Mr Wilson would not help his cause in the 1964 election campaign. The standing of a Prime Minister can be damaged, if he gives a poor performance, and a skilful interviewer may make him seem very foolish. Thus the case that the Prime Minister has been strengthened by television is not proven.

The Prime Minister if he is to remain in office must carry his leading rivals with him. He might withstand a backbench revolt with their support, but if a backbench revolt found a spokesman of leadership calibre, who could win the backing of his other colleagues, then the Prime Minister would be in a very insecure position. To avoid this fate he must woo and coax his colleagues and party to support him and his policies. He is engaged in a continual dialogue with his party both inside and outside Parliament. The Whips act as his eyes and ears, conveying to him through the Chief Whip the feelings of the Parliamentary party. The Chief Whip's job is to tell the Prime Minister what the

MPs will not stand; he restrains the Prime Minister as much as the MPs; he mediates between the two, explaining each to the other. The Whips are responsible for knowing thoroughly the views of certain groups of MPs divided into the geographical areas of their constituencies and they also attend the specialist party Committees in the House. Whenever any policy or tendency of the leadership is found to be creating displeasure then the Whips inform the Prime Minister and try to effect a reconciliation. The Whips should not be regarded as the bullying agents of the Prime Minister.[7] By other means also he keeps in close touch with the feelings of his party, through individual trusted MPs, his private secretaries, his own personal contacts in the House, in its tea room, dining room, bar and corridors and through more formal meetings with backbench committees. It would be fatal for a Prime Minister to set himself apart from his parliamentary party. It requires management. So too does the extra-parliamentary party, especially the Labour Party which has less of a tradition of loyalty to the leadership than the Conservative Party. To keep the outside party conversant with the policy of the Parliamentarians, Ministers, since the Leyton by-election, are to explain their positions to area conferences of party members all over the country and a liaison Committee has been established to mediate between the Parliamentary Labour Party and the National Executive Committee (*The Times*, 29 January, 1965). The leaders in Parliament recognise that the basis of their power would vanish if they alienated their party activists. Thus the Prime Minister is not the master of his party. Leaders can lose their parties' support and be toppled. They lead only with the sufferance and by the courtesy of their followers. A Prime Minister is only as strong as his party, and particularly his chief colleagues, let him be.

The Prime Minister's power of patronage has been exaggerated as a means of keeping his supporters loyal. Careerists can argue with great force that the way to achieve top office is not

7. On the role of the Whips see the *Listener* (1963, a, b). Hill said that 'A Chief Whip's job is to listen and to learn, to gather up the scraps of gossip, to assess other people's opinions. He is the Prime Minister's ears and eyes in the smoking room and the lobby' (1964, p. 242). See also the *Economist*, 15 July 1961.

to give loyal and silent service, but to build up a following, to gain a reputation of having expertise in a certain sphere and to make a nuisance of oneself. The Prime Minister will then be forced to give the man office to quieten down his attacks, to restrain his following and generally to keep the party contented. But once in government office the man is not necessarily neutralised and muzzled. He will still maintain his following and keep open his informal contacts with them: indeed his stature amongst his faction may be enhanced by his performance in office. Thus he will be able to bring forceful pressure to bear on the Prime Minister whenever a policy is contemplated that he thinks undesirable. And if the opponent is a leading figure in the party with a significant following, the Prime Minister will be most reluctant to force the matter so far that he will be faced with a rebellion and resignation which will injure the reputation of his Government. The Prime Minister's power to offer office and promotion to backbenchers and Ministers is not a sure-proof device for obtaining their obedience to his wishes. He is seriously checked by his major colleagues who can rally other Ministerial and formidable backbench support against him. The MPs then are not mere 'lobby fodder' for the Prime Minister, nor is the House of Commons just a 'rubber stamp' or 'talking shop'. MPs can bring their views to the notice of the Prime Minister, individually or collectively, through discussion with the Whips, in the specialist Committees, and by approaching him themselves directly. Since he depends on their allegiance, he will try to accommodate his policies to their wishes.

The Prime Minister's influence over policy has been exaggerated. Government business has so increased and involves many technical and complex factors that no one man is able to survey the whole field. Policy initiatives come from many sources, not just from the Prime Minister, but from party policy, from the recommendations of Civil Servants who have worked out schemes with various interests often before the Prime Minister knows about them, from administrative necessity, from the sheer pressure of events at home and abroad and from the demands of public opinion channelled upwards in various ways. The House of Commons itself is no negligible factor and even the Opposition is influential. On some issues the arguments of the Opposition may gain favour with the electorate and then the Government party, especially if an election is imminent, will take over some of the Opposition's suggestions as its own, so as to blunt the force of its attack. Before the last election the Labour Party frequently claimed that its policies had been filched by the Government. Debates in the House of Commons, therefore, are not a meaningless charade; they can help shape the Government's policy. The Prime Minister has also to take into account the views of his own party both in and outside the House. Through their specialist Committees MPs have opportunities for gaining expertise in the work of particular departments and can therefore keep significant checks on the policy of the Government. The coming of Independent Television indicates that a specialist Committee can even impose its policy eventually on a reluctant Cabinet (Wilson, 1961). Thus the Prime Minister is not necessarily able to initiate the policy he wants, nor shape policy as he desires. There are too many political pressures which he has to take account of.

A Prime Minister has a free hand constitutionally to form his own Cabinet, but politically he is limited. He has to include the leading figures in the parliamentary party, and they may be so influential within the party and in the country that they may even dictate which office they will have. His Cabinet must represent a cross-section of opinion in the party and contain the main faction leaders. Harold Wilson before the election said that Sir Alec Douglas-Home's Cabinet was too large. It revealed, he said, the Prime Minister's weakness, because he had had to strike a large number of bargains. He promised to form a smaller Cabinet (Wilson *et al*, 1964, p. 26). In fact it was exactly the same size, again evidence of the number of powerful figures and interests the Prime Minister had to conciliate. Moreover, the actual offices to which he allocated the individuals showed very few surprises and suggested that he had not had much freedom to manoeuvre. Most went to offices to which they had already staked a claim, as members of the Shadow Cabinet, as front-bench spokesmen, and because they had some expertise or interest in the subject. Thus the Prime Minister has not a free hand in the choice of his colleagues or the allocation of their offices.[8]

Nor has he a free hand in dismissing them. None of the Ministers who were dismissed or retired after disagreement with the Cabinet in the post-war years were men of sufficient standing in their parties to present a significant challenge to the Prime Ministers, with the exception perhaps of Aneurin Bevan. No Prime Minister [Macmillan] threw out or forced the resignation of a man who had support enough to replace him.[9] Even in the July purge of 1962 no serious contender for the leadership was removed. The Prime Minister took good care to keep in the Cabinet his main rivals. His display of butchery illustrated further the limitations on his freedom of action. It did not enhance his position, rather it damaged an already fading reputation. He appeared to be making scapegoats of Ministers who had served him loyally and carried out policies he had agreed with. He seemed to be sacrificing them to save his own skin. His actions did not increase confidence in his powers of judgement or timing. He made enemies inside the parliamentary party and inside the Conservative Party outside Parliament. He did not increase the popularity of the Government. He undermined his own position by his purge.[10] The incident also illustrated the point that loyal service is not enough to bring a Minister promotion and to prevent dismissal. None of those axed had a reputation for being awkward or nuisances or opponents of the Prime Minister. They were removed because they were easy targets and appeared to have no significant following

8. See Punnett (1964), especially on p. 70 where he says, 'On the whole there was very little change in the allocation of senior responsibilities in the transition from opposition to power, and the Ministerial duties are very largely based on the allocation of responsibilities that applied in the 1963–64 session.'

9. Attlee never threw out Bevin, Cripps or Morrison.

10. Even Crick points out (1964, p. 39) that by-election reverses continued; opposition in his own party was brought out into the lobbies when seventy backbenchers held a protest meeting against the dismissal of Selwyn Lloyd, and it led to the revolt of October 1963.

See also Hill (1964, pp. 246–8); Kilmuir (1964, pp. 322–4); Bevins said that 'In July 1962 Harold Macmillan committed political suicide more certainly than if he had himself resigned' (1965).

among the remaining leading Cabinet Ministers or the MPs generally. Thus the importance of the Prime Minister's powers of appointment and dismissal has been grossly overestimated, perhaps most of all by Harold Macmillan.

Although the proceedings of the Cabinet follow a formal protocol, the predominance of the Prime Minister suggested by the customs of Cabinet etiquette has been exaggerated. His control over the agenda is not as absolute as has been presented. He may temporarily be able to keep off the agenda an item he dislikes, but he would be unable to prevent permanently a group or even one of his major colleagues from bringing up a matter they wished to discuss. If he did try to obstruct them, he would be acting senselessly, stirring up their opposition and encouraging them to rally support amongst the rest of the Cabinet and the MPs against him. It would be very foolish for a Prime Minister to storm out of a Cabinet meeting when one of his leading colleagues brought up an issue which the bulk of the Cabinet wished to discuss. To walk out on such an occasion would seriously damage his reputation in their eyes.[11] The actual drawing up of the agenda is not solely dictated by Prime Ministerial whim. Outside pressures are significant, from his colleagues, departments, the party in and out of Parliament, public opinion and events both domestic and external. Nor is he in command of the final verdict of the meeting. His summary and decision cannot go against the sense of the meeting. He cannot impose his own views on a reluctant session, especially if the chief figures in the Cabinet oppose him. He may see his ideas modified and even rejected in the give and take of discussion.[12] To carry on as leader, the Prime Minister must retain the confidence of his Cabinet, which means that he cannot dictate to it. Just because there is little evidence of revolts against the Prime Minister within the Cabinet, does not indicate that its members are tamely subservient to him. Most likely it

11. Enoch Powell said, 'A Minister clearly has a right to bring a matter to his colleagues if he wants to. The very nature of collective responsibility implies that if a man wants his colleagues' assent or advice he can have it' (Wilson, *et al.*, 1964).

12. Lord Hill said of Macmillan that 'if he found himself in a minority he accepted the fact with grace and humour' (Hill, 1964, p. 235).

shows that the final decisions are agreed ones, reached after discussion and compromise. Harmony implies not so much obedience to the Prime Minister's will as general agreement amongst the Cabinet members, including the Prime Minister.

The charge that the Prime Minister bypasses the Cabinet through conversations with individual Ministers, cronies, Cabinet committees, and experts outside government, loses sight of the important fact that any major decisions, which such meetings come to, have to pass through the Cabinet before they can be implemented. Any participant in such sessions with the Prime Minister, who objects to any decision, can get it discussed and decided at Cabinet level, and any member of the Cabinet can query any decision of such sessions, get a discussion started and a Cabinet decision taken.[13] The doctrine of collective responsibility is still meaningful. By it, Ministers are encouraged to take an interest in the work of other departments than their own. It is a myth that a Minister is so completely absorbed in the work of his own department that he neglects the other aspects of government policy.[14] Ministers are still members of the House of Commons and members of their Party. They have to defend the whole range of Government policy and not just that of their department. Moreover, they are usually keen on promotion, and thus do not immerse themselves in a single subject to the exclusion of other topics.

It is only sensible for the Prime Minister to keep on specially close terms with his chief colleagues and major rivals. These are the men with most weight in the Cabinet; to square them would be the first stage in getting a policy through the Cabinet. This inner Cabinet has no formal structure, nor is it a collection of the Prime Minister's personal friends. He consults them not because he likes their company but because they are the most powerful men in his Government. This kind of grouping is quite different from those meetings which Churchill used to

13. Mr Wilson in the ITV broadcast on 'Power in Britain' said that it was open to any member of the Cabinet to question any of the assumptions of the Cabinet Committees, and Ministerial meetings at Chequers which he said were like Cabinet Committees (10 January 1965). Also see *The Times*, 11 January 1965.

14. See Enoch Powell's view on this point (Wilson *et al.*, 1964, p. 58).

G. W. Jones 201

hold late at night with some cronies. These were his personal friends with whom he enjoyed discussing matters, using their ideas to stimulate and sharpen his own.[15] The chief men in his Cabinet were a different set. The former had not the real influence in Government which the latter had, who could block some of Churchill's own objectives (Mackintosh, 1962, p. 435).

Harold Wilson's meetings with Ministers and officials to discuss particular topics are not innovations. Other Prime Ministers have had such meetings, and dinners with experts;[16] what is new is the publicity given to them. This is part of the technique of government, creating the impression that the Government is active.

The two instances always quoted to show the great scope of Prime Ministerial power, the decisions to produce atomic weapons and to carry out the Suez venture, have been presented in a very biased way. The decision to produce atomic weapons was taken after thorough discussion in the Defence Committee of the Cabinet; it was circulated in the Cabinet agenda, but not discussed in Cabinet because the decision was accepted by the Cabinet Ministers; the decision was also announced to Parliament, and again no discussion took place because at that time in 1948 there was no significant opposition to the manufacture by Britain of such weapons.[17] The Suez affair was not the personal policy of the Prime Minister. The policy was discussed and initiated in a Committee of the Cabinet, comprising the chief men in the Cabinet; the full Cabinet was kept informed about the Committee's decisions, and objections seem to have been raised by a few members; but clearly the majority of the Cabinet was behind the policy of the Committee (Mackintosh, 1962, pp. 435–6; Eden, 1960, p. 432). Thus in neither case were these decisions taken solely by the Prime Minister. He had to

15. Kilmuir noted that Macmillan refused to have an inner Cabinet (1964, p. 309). Note also Mackintosh (1962, p. 434). Lord Woolton points out that this was not Government by cronies (1960, pp. 377–8).

16. Harold Wilson claimed to be returning to the practices of Attlee and Churchill (Wilson, et al., 1964).

17. See the correspondence between Crossman and Strauss in *New Statesman*, 10, 17, 24, 31 May 1963, 7 June 1963, and in *Encounter*, June 1963 and August 1963.

carry with him his chief colleagues and the majority of the Cabinet.

The standing of the individual Minister has not been so depressed as some have suggested. The quotation from Lord Home, as he then was, has been overrated. It may tell us something about his relations with the Prime Minister, but nothing about Harold Macmillan's relations with other Ministers. Some said that Lord Home was appointed Foreign Secretary because Macmillan wanted a man who would agree with him, performing much the same role as Selwyn Lloyd. In any case it has long been the custom for the Prime Minister to be virtually his own Foreign Minister. Only Austen Chamberlain and Ernest Bevin since 1919 were allowed a significant measure of independence by their Prime Ministers. The Foreign Office has often succumbed to Prime Ministerial intervention. Thus, since the relations between the Prime Minister and the Foreign Secretary are of a special character, any statement about their relations is not a general statement about the Prime Minister's relations with other Ministers. A more apt quotation by a Minister about Harold Macmillan's practices comes from Iain Macleod.

Mr. Macmillan set a new standard of competence in the business of forming, controlling and guiding a Cabinet. He knew how to delegate to individual Ministers and to leave them alone. It was because the whole Cabinet worked so well and so smoothly that people formed the impression of an absolute personal ascendancy, and the notion grew up that we were changing from a Cabinet to a presidential system of government. In fact the reverse was happening. Mr Macmillan by his skill, restored a great deal of vitality to the Cabinet as a body.[18]

Sir Alec Douglas-Home in a later interview in the *Observer* (13 September, 1964), when he was Prime Minister, said, 'A good Prime Minister, once he had selected his Ministers and made it plain to them he was always accessible "for comment

18. The *Spectator*, 14 February 1964. Lord Kilmuir noted that 'Macmillan's approach to Cabinet business was businesslike and firm; all important issue [sic] would be dealt with by the Cabinet, to remove the very real possibility that some unconsidered independent action by a junior Minister might damage the Government as a whole' (Kilmuir, 1964, p. 308).

or advice", should interfere with their departmental business as little as possible.' Harold Wilson has described the task of a Prime Minister as 'conducting an orchestra and not playing the instruments oneself'.[19] The only post-war Prime Minister who claimed that he was more than *primus inter pares* and acted as such by for example interfering and fussing with Ministers and their departments was Sir Anthony Eden (Mackintosh, 1962, p. 435; Dalton, 1965).[20] His activities did not gain him the support of his colleagues, and he can hardly be called one of the more successful Prime Ministers of Britain.

The Prime Minister is at a serious disadvantage with his colleagues. Unlike most of them he has no department to keep him informed and to brief him. He is not able to check the information flowing to him from the departments and their Ministers. Without alternative sources of information he cannot easily evaluate their advice.[21] He is especially weak in that he cannot involve himself in the 'germinating stage' of a policy,[22] when the civil servants and Ministers are mulling over some proposals. He is most likely brought in when discussions are completed, and opinions have solidified. His private office and Cabinet office are not comparable to the departments behind his Ministers, nor do they approach the large number and expertise of the advisers of the American President.[23] Harold

19. In the ITV broadcast 'Power in Britain', 10 January 1965 and in *The Times*, 25 January 1965. The political correspondent of the *New Statesman* said 'The Labour leadership is composed of a full (if at times discordant) orchestra, rather than a one-man band' (29 January 1965). Earlier he had claimed that Harold Wilson showed a readiness to delegate responsibility (*New Statesman*, 22 January 1965).

20. Kilmuir points out that Eden annoyed Macmillan by interfering in his department (Kilmuir, 1964, pp. 243–4), and that Macmillan interfered far less than Eden 'unless he judged that they [departmental matters] merited Cabinet consideration' (p. 308).

21. Because he is so weak in this respect there have been suggestions that he should have a department of his own, a Prime Minister's office. The *Economist*, 8 June 1963, or Lord Shawcross in *The Times*, 11 October 1963. The *Guardian*, 26 February 1964.

22. Lord Bridges and Harold Wilson have noted the restraints on the Prime Minister's power because he was absent at the 'germinating stage' (Wilson *et al.*, 1964, pp. 68–9).

23. The following expand this point: Rose (1965, p. 195); Sampson (1962, pp. 334–5); Smith (1963); *Observer* (1964); *Sunday Times* (1964).

Wilson, before becoming Prime Minister, expressed the view that the Prime Minister needed to be served by a briefing agency to ensure that he was as fully informed as a departmental Minister, and that the Prime Minister should come in on policy discussions at an early stage (Wilson *et al.*, 1964, p. 26). Harold Wilson's sessions at Chequers, which he claims are a return to the methods of Churchill and Attlee, are attempts to bring the Prime Minister into this early stage, and his attaching to the Cabinet office of certain academics and civil servants, economists, scientists and technologists in particular, is an attempt to provide himself with new sources of information and advice. He has not added them to his private office, which has remained very much the same as before, but to the Cabinet office. It is, however, not just the servant of the Prime Minister; it has a collective loyalty to the Cabinet and its prime function is to serve that body, not a single man. Indeed Wilson's refusal to turn his private office into a strong central intelligence service for himself indicates some limits on his power. If he had done so he would have irritated his Ministers and civil servants (*Sunday Times*, 1964). To avoid their displeasure he had to strengthen the Cabinet office. But far from enhancing the position of the Prime Minister above his colleagues the Cabinet office has served to sustain the doctrine of collective responsibility, since it has been loyal to its function of serving the Cabinet as a whole.

Even if he had established a stronger private office, it is unlikely that it would have prevailed against older and larger departments. They have usually triumphed over small *ad hoc* teams of civil servants attached to new-fangled Ministries with lofty aims and no traditional establishment. Non-departmental Ministers and Prime Ministers have had little success when fighting the entrenched departments, who remain impervious to take-over bids (the *Economist*, 13 August, 1960). The civil service consists of a number of departments, each possessing a strong *esprit de corps*. It is not as centralized and monolithic as some have suggested and therefore not so easily amenable to Prime Ministerial control. His power over appointments is not such that he can put exactly whom he wants in any position he likes. He has to defer to the advice of the Joint Permanent Secretary to the Treasury and the consensus amongst the top echelons of the civil service about who should fill the major posts. Even if a personal choice is put in charge, there is no guarantee that he will remain a loyal servant of the Prime Minister. He will most likely become the spokesman of his department's view, defending its interests against all comers.

It is hard for an individual Minister to know all that is going on in his own department, and therefore even harder for a Prime Minister to know all that is going on in the whole machine of Government. If on one item he does exert himself to influence the course of a decision, he will have to expend much energy and effort, and in so doing will naturally neglect other aspects of policy. If he does prevail in one area, he fails in others, because he cannot influence everything at once (Dalder, 1964, p. 248).

The Prime Minister has no executive powers vested in him. To achieve anything he must work with and through his Ministers who have executive power vested in them (Moodie, 1964, p. 85). These men have powerful and independent departments to brief them and possess significant followings in their party who hope to see their man one day leader. To become and remain Prime Minister a man must carry these major colleagues, who are his rivals, with him. He cannot dictate to them, but must cooperate, consult and negotiate with them and even at times defer to them. Cabinet Government and collective responsibility are not defunct notions. Shared responsibility is still meaningful, for a Prime Minister has to gain the support of the bulk of his Cabinet to carry out his policies. He has to persuade it and convince it that he is right. Its meetings do not merely follow his direction. Debate and conflict are frequent. It cannot be by-passed and he cannot be an autocrat. To attempt to become one presages his political suicide.

The Prime Minister is the leading figure in the Cabinet whose voice carries most weight. But he is not the all powerful individual which many have recently claimed him to be. His office has great potentialities, but the use made of them depends on many variables, the personality, temperament, and ability of the Prime Minister, what he wants to achieve and the methods he uses. It depends also on his colleagues, their personalities, temperaments and abilities, what they want to do and their methods. A Prime Minister who can carry his colleagues with him can be in a very powerful position, but he is only as strong as they let him be.

References

ANDREWS, W. G. (1960), 'Some thoughts on the power of dissolution', *Parliamentary Affairs*, pp. 286–96.

BEVINS, R. (1965), *Sunday Express*, 17 January.

BIRCH, A. H. (1964), *Representative and Responsible Government*, Allen and Unwin.

BLONDEL, J. (1963), *Voters, Parties and Leaders*, Penguin.

CHESTER, D. N. (1962), 'Who governs Britain?' *Parliamentary Affairs*, Autumn, pp. 519–27.

CHURCHILL, R. S. (1959), *The Rise and Fall of Sir Anthony Eden*, MacGibbon Kee.

CRICK, B. (1964), *The Reform of Parliament*, Weidenfeld & Nicolson.

CROSSMAN, R. H. S. (1964), Introduction to W. Bagshot, *The English Constitution*, pp. 81–7.

DALDER, H. (1964), *Cabinet Reform in Britain 1914–1963*, Oxford University Press.

DALTON, H. (1962), *High Tide and After*, Frederick Maller.

DALTON, H. (1965), Obituary to Sir Winston Churchill in *New Statesman*, 29th January.

EDEN, SIR A. (1960), *The Memoirs of Sir Antony Eden, Full Circle*, Cassell.

EPSTEIN, L. D. (1960), 'British M.P.s and their local parties: the Suez cases', *Amer. Polical Sci. Rev.*, June, pp. 374–90.

FINER, S. E., BERRINGTON, H. B., BARTHOLOMEW, D. J. (1961), *Backbench Opinion in the House of Commons, 1955–59*, Pergamon.

HEASMAN, D. J. (1962), 'The Prime Minister and the Cabinet', *Parliamentary Affairs*, Autumn, pp. 461–84.

HILL, C. (1964), *Both Sides of the Hill*, Heinemann.

HINTON, R. W. K. (1960), 'The Prime Minister as an elected monarch', *Parliamentary Affairs*, Summer, pp. 297–303.

HUNTER, L. (1959), *The Road to Brighton Pier*, Arthur Barker.

JOHNSON, P. (1964), *New Statesman*, 14 February.

JONES, C. O. (1964), 'Inter-party competition in Britain, 1950–1959', *Parliamentary Affairs*, Winter, 1963–4, pp. 50–64.

KILMUIR, D. P. M. F. (1964), *Political Adventure*, Weidenfeld & Nicolson.

MACKINTOSH, J. P. (1962), *The British Cabinet*, Methuen.

McKENZIE, R. T. (1963), *British Political Parties*, Mercury Books.

MOODIE. G. C. (1964), *The Government in Great Britain*, Methuen.

PUNNETT, R. M. (1964), 'The Labour Shadow Cabinet, 1955–1964,' *Parliamentary Affairs*, Winter, 1964–5.

Observer (1964), interview with Sir Alec Douglas-Home, 13 September.

ROSE, R. (1964), 'Parties, factions and tendencies in Britain', *Political Studies*, February, pp. 33–46.

ROSE, R. (1965), *Politics in England*, Faber.

SAMPSON, A. (1962), *Anatomy of Britain*, Hodder and Stoughton.

SMITH, G. (1963), 'The political prisoner', *Sunday Times Colour Magazine*, 18 September.

Sunday Times (1964), interview with R. Neustadt, 8 November.

The Listener (1963a), 'The Commons in action', 19 December.

The Listener (1963b), interview with M. Redmayne, 26 December.

TRENAMAN, J., and MCQUAIL, D. (1961), *Television and the Political Image*, Methuen.

WILSON, H. H. (1961), *Pressure Group; the Campaign for Commercial Television*, Secker and Warburg.

WILSON, H. *et al.* (1964), *Whitehall and Beyond*, BBC.

WOOLTON, R. D. (1960), *The Memoirs of the Earl of Woolton*, Cassell.

13 G. A. Almond and S. Verba

Political Attitudes: The Sense of Civic Competence

Excerpts from 'The sense of civic competence', in G. A. Almond and S. Verba, *The Civic Culture*, Little, Brown, 1965, ch. 6, pp. 136–60.

Democracy is a political system in which ordinary citizens exercise control over elites; and such control is legitimate, that is, it is supported by norms that are accepted by elites and non-elites. In all societies, of course, the making of specific decisions is concentrated in the hands of very few people. Neither the ordinary citizen nor 'public opinion' can make policy. If this is the case, the problem of assessing the degree of democracy in a nation becomes one of measuring the degree to which ordinary citizens control those who make the significant decisions for a society – in most cases, governmental elites.

Recent work on the theory of influence suggests that there are numerous means by which interpersonal influence can be exerted, and that it makes a difference which means are used. In this chapter we shall be concerned with a particular type of influence that nonelites may exert on elites: a type that we label *political* influence. We shall roughly define the political influence of a group or individual over a governmental decision as equal to the degree to which governmental officials act to benefit that group or individual because the officials believe that they will risk some deprivation (they will risk their jobs, be criticized, lose votes) if they do not so act. Thus we define political influence as both the outcome of the decision and the motives of the decision makers. The outcomes will benefit the influential groups or individuals more than it would if the influence were not exercised. And the decision makers act to benefit the groups or individuals because they believe they will suffer some deprivation or, what amounts to the same thing, fail to gain a reward. The latter criterion is important. Officials may act to benefit a particular group for a variety of reasons: out of a feeling of paternalism, for instance. But it is only when officials act because they fear the consequences of not acting that a group may be considered to be politically influential and a participant in the decision. If the individual can exert such influence, we shall consider him to be *politically competent*; or if he *believes* he can exert such influence, we shall view him as subjectively competent.

So far we have defined political influence as the way in which governmental elites make decisions. Our study, however, concentrates upon the perceptions and behaviors, not of governmental elites, but of the ordinary citizen. We are concerned with the ordinary man's perception of his own influence. Thinking that one can influence the government or even attempting to influence government is not the same as actually influencing it. A citizen may think he has influence over decisions, or he may attempt to exert influence over decisions, and the government official may be unmoved. Conversely, a citizen may believe that all government decisions are made without any consideration of his needs and desires or of the needs and desires of his fellow citizens, when, in fact, government officials constantly try to calculate the way in which groups will react to their acts.

If the degree to which citizens believe they can influence the course of governmental decisions is not necessarily related to their actual level of influence, why study their subjective views of their competence? In the first place, we are interested in the state of attitudes in a country. If democracy involves high levels of actual participation in decisions, then the attitudes of a democratic citizenry should include the perception that they in fact can participate. A democratic citizen speaks the language of demands. Government officials accede to his demands because they fear some loss otherwise – the loss of his vote perhaps – or because they consider it legitimate that he make such demands. The subject, too, may want and expect beneficial outputs from the government. But he does not expect these to be accorded him because he demands them. The government official who acts to benefit him responds, not to the subject's demands, but to some other force. In a traditional society with a highly developed set of norms as to what is due each member, the government official may be responding to these traditional rules when he acts in favor of an individual. Or in an authoritarian–legalistic political system in which the behavior of government officials is circumscribed by explicit rules, he may act as he does because the individual falls within a particular category, which, according to the rules, is to receive a certain type of treatment. In these situations the official is not acting capriciously. His decision to aid the individual is determined by a set of social or legal rules. And these rules may, of course, be enforced by an administrative hierarchy to which the subject may appeal. This kind of subject influence, or administrative competence, is more circumscribed, more passive than that of the citizen. It may set in motion an action that will affect the way in which a rule is interpreted or enforced against an individual. It is not a creative act of influence that can affect the content of the decisions themselves, except in an indirect way.

Second, the perception of the ability to exert political influence is significant even if individuals rarely try to use that influence, or are frequently unsuccessful when they do try. Much of the influence that our respondents believe they have over government probably represents a somewhat unrealistic belief in their opportunities to participate. It is likely that many who say they could influence the government would never attempt to exert such influence; and it is likely as well that if they tried they would not succeed. Yet such a belief in the ordinary man's ability to participate may have significant consequences for a political system. Though individuals' perceptions of their own political ability may not mirror the objective situation, it cannot be unrelated to that situation. If an individual believes he has influence, he is more likely to attempt to use it.[1] A subjectively competent citizen, therefore, is more likely to be an active citizen. And if government officials do not necessarily respond to active influence attempts, they are more likely to respond to them than to a passive citizenry that makes no demands. If the ordinary citizen, on the other hand, perceives that government policy is far outside his sphere of influence, he is unlikely to attempt to influence that policy, and government officials are

1. Evidence that those who believe they can influence are more likely to have actual experience in attempting to do so will be presented in Table 2 on p. 216.

unlikely to worry about the potential pressure that can be brought to bear on them. Thus the extent to which citizens in a nation perceive themselves as competent to influence the government affects their political behavior.

Furthermore, the existence of a belief in the influence potential of citizens may affect the political system even if it does not affect the political activity of the ordinary man. If decision makers believe that the ordinary man *could* participate – and they certainly are not entirely cut off from the dominant social beliefs – they are likely to behave quite differently than if such a belief did not exist. Even if individuals do not act according to this belief, decision makers may act on the assumption that they can, and in this way be more responsive to the citizenry than they would be if the myth of participation did not exist. But whether myth or reality (and the statements we shall be talking about are probably a combination of both), the extent to which individuals think they can influence the government and the ways in which they believe they can do so are . . . important elements of the civic culture.

[Here] we are concerned with the perceptions that individuals have about the amount of influence they can exercise over governmental decisions. Several questions may be asked about their attempts to influence the government:

1. Under what circumstances will an individual make some conscious effort to influence the government? Direct political influence attempts are rare. For the ordinary citizen the activities of government – even local government – may seem quite distant. At the time that a decision is being made, the citizen is not aware that it is being made or of what its consequences for him are likely to be. It is probable, then, that only in situations of some stress, where a government activity is perceived to have a direct and serious impact upon the individual, will a direct influence be stimulated.

2. What method will be used in the influence attempt? Some major dimensions in this respect include: the kinds of channels of influence that are used; whether the attempt is violent or non-violent; and whether the individual attempts to influence the government alone or attempts to enlist the support of others.

3. What is the effect of the influence attempt? The extent to which the government official changes his behavior in response to some influence attempt by a citizen is a problem beyond the scope of our study. However, since we are concentrating on the perspective of the citizen, we shall consider his view of the likelihood that an attempt made by him to influence the government will have any effect.

The distribution of subjective competence

In developing our survey instrument, we took into account the fact that direct attempts to influence the government are more likely to arise in some stress situations, in which an individual perceives that an activity of the government is threatening injury to him. Our questions attempted to place the individual in such a hypothetical stress situation, so that we could ascertain how he thought he would react. We asked him to suppose that his local government or his national legislature was considering a law that he thought was very unjust and harmful. What did he think he could do about it? If the respondent thought he could do something, we probed to find out what it was. We then asked him how much effect he thought any action he took would have, and how likely it was that he actually would do something. A similar set of questions was asked about an unjust and harmful regulation being considered by the most local governmental unit. These questions were about the political branches of the government, the elected governments on the national and local levels. Through these questions we hoped to get some notion of the respondent's views on the extent of his political competence and, more important, on the strategy of influence open to him.

The results for these questions on local and national subjective competence are reported in Table 1. Two points call for comment. First, in all five countries the sense of subjective competence occurs more frequently vis-à-vis the local government than the national government. This confirms widely held views of the closer relatedness of citizens to their local governments because of their greater immediacy, accessibility, and familiarity. American and British respondents most frequently say that there is something they can do about an unjust local regulation. More than three-quarters of those we interviewed in each of the two countries expressed the opinion that they have some recourse if they believe the local government is considering a law they think unjust; only 17 per cent say that there is nothing they can do. In the other three countries over 30 per cent of those interviewed report that there is nothing they can do in such a situation.[2]

Table 1 Percentage Who say They can do Something about an Unjust Local or National Regulation; by nation*

Nation	Can do something about local regulation	Can do something about national regulation
United States	77	75
Great Britain	78	62
Germany	62	38
Italy	51	28
Mexico	52	38

*Percentages in each case apply to the total sample.

The second point brought out in Table 1 is that, although in all five countries the proportion that says it can influence the local government is higher than the proportion expressing

2. Many respondents make it quite clear that they believe there is nothing they can do, either because they consider themselves too powerless or because they consider government activities outside their sphere of competence. The following are some examples of these responses:

A German housewife: 'Nothing at all. The local council makes its decision, and there is nothing one can do about it.'

A German housewife: 'I'd say nothing because I don't understand it, and I wouldn't do it right, anyway.'

An American semiretired: 'Nothing. That's all because we put our trust in our elected people and we must feel they know more about these things than we do even though we don't always agree.'

An American housewife: 'Not anything. No "mam" not nothing . . . Nothing at all.'

A British retired office worker: 'I wouldn't have much chance to do anything, being just one insignificant person.'

An Italian housewife: 'What do you want me to do? I don't count for anything.'

A Mexican housewife: 'Nothing. I have no one with whom to talk. I wouldn't know what to do in such a case.'

national competence, this difference is relatively small in the American, British, and Mexican samples, and relatively large in Germany and Italy. Put briefly, three-fourths of the American respondents express local and national competence; more than three-fourths and a little less than two-thirds of the British respondents express local and national competence, respectively. In Germany almost two-thirds of the respondents express local competence, whereas only a little more than one-third express national competence. In Italy the proportion drops from one-half to less than one-third. And in Mexico the proportion declines from a little more than one-half to a little more than one-third. The generalization about the greater sense of competence vis-à-vis the local government holds up in our findings, but it is most apparent in Italy and Germany.

That an individual is subjectively competent does not mean that he will in fact try to change what he considers an unfair law. Ours was a hypothetical situation, and we do not really know what our respondents would do if they ever were actually faced with such a challenging situation. But we did ask them for their opinions on whether or not they thought they would act. In all countries many who say they can do something about an unjust regulation report that in fact they probably would do nothing. But the number who report that there is at least some likelihood that they would make an effort reflects the same national pattern reported above. If we consider the responses about the local government (the responses about the national government form the same pattern), we find that 58 per cent of the American respondents and 50 per cent of those in Britain say there is some likelihood that they would actually make an effort to influence an unjust regulation. In Germany 44 per cent and in Italy 41 per cent make some such affirmation. (The question was, unfortunately, not asked in a comparable form in Mexico.)

Lastly, there is some evidence that the subjective estimate of one's propensity to act in this challenging political situation is closely related to actual attempts to influence the government. In all five nations a substantially larger proportion of those respondents who say there is something they can do about an unjust local regulation (let us, for convenience, call them 'local competents') report some experience in attempting to influence the local government. (We find the same pattern in the national data.) These data are reported in Table 2. In all nations those who say they could influence the local government, in comparison with those who say they could not, are at least three times as likely to have attempted such influence.

Table 2 Percentage who say They have Attempted to Influence the Local Government, by Local Competents and Local Non-competents

Nation	Local competents		Local noncompetents	
	%	No.*	%	No.
United States	33	(745)	10	(225)
Great Britain	18	(748)	3	(215)
Germany	21	(590)	2	(365)
Italy	13	(508)	4	(487)
Mexico	9	(531)	2	(476)

*Numbers in parentheses refer to the bases upon which percentages are calculated.

Thus the sense of local and national civic competence is widely distributed among the American and British populations. In Germany and Italy local competence is widely distributed, national competence is much less widely distributed. In Mexico, though the general level of civic competence is lower than in the United States and Britain, the discrepancy between the local and national level (as reported in Table 1) is less great than in Germany and Italy. It also appears that there is a relation between subjective competence and political action.

Local competence and national competence are, as one would expect, fairly closely related. The man who believes he can influence the national government is more likely to think he can influence the local government than is the man who does not feel competent on the national level. Conversely, the man who feels competent locally is also more likely to believe he can influence the national government than is the man who does not have a sense of local competence. Earlier it was pointed out that local competence is more widespread than national competence. Furthermore, local competence is most widely distributed in nations in which local government autonomy and the accessibility of local government officials to ordinary citizens is most firmly institutionalized. Adding these three facts together – local and national competence are related, local competence is more widespread than national, and local competence is related to the institutional availability of opportunities to participate on the local level – one has an argument in favor of the classic position that political participation on the local level plays a major role in the development of a competent citizenry. As many writers have argued, local government may act as a training ground for political competence. Where local government allows participation, it may foster a sense of competence that then spreads to the national level – a sense of competence that would have had a harder time developing had the individual's only involvement with government been with the more distant and inaccessible structures of the national government. To argue this point is to speculate beyond our data on national and local competence. But in a later chapter we shall present data to the effect that the individual's belief in his ability to affect the government derives, at least in part, from opportunities to be influential within smaller authority structures such as the family, the school, and the place of work.

The strategy of influence

Another aspect of political competence is the strategy an individual would use in attempting to influence the government. The *way* in which those who report that they could influence the government say they could exert this influence is, of course, important. It makes a difference whether someone has only the vaguest notion of what he can do, or a clear view of the channels open to him for expressing his point of view. It also makes a difference what resources he believes he has available to use. Furthermore, the strategy that an individual would use will naturally affect the extent to which his subjective view of his ability to influence represents real influence potential – that is, it represents the sort of activity that has some chance of changing the behavior of the government officials. We shall deal primarily with those who think they have influence, the 'competents', and ask how they would exert that influence.

The strategies of influence that individuals report they would use in connection with the local government are summarized in Table 3. (Comparable data on the national government will be presented below.) Let us look first at the question of what social resources the individual feels he has available to him. This is highly significant for understanding the nature of his perceived relationship to his government. Government organizations are large and powerful, especially when compared to the individual. This is especially true of the national government, but even local government represents an institution whose resources are much greater than those of the ordinary man. Looking at the individual and his government, one is tempted to see him as lonely, powerless, and somewhat frightened by the immensity of the powers he faces. This is in fact one of the most frequent descriptions of the average man in modern political societies. In the theory of the "mass society" the individual is described as related directly as individual to the state. He has no other social resources to support him in this relationship and naturally feels ineffective and anxious. However valid this theory may be concerning the actual amount of power the average man has and the social resources available to him, our data suggest that a large number of our respondents do not view themselves as the model of mass society describes them. In their relationship to their government they think of themselves as neither powerless nor, what is more important, alone.

This fact is reflected in the data reported in Table 3. A number of our respondents believe that they can enlist the support of others in their attempts to influence the government. What is most striking is the variation from country to country in the numbers who feel they can call on others to aid them. In the United States 59 per cent of our respondents indicated that they could attempt to enlist the support of others if they wished to change a regulation they considered unjust. At the other extreme, only 9 per cent of the Italians mentioned the use of this social resource. In the other countries the proportions reporting that they would try to enlist the support of others varied from

Table 3 What Citizens would do to Try to Influence
their Local Government; by nation

What citizens would do	US	UK	Germany	Italy	Mexico
Try to enlist aid of others					
Organize an informal group; arouse friends and neighbors, get them to write letters of protest or to sign a petition	56	34	13	7	26
Work through a political party	1	1	3	1	—
Work through a formal group (union, church, professional) to which they belong	4	3	5	1	2
Total percentage who would enlist others' aid*	59	36	21	9	28
Act alone					
Directly contact political leaders (elected officials) or the press; write a letter to or visit a local political leader	20	45	15	12	15
Directly contact administrative (nonelected) officials	1	3	31	12	18
Consult a lawyer; appeal through courts	2	1	3	2	2
Vote against offending officials at next election	14	4	1	1	—
Take some violent action	1	1	1	1	1
Just protest	—	—	—	12	—
Other	1	2	—	3	5
Total percentage who would act alone†	18	41	41	43	24
Total percentage who would act with others or alone	77	78	62	51	53
Total number of respondents	970	963	955	995	1,007

* Total percentages are less than the total of the individual cells, since some respondents gave more than one answer.

† This row includes only the respondents who replied that they could do something but did not mention working with others. Hence the total is less than the sum of the individual cells, which contain respondents who may have mentioned both group and individual activity.

36 per cent in Britain, to 28 per cent in Mexico, to 21 per cent in Germany.[3]

Whom would citizens enlist to support them? Individuals as we know are members of a large number of social groups. They are not merely citizens of their nations; they are members of families, communities, churches, voluntary associations, trade unions, and a great variety of other groups and organizations. Basically these associations can be divided into two classes: formal organizations and informal face-to-face groups.

Much has been written about the important role of formal organizations in the political process – especially the role of political parties and associational interest groups. Both play major intervening roles between the individual and his government. They aggregate the demands of citizens and communicate these to government officials. Recently there has been growing interest in the informal face-to-face network of social groups to which an individual belongs – family, friends, work group, and neighbors. Here the main emphasis has been upon the impact of these groups on the political attitudes of their members, and on the process of communication downward; that is, to the individuals from such formal institutions as government, political parties, and the mass media.[4] Little has been said about the role of such informal associations in what we might call the 'influence-upward' process: the process by which citizens in a democracy influence the attitudes and behavior of government officials. But our findings show most strikingly that, when it comes to the support that individuals believe they could enlist in a challenging political situation, they think much more often of enlisting support from the informal face-to-face groups of which they are members than from the formal organizations to which they belong or with which they are affiliated. In all countries except Germany, less than 1 per cent of the respon-

3. Since question wording can seriously affect the response received, it is important to note here that the notion that one could enlist the support of others was in no way suggested by the question or by the interviewer's probing of the question. Interviewers were carefully instructed not to ask such questions as: 'Is there anyone you could get to help you?' or 'Would you attempt to do this alone or with other people?'

4. On the subject of the political functions of informal groups, see Verba (1961, ch. 2).

dents indicate that they would work through their political party if they were attempting to counteract some unjust regulation being considered by the local government; the German figure is about 3 per cent. Clearly, no matter how important the role of political parties may be in democratic societies, relatively few citizens think of them first as the place where support may be enlisted for attempts to influence the government.[5]

In all countries more individuals report that they would attempt to work through other formal organized groups than through political parties. But when one considers the entire range of formal organizations to which people may belong, the number who report they would enlist their support is small : no more than 3 per cent of the respondents in any country. Of course, not all respondents have some formal organization at their disposal; such organizations are more frequent in some nations than in others. And the percentage who report membership differs substantially from country to country. Furthermore, not all formal organizations are equally politically relevant.

But even among those respondents who belong to a formal organization that they report is involved in politics, the number who would invoke such membership in a stress situation is much smaller than the number who are members. In the United States, where such memberships are most frequent, 228 respondents report membership in this kind of organization, but only thirty-five of these Americans report that they would work through that organization if they were trying to influence a local regulation. In Italy, where such memberships are least frequent, we find the same pattern. Fifty-six Italians belong to some organization they believe is involved in political affairs, but only thirteen of those members would work through it if they were trying to influence a local regulation. The aid of a formal organization would be called upon most frequently in

5. To some extent the infrequent mention of a political party in this context probably understates the role of parties in this influence process. Many more respondents mentioned contacting government officials. If they explicitly mentioned that the partisan affiliation of the official was relevant in their attaining access to him, they would be coded as working through a party. But many may have considered this affiliation relevant even if they did not mention it.

Germany, but only half as frequently as the occurrence of membership in a politically relevant organization.

That formal organizations rarely would be invoked by individuals who were trying to influence the government does not mean, however, that these organizations are politically unimportant. They still may affect an individual's political influence, for he may have more influence over government officials merely by being a member of such a group, even if he makes no overt attempt to influence the government. And this sort of influence is of great significance – probably of greater overall significance than the overt influence attempts that ordinary citizens make from time to time. Furthermore, though an individual would not use his formal organization as the means to influence the government directly, his membership in itself enhances the prospects that he will believe himself capable of influencing the government and will actually make some such attempt. Thus he may, for a variety of reasons . . . develop greater self-confidence in his own political competence.

Cooperative political behavior

As Table 3 indicates, in all nations respondents less frequently mention enlisting the support of formal groups than informal groups – arousing their neighbors, getting friends and acquaintances to support their position, circulating a petition. This in itself is striking, though it ought not, for reasons given above, to be taken to imply that these informal groups play a more significant role in the political process than do formal organizations. What is most striking is not the frequency with which informal groups are mentioned in all countries, but the sharp differences in frequency among the nations.

Thus Table 4 shows that 56 per cent of the American respondents, 34 per cent of the British, and 26 per cent of the Mexicans reported that they would use this informal group strategy, as compared with 13 per cent of the Germans and 7 per cent of the Italians. If we consider the proportion of local competents who say they would cooperate with their fellow citizens in attempting to influence the government, we find that 74 per cent of American local competents would use informal groups, whereas only 13 per cent of Italian local competents and 22 per cent of the Germans would do so. In Mexico, though the proportion of local competents is relatively low, the proportion of those local competents who would work through informal groups is quite high – 50 per cent. And in Britain the proportion of local competents who say they would seek the cooperation of others is about as great – 43 per cent.

Table 4 Those who would Enlist the Aid of an Informal Group to Influence an Unjust Local Regulation

Nation	Percentage of total sample		Percentage of local competents	
	%	No.*	%	No.
United States	56	(970)	74	(745)
Great Britain	34	(963)	43	(748)
Germany	13	(955)	22	(590)
Italy	7	(995)	13	(508)
Mexico	26	(1007)	50	(531)

* Numbers in parentheses refer to the bases upon which percentages are calculated.

The notions that one can cooperate with one's fellow citizens in attempting to influence the government and that such cooperation is an effective means of increasing one's own influence dominate the bulk of the responses of the local competents in the United States and play an important role in responses in Britain and Mexico. In all five countries, however, there are individuals who would work with others in attempting to influence the government. A few illustrations may help to convey that attitude:

An American office manager: 'You can't do anything individually. You'd have to get a group and all get together and go to the proper authorities to complain.'

An American salesman: 'Get up a petition. Get together with people who have the same objection. Taking it up with the responsible person like the mayor or police commissioner.'

An American housemaid: 'I could discuss it with others and see how many others felt the same about it as I did. We could then write a letter each to some government person in charge and let him know how we felt, or we could write one letter and get a lot of people to sign it.'

An English dispatch clerk: 'Contact neighbors and friends and make a protest to the councillors. . . .'

An English foreman gardener: 'First thing – get a petition going. Take it up to the Council offices and make yourself spokesman of a group. You could try the local MP.'

An English house painter: 'You could more or less get a petition up and show the feeling. You could discuss it with your workmates and your wife.'

A Mexican shoemaker: 'Protest, join a group of citizens, and personally go to the office where it was issued and talk about it to the authorities.'

A Mexican housewife: 'I would get together all the people and send a petition to the president or the governor of the state signed by all.'

In a democratic political system, the belief that cooperation with one's fellow citizens is both a possible and an effective political action represents, we suggest, a highly significant orientation. The diffusion of influence over political decisions, by which we define democracy, implies some cooperative ability among the citizenry. This cooperation seems to be necessary, in terms of both the amount of influence the ordinary man can expect to have and the results of his influence on governmental decisions. By definition, the 'average' man's influence over the government must be small. Compared with the forces of government – and this would apply to local as well as national government – he is a frail creature indeed. If the ordinary man is to have any political influence, it must be in concert with his fellows. Second, from the point of view of the output of a democratic government, noncooperative and completely individualistic influence attempts could lead only to dysfunctional results. Every individual demand cannot be met, or the result will be chaos. If the government is to be responsive to the demands of the ordinary man, these demands must be aggregated, and the aggregation of interests implies cooperation among men. The aggregation of interests involved in the cooperation of groups of like-minded individuals is aggregation on a rather low level, but it does suggest a propensity to work together with one's fellows, which is relevant for larger political structures as well. In any case, we may suggest that the citizen who believes he can work cooperatively with others in his environment if he wants to engage in political activity has quite a different perspective on politics from the individual who thinks of himself as a lone political actor.

Furthermore, the notion that one can affect a government decision by bringing one's peers into the dispute is a highly political notion. It represents a fairly clear attempt to use political influence in one's relations with government officials. The threat that *many* make – whether it is the threatened loss of votes or of support, or the threat of public criticism – is, other things being equal, greater than the threat that *one* can make. Thus the individual who mentions getting others to join him in his dispute with the government is more likely to see himself as a citizen able to influence his government than as a subject who lacks such influence. And the variations among the five nations in the frequency with which such groups are mentioned reflect variations in such citizen competence.

It is particularly important to note what sorts of groups are involved here. The informal groups our respondents talk of forming do not exist, at least in a politically relevant sense, before the political stress situation arises. The individual perceives himself as able to create structures for the purpose of influencing the government. These structures represent a form of influence that had not been committed to politics before the politically challenging situation arose. In this sense, the ability of the individual to create structures to aid him in his disputes with the government represents a reserve of influence on his part. He has not committed his complete support to some larger social system, as has the individual in the so-called mass society; nor is he cut off from contact with the government, as is the parochial.

That a large proportion of people in a country perceive that the informal face-to-face groups of which they are members can be rallied to their support in time of political stress represents a significant aspect of the political culture of that nation. It means that some of the most basic building blocks of the social structure have been incorporated into the political system. An individual's role as citizen, particularly as a democratic, influential citizen, fuses with his other social roles. The type of political activity sparking this fusion of informal group membership and political citizenship is also highly significant. The fusion takes place because of political demands being made by citizens upon their government. They invoke their friends and neighbors in an attempt to influence their government. Thus the fusion occurs at the heart of the democratic process – the process by which the ordinary citizen exercises some control over his government. This is profoundly different from the fusion between face-to-face groups and government that has been attempted within totalitarian states. Here the government has attempted to influence the individual: family and friendship groups are penetrated by the state to support its attempts to propagandize and control. The state attempts to control these informal groups. In the countries we studied the invocation of informal groups has a contrary meaning. It is an attempt to penetrate and control government. It represents a meshing together of polity and community, rather than an assimilation of community into the polity.

Lastly, we have stressed the importance of this propensity toward cooperation with one's fellow citizens, not merely because we believe that it has significant consequences for the political system, but because we feel it is a type of behavior that can best be understood and explained by the type of study contained in this book. In the first place, the frequency with which individuals talk of cooperating with their fellow citizens to influence the government is not as dependent upon the structure of government as is the frequency with which they say they can influence the government. Whether or not someone feels he can affect the course of government action obviously depends to a large extent upon the structure of government – the extent to which it provides citizen access. But the difference between the individual who responds that he would write a letter to the local council and the one who responds that he would write a letter to the local council *and try to induce his friends to do likewise* cannot be explained by national differences in the structure and powers of their respective local councils. As we shall see shortly, these differing levels of social and economic development, while they can explain many of the political differences among the nations, cannot explain the propensity to cooperate politically. The origin of this propensity must be sought elsewhere.

Though the use of primary groups as a resource for influence is most common in the United States, Britain, and Mexico, there are several interesting differences between the United States and Britain on the one hand and Mexico on the other. The notion that one can mobilize an informal group as an aid in attempting to influence the government appears to be of greater significance for the actual exercise of influence in the former two countries. Earlier it was pointed out that those who report they can do something about an unjust local law (the local competents), compared with those who report the opposite, are much more likely to report some experience in attempting to influence the government. If we look only at the local competents and ask how those who would work through groups and those who would act alone differ in the extent of their experience in attempted local influence, we find that in the United States and Britain those who would work through groups are more likely to have had experience in these endeavors. In the United States 36 per cent of those who report they would work through informal groups (no.: 547) also report that they have at some time actually attempted to influence the government, whereas only 25 per cent of those local competents who would use some other strategy (no.: 198) report such experience. In Britain the parallel figures are 23 per cent for those who mention informal groups (no.: 315) and 15 per cent for other local competents (no.: 414). In Mexico, on the other hand, those who mention informal groups are a bit less likely to be the experienced respondents: 7 per cent of those who mention informal groups (no.: 264) report experience, as against 10 per cent of the other local competents (no.: 267).[6]

6. In Germany those local competents who mention informal groups are somewhat less likely to have had actual influence experience. Seventeen per cent of those who mention informal groups (no.: 126) report past experience, as against 23 per cent of local competents who do not mention them (no.: 460). In Italy those local competents who mention groups are somewhat

Furthermore, in the former two countries the use of informal groups as a means of influencing the government is seen, not only as a means to protest, but as the key to effective protest. In order to test the extent to which individuals felt they could influence their local government, we asked another question after asking what respondents thought they could do about an unjust local law: 'If you made an effort to change this regulation, how likely is it that you would succeed?' Of interest to us here is that a large number of American and British local competents volunteered the statement that their protest would have some likelihood of success only if others joined with them. (The percentages were 30 in the United States and 20 in Britain.) In Mexico, though a good percentage felt there was some likelihood that they would succeed if they attempted to influence their local government, fewer than one per cent of the respondents suggested that this would be the case only if they had the support of others. Though the use of informal groups is perceived as a means of influence in Mexico, it is not yet perceived as the key to effective influence.[7]

One further difference deserves mention. In the United States and Britain the use of informal groups as a means of influencing a governmental decision is considered much more appropriate on the local than on the national level. In Mexico, on the other hand, the proportion who would use informal groups is about the same on the local and national levels. The fact that in Britain and the United States, more than in Mexico, the use of such groups is closely related both to experience and to expectations of success, coupled with the fact that such strategy is considered more appropriate in connection with the local government in the former two countries, suggests that informal group strategy is based on a more realistic appraisal of the potentialities of such a strategy – a realistic appraisal deriving from actual experience with such groups on the local level. In Mexico this influence strategy is less well grounded in actual local experience. It appears to be another instance of the aspirational character of the Mexican political culture.

more likely to be experienced: 16 per cent (no.: 67), as against 13 per cent (no.: 438) of those who do not mention groups.

7. In Germany the percentage of local competents who mentioned that they would succeed only if others joined them was 12; in Italy it was 5.

Individual action

The respondents who spoke of themselves as acting alone in their attempt to influence the government show some variation, as Table 4 indicates, in the strategies they mention. In the United States and Britain respondents are more likely to say they would approach an elected government official rather than an appointed official of the bureaucracy. In Mexico and Italy respondents are as likely to say they would direct their protest toward one type of official as toward the other. In Germany, however, more respondents mention appointed officials than elected officials as the target of their protest. It is tempting to consider these results to be a reflection of a more highly developed political competence in the United States and Britain. A protest to an elected official seems to be inherently more of a political protest, in the sense of involving an implied threat of deprivation to the official if he does not comply – for the loss of the vote is the most usual deprivation with which the individual can threaten an offending official. This may partly explain the differences among the nations in the chosen targets of influence attempts; but it is more likely that these differences merely reflect national differences in the relative position and importance of elected and appointed officials within the structures of local government.

Lastly, not all of those who say they could do something about an unjust local regulation had any clear strategy in mind. As Table 3 indicates, 12 per cent of the Italian respondents said that they could protest if faced with a regulation they considered unjust, but when asked how or to whom they could protest, gave no more specific reply. The 12 per cent who would protest represent about one-fourth of all Italian local competents. While this answer shows a higher level of subjective competence than the answer that one could do nothing, it reflects little awareness of the political channels through which one might effectively approach the government.

National competence

We saw in Table 1 that in all nations fewer respondents say they could influence the national legislature than the local government and more say there is nothing they could do. In

Table 5 we report the strategies respondents say they would use *vis-à-vis* the national government. In all nations formal organizations are somewhat more often mentioned as a resource for influencing the national government than the local government. (And if one calculated the percentage as a proportion of 'national competents' rather than as a proportion of the entire sample, the difference would be sharper.) Conversely, in all nations fewer respondents mention using informal groups in connection with the national government than mentioned them in connection with the local government, though the pattern is the same; these groups are mentioned most frequently in the United States, followed by Britain and Mexico, then Germany and Italy. Generally, national influence strategies tend to rely more on the organized structures of politics, such as interest groups, political parties, and the press, or on individual approaches to elected political leaders. As we have already pointed out, this probably reflects realistic calculations. It takes a larger group and greater political skill to bring influence to bear on the national than on the local government. However, our evidence suggests that informal group competence persists significantly at the national level in the United States and Britain, even if it does not bulk as large as it does at the local level [. . .]

Table 5 What Citizens would do to Try to Influence their National Government; by nation

What citizens would do	US	UK	Germany	Italy	Mexico
Try to enlist aid of others Organize an informal group; arouse friends and neighbors, get them to write letters of protest or to sign a petition	29	18	7	6	18
Work through a political party	1	2	6	2	—
Work through a formal group (union, church, professional) to which they belong	4	3	7	2	3
Total percentage who would enlist others' aid*	32	22	19	10	20

What citizens would do	US	UK	Germany	Italy	Mexico
Act alone					
Directly contact political leaders (elected officials) or the press; write a letter to or visit a local political leader	57	44	12	7	8
Directly contact administrative (nonelected) officials	—	1	4	4	6
Consult a lawyer; appeal through courts	—	—	1	1	4
Vote against offending officials at next election	7	3	4	1	—
Take some violent action	—	—	2	1	4
Just protest	—	—	—	3	—
Other	—	2	—	2	3
Total percentage who would act alone**	42	40	18	18	18
Nothing	21	32	56	50	50
Don't know	4	6	7	22	12
Total percentage†	123	111	106	101	108
Total number of respondents	970	963	955	995	1007

* Total percentages are less than the total of the individual cells, since some respondents gave more than one answer.

** This row includes only the respondents who said they could do something but did not mention working with others. Hence the total is less than the sum of the individual cells, which contain respondents who may have mentioned both group and individual activity.

† Percentages exceed 100 because of multiple responses.

Reference

VERBA, S. (1961), *Small Groups and Political Behavior*, Princeton University Press.

14 J. P. Nettl

Consensus or Elite Domination: The Case of Business

Excerpts from J. P. Nettl, 'Consensus or elite domination',
Political Studies, vol. 13, no. 1, 1965, pp. 22–44.

This article attempts to demonstrate a general thesis from a particular segment of society. The general thesis is that the famous British consensus is not a sort of social or political ectoplasm which emanates from, and hovers over, the consentient, but a social institution with its own structure, procedures, attitudes, beliefs. Nor is it equally shared. Instead, like a magnet, it sucks in members (or servants) from the periphery – away from their own self-interested groupings. In doing so it emasculates these groups, while preserving their outward shell of autonomy and independence. Pressure group politics are therefore less 'real' than they seem – their very success in Britain, which has thrilled (American) political commentators searching for limited and orderly struggle as the highest form of organized democracy, may indeed depend on this element of shadow-boxing (Eckstein, 1960; Beer, 1956, 1957). It will be argued moreover that the consensus has its peculiar and particular exponent, both vehicle of consensus attitudes and ideal type – the higher civil service. It does not create the consensus, nor is it created by it; nonetheless it is the centre of its magnetic field, its institutional expression.

This general thesis is examined in the particular context of the business community in its relations with Whitehall. The relationship is discussed in its various aspects – social, procedural, structural, legal, and from the point of view of policy, public and sectional. The usual practice in such cases is to use the tunnel method: broad general proposition – particular and 'narrow' application including 'proof' – restatement of broad general proposition with 'proof' of the validity of the connection between the particular and the general. I shall be less orderly, shuttling back and forth from the general to the particular all the time. I believe the one makes no sense if divorced from the other, even for a short space of time.

It is a large subject and I can only sketch the problem in an article, ask more questions than I can answer and, even where an answer is attempted, indicate the manner of answering rather than provide the substantive answer itself. But perhaps this manner of approach will, if found valid, enable others to screw out answers from the intractable plethora of social relations in England.

Before we get down to any *relationship*, we must briefly examine the state of the related. I hope to show that as far as the business community is concerned, it is a state of remarkable weakness and diffuseness – compared, say, to organized labour or the professions. Lacking firm sense of their distinct identity, and belief in their distinct purpose, businessmen have been particularly vulnerable to the pressure of the consensus as emanating from Whitehall. (I have of course to show, and not merely to assume, the latter's strength and cohesiveness – indeed its very existence). The whole problem is largely virgin soil. There is a certain amount of factual material concerned with the structure and methods of government in order to be able to study its relations with the structure and methods of business. The new (in Britain) subject of pressure groups has again opened up certain aspects of business–government relations, but not in an exclusive sense; pressure groups are part of the political input process (in the broadest sense of 'political') in which business is an also-ran. Significantly the best detailed studies of pressure groups in Britain do not relate to business at all, but to professional organizations. Then there is the amorphous field known as 'economics', particularly policy and planning, in which government action on the economy has been discussed – the economy being a nameless, faceless, passive honeycomb of 'firms'. Finally business has been studied *per se* – with the government now in the role of faceless though active juggler of the parameters. Thus there is much incidental information on the relationship between government and business, but usually with the one serving as a vaguely limiting or activating factor of the other. No specific study of the dynamic, exclusive and precise relationship exists.

Nor, of course, has this relationship been used as evidence of wider social problems.

The image of business

Let us start with that mythical beast, the rugged entrepreneur: individualistic, non-conformist, aggressive, anti-social – the spider who sits at the centre of all the symmetrical webs of economists' models relating to perfect competition or the market economy. Historically, he is the product of ignorance and neglect; the government and the social forces behind it were hardly aware of his social or political existence until he had created his revolution – in the North, at the far end of the kingdom. For a long time, most of the legislation which took note of his existence was designed to inhibit him rather than positively to help those who worked for him, not to speak of helping him. The significant difference between the industrial revolution in England and elsewhere in Europe was the indifference of the central government, its failure for a long time to see any but undesirable consequences in what was happening – the ruin of agriculture. It seems to be a valid generalization in Europe that the later industrial take-off and drive to maturity took place, the greater the extent to which governments got in on the act. And, just as many of our constitutional forms relate to the eighteenth century – a gap bridged by myth – so does the popular picture of the businessman still portray the rugged individual with the Yorkshire accent, with his aggressive contempt for the bewildering allurements of wicked London. We still find him occasionally in the fiction best-sellers of the less sophisticated kind (*Room at the Top*); monotonously he croaks and snaps at us from the television screen and out of the pages of serialized fiction – where, incidentally, we must look primarily for the personalization of our more massive myths, not in the sophisticated novels of Iris Murdoch or C. P. Snow. Curiously enough we also find him deeply embedded in the common-law view of business, which holds that the only possible function of businessmen is to make money – and be very frugal about spending it.[1]

1. 'The directors must act *bona fide* in what they consider – not what the court may consider – is in the interests of the company', Lord Greene M.R. in *Re Smith* v *Fawcett* (1942) Ch. 304, 306. See also *Hogg* v *Cramp-*

Such a man dislikes and fears government and has as little as possible to do with it. A few real specimens of the type still exist, on sociological parole from Manchester and Bradford. But nowadays the rugged entrepreneur hardly exists any longer, and certainly is typical of nothing but a sentimental attachment to eccentricity. Why then does fiction predominate so grossly over fact? The reason is that this hundred-plus-year-old figure is in fact the only example of a specific business identity that we have. Nothing equally specific or exclusive has ever taken his place. There has, in fact, been a vacuum and he has survived in it. Nor is it an entirely accidental vacuum. The sturdy British businessman to whom successive Presidents of the Board of Trade refer – this is he; Harold Macmillan's reminder that exporting is fun could only have been nostalgically addressed to such as him – he being a man uncouth enough to derive satisfaction out of 'doing' foreigners. As a type the rugged entrepreneur exists largely in the mind of the remoter members of both political parties – and in popular fiction.

This is not an image that businessmen like or even accept, but the point is that try as they might, they have never been able to find a better common image with which to displace it. Literature has not helped. In England, unlike America, business novels are not a recognized literary form; business *characters* in novels do not usually rise above the grotesque antics of John Braine's Brown.[2] 'It is simply that here [in England] we know our audience. Any reading public is a tiny minority of the whole population; with us . . . the minority shares enough assumptions to be a good audience'.[3] And one of the assumptions shared is

thorn as discussed in *Journal of Business Law* (1964), pp. 51–53; also the note on commercial firms as potential patrons of the arts in *New Society* no. 83, 30 April 1964, p. 5, where Lord Greene's remarks are misquoted. The mandatory obligation on businessmen to act like businessmen is enhanced by the fact that their fiduciary duty is not to the shareholders (who might conceivably have notions of public interest) but to the company which by definition cannot have.

2. Of course there are stories about business families like *The Crowthers of Bankdam*, and businessmen – usually stereotyped – parade through many novels. But there is little interest in business as a social problem. An honourable exception is Anthony Trollope, *The Way We Live Now*.

3. C. P. Snow, 'Which Side of the Atlantic: The Writer's Choice', *New Statesman*, vol. 56 (1958) p. 287–8.

expressed by one of C. P. Snow's own fictional characters in *Strangers and Brothers*: 'I'm still convinced that successful business is devastatingly uninteresting'. The pathetic best that advertising has tried to do for business is the figure of the benevolent public benefactor (the bank manager who really looks like a doctor and family solicitor rolled into one, and apparently working for no fee) or the anonymous corporation whose only concern is working for the benefit of the public – and occasionally its employees.

Business in England thus lacks a social identity of its own. The effects are far-reaching. I have, in a different context, previously dealt with the *economic* impact of this problem on profit maximization (Nettl, 1957, p. 87). In our society there is a general and a more particular reason for this lack. The general reason – extending beyond business – is that while we like to think of ourselves as essentially 'individuals', and both admire as well as sustain the articulation of eccentricity – laughing at regimented nations like the Germans – the real social situation is precisely the other way about. It is the Germans who are educated and trained to accept individuality and loneliness – hence the Hegelian State as substitute father – while our education is towards group activity, public virtues, team spirit, and the fancy that we are sufficiently cohesive not to need such a state. Having a notion of the public good instilled into us, we do not need to search for it – it emerges. Having group identities *ab ovo* we do not need to create them artificially. Thus there are existing social cohesions which surpass the strength of any specific group identity for businessmen – or teachers or farmers or politicians. One is *either* a rugged individual entrepreneur *or* a public figure, full of public spirit and consensus illumination, who happens to spend working hours in a business firm (but could just as well do so elsewhere).

The more specific reason lies in our attitude to ascription of merit. We do not recognize 'separate but equal' or parallel careers; like the American Supreme Court – though with more success – we enforce integration, at least at the top. Our honours list is a general one, barely divided into civil and military at odd points; businessmen get the same honours as scientists, footballers, professors, politicians – and, most important, civil servants.[4] This applies to an OBE as much as to a peerage. In France, and even more in Germany and Austria, the business-man has, or had, until recently, his own hierarchy of status and honour. The British businessman thus competes for honours designed for entirely different social groups. He is expected, in return, to adopt some of the attitudes that go with, say, membership of the House of Lords – to follow the example of the more regular and 'normal' recipients of honours. The granting of honours – at least higher ones – thus becomes a cooption more than a reward. A well-known sub-category of the rugged entrepreneur in literature – charged with special functions of hilarity – is the rugged entrepreneur in ermine. I have always wondered whether the honours scandal under Lloyd George was not so much due to the manner of obtaining the peerages in question as the *continuing* 'rugged' and unreconstructed be-haviour of the recipients. Once more we have the well-known absorption effect of British society embracing the business world – but at a price of group self-effacement.[5]

It is an extraordinary and unique feature of British society that those considered worthy of higher bracket honours – a growing 'safety valve' category – should thereby be promoted to the legislature as well. A title can be a reward – and always was; appointment as royal counsellor was another reward for entirely different services, and one imposing obligations of service; only a special kind of philosophy assumes that both needs can be met with one and the same reward. A philosophy which assumes people – certain people – to be capable of playing a variety of quite different roles with equal distinction, and with-out conflict between one and the other. This notion necessarily reduces roles to the inferior status of a charade (a typically British game), limited and controlled by that obstinate, perva-sive insistence of the common good ('general will' if you like) emerging through all institutional and role disguises by virtue

4. cf. Marx's category of economic parasites (1883): 'King, priest, professor, prostitute, soldier, etc.' who 'draw their revenues by grace of their social function . . .'.

5. The sociological effect of, and justification for, the award of honours in different modern societies deserves more study, particularly the question whether honours (other than for valour) relate to the quality of persons or acts.

of – what? The public virtues of education, of team spirit, of social cohesion, in short of consensus.[6]

Consensus

This I believe to be the central mechanism of British society and its sub-function, government. The notion of a division of powers originated in this island, from where it was transported into the practice of the American constitution and the theory of Montesquieu. Here in the last 150 years it has been neither applied nor specifically contradicted, it has simply been gobbled up by the assumption that its positive benefits can somehow always be retained by the unique British capacity for charades. A civil servant can be a judge, a minister of the crown can be a legislator, a businessman can be a civil servant or tax collector, an arts graduate can be a science boss – providing he declares his role and providing he adopts the relevant procedures. Institutional and personal separation, the classical division of powers applied in America and . . . revived by De Gaulle in France, became an unnecessary (and unspoken) nuisance in Britain and was quietly but effectively emasculated. Today only lawyers and very old fashioned professors of government discuss it as a factor to be reckoned with. What counts are people – flexible, independent, selfless people able to fill any role with unblemished distinction. The only similar notion I have ever discovered elsewhere in the modern world is in the Soviet Union where party members are supposed to be equally able to tackle any assignment with the virtuosity of the allrounder (i.e. Communist).

In C. P. Snow's *The Masters* and again in *The Affair* there is a very pompous and irritating Master of a College, Crawford, who prefaces almost every one of his pontifical, uninteresting and usually obvious remarks with the phrase: 'Speaking now as a scientist' (or 'as a private individual' or 'as Master of the College' or 'as an impartial judge'). None of the characters

6. I now find that the theatrical analogy of roles and the dramaturgical method of analysis has already been very ably used by Goffman (1959). Though not immediately relevant to this political context, I can but assert in my own defence that this interesting work only came to my notice after this article had been completed.

in the book, or Snow himself, ever for one moment challenge his right to change hats in this fashion – for Crawford only says what others do without saying. A great critic has called *The Masters* 'a paradigm of political life' (Trilling, 1956, p. 130) – and so it is, for the roles and functions of the college officers are – and are intended to be – perfectly capable of transplantation into government, or for that matter into business. I make, incidentally, no apology for the frequent subpoena of C. P. Snow because he has lived in the stratosphere of the higher consensus and has tried to report it – in all its implications.

This then is the declaration of roles. In practice it operates very much as in literature. Only the English civil service and armed services have developed the special ghost category of 'acting' and 'temporary' positions, in which someone plays a superior role with all the attributes of the acquired rank save one – permanence (and partly pay). The impartial tribunal or commission, indiscriminately composed from among the higher consensus and confronted by the 'expert' (i.e. committed) witness, is another example of role-playing. Of course, experts sit on commissions or tribunals too, but those who become deeply committed (i.e. criticize the government too strongly) are often left to cool off in a commissionless tundra for a while. Unpaid magistrates, drawn from a very wide consensus list, are another example. And finally, as we shall see, most extraordinary and least known of all; businessmen 'regulating' their industry on a ministry's behalf[7] [. . .]

In emphasizing role-playing as the structural myth of the British Constitution or polity, I believe that I am close to the central lubricant of British political and social life, for this seems to be the explanation of how the system works, why it works at all. The whole institutional paraphernalia of functional differentiation has been vitiated or scrapped, yet we speak of Executive, Legislature and Judiciary as though they were distinct entities; we speak of business, the professions, government as though these were wholly separate worlds. To see the real potential of our constitution we need only look at daughter

7. It is curious that Britain, with its very real consensus, has no popular word for it – unlike nations where consensus is much less well established; cf. the Italian expression *la gente per bene*.

versions operated without our myths – Ghana or South Africa. Yet the role playing capacity of the amateur is a myth – unless the British really are a kind of *Herrenvolk*. All roles cannot be equal, one must dominate, for procedural reasons if no other, but more probably because, as Khrushchev has stated, no men are neutral. Just as every conversation between two people is a mild form of tussle for control, so every role played conflicts somewhere with another, played already or yet to be played. As an adequate political system charades, however well acted, are not good enough [. . .]

The consensus I have in mind is not . . . simply an emanation of some unique British quality – though it has something of that too. Nor is it just the product of conscious compromise and group self-denial. I believe that to have a consensus *at all*, you need an ideal type, a model of attitudes, procedures, institutions – an elite. This must not be socially so remote as to make emulation and effective entry impossible. You also need a vehicle that will effectively carry the consensus into society. In Britain this is the higher civil service. It has the access. Its methods, social and functional attitudes, values are being ever more widely adopted. It allocates honour and rewards much in accordance with its internal scale. It has all the strength of adulation in popular as well as sophisticated literature.[8]

Now from the general to the particular. As I have already stated, the relationship of government and business has not been examined in this context. On the input side (business to government) the student of politics has briefly identified pressure groups. On the output side (government to business) it has been the economists' pigeon. I believe, and will try to show, that in the social relationship between the institutions of government on the one hand and business on the other, the lack of social identity of the latter has been fostered, exploited and pre-empted by government (i.e. the civil service), and that this has led to something like schizophrenia in the world of business.

8. An examination of how the civil service came to play this role – how the consensus came to be created and how it is maintained – is outside the scope of this paper. Probably one of the key factors is the higher educational system – and the absence of social immersion in a continental or American type of compulsory military service. The army is part of the general consensus in Britain, not a separate establishment.

Structure

The first problem is a structural one. In a society which approves of growing economic regulation and on the whole sees its libertarian requirements fulfilled by checks on policy orientation through public discussion and a notion of popular representation or even mandate, the structure of administration will proliferate almost unseen. Contrary to the general belief implicit in an *ad hoc* philosophy of government, agencies are created not in the wake of urgent requirements but early on in the articulation of need; the *ad hoc* or higgledy-piggledy predilection is fulfilled by the informality, the untidy manner of their growth, and by the extraordinary unreason of their 'subordination' (*podchinenie*: the Soviet Russian word for the place at which any institution is hooked on to the hierarchical chart). But the point is that the growth of administrative and governmental structure takes place from the centre outwards, not inwards from the periphery. The need is central and the structural remedy universal.[9] With business particularly, the government's obligation (often statutory) to consult has led to the dilemma of having no one very obvious or representative to consult with. A planet cannot deal with satellites, it can only control them. Thus historically, we find ministries, especially the Board of Trade, encouraging the formation of representative industrial organizations and associations, especially during the time when government regulation of the economy was growing most rapidly. This was the period of the Second World War and the lean years immediately following, but it has continued ever since (PEP, 1957, pp. 31–45). As the need for contact between business and government grew, more industries organized for representational purposes; in many industries where representation was split or divided the relevant government department cajoled the industry into a representational structure which would make a suitably Procrustean bedfellow for itself. Representation was not of course the sole purpose of

9. Significantly the demand for structural remedies greatly outruns even the substantial supply. When well-known and self confessedly rebel intellectuals demand a Ministry of Leisure the social aspect of structural 'inflation' has clearly reached a very high level. So apparently rebellion consists, not of opposing government, but demanding the impossible from it.

organization, nor its only historic cause, and very often (as in the motor industry as well as in Calico Printing) internal regulatory or oligopolistic functions provided a structure on which representation could readily be superimposed. But the whole point about representation is that it is so largely government-sponsored – or at least government-encouraged; neither offensive nor defensive but essentially participatory.

Nothing shows this more clearly than the functional division of organizations; by industry, by product, by industrial process. It is a breakdown along technical lines. It is also a form of organization that unites what are essentially direct, complete, irreconcilable competitors at their most precise point of conflict. This aspect has almost entirely escaped attention. After all, industrial organization can be vertical as well as horizontal – above all it can be (and elsewhere often is) regional. And there are regional organizations in this country too, of very ancient vintage (Chambers of Commerce and Trade) but now with little power or representational influence.[10] Industry has a respectable regional tradition in this country; the fact that industrial associations do not follow a basically regional pattern seems to indicate the connection of associational purpose with government. Yet the form chosen (technical horizontal organization) happens also to be the most conducive to oligopoly and restraint of trade. This is part of the schizophrenia to which I shall return later. Meanwhile it is worth pointing out that this makes Britain uniquely comparable to countries with a false mythology of free trade covering what is in fact a highly organized market, like Switzerland or Austria – the most rigidly corporative economy of them all. The organizational emphasis is very similar; all that differs – a big difference though – is public policy.

That the flow of influence is greater from the government towards organized industry than from industry inwards can be

10. A curious example. Trade arbitration procedures were a traditional Chamber of Commerce preserve; now they are being increasingly handed over to the Trade Association concerned. Thus domestic contracts stipulate arbitration by the industrial association concerned in case of dispute, but foreign contracts more often still maintain the more respectable-looking procedure of arbitration led by the local Chamber of Commerce.

seen from the position of the very big corporations. In industries organized for defence or attack these would be the natural 'leaders' of the organization. In fact, they are no more than participants, whose size is reflected by the provision of services and personnel to the association rather than by any shouldering of combat responsibility. Firms like ICI and Lever Brothers in fact carry out a 'civil service' function for many of the associations to which they belong – with all the attributes of compromise and neutrality that this implies. ICI belongs to eighty associations, Lever to between forty and fifty. 'They are at pains to avoid dominating associations . . . [and] for large firms the benefits of membership are often difficult to define' (PEP, 1957, pp. 185, 240). PEP, the authors of these statements, recognize the predicament of such scattered membership for very large firms, and the difficulty of pinpointing the purpose of their membership. But they did not investigate the corollary: that none of these big firms use associations in order to talk to the government about their business concerns, nor does the government in order to talk to them. Membership of an association means participation in regulating the market (in the minority of cases where this is done); it always means a listening post with competitors; above all it is an additional means of government influence on industry as a whole – only the one big firm has then to be persuaded in its role as association 'uncle'.

The most flagrant example of colonization of 'big firms' by Whitehall – even without benefit of association – is the function of the joint stock banks as agents of the Bank of England. With little discretion or authority of their own, their job is to pass on applications, to sniff out transgressions – how right the French are to use the word *agents* for policemen – and to process inward demands for obvious irrelevance and unlikelihood of eventual acceptance. The result? Joint stock bank procedures mirror those of middle and lower-middle Whitehall. One wonders to what extent it is this that provides a rapidly growing market for Merchant Bankers.[11]

11. During the credit squeeze of 1958–9, the Joint Stock banks adhered fairly rigidly to Government guidance about credit limits, while the Merchant Banks were able to increase their clientele by a less severe interpretation of credit self-discipline.

Business divides into two; firms large enough to deal smoothly and regularly with government direct, and the atomized world which can only articulate or be addressed through an organization. Differences in size caked with an egalitarian philosophy unrealizable in practice (equality before the law etc.) are anyhow conducive to schizophrenia and this built-in class difference between a direct and an indirect-collective approach to government only enhances it. One has to have been in industry to appreciate the occasional humiliations involved for the medium-sized firm – for instance in being told by Whitehall with a slight (and falsely modest) frown: 'We seem to recollect dealing with this point in correspondence with your association's Mr. Snooks a little while ago. . . .' Not that access is denied to smaller firms; it is the gentle reminder that one has come and disturbed unnecessarily, and the difficulty of finding the right man in Whitehall in the first place. Dealing with Whitehall is a professional business, or rather an institutional one; odd occasional visitors have neither status nor privilege. Only associations and very large firms can institutionalize their Whitehall contacts.

The extent to which industrial associations take over governmental functions – and are universally understood to do so – becomes clear from this rather smug sentence: 'The (government) department knows that a reputable association would not take up a case unless the *responsible officers* of the association believed that it should be pressed' (*Report of the Committee of Intermediaries* (March 1950), Cmd 7904, p. 50). Responsible – to whom?

Procedure

Procedures correspond to the charade rules. It is said that the difference between White and Indian in South America is not race, colour, religion, or even class; it is the manner of living, the role. One 'lives' white or Indian. Similarly in this country one 'acts' like a civil servant. No one will challenge the existence of informal but well-defined civil service procedures. There are no business procedures to compete with them.

Now it may be said that civil service procedures are optimal, the product of large size and great experience, and that to say there are no business procedures to compete with them is merely to admit the predominance of the best over the second best. There may indeed be such a thing as optimal procedure for large organizations and they may conceivably even apply equally to government and industry (but surely not necessarily)— in America, however, it is business that claims to originate and develop them, and is usually admitted to do so. We have, therefore, a double problem. Whether business calls for the same procedures as government (no one claims judicial and administrative procedures to be similar or substitutable; indeed it is mainly by procedure that Crawford the civil servant can be distinguished from Crawford the judge) I am not competent to answer. The other problem is the direction of procedural influence. In this country it is clearly outwards, government to business.

There seem to be at least two main factors. In explaining government policy to 'our people' association officials increasingly use government terminology and methods. They are, after all, temporary civil servants for much (an increasing part) of the time. They see and hear from their opposite numbers in Whitehall much more frequently than many of their own members. In many associations the proportion of the industry represented is small, the proportion who participate actively in the affairs of the association even smaller. The 'permanent' association officials (how they do get re-elected) are solicitors or accountants. The *Lorelei* appeal of the predictable and well-mannered Whitehall methods has a great and often natural appeal. They will bargain hard for the industry's obvious interests where these are clearly threatened – or can in some way be indentified (this question belongs to public policy) but it is through the small change of regular contact that Whitehall exercises its influence. And this small change is essentially procedural. Where civil servants with real if not official powers to negotiate 'cannot commit their ministers to more than this', businessmen with equally real powers 'cannot commit their boards to less than that'. The one is the consequence of the other. Thus the board of directors becomes the businessman's deterrent in response to the procedural strategy of Whitehall. The validity of the pre-war distinction between 'officials' and 'unofficials' has largely disappeared (Dale, 1941, p. 180). The weapon of constitutional *non possumus,* with which American diplomats used to ward off dangerous foreign commitments by conjuring up an implacable Senate, has become an everyday fiction in the relationship between government and business.

The second factor arises from the situation that Whitehall has a distinct social identity and business has not. The value of official procedures is not only based on performance but on ascription – which, sociologists keep telling us, has an obstinate capacity for survival in an otherwise increasingly achievement-orientated society. I have attended at least half a dozen lectures by senior business negotiators on 'how to deal with government' – and while these lectures purported to be technical, they were in fact social: restraint, moderation, give-and-take, 'never over-state your case'. All the lecturers were phenomenally agreed (consensus). And the ideal type that emerged from their revealed wisdom was the precise opposite of the rugged entrepreneur. It is not merely that if you want things from government you have to follow its methods of going about its business, but the secondary spread of these habits into the internal conduct of business – especially in large firms. For instance, the rapid growth in the functions and status of secretaries, the impersonal award of status symbols and privileges to go with the job and not the individual, the vital destruction of the old business principle of dealing whenever possible with the boss – all are Whitehall habits.

Finally we must differentiate these contacts between government and business as regulator and regulated from those of government as purchaser or seller with industry as supplier or consumer. The charade will have it that here – and here only – commercial considerations must apply. Civil servants are under constant pressure to act as businessmen, as rugged entrepreneurs. In fact they are expected to outdo businessmen at their own profession.[12] It is here that the latent role conflict inherent in charades – usually subsumed only by the admitted recogni-

12. In this connection the recent Ferranti case sheds much light on the attitude of the civil service towards its own members acting as purchasers. One of the Ministry of Defence's shortcomings was its failure to estimate correctly the profit ratio of the firm supplying the weapons system. Not even the sharpest tycoon is expected to know that much about his suppliers.

tion of the postulated 'public interest' – comes out into the open. Businessmen in the role of civil servants must, to be successful, be wholly committed to their role – and even as businessmen they are often expected to behave *à la façon de* Whitehall – but civil servants in the role of businessmen must outdo businessmen and yet not cease to be civil servants. That surely is the essence of the implied philosophy behind the Nationalized Industries in Britain; the combination of business acumen and efficiency with public accountability and all the glare of publicity – a combination that is in fact a conflict. Especially in recent times the commercial rationality has been emphasized more strongly than ever, yet it has been matched by greater demands for parliamentary control (Committee on Nationalized Industries). Beeching has to make his profit – but at the same time follow the tortuous system of consultations and public appeals against his decisions.

Yet contacts between civil service and industry must not on the other hand become too loose and informal. Fourteen years ago a select committee examined the structure of commercial contact with government in detail, with special reference to the temporary problem of administering post-war scarcity (*Report of the Committee on Intermediaries*, March 1950, Cmd 7404). On the subject of our problem, the committee had nothing but praise for the logic of industrial association. 'As the scope and extent of government activity . . . has increased, it has been only natural for the government to consult bodies which it knew *to be representative* of the interests which government activity increasingly affected (p. 43).

The social aspect

Important as it is, the social aspects of any confrontation between structured groups are the most difficult to identify behind and around the more formal aspects of institutions and procedure. I can offer little evidence other than direct observation and – yet again – the informal illuminations of literature. But as this social aspect is central to my argument I am bound to try and deal with it.

The division between big business (plus business negotiators and administrators) and small business is most noticeable in social terms. Within firms like the ICI, Lever and the big oil companies, there is an immense hierarchical break between the centre and the periphery (main board and divisions in ICI, main board and subsidiary boards in Lever, main board and field units in the oil companies). I well remember an immensely successful ICI divisional sales director, enlivened by alcohol, explaining that he had everything – power, salary, perks – except the slightest chance of promotion to main board. 'As a successful sales director I am not the type.' And he wasn't. *In whisky veritas* he saw his disability not in terms of capacity or technical education, but as a social bar. Yet it was not simply a matter of 'class' but a matter of his capacity for playing the essential charades. As sales director he was expected to play at (and with) rugged entrepreneurs; this was one role that could not be combined with the easy flexibility required at the centre. In his own words, he 'was not the sort ever to be *persona grata* in Whitehall'.

So he and many others are shunted off into the 'expense account' world. This is *not* the top of the business pyramid, as is often believed (largely by academics) but the resting place of those who will never get to the top. Insidiously the tax system and the philosophy behind it, which have created the expense account world, recognize the consolation aspect; they despise it and yet permit it, almost as necessary sop for social deprivation. Thus I think most senior civil servants would privately agree with Titmuss about the inequitable distortion of our tax laws, but underlying this disapproval of the expense account mentality is a feeling of relief at the diversion of the wild beasts into hedonistic channels instead of those of social or (still worse) political ambition. The 'top' businessmen would never be seen dead at a typical expense account establishment – and those few who choose to be seen there alive often get their come-uppance with a savagery out of all proportion to any technical offence which they may have committed (Sir Bernard Docker). The rugged entrepreneur – the real one – would not go there either, and would not be expected to go. The ostentatious expense account businessman is really a social deviant, assisted by specially framed tax laws. It is curious how the real expense account industries (Films, Ladies' fashions) are still socially taboo.[13]

Again I have found that members of (and aspiring candidates to) main boards move socially in Whitehall circles to a remarkable extent. The consensus operates even more strongly in silence (socially) than in speech (politically). Unlike America or Germany, where social entertainment is professionally enclosed all the way up the pyramid, it opens out in England to that platform where everyone can play charades – and where people are 'themselves' only in their own homes. It would be invidious to give names, but all the top businessmen I know would never move in what they would describe as 'business' circles (except bankers who alone have a recognizable social identity of their own, and move in something called 'bankers' circles', but which in turn are permeated by Whitehall mores). Perhaps the best way of obtaining a grip or focus on the imprecise is to study its negation; the sons of the rugged entrepreneurs (thrift) support and drive forward the teenage consumption boom (spendthrift); the offsprings of the higher consensus, including top businessmen (public spirit) wear jeans and help motivate the total negation of consensus (extreme egocentricity).[14] There emerges an ideal type of personality representing this upper social platform of consensus – immaterial whether he be lawyer, civil servant, doctor, don, or businessman. One of the rare British novels interested in this problem of the indifference of profession compared to the importance of the role, a novel which emphasizes the ability of the ideal type to substitute one role for another with equal success, describes the type like this – through the eyes of a jeans-wearing detractor: 'London man, 1959, middle to upper class, brain worker . . . but functional, entirely functional . . . only this is what makes him interesting' (Norwood, 1960, p. 232). And from the inside, from the platform

13. The expense account businessman is in a different position under the common law, which traditionally reflects the consensus of role expectations of the day before yesterday. 'There are to be no cakes and ale except such as are required for the benefit of the Company.' *Per* Bowen L. J. in *Hutton* v *West Cork Ry.* (1883) 23 Ch. D. 654 at p. 674, Court of Appeal. This is still quoted as official doctrine.

14. For this eminently respectable social-psychological thesis see e.g. Lasswell (1959 pp. 3–18), also Huntington (1962, pp 63–64).

itself, comes this demand on the consensus member: the businessman who wants to be heard in Whitehall must 'moderate the direct selfish interests which it is his duty to promote by a decent sense of his obligations to the community at large'.[15]

It is obvious that the consensus is not one of organic growth, of fusion; it is essentially the role of the public servant, of Upper Whitehall, that dominates it. 'Public interest', the sense of the community at large, is their peculiar property, goes naturally with the job, but it does not go naturally with business – indeed the rugged entrepreneur is almost by definition barred from suffusion by it. The extreme disparity of roles demanded here must produce either schizophrenia or the more common phenomenon of ceasing altogether to be a businessman and simply becoming a civil servant in business. It is this latter drift which has caused the frequent ministerial (mostly Tory) wails against a background of dollar crises and relatively declining exports: 'What has happened to the traditional (sturdy, aggressive, etc.) British businessman?'[16]

As in the case of the nationalized industries, charades do not apparently trouble the consensus member called upon to play entrepreneur. The obvious example is the large number of senior civil servants who not only join industry (at main board level of course) but fit the role beautifully. The only recent case of incompatibility was that of Lord Mancroft (a former junior minister) – and it was his company that was incompatible (with their 'commercial' viewpoint and their rash statements in public), not Lord Mancroft (with his restraint, his anonymity, his conscience). In fact, stripping away all racial and religious overtones, we are left with widespread public assumptions about the compatibility or incompatibility of the roles of Lord Mancroft as director of a strongly Zionist group of firms, and Lord Mancroft as director of a neutral and hopefully ubiquitous international insurance company. More explicitly, the same problem was ventilated by the Bank Rate Tribunal examining the impartiality of Keswick's roles. But perhaps the most re-

15. Street, Chairman of the Cotton Board (1959, p. 1), and quoted by Grove (1962, p. 145).
16. Compare the same preoccupation, but with a different emphasis and analysis, by Balogh (1959 p. 93 ff).

markable example of the expected capacity of consensus role-players is the case of Dr Beeching, invited to leave the ICI main board and outdo all rugged entrepreneurs at rugged entrepreneurship in publicly owned British Railways, and in the course of executing public policy to make the railways pay. For he is not a rugged entrepreneur at all, but a consensus figure acting like one – by order. We have already noted the curious lacuna in consensus attitudes where the government's commercial operations are concerned [. . .]

Conclusion

Though specially strong in Great Britain, the notion of consensus is not uniquely British. It is a feature of all sophisticated societies. But the first problem is: whose consensus? For consensus is not so much the product of compromise as of elite ascendancy and its acceptance. In Britain it is, I maintain, presently a Whitehall consensus. It was not always so. But the political emasculation of the aristocracy as a condition of its survival, together with the remarkable decline of importance of formal politics (House of Commons, Party conferences, grass roots) in favour of the executive and its chief, the Prime Minister, have led to the quiet emergence of the Snowmen, the upper civil servants and their mores. Their influence on the professions was socially logical and predestined, their influence over business a more drawn-out and difficult process. Efforts are being made to draw in the Trade Unions and the arts, though with only limited success as yet.

In America it is just the other way about. There is consensus too (though weaker) and it comes *from* the business community.[17] Top businessmen join the administration – not to be businessmen (like Beeching) but to be administrators (Macnamara). When Americans think of 'organization' or 'administration', they visualize big business as often as government, at least they did until the end of the last war. Significantly the dichotomy

17. The most up-to-date and suggestive study of this problem in the United States is Bauer *et al.* (1963). See also Lowi (1964, pp. 677–715). I think this book bears out my general thesis very well (see pp. 150, 209 on consensus, and p. 125 on location of elite).

individual/organization in American fiction is a business problem, from Dreiser to Marquand; it was not until the McCarthy era that Merle Miller first used government as the personality-crushing octopus of fiction.[18] Not that the theory of organization meets with universal approval in literature; the optimal view is size and growth *plus* a 'mood of nostalgic reverie for the company town, the home of paternalistic order, domestic virtue and productive work . . . assumptions – far from being 'capitalistic' or contemporary – are actually Populist and Veblenian' (Larrabee and Riesman, 1957, pp. 236–7). There is here a view of business as a social philosophy and both nostalgic 'good' and contemporary 'bad' are more sophisticated – and a much more popular subject for fiction – than the rugged North country millowner of Britain.

In American fiction and in European fact, the choice is between the individual and the corporation – with a happy ending ensuring the triumph of the former (integrity) over the latter (corruption) – or his utter degradation. Only in the English novels of C. P. Snow do the needs of individual and organization have to be reconciled; justice for the former, respectable self-preservation for the latter. The Continent has been fascinated by Snow's proposition, indeed by the whole 'typically English' problem. There the consensus (in so far as it exists) is not concerned either with business or with administration but with questions of political philosophy; business and government are – and are expected to be – in a state of permanent friction, fighting and subverting each other (influence is too polite a word).

I think only Sweden can fairly be compared with Britain. Those, like Gunnar Myrdal, who believe that consensus, self-regulation and widespread charades are the hope of civilized democracy (with perhaps more tolerant public policies in the international 'state of nature') put Sweden first as an example, then Britain. But it seems to me that this system is in many ways a self-denying ordinance, which Switzerland and Sweden have

18. Miller, *The Sure Thing*, 1952. The title of a businessman's reminiscences of Washington – Merson, 'My education in Government' (1954) – where he compares 'Expediency v. Efficiency: a businessman's misadventures in the Eisenhower administration'. I owe this, and two other American references, to my colleague Professor Millgate, now of Toronto.

accepted (one might suggestively for once list the things these countries have to do *without*) but for which this country is not yet ready. For Britain, the austere consensus at home is not at all austere in the field of international relations, public policy still demands greatness (at least the equipment that goes with it). Hence the importance of the essentially British make-believe of charades, propagated and best played by Whitehall [. . .]

References

BALOGH, T. (1959), 'The apotheosis of the dilettante', in H. Thomas (ed.), *The Establishment*, London.

BAUER, R. A., DE SOLA POOL, I., and DEXTER, L. A. (1963), *American Business and Public Policy: The Politics of Foreign Trade*, New York.

BEER, S. H. (1956), 'Pressure groups and parties in Britain', *Amer. Polit. Sci. Rev.*, March.

BEER, S. H. (1957), 'Representation of interests in British government', *Amer. Polit. Sci. Rev.*, September.

DALE, H. E. (1941), *The Higher Civil Servant in Britain*, London.

ECKSTEIN, H. (1960), *Pressure Group Politics: The Case of the British Medical Association*, London.

GOFFMAN, E. (1959), *The Presentation of Self in Everyday Life*, Allen Lane The Penguin Press.

GROVE, J. W. (1962), *Government and Industry in Britain*, Longmans.

HUNTINGTON, S. P. (ed.) (1962), 'The garrison-state hypothesis today', in *Changing Patterns of Military Politics*, Free Press.

LARRABEE, E., and RIESMAN, D. (1957), 'Company-town pastoral: the role of business' in *Executive Suite*, in Rosenberg and White (eds), *Mass Culture: The Popular Arts in America*, Free Press.

LASSWELL, H. D. (1959), 'Political constitution and character', *Psychoanalysis and Psychoanalytic Review*, vol. 46, pp. 3–18.

LOWI, T. J. (1964), Review in *World Politics*, vol. 16, no. 4, July.

MARX, K. (1883), *Das Kapital*, translated Untermann, 1906, Kerr.

MERSON, M. (1954), 'My education in government', the *Reporter*, 7 October.

MILLER, M. (1952), *The Sure Thing*, New York.

NETTL, J. P. (1957), 'A note on entrepreneurial behaviour', *Rev. Econ. Stud.*, vol. 24, no. 2.

NORWOOD, P. (1960), *Prizegiving*, London.

PEP (1957), *Industrial Trade Association*, London.

SNOW, C. P. (1958), 'Which side of the Atlantic: the writer's choice', *New Statesman*, vol. 56, pp. 287–8.

STREET, Sir R. (1959), 'Government consultation with industry', *Public Administration*, Spring.

TRILLING, L. (1956), *A Gathering of Fugitives*, Secker & Warburg.

15 J. W. Grove

The Collective Organization of Industry

Excerpts from 'The collective organization of industry', in J. W. Grove, *Government and Industry*, Longmans, ch. 5, 1962, pp. 125–161.

Introductory

The complexity of the central government's departmental organization . . . matches the diversity of the economy that it is designed to guide and direct. But the 'economy' is not simply an accumulation of separate business enterprises, a collection of individual employers, managers, workers, and farmers. It is also a very large number of organizations whose business it is to represent the common interests of whole industries and trades, crafts and professions, skills and technologies. Today, the economy is honeycombed by associations and it is through them, to an important extent, that the actions of the central government are shaped. This section gives a short account of their nature and functions, and their role in relation to national economic policy and administrative procedures.

Forms of organization

No classification of these variegated forms can ever be wholly satisfactory, but we may identify four important categories. The most important, in the present context, are the *sectional groups*, so called because they represent (or purport to represent) the special interests of sections of economic life, and are distinguished by the fact that they are all based on identity of industrial, or commercial, or professional, or vocational interest. They include *trade unions* and *trade associations*, representing the traditional distinction between labour and capital; *vocational associations* that bring together groups of 'workers by hand and brain' but are not primarily trade unions; and what may be called, for want of a better name, *technical associations*, bodies that are concerned with advancing the science and art of industrial and trade processes, but, unlike trade associations, are not immediately concerned with the commercial or financial interests of their members. Some of these bodies – the National Federation of Building Trades' Employers and the Transport and General Workers' Union are well known, at least by name, to the public. Others – such as the Eel and Pie Traders' Association – are perhaps more obscure, but not necessarily less important in their own field.

The second category consists of *geographical groups*, bodies that exist to promote the development of industry and trade in a particular geographical area, regional or local. Some of these – Chambers of Commerce and Chambers of Trade, for instance – are akin to trade associations; others – like, the Industrial Development Associations – are very different.

Thirdly, there are a number of national *peak associations*, like the Association of British Chambers of Commerce and the Federation of British Industries, which draw together a whole range of sectional or geographical associations, and sometimes both.

Finally, there are *pressure groups* properly so called:[1] bodies that exist, in some cases exclusively, to advocate certain lines of public economic policy, and draw their members, not from specific sectional or geographical areas, but from a wider community. They are usually based on acceptance of a political programme rather than on identity of economic or local or regional interest, and they represent general attitudes rather than sectional views. Sectional and geographical groups and their national peak associations may, and frequently do, act as pressure groups, but that is not their sole, or even their main, purpose.

Sectional groups

1. The term *trade association* covers many types of activity. The Restrictive Trade Practices Act of 1956 defines it as 'a body of

1. The term 'pressure group' defines a class of activity rather than a species of association, and is not, in any case, a particularly happy term because of its emotive overtones; 'attitude group' is perhaps a better label for this kind of association.

persons (whether incorporated or not) which is formed for the purpose of furthering the trade interests of its members or of persons represented by its members' (sec. 6 (8)).

Included in this category are employers' associations – a term usually reserved for trade associations whose sole object, or one of whose principal objects, is to negotiate with trade unions about wages and conditions of work; but it should be noted that a trade association is not necessarily or exclusively an organization of employers. It is an association of business enterprises rather than of individual persons (though as usual there are one or two exceptions),[2] but, outside manufacturing industry, the typical business enterprise may be the one-man or family business, and many trade associations include such businesses in their membership (e.g. the National Federation of Ironmongers).

No complete census exists, and because of difficulties of definition it would not be an easy matter to take one, but there are some partial indicators. PEP, in its report on trade associations (1957), lists some 1300 associations in manufacturing industry, known to be operating in 1956; but, with a few exceptions, this figure excluded local and regional bodies. The Ministry of Labour Directory of Employers' Associations enumerates roughly two thousand national, regional, and local employers' associations; these include some associations on the PEP register (i.e. those national associations in manufacturing industry that have collective bargaining as one of their functions), but no record is available of associations that are neither employers' associations nor concerned with manufacturing industry.

Nor, even, is there any reliable estimate of numbers. The figure usually quoted is 2500, but this is taken from a PEP broadsheet published as long ago as 1944;[3] it was a very rough guess based on a sample which the authors admit was biased. From random inspection of commercial directories and lists of

2. E.g. the National Chamber of Trade, a national federation of trade associations and firms which also includes a large number of individuals among its members.

3. The sample included a high proportion of manufacturers' as against other types of association.

bodies offering evidence to official committees of inquiry, it is fairly certain that the figure is much larger than this. But this is of no great importance; what is important is that there are today few sectors of the economy, however small – whether in manufacturing or extractive industry, wholesale or retail trade, the consumer services, transport and communications, banking, insurance, or finance – without at least one representative association. The only major exception in manufacturing and extractive industry, for example, is the oil industry.

The pattern of trade association organization is intricate. Associations are organized in various ways: on the basis of product, process used in manufacture, or type of business or service provided. Local associations may be affiliated to regional or national associations and sometimes to both; national associations may join with others in federations or confederations claiming to represent the whole or large sections of a single industry or trade, or a group of related industries and trades. Associations representing different sectors of industry or trade but having certain aims in common may affiliate to one another. A few associations integrate producers, wholesalers and retailers and sometimes importers and exporters as well. The pattern is further complicated by overlapping in coverage and by multiple- and cross-membership, so that a firm may belong to several trade associations directly and to many more indirectly through affiliation. In manufacturing industry large firms producing a number of commodities may belong to two, three or even a dozen or more different associations.[4]

Associations vary tremendously in strength, in size of membership (both absolutely and in relation to the total number of available businesses), in wealth, and in the number of staff employed. In some cases, a high proportion of the available businesses are non-members; in others there is almost a one hundred per cent 'shop'. Some large associations employ a considerable private bureaucracy and are highly organized, conducting their business through an elaborate structure of councils and committees; others, even quite large ones, run their

4. Imperial Chemical Industries belongs to about eighty trade associations, Lever Brothers to about fifty, the Co-operative Wholesale Society to about seventy.

affairs very informally and with little paid assistance. The largest employ from two to three hundred people, including perhaps (depending on the nature of the association) professional engineers, accountants, architects, and solicitors, and their annual incomes run into six figures. But the majority of associations are small. Some are little more than organizations 'on paper'. They meet infrequently, employ a firm of accountants or solicitors, another trade association, or the local Chamber of Commerce to do their secretarial work, and have an annual income of a few pounds.

Functions are equally varied. All trade associations provide a forum for the exchange of information and discussion of common problems; all give some attention, and most devote a great deal of attention, to mutual defence, and to the representation of their collective interests to outsiders – particularly to government departments, nationalized boards, local authorities, and other public bodies, but also to other industries, trades and businesses. 'Representation' is probably the most important of the services they offer, except for the rather special class of employers' associations[5] which exist primarily to bargain with employees and to deal with related labour matters like welfare, training schemes, and workmen's compensation. Many industrial associations provide common services, including cooperative advertising, the organization of trade fairs and exhibitions, and the collection and publication of statistics and trade intelligence. Some provide protective services in the form of trademark registration, the sharing of information about customers' credit, legal advice, the conduct of litigation on behalf of members, and the settlement of disputes between members by private conciliation or arbitration. Others, again, provide (sometimes with government support) services intended to improve efficiency and productivity in the industry, including cooperative research, standardization of products, and the improvement of quality and design. Only a shrinking minority operate restrictive

5. Some sections of industry possess both a general trade association and an employers' association. To take an example at random, in the shipbuilding industry the Shipbuilding Conference is the main national trade association, the Shipbuilding Employers' Federation is the employers' association.

trading agreements because the agreements of manufacturing and distributing associations (though not all trade associations) are now subject to the Restrictive Trade Practices Act 1956. These must be registered, and may be scrutinized and terminated by the Restrictive Practices Court, and many are being abandoned voluntarily.

2. In law, a *trade union* may be either an association of workers or an association of employers, but in everyday usage the distinction between a trade union and a trade association is perfectly clear. According to the official definition used by the Ministry of Labour a trade union is

an organization of employees – including those of salaried and professional workers, as well as those of manual wage-earners – which is known to include among its functions that of negotiating with employers with the object of regulating conditions of employment.

This is a serviceable definition, but it does not clearly distinguish a trade union from the many vocational associations that do not actually exclude a concern about conditions of employment even though they are not continuously engaged in negotiations with employers.

Like trade association organization, the structure of the trade union movement is extremely complex. There are about 650 unions, but the field is dominated by the largest unions, which are predominantly general and industrial unions, though they include some very large craft unions like the boiler-makers' and the building trades workers'. The seventeen largest unions account for about 70 per cent of the membership.[6] The medium-sized unions are mostly craft unions, the oldest form of union. The 300 smallest unions have less than half of 1 per cent of the total membership, and if 'small' is defined as 'having less than 5000 members', over 520 unions are small. Only thirty-six unions have a membership of more than 50,000. The trend towards bigness, of which the formation in 1945 of the National Union of Mineworkers and the amalgamation in 1947 of two

6. The big six (the Transport and General Workers' Union, the National Union of General and Municipal Workers, the Amalgamated Engineering Union, the National Union of Mineworkers, the National Union of Railwaymen, and USDAW) have between them about half the membership of the movement.

large unions to form the Union of Shop, Distributive and Allied Workers may stand as examples, has been accompanied by the growth of federations of unions in various industries, importantly, in shipbuilding, engineering and the building trades, usually for joint action in bargaining with employers' federations,[7] even though the federating unions may retain their autonomy for other purposes [. . .] On the whole, however, the largest industry trade unions, like the largest industry trade associations,[8] tend to devolve considerable powers on to 'sections' representing the interests of the members in particular parts of the industry.

Little is publicly known about the representativeness of trade associations beyond the fact that some associations have a more inclusive membership than others; the representativeness of trade unions, on the other hand, is public knowledge, at least in general terms. Rather more than half of all men employees and rather less than a quarter of all women employees are members of a trade union, according to Ministry of Labour figures. Total trade-union membership is estimated at about $9\frac{1}{2}$ million, or about 40 per cent of the working population. The extent of unionism varies greatly in different sections of the economy. The mineworkers are the most highly unionized with a trade-union membership of over 90 per cent, and they are closely followed by the railwaymen, the shipbuilding workers, and workers in the printing trades, all with around 80 per cent. In many industries the percentage varies between 40 per cent and 60 per cent, and in the distributive trades and some of the consumer services it is less than 20 per cent. In a few cases it is less than 10 per cent. In general, as might be expected, it is much greater in manufacturing industry than in occupations like agriculture and the distributive trades where the organization of workers is exceptionally difficult; but it is less than 50 per cent in a number of important manufacturing industries, including not only textiles which employ many women, but also chemicals in which employment is almost entirely

7. E.g. the Confederation of Shipbuilding and Engineering Unions which brings together thirty-eight unions for cooperation in collective bargaining.
8. E.g. the British Iron and Steel Federation, and the Food Manufacturers' Federation. There are many others.

male. Of the 12½ to 13 million non-unionists (of whom about 6 million are women) probably about 4¼ million are employed in manufacturing, including the manufacture of food, drink and tobacco, with a further 1¼ million in building, civil engineering, and transport. The general trend of trade-union membership over the past two decades, when conditions have been exceptionally favourable for the trade-union organizer, indicates that there is likely to be a permanent majority of non-unionists in industry.

Some unions, like some trade associations, have large permanent staffs; but most unions employ no more than an organizing secretary and a few typists. In general, the trade union bureaucracy is small in relation to the size of the membership: the ratio of full-time officials to members is about one in nine hundred, compared with about one in three hundred in the United States. Trade-union secretaries are paid much less than trade association secretaries. It has been said that no other organization with the possible exception of the churches places so much reliance on voluntary effort.

Apart from their primary function of collective bargaining, trade unions provide many services for their members. Their friendly society activities are still of substantial importance (friendly benefits in recent years have totalled roughly £4–4½ million a year, or about a third of all trade-union expenditure). Like trade associations, unions may engage in restrictive practices to protect their members' status and bargaining power. Some unions have even supported the trade associations in their industry in operating agreements restricting competition. Recently, many unions have turned their attention to problems formerly left to management, such as industrial efficiency and productivity, often (as with trade associations) at the request of the government. Their representational functions are, within their own field, hardly less important today than those of trade associations; and some unions, like the miners' and engineers', have a long history of political action. In the nature of things, however, a great deal of business with government on labour matters affects organized labour as a whole and is channelled through the TUC.

3. Side by side with trade associations, employers' associations,

and trade unions, there now exist hundreds of voluntary associations (the exact number is not known) representing the socially recognized professions, vocations seeking recognition as professions, and groups with a common interest in a particular branch of technology or expertise. These *vocational and technical associations* are very diverse in character; generalization is difficult; and it is seldom easy to place a body firmly in one category [...]

Geographical groups

There is often very little in their functions to distinguish Chambers of Commerce from a great many trade associations, and some Chambers (for example, the Manchester Chamber of Commerce) tend to be identified with the industry that predominates, or has predominated in the past, in their locality. Their distinguishing characteristics lie not in their methods or in the services they provide but in the fact that they aim to draw together all the commercial interests of a large city or town and its surrounding area. They usually claim to speak for 'all sections of the industrial and commercial community'. Chambers of Trade are similar, in principle, but mostly represent small-scale private enterprise; they concern themselves with local affairs and with the impact on local affairs of national administration, rather than with national economic policy.

The trade unions might be said to possess a similar form of organization in local trades councils. These bodies (of which there are now about five hundred, grouped in some two dozen county federations) bring together local branches of large unions and small local unions in each industrial area. But, though historically of great importance (they were at one time the main agencies through which the Labour Representation Committee, and later the Labour Party, worked in the constituencies) they are now relatively insignificant politically, and they have no influence whatever on national policy in the trade-union movement, though they occasionally act informally as a kind of regional organization for the TUC.

Apart from local bodies of this sort, there are a variety of organizations which cover wider areas and usually have more specialized aims, drawing their members from firms, trade associations, Chambers of Commerce and Trade, trade unions, and local authorities alike. Among them are the Industrial Development Associations, which try to attract industry to their area and advertise its advantages. They sponsor economic and social research, and act as pressure groups, lobbying and drawing public attention to the needs of the community. Typical examples are the Mid-Wales Industrial Development Association, the North-East Development Association, and the Lancashire and Merseyside Industrial Development Association. These bodies grew up in the 1920s and 1930s, and for a time the 'industrial development movement' enjoyed some prestige; but it now seems to be suffering a decline. On the other hand, several important national bodies have made their appearance: the Scottish Council (Development and Industry), the Scottish Tourist Board, the Welsh Economic Development Council, and the Development Corporation for Wales.

Peak associations

The oldest of the national 'peak' associations, the *Association of British Chambers of Commerce,* has a membership of about a hundred Chambers of Commerce in the United Kingdom. These are mostly found in the larger towns and cities. This gives the Association a nominal membership of something like sixty thousand firms, but about a quarter of these firms are members of the London Chamber of Commerce, and about half of them are accounted for by the London, Manchester, and Birmingham Chambers. A number of large trade associations are represented on the governing council of the ABCC; these include the Chamber of Shipping, the National Farmers' Unions, the British Bankers' Association, and the British Insurance Association. *The National Chamber of Trade* links at the national level about nine hundred local Chambers of Trade, smaller Chambers of Commerce and similar bodies. Some thirty or forty national trade associations are 'allied' to it.

The two major peak associations in manufacturing industry are the *Federation of British Industries* [now known as the Confederation of British Industries] and the *National Union of Manufacturers*. The former links together about three hundred trade associations, and some seven thousand individual firms are also members. Though the Federation speaks mainly for big industry, and its governing councils are dominated by the 'millionaire industrialists' (most of the largest firms and the major associations are members), about 40 per cent of its membership, it is said, consists of firms employing less than a hundred workers. The NUM, on the other hand, stands for free enterprise, and speaks, unequivocally, with the voice of the small and medium-size firm. Its membership includes about five thousand firms and some seventy trade associations. About half of its member associations have no full-time staff of their own, and the NUM provides them with secretarial assistance at cost. Some firms and associations are members of both bodies, but they are not in an important sense rival organizations. The FBI has a large staff and . . . its own private diplomatic service of full-time and part-time representatives overseas, and a foreign office (its Overseas Department) at its headquarters in Tothill Street, which employs about a quarter of the total headquarters staff. The NUM is built on a more modest scale (its income, for example, is only about a quarter of that of the FBI) but it is more active in the provinces. Both bodies provide their members with a range of services, including information about government regulations and legislation, but their major interest is representation—the formation of policy affecting industry as a whole. Their influence is difficult to assess, but it is certain that it is not as great as has frequently been asserted. Government departments do not go to them for advice and information about *specific* industrial questions; they go to the trade associations concerned. It is these associations collectively, rather than the FBI or NUM, who are the real 'voice of industry'. Their most important function, perhaps, is to act as a kind of sub-Parliament for industry which throws up its own industrial 'Ministers' – a relatively small number of leaders of the business world on whom the government can rely for guidance on a wide range of issues, and to whom, because of their standing in the business community, it can entrust the job of fostering sympathetic attitudes to official views and policies. On the other hand, the importance of an all-industry association like the FBI should not be underrated. The bureaucracy of the FBI is useful to government in a number of ways [. . .]

The British Employers' Confederation, though in one sense the FBI in another hat, is a retiring body, shunning the publicity that the FBI continually and successfully seeks. Unlike the FBI it has no member firms, but it claims that its member employers' associations cover approximately three-quarters of the total working population employed by private enterprise. These associations are drawn from the whole field of industry and commerce so that its membership is wider than that of the FBI. In practice its authority over its constituents is much less than that of the *Trades Union Congress,* which, acting through its General Council, speaks on behalf of its 180 affiliated unions for about ninety per cent of organized labour. The TUC is immensely influential in many ways, both inside and outside the movement, but it is cautious and slow-moving and has few constitutional powers over its affiliated unions. It is concerned, in broad terms, with the promotion and coordination of industrial action and with the adjustment of disputes between and within unions (in these matters it moves very circumspectly, always seeking to carry the union leadership with it), but in practice its most important function is to represent the interests of organized labour to the government, to the Labour Party, to industry and the employers' associations, and to the general public. Its annual income compares favourably with the income of the largest trade associations (that of the FBI is roughly the same), but its whole-time staff is small (about seventy).

The 'peak organization' for the cooperative movement is the *Co-operative Union*. The Union itself is registered as a cooperative society under the Industrial and Provident Societies Acts, but its membership consists solely of cooperative societies (mainly retail societies), and no individual person is admitted. It is governed by the annual Co-operative Congress to which all member societies send delegates. It is an employers' association, advising its members on negotiations with the trade unions within the movement. Through its Parliamentary and National Policy Committees it initiates action on legislation and administration affecting the cooperative trades and it links the movement to party politics through its delegates on the National Committee of the Co-operative Party, and on the (advisory) National Council of Labour which brings together representatives of the Co-operative Movement, the Labour Party and the Trades Union Congress.

Pressure groups

Economic pressure groups have a long history, though few have been as successful as their prototype, the Anti-Corn Law League. They were more important, perhaps, in the nineteenth century when the power of Parliament was greater than it is now, and before the rise of permanent sectional groups and a central government bureaucracy. In the nature of things, their influence must largely be gained through lobbying MPs and through publicity campaigns rather than by establishing channels of contact with Ministers and permanent officials. Nevertheless, they are still to be found in great numbers, some of them as 'front' organizations for sectional groups [. . .] Recent groups of this kind include the Fair Prices Defence Committee (supporting resale price maintenance), Aims of Industry and the misleadingly named Institute of Directors (both opposing nationalization). Governments must take heed of these groups, but their influence on affairs is generally much less than that of sectional interests. There are also groups which speak, either peripherally or directly, for the consumer [. . .]

This complex group organization is not confined to the private sector. Public bodies have their own representative trade associations and public officials concerned with the regulation of trade have their own professional institutes. There is much overlapping, reflecting the mixed character of the economy. Thus public officials belong to professional bodies that draw their members from private and public industry alike . . . ; general trade unions like the Transport Workers' draw members from public as well as private industry; so too do trade associations like the British Coking Industry Association which numbers among its members the National Coal Board and the Gas Council, and the Public Transport Association, to which both private and public omnibus undertakings belong. . . .

Collective organization and the administration of control

Few collective organizations, apart from pressure groups, are primarily concerned to propagate political principles; they exist first and foremost to serve the domestic interests of their members and their craft or vocation. Few, outside the cooperative societies, and some, though not all trade unions, are closely allied to a political party; but as the State has increasingly assumed responsibility for the management of economic matters, organized groups have come to play a major part in the political as well as in the economic and social life of the country. They have sought to protect and advance their interests at the vital point by trying to obtain a share in shaping public policy and administrative practice. These ends may be pursued through Ministers and civil servants, and through independent administrative bodies and advisory committees appointed by Ministers, through Parliament, through the political parties, and through most of the organs of public opinion. Of these channels of influence, the first is the most effective for the majority of organized interests, though not always the most readily available.

The British political system (unlike the political systems of most other Western democracies) is characterized by the almost complete dominance of the Executive in policy-making as well as in the direction of day-to-day business, by the correlative weakness of the Legislature, and by the monolithic character of the two great political parties which makes for a high degree of party discipline in Parliament and a unified approach in matters of party policy. Thus, a British interest group seeking to promote or to block some change of policy thinks first of the appropriate Minister and his department where an American interest group, for example, thinks first of Congress and its legislative committees. It is an exaggeration, but a justifiable exaggeration, to say to the British interest group: 'If you can bring over the Minister and the Chancellor of the Exchequer you have not much else to worry about' (Beer, 1956).

The centralization of decision-making power in Britain does not mean that organized groups are indifferent to what happens in Parliament, nor does it imply that they ignore the policies of the political parties; it does mean that consultation and pressure now find their focus primarily in the central administration, and that securing access to a Minister and officials is of much greater long-term importance than lobbying MPs or seeking the return to Parliament of Members representing the group's views. This is particularly true of sectional groups, for whom the more openly political activities of lobbying tend to be at best a second line of attack or defence when they are unable to pursue their aims more directly. Lobbying is important when the group lacks good 'access' to its Department, or when it is urging some highly political course of action which civil servants are not permitted to discuss. But, in practice, the bread-and-butter work of sectional economic groups is conducted at a much less exalted level than that of major controversial policy. As a leading trade-association official has expressed the matter:

the great bulk of the work of government is administration not policy. . . . Industry may or may not like the policy . . . but when the issue is decided it may make a world of difference to industry how the policy is implemented and translated through administration into action (Kipping, 1954, p. 6).

It is, in fact, rather rare for a sectional group with good 'access' to engage in openly political activities; these will, as a matter of tactics, be more often conducted by pressure groups representing attitudes to economic affairs (to which, of course, firms or individuals in the sectional group may belong), or by a 'peak' association, or by individual firms. No officially recognized group is likely to risk jeopardizing its privileged position by deliberately antagonizing or embarrassing its Minister and his department.

The amount of interaction between government departments and a sectional group depends on a number of factors, not least on the size and national importance of the industry, trade or profession concerned, and (the two are nowadays opposite sides of the same coin) the extent to which the government seeks to regulate it or to promote its well-being. It would, theoretically, be possible to construct a hierarchy into which all known sectional economic groups could be fitted according to the extent of their contacts with the central administration and their other, more political activities. At the top there would be a relatively small number of organizations of great national importance with well-established links with Ministers, leading Opposition spokesmen, officials, and back-bench MPs and, perhaps, with the great political party organizations outside Parliament, actively fostering a climate of official opinion favourable to their objects, with considerable private bureaucracies and a substantial body of expert information and opinion to offer. The pyramid would broaden gradually, leaving at the bottom a relatively large number of organizations whose parliamentary activities would be spasmodic and perhaps confined to occasional lobbying, lacking the resources or perhaps the inclination to spend much money and effort on educating public opinion, and whose contacts with officials would be infrequent and rather formal, perhaps taking the form of an occasional 'delegation to the Minister' or the submission of a memorandum. But the consequence of the system is that every economic department – and practically every division and branch of the department – has its retinue of organized interests which accompany it around as the pilot fish swim along with the shark; and it by no means follows, because some fish are smaller and more insignificant than others, that they will pass unnoticed. The Board of Trade is likely to have more business with the Association of Chemical Manufacturers than with the Shroud Manufacturers' Association, and the Ministry of Agriculture more business with the Food Manufacturers' Federation than with the Association of Bee-Keeping Appliance Manufacturers; but we may be sure that there is someone in the Ministry of Agriculture whose job it is to know the affairs of the bee-keepers; just as those in Whitehall who have to do with civil defence in a limited war are not unmindful of the potential importance of shrouds.

Thus, the departments stand, as it were, at the centre of a series of concentric circles of contending interests and pressures. Consultation takes place directly between Ministers and office-bearers in the various associations and between officials in the Departments and their 'opposite numbers' on the permanent staff of the associations; pressures reach the Departments indirectly from groups acting through independent administrative agencies and through Parliament, from groups acting on Parliament through the political parties, and from groups acting on the parties through the organs of public opinion.

The system of 'consultation'

It has long been accepted official practice that Ministers, and civil servants acting in the name of Ministers, should seek the views of responsible organizations representing the affected interests before making changes in the law. The need for consultation before making regulations (Statutory Instruments) has been recognized in statutes since at least the turn of the century. The principle was firmly established by the end of the First World War, and Sir Cecil Carr suggested, in his *Delegated Legislation,* published in 1921, that consultation with interests was one of the essential safeguards of Departmental lawmaking. The practice of consultation has grown less formal with the passage of time, and its scope has been broadened to include a mass of administrative procedure. Formal machinery set up by statute for consultation about draft regulations has been supplemented, if not supplanted, by informal day-to-day contact between government and industry on all matters of mutual concern. Today, interests will usually press for statutory recognition of their right to be consulted only when they feel uncertain of securing the attentions of a department. From the administrator's point of view, legal requirements for consultation can be embarrassing since they may well lead to questions about procedural powers: is consultation mandatory under the Act? with whom is the Minister bound to consult? what is a 'representative' organization? and what meaning is to be attached to the word 'consultation'? If, for example, the Minister is required by the Act to consult with 'representative associations of employers and workers', a failure to consult a particular employers' association or trade union might render the Minister's subsequent actions *ultra vires*. What constitutes a 'representative' organization would probably be a matter for the Minister rather than for a Court to decide, but that this is not always certain is emphasized by the use in some statutes of such phrases as 'such representative organizations as the Minister thinks fit', or 'such organizations as appear to him to be representative', or even[9] 'such bodies (if any) as appear to him to represent . . .'.

9. Sea Fish Industry Act 1938, s. 2 (5).

These legal formulae emphasize an important fact about the system: namely, that the right to be consulted is not open to all unconditionally and without restriction. The central administration is, in one sense, the chief guardian of that much-abused ideal, the public interest. Access to the administration may be achieved by influence, but it can usually be retained, and what is more important, be exploited successfully, by persuading Ministers and their officials that there is some public advantage to be had from it. Interest groups will always maintain, of course, that they are motivated by a concern for the public interest, nor are they necessarily insincere when they make this claim. As Dicey (1914, p. 15) put it, 'men come easily to believe that arrangements agreeable to themselves are beneficial to others. A man's interest gives a bias to his judgement far oftener than it corrupts his heart.' But it is for the administrator to decide where the public interest lies, and he will be more easily persuaded by a group with something to offer than he will by one that uses threats or even, indeed, reasoned argument. 'Recognition' which gives a sectional group good access to the administration may be said to depend on three factors. The first is that Ministers and officials should be prepared to place some trust in the leadership of the group, and this will depend, at least in part, on the extent to which the group can demonstrate that it is led by men 'who moderate the direct selfish interests which it is their duty to promote by a decent sense of their obligations to the community at large' (Street, 1959). Secondly, the administrator must be persuaded that the group is in some sense 'representative' of those on whose behalf it claims to speak. This is a criterion which can rarely be made explicit – it is by no means always necessary, for example, for a trade association to show that it speaks for 50 per cent or more of the firms in its industry – and it is, therefore, one which it is not always easy to satisfy. Thirdly, recognition will be easier to obtain the more useful the group can make itself to the administrator, whether by providing expert information which the civil servant does not possess, by acquiring a reputation for supplying sound advice, or by a willingness to cooperate in performing specific and sometimes onerous administrative tasks. No successful administrator needs to be reminded that smooth administration depends on securing the willing cooperation of 'those whom the laws most affect'. No civil servant can do his job efficiently unless he has frequent recourse to technical information of which the sectional group may sometimes have a monopoly, but which in any case it can usually provide more quickly and accurately than any other source. Thus, the conditions that are the price of recognition are also weapons in the hands of the sectional group that seeks it, and, if the conditions are satisfied, recognition can seldom be withheld. So important to good administration, indeed, is the system of consultation that in the absence of representative organizations, the government may take the lead in creating them. Sometimes, on the other hand, there may be too many 'representative' organizations in the industry. A classic case occurred in the building materials industries, where, in 1945, the Ministry of Works took the initiative in setting up a National Council of Building Producers, bringing together forty-one separate trade associations for common action in dealing with the Department.

These remarks suggest that consultation consists, in practice, of three separate though interdependent elements, which we may call negotiation, communication, and cooperation.

1. It is clear, looking at the matter from the point of view of industry, that much business with government departments is essentially *negotiation* about the terms of new legislation, statutory instruments, and administrative rules, and about the nature and extent of benefits, such as subsidies, and the conditions that must be met to qualify for them. In strict constitutional theory it is impossible for a department to 'negotiate' with outside interests, for no civil servant may commit his Minister, and no Minister may commit either the Crown or the House of Commons. It is for this reason more usual for both sides to talk of 'consultation' even where there is haggling and a bargain is struck. This limitation has the effect of introducing a certain polite wariness and 'roundaboutness' into the proceedings which is not normally found outside a government department. The atmosphere has been captured in a passage in the late H. E. Dale's book on the higher Civil Service:

The conversation will preserve all proper forms. The unofficials will inquire of the official, not 'Will you agree to this?' but 'Do you think the Minister will agree?' The official replies 'No, I feel sure he won't go as far as that; but I think he will probably consent to do so much, on the understanding that the rest is left over until next year.' The unofficials answer: 'Well, we think we can persuade our people to be content with that for the present.' And they part with mutual expressions of affection and esteem, each side understanding perfectly that pledges have been given and received to the effect that the Department will go some way to meet its unofficial critics, and that the critics will make no trouble in the House of Commons or elsewhere because it does not at once go the whole way (1941, pp. 182–3).

The constitutional forms are not a sham, because they emphasize the fact that, in the last resort, the parties are *not* equal and the interests cannot claim a right. Nor is the subordination of officials to the wishes of their political masters merely a fiction [. . .]

2. Collective organizations also act as channels of *communication* between their members and the administration. This is not so much a matter of giving advice or practical assistance as of providing a mechanism through which the consent and views of the membership can be obtained. A department hopes when it listens to a group organization that it is hearing the authentic voice of the interests concerned; when it speaks to it, it hopes that its message is being transmitted to the group as a whole, not merely to the bureaucracy and the leadership. Whether and to what extent theory corresponds to reality is a large question which we cannot enter into here. We can only assert the truth of Edmund Burke's words (1790) that 'in all bodies, those who lead must also, to a considerable degree, follow. They must conform their propositions to the taste, talent and disposition of those whom they wish to conduct'. The public servant is not much concerned with the internal organization and tactics of sectional groups (though he must be aware of them), and it is a matter of comparative indifference to him whether the association includes 80 per cent, 30 per cent, or only 10 per cent of the potential membership. What he needs is the knowledge that the leadership can provide him with reasonably accurate soundings of members' reactions and opinion, that the members constitute a fair cross-section or sample of the whole interest,

and that the leaders are men who command respect and attention in their industry.

3. Sectional groups *cooperate* with the administration in many ways. This holds many advantages short of those that can be obtained by direct negotiation, and is partly a return for the privilege of recognition. The most important general and continuing function is that of providing information and advice. This comes, necessarily, from the bureaucracy and chief office-holders rather than from the membership at large, and is provided informally in discussion from day to day, and formally through the medium of advisory councils and committees, some permanent, some *ad hoc*, with which every department nowadays surrounds itself.[10] A long list would be pointless, but among the many important permanent advisory committees on which interested parties are directly represented are: the Consultative Committee for Industry, the Cinematograph Films Council, and the Engineering Advisory Council [. . .]

Where sectional groups are not directly represented (which is usual in the case of *ad hoc* committees) the interested parties are almost always given an opportunity to submit evidence, oral as well as written. Moreover, most departments have a few specialist advisers with formal status who are not civil servants but prominent office-holders in the relevant trade, professional, or technical associations.

Sectional groups may be directly represented on bodies having executive functions. The Cotton Board, for example, includes members 'capable of representing the interests' of managements and workers in the various sections of the Lancashire textile industries, that is, members drawn from the appropriate trade associations and trade unions [. . .]

It is generally agreed that informal day-to-day contacts with officials are the most important form of consultation, outweigh-

10. There are at present about five hundred national standing advisory committees (and many more at regional and local level). Of the five hundred, the Board of Trade can lay claim to thirty-eight, the Ministry of Labour to forty, the Ministry of Agriculture to fifty-four, the Ministry of Transport and the Ministry of Aviation to sixty, and the Ministry of Power to eighteen. For a full account of the role of advisory committees in central government, see PEP, *Advisory Committees in British Government* (1960), from which these figures are taken.

ing the more formal methods of *ad hoc* and permanent advisory committees and conferences, though these may have their uses as sounding-boards for the expression of general views and opinions, and as a means of coordinating or reconciling the views of different interests. According to the National Union of Manufacturers:

Informal contacts include everything from the meeting of senior officers of the industrial organization with Ministers or Permanent Secretaries to telephone conversations between junior officials on both sides. The essence of the matter is that representatives at appropriate levels on both sides should be known to each other; that the industrial representative should be able to approach the right official on the right subject; and that . . . officials should recognize such approaches as informed and responsible ones. . . . These requirements are in general fulfilled (Select Committee on Estimates, 1960).

'So far as it is possible to generalize,' the Union continues:

it is probably true that of these methods of contact the most formal is the least effective. . . . The special committee and the formal approach . . . are the preferred and most effective methods of contact on policy matters and particularly on projected legislation. For the multitude of individual cases informal contact is the rule; and an industrial organization tends to be judged by its constituents or members on the degree to which this kind of contact exceeds in speed and effectiveness anything which the individual member can achieve for himself. In such cases it is regarded as the primary function of the organization, not necessarily to obtain the desired result, but at least to obtain a hearing and a decision (p. 303).

Parliament, parties and public opinion

Today, the role of Parliament is much reduced; as a collective body it sanctions, but it does not initiate. The government controls the course of business because it can usually rely on its majority in the House of Commons to force ready-made policies through or to block the adoption of policies with which it does not agree. The real work of Members is done outside the Chamber. The once powerful select committees, which in the nineteenth century played a vital part in policy-making, have been replaced by Royal Commissions appointed by the Crown and by committees of inquiry and standing advisory councils appointed by Ministers. This change is reflected in the activities of interest groups. Thus, the formal Objects of the National Association of Colliery Managers (as set out in their articles of association) include that of 'petitioning Parliament'; the Objects of the Federation of British Rubber Manufacturers' Associations contain no mention of Parliament, but state that the Association acts 'on behalf of the rubber and allied industries as a central medium of communication with the government and its departments on questions affecting such industries generally'. The National Association of Colliery Managers was founded in the 1880s, the Rubber Manufacturers' Federation in 1946. Nevertheless, in spite of the limitations imposed on the Private Member by present-day demands of party, public business, and Parliamentary procedure, he is not powerless. The government is in the saddle, but it must keep its majority in order to stay there. It must listen to the views of its supporters, and to the views of interests expressed by its supporters, as these are made known through the Whips, through the Parliamentary Party organization, and through the specialist committees of back-benchers. It will listen to the views of the Opposition expressed privately through its leaders, and in debate in the House. It will listen to Members on both sides of the House in Committee, whether of the whole house, or in standing committee when Bills are considered 'upstairs', and in the Select Committees of Estimates and Public Accounts. Ministers and their officials pay careful attention to views expressed by Private Members in the course of Parliamentary proceedings which have a bearing on the work of their departments and a small attendance in the Chamber does not necessarily mean that the Member's words are falling on empty air.

For all these reasons, sectional groups are unlikely to neglect the importance of seeking the support of back-benchers or of Opposition leaders; and, as already suggested, weakly organized interests (of which the domestic consumer groups are an extreme example) may be compelled to cultivate this support because they lack adequate 'access'. For the majority of well-organized groups, however, the main advantage lies in having open a second channel to which resort may be had at those points at which a frontal assault on the department has failed.

An argument lost in negotiation with civil servants may be won in a parliamentary committee, and parliamentary support for the group's views, skilfully mobilized, may be a useful bargaining point. All governments try to get their business through with a minimum of fuss, and the suggestion of trouble in the House (no government is likely to accept an openly expressed threat) may be sufficient to carry many points that are not points of major principle. It follows, on the other hand, that it may not be sufficient for a group to convince the Minister and his advisers of the general desirability of a piece of business; it may also be necessary to give them an assurance that the measure will not meet obstruction in the House. Thus, the group may be required to conciliate the interests that are likely to oppose it.

An MP is associated with outside interests at several points. He is expected to concern himself with the welfare of the industries and trades in his constituency and of the people, not all of whom are necessarily his constituents, who work in them. This is particularly important politically where Members represent constituencies in which a single industry or group of related industries predominates – the cotton industry in south-east Lancashire, the motor-car and light engineering industries in Birmingham, the steel industry in Sheffield, arable farming in East Anglia and dairy-farming in the south-west of England. Secondly, he will usually have interests or sympathies of his own in a particular industry or trade, as a company director, a shareholder, a farmer, an ex-miner, a former steel worker, and so on. Thirdly, he may take up the cause of a particular sectional economic group from a general feeling for its aims or simply because he is looking around for a cause to espouse (and many organizations are glad to associate MPs with their work by electing them as Honorary Vice-Presidents). Fourthly, he may be the spokesman for a particular group in a more formal sense, either because he serves or has served in an official capacity on its staff or governing board, or because the group provides him with financial and political backing, or perhaps both.

It is clear that few sectional groups now need to sponsor MPs financially in order to achieve such limited ends as can be gained through Parliament, since they can secure all the representation they need without paying for it. The trade-union MPs are a special case. Since 1918 there has been a formidable body of trade-unionists in the House. But a large block of the trade-union MPs are miners' MPs, and a great many important unions have no direct representation at all. The most important reason, for the trade unions, for continuing the system of sponsoring – apart from tradition and sentiment – is that it enables them to keep a hold on the Parliamentary Labour Party; but the unions represented in the House would suffer very little if the system were abandoned. The Co-operative Movement has its own party, but the greatest number of 'Co-op MPs' in any Parliament since its first success in 1918 was twenty-three (in the Parliament of 1945), and it could not survive apart from its alliance with the Labour Party.

It may be important for groups to secure influence in the constituencies. The electoral map of Britain is such that the result of an election is a foregone conclusion in more than half the constituencies, and in choosing a candidate the local majority party organization is in fact choosing a Member of Parliament. The trade unions have long been aware of the importance of constituency influence, and it is significant that the National Farmers' Unions now encourage their local branches to play an active part in constituency politics and if possible to get their members on to party selection committees. It is not known how far this practice has been followed, nor to what extent it is followed by other groups; but it shows a lively appreciation of the true sources of influence in the political system.

Nationally, sectional groups prefer to keep clear of close party affiliations and to avoid committing themselves publicly on highly controversial questions, except perhaps on very large issues of principle such as the nationalization or denationalization of their industries where it is necessary to impress on those in the higher councils of government – the Cabinet and its committees, and the leaders of the national parties – the support for their cause. The reasons for avoiding political entanglements are clear. Both main parties accept the minor premises of the mixed economy. About six million manual wage-earners (and the number is at present increasing) regularly vote Conservative, and about two million business, professional, and white-collar workers still support the Labour Party. The more successful the group is in securing a foothold in the administrative process, the less likely is it to commit itself to one party. Even the trade-union movement, which provides the Labour Party with the majority of its members and about three-quarters of its income, is non-political in this sense. Its party links[11] have little effect on day-to-day business with Departments, and the TUC, which is not itself affiliated to the Labour Party, carefully stresses its independence of Labour Party direction and its place as guardian of the interests of the organized workers against all comers.

A sectional economic group may try to influence the government, Parliament, and the political parties by direct appeals to 'public opinion', but this is rare if set against the thousands of contacts that take place every day between groups and Westminster and Whitehall. No organized group can be wholly indifferent to public opinion, but for the majority, 'education' and 'information' (i.e. propaganda) is directed more often towards their own members, to rally flagging spirits and whip up support for current policy, than to the public at large. Even for pressure groups proper, Press and publicity campaigns are dangerous weapons that may recoil with stunning effect; they are more useful when a group is seeking to oppose (which most pressure groups do), than when it is seeking to promote, some new line of policy. Prestige advertising is used by a few large trade associations (and by organizations that are 'fronts' for large trade associations), but it is used far less than in the United States where belief in the power of advertising is greater and where government is more readily influenced by mass opinion. Political advertising in the Press, particularly when an election is approaching (which is the only time it is likely to be seriously considered) is perhaps to be avoided, not because it is likely to fall foul of the law, but because of the danger that it may produce the opposite effect to that intended, the British, in general, taking the view that businessmen ought not to meddle in elections [. . .]

11. 186 unions are affiliated to the Labour Party; of these, eighty-four are empowered by law to collect contributions for a political fund.

The large firm and the public corporation

The largest firms are so large that they can deal with government departments direct; if they are also leaders in the relevant trade and employers' associations, this is because they think it necessary to maintain good public relations with the smaller firms, not because they anticipate any great advantage from participation. (They may even bargain directly with their employees' unions, though the fact that the British Employers' Confederation refuses to admit individual firms to membership exerts some pressure to conform.) In these matters they are akin to the public corporations which, though they stand in a rather special relationship to the government, are not simply creatures of a Minister, but independent bodies of great economic importance with a highly-developed and perfectly legitimate sense of their own standing as parts of the public service at least the equal of any government department.

There is something to be said for the contention that the modern business leader, whether in large-scale private enterprise or publicly-owned industry, is becoming more and more a 'politician' and a bureaucrat in outlook and action just as the high-ranking civil servant is forced to become a 'businessman', or, at least, to study and imitate his habits. Changes in the recruitment policies of the biggest firms bring them into line with the nationalized industries; both increasingly look for their future leaders in the educational ranks from which the higher civil service is drawn: honours graduates in arts from the Universities of Oxford and Cambridge ('we like to take boys who have learnt Greek', a director of Shell is reported to have said in 1959, 'we find they sell more oil'), as well as honours graduates in science and technology from London and from Manchester, Bristol, and other major provincial universities. Top businessmen in private industry today acquire prestige, not simply by making profits for their firms, but by following 'more enlightened' policies which it is the business of the public industries and of government officials to foster. They seek, not only business success, but esteem as advisers to Ministers and senior civil servants, and as members of the boards of public enterprises.

On the other hand, senior civil servants are encouraged, and not merely allowed, to take up positions on the boards of private companies when they reach retiring age and they may even be permitted to retire early, with full pension rights, for this purpose. They move to trade associations more rarely, though there are some notable exceptions [. . .] There are clear advantages to both sides in these arrangements, but there are equally obvious dangers. There is a well-known Treasury rule that the permission of the Minister and the Chancellor of the Exchequer must be obtained before high officials can take outside posts within two years of retirement, but this does not wholly dispose of the risk that some men who remain in the service 'will also wish to do well and will therefore be – in most cases quite unconsciously – inclined to take a general view of things not awkward to large private interests' (Balogh, 1959, p. 96).

There is, however, some attempt to guard against the more obvious dangers by moving senior civil servants about from division to division at frequent intervals. Trade associations do not like this, since it makes routine contacts more difficult.

Conclusion

This system, which has been permitted to grow in response to administrative need, is not without its difficulties and problems. First, as has been said (Wheare, 1955, p. 67), the system has immensely strengthened Whitehall at the expense of Westminster. It is going much too far to argue that 'acts of policy are now decided by the interplay of thousands of conflicting interest groups, and Cabinet Ministers . . . play virtually no part in shaping decisions which they subsequently defend with passion' (Johnson, 1957). It *is* true that a large part of the nation's economic business is now settled with only the barest reference to the electors' representatives in Parliament. 'If Whitehall can claim the monopoly of knowledge and the agreement of the interested parties, what can Westminster do?' (Wheare, 1955). Secondly, there is a danger that officials may be liable, collectively, to 'capture' by organized interests; that is, that they may come to identify the interests of a particular sectional group or groups with the public interest which it is their duty as officials to try to identify and serve. This phenomenon is so well known in the United States that it has been given a name: 'clientalism'. The Interstate Commerce Commission (which regulates the railroads), the Civil Aeronautics Board, and the Federal Communications Commission are familiar examples. If the danger is less real in Britain, this is because British departments usually cater, under one Minister and one set of top officials, for a variety of (often conflicting) interests, because all 'independent' administrative bodies are in the last resort subject to Ministerial direction, and because the political system provides a series of more or less effective counterweights to the direct pressure of groups. There is, for example, no 'appropriation struggle' in the American sense. The control of public funds is in the hands, not of legislators free from the shackles of party discipline, but of the Cabinet and the Treasury. In so far as there is an appropriation struggle in Britain, it takes place within the walls of the Treasury – and the Treasury is not an interest-group department, whatever else it may be. It is the battlefield on which the various divisions of the various departments contend for public funds, but the progress of the battle is largely conditioned by major Cabinet decisions about 'what the nation can afford'. And the Cabinet is, in a very real sense, beyond the direct reach of narrowly sectional interests. Public funds, however, are not always in question, and the very conception of production departments implies that the danger, though it may be less real than in America, is not wholly absent. The controversy over the amalgamation of the Ministries of Agriculture and Food in 1955, for example, turned largely on the extent to which a department whose job it was to look after the farmers could at the same time be expected to attend (as the old Ministry of Food had attended) to the needs of the consumer.

A related question is to what extent sectional groups may succeed in so modifying the structure and powers of an administrative organization that they prevent it from carrying out its functions effectively. This is another familiar American occurrence. It has happened here: examples include the highly successful efforts of the Mining Association of Great Britain to thwart the operation of the amalgamation provisions of the

Coal Mines Act 1930; and the attack by industrial interests on the scheme for Industrial Development Councils, introduced by the Labour Government in 1947. The counter-danger (capture of the sectional group by a Department) is, on the other hand, more marked in Britain than elsewhere. There is a real danger that a group may be drawn so closely into the machinery of government that its wings are effectively clipped.

References

BALOGH, T. (1959), 'The apotheosis of the dilettante', in H. Thomas (ed.), *The Establishment*.

BEER, S. H. (1956), 'Pressure groups and parties in Britain', *Amer. Polit. Sci. Rev.*, vol. 50, no. 1, pp. 56.

BURKE, E. (1790), *Reflections on the Revolution in France*, O'Brien (ed.), Penguin.

CARR, C. (1921), *Delegated Legislation*.

DALE, H. E. (1941), *The Higher Civil Service in Great Britain*.

DICEY, A. V. (1914), *Law and Opinion, Lectures on the Relation between Law and Public Opinion in England during the Nineteenth Century*, Macmillan.

JOHNSON, P. (1957), *New Statesman*, 12 October.

KIPPING, N. (1954), *The Federation of British Industries*.

PEP (1944) *Planning*, no. 221, p. 20, PEP.

PEP (1957), *Industrial Trade Associations*, PEP.

PEP (1960), *Advisory Committees in British Government*. PEP.

Select Committee on Estimates (1960), *Report*, session 1959–60, Board of Trade.

STREET, SIR R. (1959), 'Government consultation with industry', in *Public Administration*, Spring.

WHEARE, K. C. (1955), *Government by Committee*, Oxford University Press.

Part Three
Decision Making and the Structure of Society

If we were able accurately to describe the pattern of decision making within a society and over a period of time, then we would be able to say who rules in that society, for whom, and for what purposes. Clearly, that would be an impressive achievement, of interest presumably to everyone. Social scientists are, as has already been indicated, a long way from achieving that degree of accuracy. There do exist, however, several models of the distribution of power; and social scientists who study decision making in society use either one or another of these models as working assumptions, or explicitly set out to test hypotheses derived from one of them. It is primarily for this reason that we present, in this final section, four important models: ruling class, elitism, pluralism, egalitarian democracy. We briefly outline their central features in this introduction and indicate some of the problems involved in obtaining evidence in relation to three of them. The selections in Part Three of the Reader are designed to fill out the bare bones presented here and to expose some of the strengths and weaknesses of each model.

1. *The ruling class.* The ruling class model owes its origin and subsequent development to the social theory of Marx.

Let us give a summary of the main elements in the model.

The structure of society is divided between a class that rules or exploits, and a class or classes which is ruled or exploited. What divides the ruling class from the subject classes is their different relationships to the major instruments and processes of economic production. The ruling class own and control the means of production; the subject classes do not. There is perpetual struggle between the ruling class and the subject classes. The economic dominance of the ruling class is its source of power in this struggle. Their dominance is sustained by their ownership of property which is transferred within families through the laws of inheritance and in other ways from generation to generation, by their control over military force, and by their heavy influence in the production of ideas. Their power is deployed to control the major decisions taken in the society for their own benefit.

The major distinction between the ruling class and the elitist models is that in the former model, class struggles with class, both of which are cohesive groupings; whereas in the latter an organized minority confronts an unorganized majority. Marx's social theory accounts for the existence of classes, or coherent social groupings, in at least two ways. Firstly, the members of each class have common economic interests; for the ruling class a primary interest is to perpetuate their ownership of property. Secondly, the classes are in conflict, and out of that conflict are developed and sustained their self-awareness and solidarity.

The class analysis of power and decision making is not well represented in social science literature. This may be so in part because Marx himself was unable to address his attention directly to the subject, although his notes suggest that he had planned to do so. We are left with the assertion, which he did not elaborate, that the state is basically the coercive instrument of the ruling class, summarized in the celebrated formulation: 'The executive of the modern state is but a committee for managing the common affairs of the whole bourgeoisie'. Marx's followers have accepted this thesis as more or less self-evident. Consequently, it has not been a central concern of Marxists to analyse government and politics in advanced capitalist societies. There are scattered references, however, from which we have selected two as illustrations of Marxist analyses of the state (Miliband; Baran and Sweezy). A third selection related to this model provides a critique of Marxist theory in terms of its applicability to contemporary Britain (Crosland).

2. *Elitism and Pluralism*. Both elitism and pluralism reject the perspective of society characterized by classes and class conflict. Both adopt the perspective of society as being made up of a minority of leaders or representatives, who make political decisions in the society, and a mass which is in the majority and within which particular interests may be organized. Both can also be most usefully defined as the obverse of each other along a common set of dimensions. For these reasons we take the somewhat unusual step of bracketing them together.

Pluralism may be said to characterize the distribution of power in a society if the following conditions exist:

(a) Competing centres with different bases of power and influence exist within a society.
(b) There are opportunities for individual and organizational access into the political system.
(c) Individuals actively participate in and make their will felt through organizations of many kinds.
(d) Elections are a viable instrument of mass participation in political decisions including those on specific issues.
(e) A consensus exists on what may be called the 'democratic creed'.

Elitism is the antithesis of pluralism, and thus may be defined as domination of the decision-making process by a single group, limited rank-and-file access, little or no opposition, dissensus *vis-à-vis* a political creed, and failure on the part of most of the adult community to use their political resources to influence important decisions.

More restricted definitions which also appear in the literature, especially in very recent studies, are that pluralism exists if no single elite dominates decision making in every substantive area, and elitism exists where there is no competition between elites. These several definitions are amplified in the essay by Presthus.

Both elitism and pluralism, in contrast to the ruling class model, leave open the question of who benefits from the decision-making process. An elite may be benign, and exercise its power in such a way as regularly to meet the genuine needs of the mass; it is equally possible within the logic of the model for the elite consistently to exercise its power to its own advantage and to the disadvantage of the mass; and there are other possible relationships between elite and mass. There is similar openness in the case of pluralism. Those special interests with effective organizations to represent them may benefit more from the decision-making process than other social groups less well organized; or large electoral constituencies lacking efficient organizations, may benefit more from a particular decision than well-organized minority interests; and so forth. The point is that relationships between the decision makers and the rest of the society, in terms of who benefits, is not given in the models, and thus must be determined in each case. And since both elitist and pluralist models presuppose a society in which human beings have differential status, prestige and resources, then it follows that some benefit more than others.

Most research by social scientists on the structure of decision making in societies proceeds on the basis of these models or in accordance with the assumptions on which they rest. Fairly lively critiques of pluralism and elitism run through the theoretical literature on the subject. We include five essays in this section of the Reader which should provide an entrée to the nature of those critiques and thereby suggest the limitations of each model, depending on your point of view.

3. *Problems of specification.* In order for a decision-making system to be characterized in terms of ruling class, elitist, or pluralist models, a number of empirical criteria must be met, and the specification of these criteria gives rise to a number of problems. We indicate some of them here in relation to the selections appearing in Part Three of the Reader.

(a) *The specification of power and influence.* One must begin by stating flatly that there are enormous difficulties in measuring power and influence (Gamson). These difficulties beset any attempt at deploying either ruling class, elitist or pluralist models as concrete cases, since all three require a fairly accurate specification of the relationships between those who make important decisions and those who do not. Beyond these general difficulties, there are further problems regarding specification which are peculiar to each model.

Both the ruling class and the elitist models contain a basic premise that there is an ordered structure of decision making in society, with a particular class or group which consistently wields power and influence. The question 'who wields power?' then becomes the central concern in research. One objection to these models lies in this initial premise. The basic formulation of the models, it is argued, is rather like the question 'have you stopped beating your wife?', in that virtually any attempt to answer the question within the premises of the model will supply the researcher with the power elite or ruling class he is looking for (Bachrach and Baratz), and it excludes from consideration the possibility that no one consistently wields powers and influence ('I never beat my wife in the first place').

A second major objection to these models has to do with equations which are often made between potential power and actual power (Finer; Dahl). For example, the question is raised: what sort of evidence exists to establish that the influence of a ruling class or specified elite is sufficient to control the major decisions in a society? Taking for the moment the business community as representative of both a specified elite and the bourgeoisie, it can be shown that business enterprises have at their disposal a wide range of devices by which they could influence decisional choice (Finer). These include the advantages conferred by organizational concentration, wealth, access to those in authority provided by ties of family and acquaintanceship, patronage, and the ability to thwart the government by only acting as they are obliged to by law. However, a knowledge of what business can do in terms of exerting influence tells us nothing about what is actually done. In one country, business may utilize its wealth to bribe politicians to take decisions advantageous to its own interests; in another, the political culture may be such as virtually to rule out this means of influence as a practical possibility (Finer).

Generally speaking, elitist and ruling class models are concerned more with the specification of sources of power, the mobilization of bias inherent in the structure of society, and the groups or classes advantaged by the structure. The pluralist model, on the other hand, is concerned more with the exercise of power in particular situations, with power meaning 'participation in decision making'. The problems of specification for the pluralist researcher are 'firstly to select for study a number of "key" as opposed to "routine" political decisions, secondly to identify the people who took an active part in the decision-making process, thirdly to obtain a full account of their actual behaviour while the policy conflict was being resolved, and lastly to determine and analyse the specific outcome of the conflict' (Bachrach and Baratz). The major objections to the pluralist model are not concerned so much with this programme of research as they are with what is left out as a result of the implicit assumptions on which the whole enterprise rests.

One objection is that the application of the pluralist model, in which decision makers are forced to accommodate themselves to organized interests, among which a rough balance is maintained, always favours existing (particularly business) groups against those who happen not to be well organized, e.g. consumers, farm labourers, migrant workers, the aged, the unemployed, women. In consequence, the model has a built-in conservative bias : 'the doctrine of the harmony of interests thus serves as an ingenious device invoked, in perfect sincerity, by privileged groups in order to justify and maintain their dominant position' (Carr, cited in Playford). The model, therefore, not only presents a very partial view of the structure of power in society; its application to social reality produces social science research which implicitly supports inequality and injustice by ignoring the existence of legitimate social interests (Playford).

A second major objection to the pluralist model is that, by focusing on the decision-making process, it ignores the fact that power is often exercised to confine the scope of decision making to relative 'safe' or innocuous issues (Bachrach and Baratz). It thus may be that the structure of power in society is such that the really fundamental political conflicts in society never appear in the decision-making arena at all. Schattschneider summarizes the point (cited in Bachrach and Baratz):

All forms of political organization have a bias in favour of the exploitation of some kinds of conflict and the suppression of others because *organization is the mobilization of bias*. Some issues are organized into politics while others are organized out.

(b) *The level of decision making.* For those who attempt to discover the bias of a decision-making system by looking at the decision makers themselves, a real problem is raised by the difficulty of specifying the exact point at which a decision is reached. The procedures of decision making may be such as to create a filtration process in which the identification of the time and place of the decisional choice becomes virtually impossible, as both Barnard and Brown indicated in Part One. This creates a problem, because whilst it may be possible to identify general groups of important decision makers, it is not usually possible to relate a given decision to a given group of decision makers. This point may be exemplified by looking at the situation of government administrators, who are generally recognized as being of vital decision-making importance in the context of the modern state (Miliband; Nettl). The empirical issue immediately becomes one of where we draw the line between administrators who have a real influence on important decisions and those who do not. The usual level of demarcation, in Britain at least, used to be that dividing the former administrative and executive grades of the civil service. However, organizational procedures of decision making may be such that officials in what used to be the executive grade have played a significant role in pre-empting certain courses of action. Alternatively, it might be suggested that the gap in decisional power between the grades of Principal and Assistant Principal and more elevated levels in the civil service make it sensible to draw the line here. The point is that, given the uncertainty as to the level at which decisions are made, all characterizations of the important decision makers are necessarily arbitrary.

Indeed, it may be suggested that the proponents of various models of the distribution of power resulting from the decision-making process are not infrequently talking past each other. Miliband argues that there is an identifiable elite of top decision makers in Britain, including Cabinet Ministers, military chiefs, higher civil servants, business leaders, 'the great and the good', and so on. On the other side, Crosland argues that since the Second World War there has been a transfer of economic power to the state, and that the state can be, and has been, influenced in its decision making by the working class interest represented by the Labour Party. The point here is again one of the levels at which major decisions are taken, for if it is at the level of Cabinet government alone, it is obvious that the accession of a Labour government will make all the difference in the world to the content of decision making. If, on the other hand, the level at which decisions are taken is a wider one, a group of decision makers may be isolated, whose social characteristics (and possibly interests), whilst they may have altered somewhat over recent decades, are still substantially those of the world of business and property and the professional middle classes. This sort of disagreement, based as it is on a differential attribution of the level of strategic decision making, can only be settled by a prior definition of the characterizing features of a major decision and empirical investigation of the level at which they occur.

4. *Egalitarian democracy*. Beyond the ruling class, the power elite, and representation by competing elites is another model to which we affix the label egalitarian democracy. A terse definition of egalitarian democracy would be government by all the people for all the people. The model is perhaps a special case as it is less an analytic tool for the understanding of any known society, since no such society at present exists, than it is a reference point for other models. The model can be said to form part of Marxist theory, in that the promise of a classless society would appear to be a necessary precondition of egalitarian democracy. Some social scientists would also contend that egalitarian democracy is an extension of pluralism. But the model figures in various ways in the political thought of all ages. One could say that it is the preserve of no single school of thought, and the birthright of all.

There is no literature related to this model, since social scientists are (unfortunately, perhaps) concerned these days only with what is, not with what could be. We include one essay (Bottomore), however, which does refer to this type of model as a reference point for discussion of ruling class, elitist and pluralist models. It thereby provides a useful conclusion to the subject as a whole.

The Ruling Class

16 R. Miliband

The State Elite

From 'The state system and the state elite', in R. Miliband, *The State in Capitalist Society*, Weidenfeld & Nicolson, 1969, pp. 55–67.

[. . .] Writing in 1902, Kautsky observed that 'the capitalist class rules but does not govern', though he added immediately that 'it contents itself with ruling the government' (1903, p. 13). This is the proposition which has to be tested. But it is obviously true that the capitalist class, as a class, does not actually 'govern'. One must go back to isolated instances of the early history of capitalism, such as the commercial patriciates of cities like Venice and Lübeck, to discover direct and sovereign rule by businessmen. Apart from these cases, the capitalist class has generally confronted the state as a separate entity – even, in the days of its rise to power, as an alien and often hostile element, often under the control and influence of an established and land-owning class, whose hold upon the state power had to be broken by revolution, as in France, or by erosion, as in England in the nineteenth century, that process of erosion being greatly facilitated, in the English case, by the constitutional and political changes wrought by violence in the seventeenth century.

Nor has it come to be the case, even in the epoch of advanced capitalism, that businessmen have themselves assumed the major share of government. On the other hand, they have generally been well represented in the political executive and in other parts of the state system as well; and this has been particularly true in the recent history of advanced capitalism.

This entry of businessmen in the state system has often been greatly underestimated. Weber, for instance, believed that industrialists had neither the time nor the particular qualities required for political life (see Bendix, 1960, p. 436); and Schumpeter wrote of the 'industrialist and merchant' that

there is surely no trace of any mystic glamour about him which is what counts in the ruling of men. The stock exchange is a poor substitute for the Holy Grail . . . A genius in the business office may be, and often is, utterly unable outside of it to say boo to a goose – both in the drawing-room and on the platform. Knowing this he wants to be left alone and to leave politics alone (1950, pp. 137–8).

Less dramatically but no less definitely, Aron has more recently written of businessmen that:

they have governed neither Germany, nor France, nor even England. They certainly played a decisive role in the management of the means of production, in social life. But what is characteristic of them as a socially dominant class is that, in the majority of countries, they have not themselves wanted to assume political functions (1964, p. 280).

Businessmen themselves have often tended to stress their remoteness from, even their distaste for, 'politics'; and they have also tended to have a poor view of politicians as men who, in the hallowed phrase, have never had to meet a payroll and who therefore know very little of the *real* world – yet who seek to interfere in the affairs of the hard-headed and practical men whose business it is to meet a payroll, and who therefore do know what the world is about. What this means is that businessmen, like administrators, wish to 'depoliticize' highly contentious issues and to have these issues judged according to the criteria favoured by business. This may look like an avoidance of politics and ideology: it is in fact their clandestine importation into public affairs.

In any case, the notion of businessmen as remote from political affairs, in a direct and personal way, greatly exaggerates their reluctance to seek political power; and equally underestimates how often the search has been successful.

In the United States, businessmen were in fact the largest single occupational group in Cabinets from 1889 to 1949; of the total number of Cabinet members between these dates, more than 60 per cent were businessmen of one sort or another. Nor certainly was the business membership of American Cabinets less marked in the Eisenhower years from 1953 to 1961. As for members of British Cabinets between 1886 and 1950, close to one-third were businessmen, including three Prime Ministers – Bonar Law, Baldwin and Chamberlain. Nor again have businessmen been at all badly represented in the Conservative Cabinets which held office between 1951 and 1964. And while businessmen have, in this respect, done rather less well in some other advanced capitalist countries, nowhere has their representation been negligible.

But the government itself is by no means the only part of the state system in which businessmen have had a direct say. Indeed, one of the most notable features of advanced capitalism is precisely what might be called without much exaggeration their growing colonization of the upper reaches of the administrative part of that system.

State intervention has gone further and assumed more elaborate institutional forms in France than anywhere else in the capitalist world. But both in the elaboration of the French Plans and in their execution, men belonging to the world of business, and particularly of big business, have enjoyed a marked, almost an overwhelming preponderance over any other occupational or 'sectional' group. As Schonfield notes (1965, p. 128), 'in some ways, the development of French planning in the 1950's can be viewed as an act of voluntary collusion between senior civil servants and the senior managers of big business. The politicians and the representatives of organised labour were both largely passed by'.

Much the same kind of business predominance over other economic groups is to be found in the financial and credit institutions of the state, and in the nationalized sector. The creation of that sector has often been thought of as removing an important area of economic activity from capitalist control and influence. But quite apart from all the other forces which prevent a subsidiary nationalized sector from being run on other than orthodox lines, there is also the fact that business has carved out an extremely strong place for itself in the directing organs of that sector; or rather, that business has been invited by governments, whatever their political coloration, to assume a major role in the management and control of the public sector. In comparison, representatives of labour have appeared as very poor parents indeed – not, it should be added, that the entry of a greater number of 'safe' trade union leaders would make much difference to the orientation of institutions which are, in effect, an integral part of the capitalist system.

The notion that businessmen are not directly involved in government and administration (and also in parliamentary assemblies) is obviously false. They are thus involved, ever more closely as the state becomes more closely concerned with economic life; wherever the state 'intervenes', there also, in an exceptionally strong position as compared with other economic groups, will businessmen be found to influence and even to determine the nature of that intervention.

It may readily be granted that businessmen who enter the state system, in whatever capacity, may not think of themselves as representatives of business in general or even less of their own industries or firms in particular. But even though the *will* to think in 'national' terms may well be strong, businessmen involved in government and administration are not very likely, all the same, to find much merit in policies which appear to run counter to what they conceive to be the interests of business, much less to make themselves the advocates of such policies, since they are almost by definition most likely to believe such policies to be inimical to the 'national interest'. It is much easier for businessmen, where required, to divest themselves of stocks and shares as a kind of *rite de passage* into government service than to divest themselves of a particular view of the world, and of the place of business in it.

Notwithstanding the substantial participation of businessmen in the business of the state, it is however true that they have never constituted, and do not constitute now, more than a relatively small minority of the state elite as a whole. It is in this sense that the economic elites of advanced capitalist countries are not, properly speaking, a 'governing' class, comparable to pre-industrial, aristocratic and landowning classes. In some cases, the latter were able, almost, to dispense with a distinct and fully articulated state machinery and were themselves practically the state. Capitalist economic elites have not achieved, and in the nature of capitalist society could never achieve, such a position.

However, the significance of this relative distance of businessmen from the state system is markedly reduced by the social composition of the state elite proper. For businessmen belong, in economic and social terms, to the upper and middle classes – and it is also from these classes that the members of the state elite are predominantly, not to say overwhelmingly, drawn. The pattern is monotonously similar for all capitalist countries and applies not only to the administrative, military and judicial elites, which are insulated from universal suffrage and political competition, but to the political and elective ones as well, which are not. Everywhere and in all its elements the state system has retained, socially speaking, a most markedly upper- and middle-class character, with a slowly diminishing aristocratic element at one end, and a slowly growing working-class and lower-middle-class element at the other. The area of recruitment is much more narrow than is often suggested. As Dahrendorf notes, 'the "middle class" that forms the main recruiting ground of the power elite of most European countries today, often consists of the top 5 per cent of the occupational hierarchy in terms of prestige, income and influence' (1964, p. 238).

One main reason for this bourgeois predominance in the appointive institutions of the state system has already been discussed in relation to the economic and social hierarchies outside that system, namely that children born of upper- and middle-class parents have a vastly better chance of access than other children to the kind of education and training which is required for the achievement of elite positions in the state system. Greatly unequal opportunities in education also find reflection in the recruitment to the state service, since qualifications which are only obtainable in institutions of higher education are a *sine qua non* for entry into that service.

Thus in France the main means of entry to top administrative positions is the *École Nationale d'Administration*. But professor Meynaud notes that in the year 1962, fifty-six out of seventy-one university students who were successful in the examinations for admission to the ENA belonged by social origin to '*la partie la plus favorisée de la population*'; and of the twenty-two success-ful candidates from the civil service itself, ten belonged to the same class. Of the university students who presented them-selves, there was not a single one whose parents were workers or peasants. '*Dans l'ensemble,*' Meynaud comments, '*la sélec-tion sociale de la haute fonction publique reste essentiellement inégalitaire. Autrement dit, malgré la réforme de 1945, la "démocratisation" demeure très limitée*' (1964, p. 51). The same is also true of the French military and of the French judiciary.

Not of course that France is notably more 'undemocratic' in this respect than other capitalist countries. Thus the bulk of British higher civil servants has to a remarkable degree con-tinued to be drawn from a narrowly restricted segment of the population, much of it public school and Oxbridge educated; and the same marked upper- and middle-class bias has remained evident in the higher reaches of the British army and the judiciary.

The picture is not appreciably different for the United States, where . . . inequality of educational opportunity . . . has . . . helped to narrow the area of recruitment to the state service. As Matthews notes:

Those American political decision makers[1] *for whom this informa-tion is available* are, with very few exceptions, sons of professional men, proprietors and officials, and farmers. A very small minority were sons of wage-earners, low-salaried workers, farm labourers or tenants . . . the narrow base from which political decision makers appear to be recruited is clear (1954, pp. 23–4).

In the case of the United States military it has also been noted that 'on the whole, the high officers of the army and navy have been men of the upper-middle rather than truly higher or definitely lower classes. Only a very small percentage of them are of working-class origin' (Mills, 1956).

As for Supreme Court Justices, it has been remarked that:

throughout American history there has been an overwhelming tend-ency for Presidents to choose nominees for the Supreme Court from among the socially advantaged families . . . In the earlier history of the Court he very likely was born in the aristocratic gentry class,

1. 'Political decision makers' here includes 'high-level civil servants'.

although later he tended to come from the professional upper-middle class (Schmidhauser, 1959, p. 45).

The same kind of upper- and middle-class preponderance is yet again encountered in Federal Germany:

while less than 1 per cent of the present population of the Federal republic [one writer notes] carries a 'von' in the family name, the bearers of aristocratic titles may actually have increased among senior civil servants. Senior civil servants claiming descent from working-class families remain as conspicuous by their absence as ever (Edinger, 1961, p. 27).

Similarly, Professor Dahrendorf notes that:

despite the break up of the old monopoly and the consequent dwindling significance of nobility, German elite groups from 1918 to the present [including the state elite] have been consistently recruited to a disproportionately great extent from middle and higher groups of the service class and the middle class as well as from their own predecessors in elite positions (Dahrendorf, 1968, p. 228).

And much the same story is told for Sweden and Japan.

While inequality of educational opportunity, based on social class, helps to account for this pattern, there are other factors which contribute to its formation. Here too, as in the case of access to elite positions outside the state system, there is also the matter of connections. Certainly, the more spectacular forms of nepotism and favouritism associated with an unregenerate aristocratic and pre-industrial age are not part of the contemporary, middle-class, competitive state service: the partial liberation of that service from the aristocratic grip was indeed one of the crucial aspects of the extension of bourgeois power in the state and society. But it would, all the same, be highly unrealistic to think that even in an examination-oriented epoch membership of a relatively narrow segment of the population is not a distinct advantage, not only in terms of entry into the higher levels of the state service, but also, and hardly less important, of chances of upward movement inside it. Such membership affords links of kinship and friendship, and generally enhances a sense of shared values, all of which are helpful to a successful career. Two French authors put the point well, and what they say can scarcely be thought to apply exclusively to France:

If a student of modest origin has successfully negotiated his university course, the entrance examination of the ENA and even, why not, the final examination where the 'cultural' sifting is perhaps more severe than on entry, he will not, nevertheless, be on the same level as the offspring of great bourgeois families or of high officials: the spirit of caste and personal family relations will constantly work against him when promotions are made (at the highest level, promotion is more uncertain than at lower ones) (Bon and Burnier, 1966, p. 165).

Those who control and determine selection and promotion at the highest level of the state service are themselves most likely to be members of the upper and middle classes, by social origin or by virtue of their own professional success, and are likely to carry in their minds a particular image of how a high-ranking civil servant or military officer ought to think, speak, behave and react; and that image will be drawn in terms of the class to which they belong. No doubt, the recruiters, aware of the pressures and demands of a 'meritocratic' age, may consciously try to correct their bias; but they are particularly likely to overcome it in the case of working-class candidates who give every sign of readiness and capacity to adapt and conform to class-sanctioned patterns of behaviour and thought. 'Rough diamonds' are now more acceptable than in the past, but they should preferably show good promise of achieving the right kind of smoothness.

Weber claimed that the development of bureaucracy tended 'to eliminate class privileges, which include the appropriation of means of administration and the appropriation of authority as well as the occupation of offices on an honorary basis or as an avocation by virtue of wealth' (1947, p. 340). But this singularly underestimates the degree to which existing class privileges help to restrict this process, even though they do not arrest it altogether.

It is undoubtedly true that a process of social dilution has occurred in the state service, and has brought people born in the working classes, and even more commonly in the lower-middle classes, into elite positions inside the state system. But to speak of 'democratization' in this connection is somewhat misleading. What is involved here is rather a process of 'bourgeoisification' of the most able and thrusting recruits from the subordinate classes. As these recruits rise in the state hierarchy, so do they become part, in every significant sense, of the social class to which their position, income and status gives them access. As was already noted about working-class recruitment into the economic elite, this kind of dilution does not materially affect the class character of the state service and may indeed strengthen it. Moreover, such recruitment, by fostering the belief that capitalist societies are run on the principle of 'the career open to the talents' usefully obscures the degree to which they are not.

Given the particular hierarchies of the existing social order, it is all but inevitable that recruits from the subordinate classes into the upper reaches of the state system should, by the very fact of their entry into it, become part of the class which continues to dominate it. For it to be otherwise, the present intake would not only have to be vastly increased: the social order itself would have to be radically transformed as well, and its class hierarchies dissolved.

Social dilution of an even more pronounced kind than in the appointive institutions of the state system has also occurred in those of its institutions whose staffing depends, directly or indirectly, on election, namely the political executive and parliamentary assemblies. Thus, men of working-class or lower-middle-class origin have not uncommonly made their way into the Cabinets of advanced capitalist countries – some of them have even become Presidents and Prime Ministers; and an enormous amount of personal power has on occasion been achieved by altogether *déclassé* individuals like Hitler or Mussolini.

What significance this has had for the politics of advanced capitalism will be considered later. But it may be noted at this stage that men drawn from the subordinate classes have never constituted more than a minority of those who have reached high political office in these countries: the large majority has always belonged, by social origin and previous occupation, to the upper and middle classes.

To a somewhat lesser degree, yet still very markedly, this has also been the pattern of the legislatures of advanced capitalist countries. The growth in representation of working-class parties (save of course in the United States) has brought into these assemblies, though still as a minority, men (and occasionally women) who were not only born in the working classes but who, until their election, were themselves workers or at least closely involved in working-class life; and even bourgeois parties have undergone a certain process of social dilution. Nevertheless these latter parties, which have generally dominated parliamentary assemblies, have remained solidly upper and middle class in their social composition, with businessmen and others connected with various kinds of property ownership constituting a sizeable and often a very substantial part of their membership (see Guttsman, 1963). In terms of class, national politics (and for that matter, sub-national politics as well) has continued to be an 'activity' in which the subordinate classes have played a distinctly subsidiary role. Guttsman writes for Britain that:

> if we ascend the political hierarchy from the voters upwards, we find that at each level: the membership of political parties, party activists, local political leaders, MPs, national leaders – the social character of the group is slightly less 'representative' and slightly more tilted in favour of those who belong to the middle and upper levels of our society (p. 27).

The tilt is in fact much more than slight; and the point does not apply any the less to other countries than to Britain.

What the evidence conclusively suggests is that in terms of social origin, education and class situation, the men who have manned *all* command positions in the state system have largely, and in many cases overwhelmingly, been drawn from the world of business and property, or from the professional middle classes. Here as in every other field, men and women born into the subordinate classes, which form of course the vast majority of the population, have fared very poorly – and not only, it must be stressed, in those parts of the state system, such as administration, the military and the judiciary, which depend on appointment, but also in those parts of it which are exposed or which appear to be exposed to the vagaries of universal suffrage and the fortunes of competitive politics. In an epoch when so much is made of democracy, equality, social mobility, classlessness and the rest, it has remained a basic fact of life in advanced capitalist countries that the vast majority of men and women in these countries has been governed, represented, administered, judged, and commanded in war by people drawn from other, economically and socially superior and relatively distant classes.

References

ARON, R. (1964), *La Lutte des Classes*.

BENDIX, R. (1960), *Max Weber: An Intellectual Portrait*, Methuen.

BON, F. and BURNIER, M. A. (1966), *Les Nouveaux Intellectuels*,

DAHRENDORF, R. (1968), 'Recent changes in the class structure of European societies', *Daedalus*.

DAHRENDORF, R. (1964), *Society and Democracy in Germany*, Weidenfeld & Nicolson.

EDINGER, L. J. (1961), 'Continuity and change in the background of German decision-makers', *Western polit. Quarterly*, vol. 14.

GUTTSMAN, W. L. (1963), *The British Political Elite*, MacGibbon & Kee.

KAUTSKY, K. (1903), *The Social Revolution*.

MATTHEWS, D. R. (1954), *The Social Background of Political Decision-Makers*, Random.

MEYNAUD, J. (1964), *La Technocratie*.

MILLS, C. W. *The Power Elite*, Oxford University Press.

SCHMIDHAUSER, J. R. (1959), 'The Justices of the Supreme Court – a collective portrait', *Midwest Journal of Political Science*, vol. 3.

SCHONFIELD, A. (1965), *Modern Capitalism*, Oxford University Press.

SCHUMPETER, J. (1950), *Capitalism, Socialism and Democracy*, Allen & Unwin.

WEBER, M. (1947), *The Theory of Social and Economic Organisation*.

17 P. Baran and P. Sweezy

Monopoly Capital and Government

Excerpts from 'Civilian government', in P. Baran and P. Sweezy, *Monopoly Capital*, Penguin, 1968, pp. 157–75.

[. . .] Except in times of crisis, the normal political system of capitalism, whether competitive or monopolistic, is bourgeois democracy. Votes are the nominal source of political power, and money is the real source: the system, in other words, is democratic in form and plutocratic in content. This is by now so well recognized that it hardly seems necessary to argue the case. Suffice it to say that all the political activities and functions which may be said to constitute the essential characteristics of the system – indoctrinating and propagandizing the voting public, organizing and maintaining political parties, running electoral campaigns – can be carried out only by means of money, lots of money. And since in monopoly capitalism the big corporations are the source of big money, they are also the main sources of political power.

It is true that there is a latent contradiction in this system.[1] The non-property-owning voters, who constitute the overwhelming majority, may form their own mass organizations (trade unions, political parties), raise necessary funds through dues, and thereby become an effective political force. If they succeed in winning formal political power and then attempt to use it in a way which threatens the economic power and privileges of

1. Marx (1850) wrote of the democratic French constitution adopted in 1848: 'The most comprehensive contradiction of this constitution consisted in the following: the classes whose social slavery the constitution is to perpetuate, proletariat, peasants, petty bourgeois, it puts in possession of political power through universal suffrage. And from the class whose old social power it sanctions, the bourgeoisie, it withdraws the political guarantees of this power. It forces its rule into democratic conditions, which at every point help the hostile classes to victory and jeopardize the very foundations of bourgeois society.'

the money oligarchy, the system is confronted by a crisis which can be resolved according to its own rules only if the oligarchy is prepared to give up without a fight. Since to the best of our knowledge there is no case in history of a privileged oligarchy's behaving this way, we can safely dismiss the possibility. What happens instead is that the oligarchy, which controls either directly or through trusted agents all the instrumentalities of coercion (armed forces, police, courts, etc.), abandons the democratic forms and resorts to some form of direct authoritarian rule. Such a breakdown of bourgeois democracy and resort to authoritarian rule may also occur for other reasons – such as, for example, a prolonged inability to form a stable parliamentary majority, or successful resistance by certain vested interests to reforms necessary for the proper functioning of the economy. The history of recent decades is particularly rich in examples of the substitution of authoritarian for democratic government in capitalist countries: Italy in the early 1920s, Germany in 1933, Spain in the later 1930s, France in 1958, and many more.

In general, however, moneyed oligarchies prefer democratic to authoritarian government. The stability of the system is enhanced by periodic popular ratifications of oligarchic rule – this is what parliamentary and presidential elections normally amount to – and certain very real dangers to the oligarchy itself of personal or military dictatorship are avoided. Hence in developed capitalist countries, especially those with a long history of democratic government, oligarchies are reluctant to resort to authoritarian methods of dealing with opposition movements or solving difficult problems, and instead devise more indirect and subtle means for accomplishing their ends. Concessions are made to pull the teeth of trade-union and labour political movements professing radical aims. Their leaders are bought off – with money, flattery, and honours. As a result, when they acquire power they stay within the confines of the system, merely trying to win a few more concessions here and there to keep the rank and file satisfied, yet never challenging the real bastions of oligarchic power in the economy and in the coercive branches of the state apparatus. Similarly, the oligarchy alters the machinery of government to the extent necessary to prevent any stalemates and deadlocks which might involve the breakdown of democratic procedures (for example, the number of political parties is deliberately limited to prevent the emergence of government by unstable parliamentary coalitions). By these methods, and many others, democracy is made to serve the interests of the oligarchy far more effectively and durably than authoritarian rule. The possibility of authoritarian rule is never renounced – indeed, most democratic constitutions make specific provision for it in times of emergency – but it is decidedly not the preferred form of government for normally functioning capitalist societies.

The United States system of government is of course one of bourgeois democracy in the sense just discussed. In constitutional theory, the people exercise sovereign power; in actual practice, a relatively small moneyed oligarchy rules supreme. But democratic institutions are not merely a smoke screen behind which sit a handful of industrialists and bankers making policies and issuing orders. Reality is more complicated than that.

The nation's founding fathers were acutely aware of the latent contradiction in the democratic form of government, as indeed were most political thinkers in the late eighteenth and early nineteenth centuries. They recognized the possibility that the propertyless majority might, once it had the vote, attempt to turn its nominal sovereignty into real power and thereby jeopardize the security of property, which they regarded as the very foundation of civilized society. They therefore devised the famous system of checks and balances, the purpose of which was to make it as difficult as possible for the existing system of property relations to be subverted. American capitalism later developed in a context of numerous and often bitter struggles among various groups and segments of the money classes – which had never been united, as in Europe, by a common struggle against feudal power. For these and other reasons, the governmental institutions which have taken shape in the United States have been heavily weighted on the side of protecting the rights and privileges of minorities: the property-owning minority as a whole against the people, and various groups of property owners against each other. We cannot detail the story here –

how the separation of powers was written into the Constitution, how states' rights and local autonomy became fortresses for vested interests, how political parties evolved into vote-gathering and patronage-dispensing machines without programme or discipline. What interests us is the outcome, which was already shaped before the end of the nineteenth century. The United States became a sort of utopia for the private sovereignties of property and business. The very structure of government prevented effective action in many areas of the economy or social life (city planning, for example, to cite a need which has become increasingly acute in recent years). And even where this was not so, the system of political representation, together with the absence of responsible political parties, gave an effective veto power to temporary or permanent coalitions of vested interests. The positive role of government has tended to be narrowly confined to a few functions which could command the approval of substantially all elements of the moneyed classes: extending the national territory and protecting the interests of American businessmen and investors abroad, activities which throughout the nation's history have been the first concern of the federal government;[2] perfecting and protecting property rights at home; carving up the public domain among the most powerful and insistent claimants; providing a minimum infrastructure for the profitable operation of private business; passing out favours and subsidies in accordance with the well-known principles of the log-roll and the pork barrel [. . .]

In the case of almost every major item in the civilian budget, powerful vested interests are soon aroused to opposition as expansion proceeds beyond the necessary minimum. This occurs whenever a significant element of competition with private enterprise is involved, but it is also true of other items where competition with private enterprise is largely or even wholly absent.

There are many urgent social needs which government can satisfy only by entering into some form of competition with

2. Failure to understand this is one of the greatest weaknesses of most American historical writings. There are exceptions, however. See, e.g., Van Alstyne (1960), where the decisive character of foreign relations in shaping the nation's development from earliest times is correctly appreciated.

private interests. River valley development, for example, an area in which private enterprise could never hope to operate effectively, is essential for flood control, water conservation, rebuilding eroded soils, etc. But it also produces electric power which competes with private power and thus provides a yardstick by which the performance of the private power monopolies can be measured. For this reason, river valley development is bitterly opposed not only by the utilities themselves but also by the entire Big Business community. The history of the Tennessee Valley Authority affords eloquent testimony to the effectiveness of this opposition. TVA had its origin in the government's need for nitrates during the First World War. A dam, hydro-electric generating facilities, and a nitrate plant were built at Muscle Shoals, Alabama, to satisfy strictly military requirements. During the 1920s, a campaign to turn Muscle Shoals into a broad river valley development scheme was led by Senator Norris of Nebraska; but, in this period of capitalist prosperity, nothing came of it, and even the original investment was allowed to deteriorate in idleness. It was only during the 'Hundred Days' after Roosevelt's inauguration in 1933 – a period of near-panic for the moneyed oligarchy – that Norris's determined efforts were crowned with success. And the oligarchs have been regretting their moment of weakness ever since. From their point of view, the trouble with TVA was that it was a tremendous success. It gave the American people their first glimpse of what can be achieved by intelligent planning under a governmental authority equipped with the powers necessary to carry out a rational programme. To cite only one of its achievements, by the later 1950s a typical household in the TVA area was paying only half as much for its electricity and consuming twice as much as the national average. And on a world-wide scale, TVA had become a symbol of the New Deal, a light showing others the way to democratic progress. Under these circumstances, the oligarchy did not dare destroy TVA outright. Instead, it organized a long-range campaign of unremitting criticism and harassment destined to hedge TVA in, curtail its functions, force it to conform to the norms of capitalist enterprise. And this campaign has achieved considerable successes: TVA has never been allowed to realize anything like its full potential. Nevertheless, its popularity with the people of the seven-State area in which it operates has protected it from being gutted and perverted from its original aims. The greatest triumph of the anti-TVA campaign, therefore, has been its total success in keeping the principle of the multi-purpose river valley authority from being applied to any of the other numerous river valleys of the United States where it could so richly further the people's welfare. The need for more TVAs is easily demonstrable to any rational person; during the 1930s and later, expanded government outlays on river valley development would frequently have made excellent sense as a partial solution to the problem of inadequate surplus absorption. But what Marx called the Furies of private interest, having been thoroughly aroused, easily repelled any further encroachment on their sacred domain.

Public housing, potentially a vast field for welfare spending, is another activity which encroaches upon the realm of private enterprise. A really effective low-cost housing programme would necessarily call for extensive building in open spaces, which abound in most cities in the United States. But this is precisely what the powerful urban real estate interests are against. On the rock of this opposition, all attempts to launch a serious attack on the twin problems of insufficient and inadequate housing have foundered. Instead we have had fine-sounding 'slum clearance' or 'urban renewal' programmes, which, while liberally rewarding the owners of run-down property, typically throw more people on the streets than they house. Moreover, the mausoleum-like 'project' which is the usual embodiment of public housing is no kind of environment in which a viable community could take root and grow. 'Slum clearance' is thus in reality slum creation, both off-site and on-site; and 'urban renewal' is a system of outdoor relief for landlords in the decaying 'grey belts' which are inexorably creeping out from the centres of our big cities. So grim indeed has been the American experience with public housing since it first became a political issue during the 1930s that today it no longer commands even a modicum of popular support. 'Back in the '30s,' writes Seligman, an editor of *Fortune* magazine, 'proponents of public housing were possessed of a missionary fervour. New housing, they believed, would by itself exorcise crime and vice and disease. But public housing didn't do what its proponents expected. Today, public-housing people are searching for a new rationale and their fervour is gone; the movement today is so weak that most real-estate groups hardly bother to attack it any more' (Whyte, 1958, p. 93). A deliberate plot to sabotage public housing could hardly have succeeded more brilliantly: the private interests don't have to oppose any more – the public does it for them.

River valley development and public housing are but two examples of government activities which trespass upon the territory of private interests. In all such cases, since private interests wield political power, the limits of government spending are narrowly set and have nothing to do with social needs – no matter how shamefully obvious. But it is not only where there is competition with commercial enterprise that such limits are imposed: the same thing happens in areas like education and health where direct competition is either non-existent or of relatively minor importance. Here too the opposition of private interests to increased government spending is soon aroused; and here too the amounts actually spent bear no relation to demonstrable social need.

The reason for this is by no means obvious. It is no explanation to say that by far the greater part of these non-competitive government activities fall within the sphere of state and local governments. True, no significant increases in government spending are likely to be initiated at the state and local levels, but this is essentially beside the point. The federal government can play a larger role in these matters, both directly and via grants-in-aid to state and local units; and in fact it has been doing so in recent years, though on a very modest scale. The problem here is to explain why, in a period when the health of the economy urgently demanded a steadily rising volume of federal spending, so small a proportion of the increases has been devoted to satisfying society's communal consumption requirements. Why does the moneyed oligarchy, for example, so consistently and effectively oppose the proposals for increased federal aid to education which are put before the Congress year after year by Presidents who are themselves anything but radical crusaders? The need – for more schools and classrooms, for more teachers, for higher teachers' salaries, for more scholarships, for higher standards at all levels – is obvious to any citizen who keeps his eyes open; it has been proved time and again in government reports, scholarly treatises, popular tracts. The spectre of being outclassed by the Soviet Union has been held up to the country with frantic urgency ever since the first Sputnik went into orbit in 1957: the race between the systems, we are told, will eventually be won by the side not with the greatest firepower but with the greatest brainpower. And, despite all this, President Kennedy began a news conference on 15 January 1962, more than four years after Sputnik I, with these ominous figures:

In 1951 our universities graduated 19,600 students in the physical sciences. In 1960, in spite of the substantial increase in our population during the last ten years and in spite of the fact that the demand for people of skill in this field has tremendously increased with our efforts in defence and space, industrial research, and all the rest, in 1960 the number had fallen from 19,600 to 17,100.

In 1951 there were 22,500 studying in the biological sciences. In 1960 there were only 16,700.

In the field of engineering, enrolment rose from 232,000 to 269,000 in the period 1951 to 1957. Since 1957, there has been a continual decline in enrolments. Last year the figure was down to 240,000.[1]

How are such things possible with the national interest at stake – in the simplest and crudest sense of the term, one that should be easily understandable to the dullest member of the oligarchy? How can it happen that even the modest increases in federal aid to education are so often turned down?

The answer, in a nutshell, is that the educational system, as at present constituted, is a crucial element in the constellation of privileges and prerogatives of which the moneyed oligarchy is the chief beneficiary. This is true in a triple sense.

First, the educational system provides the oligarchy with the quality and quantity of educational services which its members want for themselves and their offspring. There is no shortage of expensive private schools and colleges for the sons and daughters of the well-to-do. Nor are the public schools of the exclusive suburbs and exurbs starved of funds, like the schools which serve the lower-middle and working classes in the cities and the

1. *New York Times*, 16 January 1962.

countryside. The educational system, in other words, is not a homogeneous whole. It consists of two parts, one for the oligarchy and one for the rest of the population. The part which caters to the oligarchy is amply financed. It is a privilege and a badge of social position to go through it. And the very fact that it serves only a small part of the population is precisely its most precious and jealously guarded feature. This is why any attempt to generalize its benefits is bound to be stubbornly fought by the oligarchy. This is also perhaps the most basic reason for the strength of the opposition to expanded programmes of federal aid to education.

Second – the other side of the same coin – that part of the educational system which is designed for the vast majority of young people must be inferior and must turn out human material fitted for the lowly work and social positions which society reserves for them. This aim of course cannot be achieved directly. The egalitarianism of capitalist ideology is one of its strengths, not to be lightly discarded. People are taught from earliest childhood and by all conceivable means that everyone has an equal opportunity, and that the inequalities which stare them in the face are the result not of unjust institutions but of their own superior or inferior natural endowments. It would contradict this teaching to set up, in the manner of European class-divided societies, two distinct educational systems, one for the oligarchy and one for the masses. The desired result must be sought indirectly, by providing amply for that part of the educational system which serves the oligarchy while financially starving that part which serves the lower-middle and working classes. This ensures the inequality of education so vitally necessary to buttress the general inequality which is the heart and core of the whole system. No special arrangements are needed, however, to achieve this force-feeding of one part of the educational system and starving of the other. The private schools and colleges are in any case well provided for, and the established system of local control and financing for public schools automatically results in extremely unequal treatment for the suburban and exurban public schools in contrast to the urban and rural schools. What is crucial is to prevent this delicate balance from being upset by massive federal invasion, with the enormous taxing and spending powers of the national government being used to implement the educational reformers' age-old ideal of equal and excellent educational opportunity for all. Here we have a second compelling reason for the oligarchy to keep government spending to a minimum in an area which reason tells us could beneficially absorb a large proportion of society's surplus product.

The third sense in which the educational system supports the existing class structure is complementary to the first two. Every viable class society must provide a method by which brains and talent from the lower classes can be selected, used by, and integrated into the upper classes. In Western feudal society, the Catholic Church provided the necessary mechanism. Competitive capitalism made it possible for able and aggressive lower-class boys to ascend a purely economic ladder into the oligarchy. Monopoly capitalism has effectively blocked this channel of upward mobility: it is now rarely possible to start a small business and build it up into a big one. A substitute mechanism has been found in the educational system. Through low-tuition state universities, scholarships, loans and the like, boys and girls who are really able and ambitious (desirous of success, as society defines it) can move up from the inferior part of the educational system. Accepted into the better preparatory schools, colleges and universities, they are given the same training and conditioning as upper-class young people. From there the road leads through the corporate apparatus or the professions into integration in the upper-middle and occasionally the higher, strata of society. The superficial observer, having heard the slogans about equal opportunity, may see evidence here that the educational system works to undermine the class structure. Nothing could be further from the truth. The ideal of equal opportunity for all could be realized only by abolition of the special privileges of the upper classes, not by making these privileges available to a select group from the lower classes. This simply strengthens the class structure by infusing new blood into the upper classes and depriving the lower classes of their natural leaders.[1] And these are the objectives that are actually served by

1. 'The more a ruling class is able to assimilate the most prominent men of a ruled class,' Marx (1890, vol. 3, ch. 36) wrote, 'the more solid and dangerous is its rule.'

currently fashionable educational reforms, including such modest increases in federal aid as the oligarchy is prepared to put up with. Any serious attempt to meet the real educational needs of a modern technologically and scientifically advanced society would necessitate a totally different approach – including a commitment of resources on a scale that no dominant oligarchy intent on preserving its own narrow privileges would even dream of.

It would be possible to run through the gamut of civilian spending objects and show how in case after case the private interests of the oligarchy stand in stark opposition to the satisfaction of social needs. Real competition with private enterprise cannot be tolerated, no matter how incompetent and inadequate its performance may be; undermining of class privileges or of the stability of the class structure must be resisted at any cost. And almost all types of civilian spending involve one or both of these threats. There is just one major exception to this generalization in the United States today, and it is very much the type of exception which proves the rule: government spending on highways.

There is no need here to detail the importance of the automobile to the American economy. We need only say that the main business of several of the largest and most profitable corporations is the production of motor vehicles; the petroleum industry, with some ten corporations having assets of more than a billion dollars, makes most of its profits from the sale of petrol for use in motor vehicles; several other major monopolistic industries (rubber, steel, glass) are crucially dependent on sales to automobile makers or users; more than a quarter of a million persons are employed in the repair and servicing of automobiles; and countless other businesses and jobs (trucking, motels, resorts, etc.) owe their existence, directly or indirectly, to the motor vehicle. This complex of private interests clustering around one product has no equal elsewhere in the economy – or in the world. And the whole complex, of course, is completely dependent on the public provision of roads and highways. It is thus only natural that there should be tremendous pressure for continuous expansion of government spending on highways. Counter-pressures from private interests do exist – notably from the railways, hard hit by the growth of highway transportation, but the railways have been no match for the automobile complex. Government spending on highways has soared; limitations posed by state and local finances have been overcome by increasingly liberal federal grants-in-aid. And today highways are second only to education as an object of civilian government spending.

This fact does not in itself prove that spending on highways has gone beyond any rational conception of social need. What does prove it – dramatically and overwhelmingly – is the frightful havoc which has been wreaked on American society by the cancerous growth of the automobile complex, a growth which would have been impossible if government spending for the required highways had been limited and curtailed as the oligarchy has limited and curtailed spending for other civilian purposes. Cities have been transformed into nightmares of congestion; their atmosphere is fouled by disease-bearing pollutants; vast areas of good urban and rural land are turned into concrete strips and asphalt fields; peaceful communities and neighbourhoods are desecrated by the roar and stench of cars and trucks hurtling past; railways, which can move goods and passengers efficiently and unobtrusively, lose traffic and correspondingly raise rates in a vicious circle which threatens the very existence of commuter service for our biggest cities; urban rapid transit systems are at once starved and choked, so that getting around the downtown area of New York, Chicago, and dozens of other metropolises becomes an ordeal to which only the necessitous or the foolhardy will submit. And the usual remedy for this increasingly frightful and frightening state of affairs? More highways, more streets, more garages, more parking areas – more of the same poison that is already threatening the very life of an increasingly urbanized civilization. And all this is made possible by lavish grants of public funds, eagerly sought and approved by an oligarchy of wealth which fights tooth and nail against every extension of those public services which would benefit the great body of their fellow-citizens. Nowhere is the madness of American monopoly capitalism more manifest, or more hopelessly incurable [. . .]

References

MARX, K. (1890), *Capital*, University of Chicago Press.
MARX, K. (1850), *The Class Struggles in France:* International Publishers.
VAN ALSTYNE, R. W. (1960), *The Rising American Empire*, Oxford.
WHYTE, W. H. *et al.* (1958), *The Exploding Metropolis*, Doubleday.

18 Anthony Crosland

The Decline in the Economic Power of the Capitalist Class

Excerpts from 'The transfer of economic power', in Anthony Crosland, *The Future of Socialism*, Cape, 1956, pp. 5–22.

The pre-war power of the business class

[A basic] Marxist assumption, on which . . . much pre-war socialist analysis was based, was that society was effectively controlled by a capitalist ruling-class which held all or most of the important levers of power. Now Marxist theory does not . . . provide a satisfactory basis for the analysis of either the class system or the distribution of power; its scope is too restricted, and the categories too narrow.

Nevertheless, if we confine ourselves to one particular aspect of *economic* power, and accept that we are not discussing the whole subject of power in modern society, we may say that the pre-war 'capitalist' class possessed this power to a marked degree, and wielded it with a good deal of ruthlessness.[1] This is the power to make, or at least predominantly influence, both the major production decisions (whether, how much, how, what, and where to produce) and distribution decisions (about the division of the national income between different social groups), the first being of course much easier to determine than the second. Such power requires effective control both at the perimeter (that is, in the firm or industrial unit) and at the centre (that is, at the seat of government).

1. The adjective 'capitalist' is not, it is true, entirely exact, since it has to embrace salaried business executives as well as industrialists drawing their power from the traditional capitalist source of industrial property-ownership. Nevertheless it is a not wholly misleading shorthand for the pre-war class of business leaders, many of whom still retained a considerable ownership stake in industry; while even those who did not continued to adopt a predominantly capitalist standpoint in the sense that they held the interests of property to be paramount.

The pre-war capitalist class broadly possessed this control. In some respects, it is true, its economic power had contracted over the years with the steady accretion of influence to both the political and industrial Left, and the general growth of democratic sentiment and social conscience. Yet in other ways it had grown as a result of technical and economic changes. The trend towards large scale in industry, and the inter-war trend towards monopoly, meant that the decisions of a single firm or cartel had an increasing impact on society; a smaller number of individuals took decisions that affected a larger number of their fellow-citizens. At the same time, the growth of monopoly weakened the element of consumer influence which competition to some extent preserves.

The economic power of the business class both at the perimeter and the centre can best be gauged by recalling what was in some ways the most symbolic, as in others it was the most traumatic, incident of the 1930s – the story of Jarrow.[2] Jarrow was condemned, physically to a decade without jobs, psychologically to a decade without hope, as a result of two decisions: first, to close down the shipyard on which almost the whole town depended for its livelihood; secondly, to prevent, by the refusal of a guaranteed share in a fully-controlled home market, the construction of a modern, integrated steel plant.

Now the immediate issue is not whether these decisions were right or wrong from a strictly economic point of view, but what they implied for the distribution of economic power. Both were taken by private monopoly bodies (National Shipbuilders Security Ltd and the Iron and Steel Federation). Both were taken over the passionate protests of the workers and the local community, and in the face of a public opinion strongly aroused by such dramatic incidents as the famous Jarrow hunger-march, as well as by the flood of stories of local suffering and distress. Both were taken solely in the light of short-term profit considerations, and were influenced neither by the social and humanitarian arguments on the other side, nor by the long-term public interest in the capacity and location of two such strategically important industries. And both were taken with the sanction of the Government, despite the storm of protests and appeals.

2. For an account of this episode see Wilkinson (1939).

The refusal of the Government to intervene afforded striking evidence of the continued subservience of the political authority, despite the revulsion caused by the Great Depression, to the interests of business. Right-wing governments, largely composed of businessmen and wedded to an ideology of *laisser faire,* were firmly opposed to interfering in the 'legitimate preserve' of private industry. When they did intervene, it was not to limit the economic power of private enterprise, but on the contrary to give additional sanction or support to its policies. Tariffs, industrial subsidies, Marketing Boards – all these interventions were at the behest of the producers concerned, and designed to strengthen their monopoly position. The weight attached by the Government to the (supposed) interests of the business class was most conspicuously (and painfully) demonstrated by its refusal to adopt any effective employment policy, whether the sort of expansionist anti-depression policy being widely tried out in other countries, or even a more limited policy of locating new factories in the distressed areas.

The loss of power by the business class to the state

To-day the capitalist business class has lost this commanding position. The change in the balance of economic power is reflected in, and may be inferred from, three developments. First, certain decisive sources and levers of economic power have been transferred from private business to other hands; and new levers have emerged, again concentrated in other hands than theirs. Secondly, the outcome of clashes of group or class economic interests is markedly less favourable to private employers than it used to be. Thirdly, the social attitudes and behaviour of the business class have undergone a significant change, which appears to reflect a pronounced loss of strength and self-confidence.

The most direct and obvious loss of economic power has been to the political authority, which now exerts control over a much higher proportion of economic decisions than before the war. The public authorities today not only employ 25 per cent of the total employed population, and are responsible for over 50 per cent of total investment, but they wield a substantially greater power over business decisions even when these remain nominally in private hands.

This is largely a consequence of the explicit acceptance by governments of responsibility for full employment, the rate of growth, the balance of payments, and the distribution of incomes. The main instrument for exercising this responsibility is fiscal policy. Acting mainly through the Budget, though with the aid of other instruments, the government can exert any influence it likes on income-distribution, and can also determine within broad limits the division of total output between consumption, investment, exports, and social expenditure.

But it also exerts a powerful influence on production-decisions in individual industries – not only through a wider range of positive and negative indirect taxes (especially purchase-tax), which alter the pattern of demand and hence the relative attraction to producers of different lines of conduct; but, more important, through monetary, legislative, physical, and hire-purchase controls. It often fails to use these controls as effectively as the critics would like. Nevertheless, it uses them to an extent which severaly limits, as compared with the position under pre-war capitalism, the autonomy of business decisions.

Naturally the greater influence of the government would signify little if it were simply used to buttress the power, and underwrite the actions, of private business – if the state, in the Marxist phrase, were still the 'executive committee' of the capitalist class. But of course it is no such thing. The policies and attitudes of government are by no means the same as they were in the 1930s. The change is due mainly to a Leftward shift in the balance of electoral opinion, reflected not merely in six years of post-war Labour rule, but also in the significantly reduced majorities, by pre-war standards, of the succeeding Conservative governments. Conscious of the slender electoral margin now separating the parties, and sensitive also to a fundamental change in public attitudes towards full employment and social welfare, these administrations have largely preserved the changes introduced by the Labour Government; and this has required the exercise of economic power on a scale, and in a direction, which would never have been countenanced by pre-war Conservative governments.

The reality of the change is attested by the different outcome of clashes of group economic interests. These most obviously take the form of disputes over the distribution of income. Since 1939, a considerable redistribution of personal incomes has occurred; and the gains have accrued largely to the workers, while the losses are at the expense of property-incomes – the share of net dividends, in particular, is much reduced. In addition, and indeed partly responsible for the smaller share of dividends, the taxation of profits is now much heavier than before the war despite an unceasing chorus of protests from business leaders. When private industry cannot even win its taxation battles against the government, something quite important must have changed.

Equally significant is the distribution of economic sacrifices in a crisis, for this reflects perhaps more accurately than anything else the ultimate location of power. Before the war, it was always the working class which bore the brunt. Since the war, the outcome has been quite different. It was a shrewd, though not overfriendly, American observer who remarked of the 1947 crisis that 'for the first time in British history the brunt of an economic crisis is not being borne by the workers' (Matthews, 1947). The best evidence of the change, at least during the period of Labour Government, was to be found in the intense antagonism of the better-off classes.

Herein lay the whole secret of the middle classes' attitude to the Government, which ranged from white fury to hurt bewilderment. In 1921 they had suffered severely, but the working class had suffered too. . . . It was the same in 1931. . . . But now the Labour Government was talking about 'equality of sacrifice', and the working class was not sacrificing anything; there weren't even any unemployed (Lewis and Maude, 1949).

Certainly the middle classes have come off distinctly better under the Tories. Yet a repetition of 1921 or 1931 is unthinkable even now; the national shift to the Left, with all its implications for the balance of power, may be accepted as permanent.

The other test lies in social and political attitudes. Here the contrast with both the facts and the expectations of the 1930s was complete, most obviously during the period of Labour rule.

Pre-war socialists often anticipated violent, if not unconstitutional, opposition from private business; and a whole theory of 'capitalist sabotage', ranging from a flight of capital abroad to a 'strike of capital' at home, was constructed on this premiss. The event was very different. Investment proceeded briskly, and indeed had to be restrained; the opposition to nationalization, although vocal, was never violent; firms and Trade Associations cooperated amicably wth Labour Ministers; there was no hint of sabotage; and generally the atmosphere was one of amiable amenability, not untinged with nervousness.

All this was partly, of course, a reflection simply of the extreme unplausibility of pre-war Marxist analysis. But it also reflected a consciousness on the part of industry that the balance of power had altered. This consciousness (and also the diminished capitalist influence within industry itself) was most conspicuously demonstrated by the acceptance of voluntary dividend restraint during the Crippsian era. Despite the outcry in the City press, the degree of cooperation was remarkable, and a striking sign of weakened capitalist self-confidence. Certainly company chairmen continued to fulminate in their annual speeches; but their actions were the reverse of aggressive.

The fact that governments now exercise this pervasive economic power, and that they do so from motives other than a desire to prop up private business, would be sufficient by itself to outmode most pre-war, semi-Marxist analyses of class power. 'Whatever the forms of state', wrote Laski in 1937, 'political power will, in fact, belong to the owners of economic power.' This was hardly a very helpful or plausible statement even in 1937, in the light of the history of Nazism and Fascism. But if we are to make misleadingly simple statements of this kind, it would be more accurate to turn Laski's statement on its head: whatever the modes of economic production, economic power will, in fact, belong to the owners of political power. And these to-day are certainly not the pristine class of capitalists.

The effects of nationalization on the distribution of power

A second transfer of economic power has followed from the nationalization of the basic industries. This has clearly diminished the power of the capitalist class. But more than this one cannot easily assert, for while everyone agrees on who has lost the power, not everyone agrees on who has gained it. The political authority now has, it is true, the power of Ministerial directive, of parliamentary debate, and of investigation by select committee. On the other hand, many of the nationalized boards consistently act in a very independent manner, which provokes constant complaints alike from workers, politicians, and economists. Indeed, some people think that the boards are actually less 'accountable', and amenable to governmental control, than many private managements.

For practical purposes, therefore, economic decisions in the basic sector have passed out of the hands of the capitalist class into the hands of a new and largely autonomous class of public industrial managers. But since the political authority has at the same time acquired an explicit legal power over these new managers, even though it often chooses not to use it, the change does represent, in the last resort, an increase in the economic power of the state – though of course this leaves open the question of whether nationalisation is always the only, or the best, method of achieving this result [. . .]

The psychological revolution within industry and the altered role of profit

So far we have considered the loss of economic power by the business class as a whole to forces external to itself. But internal changes have also occurred within industry which significantly reduce the power of the capitalist class relative to other managerial classes. These changes were already perceptible before the war; but they have accelerated in the last decade.

The first, a consequence of the growing scale, complexity and technical intricacy of modern industry, is the increasingly specialised nature of business decisions. The gifted amateur is more and more at a discount; and even the professional top executive sometimes finds his decisions almost predetermined (especially in regard to investment) by technological or research considerations. As a result, although the ultimate power of course remains in the hands of the top 'lay' management, more and more influence passes to the technical experts and specialists – the new 'organization men' with the 'long-haired know-how', to use the current American slang: the plant engineer, the research chemist, the market research experts, the corporation lawyers, and the like. This partial change in the character of the decision-making function naturally calls for men with a different outlook and equipment, and therefore different interests and motives, from those of the traditional capitalist. One sign of the change is the growing number of scientists and specialized technicians appointed to boards of directors.

But much more significant, though many socialists are reluctant to admit it, is the change in the psychology and motivation of the top management class itself. This is partly, though by no means solely, a consequence of the now well-documented change in the composition of the business-executive class. The divorce between ownership and management, and the relative growth of the joint-stock corporation with fragmented shareholding, were of course already evident before the war. But the process has been further accelerated since by the continued growth in the scale and hence the financial requirements of industry, by a level of taxation which bears relatively more heavily on the small private business than on the public company, and by the effect of higher death duties in compelling the conversion of private into public companies. Business leaders are now, in the main, paid by salary and not by profit, and owe their power to their position in the managerial structure, and not to ownership. Meanwhile, the nominal owners have largely lost even the residue of control which they retained before the war.

And top management today is independent not only of the firm's own shareholders, but increasingly of the capitalist or property-owning class as a whole, including the financial institutions. As compared with the inter-war period, a higher proportion of profits is ploughed back into the business, and a higher proportion of capital expenditure is financed internally and not by recourse to outside capital. It is true that the Marxist prophecy of the transition to 'finance-capitalism', as industry fell more and more into the clutches of the City and the banks, was never at any time wholly fulfilled in Britain. But the financial difficulties created by the depression caused at least a trend in that direction before the war; and there were certain important industries in which management was, in consequence, extremely susceptible to outside financial pressure.

Today, however, a decade of prosperity and high gross profits, combined with a lower ratio of dividend distribution, has greatly fortified the financial strength and independence of most public companies. Despite the increased weight of taxation, undistributed profits are normally sufficient (taking industry as a whole) to finance the whole of industrial capital formation – with a good deal, indeed, to spare. Naturally some firms still need to borrow or make new issues of share-capital; but internal company savings, relative to investment, are now higher than before the war. The economic power of the capital market and the finance houses, and hence *capitalist* financial control over industry (in the strict sense of the word), are thus much weaker. This change alone makes it rather absurd to speak now of a capitalist ruling-class.

The decline of capitalist control does not of course mean that the profit-motive has disappeared, or that profits are less important. It is a mistake to think that profit, in the sense of a surplus over cost, has any special or unique connection with capitalism. On the contrary, it must be the rationale of business activity in any society, whether capitalist or socialist, which is growing and dynamic. But with the divorce between ownership and management, the role of profit has undergone a subtle change, which leads to a consequential change both in the distribution of profit, and in the intensity with which maximum profits are pursued.

The contemporary business leader does not want high profits primarily as a source of high personal income or consumption; since he does not own the business, he cannot, as his capitalist predecessor often used to do, withdraw large sums from it for his own enjoyment. Nor does he seek high profits primarily in order to maximize the reward of shareholders. He seeks them, partly, of course, because in the long run his own remuneration depends on the success of the company, but mainly because his social status, power, and prestige depend directly on the level of profits. This is both the conventional test of business performance, and the source of business power. It determines both the strength and prestige of the firm, and the power and social status of its executives. Thus profit remains an essential personal and corporate incentive – but largely as a source of strength and influence, and not as an avenue to a privileged consumption-position for the capitalist. The implications for the distribution of income, as the shareholders' champions well realize and the figures of dividend payments demonstrate, are of course profound.

A further result of this change is a less aggressive pursuit of maximum profit at all costs. Profits are seen partly as a source of social prestige. But in the climate of the welfare state, they are far from being the only such source. The business leader can also acquire prestige by gaining a reputation as a progressive employer, who introduces co-partnership or profit-sharing schemes: or by being known to possess a high standing in Whitehall, and to have the ear of Ministers, an obvious candidate, perhaps, for Royal Commissions and National Advisory Councils; or by enjoying an outstanding local and civic reputation, as a benefactor, a helpful friend to the City Council, a member of the Court of the civic University; or by displaying obvious patriotism, and devoting a lot of time to the British Productivity Council; or simply by being an intellectual, who broadcasts and writes in Bank Reviews, or makes speeches at the British Institute of Management or Nuffield Conferences at Oxford. Such activities are increasingly common and well-regarded.

All this represents, I believe, a profound change in the social climate, which communicates itself even to the sphere of business decisions. Thus private industry today tends to be very sensitive to public opinion, and to its own notion of the public interest, even though no specific threat or sanction may have to be feared either from the government or from labour. This is evident even in respect of price policy. Price-determination is not now simply a matter of crude profit-maximization, or invariably directed to the greatest possible exploitation of the consumer. It is at least influenced by notions of what constitutes a conventionally fair and reasonable price, which will be acceptable as broadly in the public interest, and immune from accusations of over-charging. For a long time after the war, for example, there were many goods, such as motor-cars, for which a huge pent-up demand existed, and which would have commanded an enormous price in a free market. Yet manufacturers, almost without exception, held prices down to what they considered a 'fair' and 'reasonable' level, well below the market or profit-maximizing price. No doubt considerations of long-run goodwill played a part in this deliberate moderation; but the prevailing social climate also played a part.

The traditional capitalist ruthlessness has largely disappeared from other spheres as well: from that of investment policy – few firms today, quite apart from the certainty of government intervention, would even try to repeat the Jarrow story; or policy towards competitors, dealers or suppliers, who are seldom driven into bankruptcy with quite the vigorous *élan* of thirty years ago; and most obviously, in the many ways described above, from labour policy.

The talk, and part of it at least is genuine, is now of the social responsibilities of industry – to workers, consumers, the locality, retiring employees, disabled workers, and in America, where business benefactions are on a gigantic scale, to universities, research foundations, and even symphony orchestras. Aggressive individualism is giving way to a suave and sophisticated sociability: the defiant cry of 'the public be damned' to the well-staffed public relations department: the self-made autocratic tycoon to the arts graduate and the scientist: the invisible hand, in Mr Riesman's phrase, to the glad hand. Private industry is at last becoming humanized.

I do not mean that all businessmen now behave as though they were *manqué* philanthropists or social reformers – many manifestly do not. But I do believe that the trend is in the direction I describe: that most businessmen are at least tinged by these more social attitudes and motives: and that those who most obviously express the change are coming to set the tone for industry as a whole. At any rate, we have here a definite contrast with a generation ago.

This psychological change of course fuses with, and reinforces, the change in attitudes to the state and the Trade Unions described above, and due simply to the loss of economic power. In practice one cannot disentangle the two influences, or say precisely which is cause and which effect. Nor indeed does it very much matter. Even supposing the motives behind the more diplomatic and humane behaviour to be of the narrowest and most self-interested kind, deriving solely from a consciousness of weakness, it would make no difference to our analysis – indeed it would be the more convincing proof of the altered configuration of power. And no doubt a large part of the change is to be so explained. Yet I doubt if this is the whole explanation – especially as the decline in the ideology of aggressive individualism even has its reflection within the business itself, where decision making is more and more passing from the individual to the team.

This is not due solely to such technical influences as the greater number of variables and their increasingly specialized character, which virtually compel a group approach to decision-making. It is also due to a change in ethos, from the cult of the individual to the cult of teamwork. This explains the almost obsessive contemporary emphasis on cooperation, participation, communication, 'democratic leadership', 'permissive management', and all the rest of the slogans of 'progressive' management. The old-style capitalist was by instinct a tyrant and an autocrat, and cared for no one's approval. The new-style executive prides himself on being a good committee-man; and subconsciously he longs for the approval of the sociologist. He dreads any suggestion of high-handedness, or hint that he has failed to consult his colleagues. Above all the staff must work as a team; and where once the apt analogies for business behaviour were taken from war, now they are taken from sport. As one of the shrewdest observers of American industry has written: 'If our society comes to an end it will not be with a bang or a whimper. The sound track will be the soft tinkle of rimless glasses on a conference table' (Whyte, 1952, p. 223).

The political power of private industry

[. . .] Whatever may or may not be happening in the realm of managerial psychology, it is indisputable that the economic power of the capitalist (i.e. industrial property-owning) class is enormously less than a generation ago; while even that of the managerial business class is significantly restricted by the new economic activism of governments, and the greater strength of organized labour [. . .]

Of course the arguments presented [here] relate only to one manifestation of power in modern society, and that, in my view, of diminishing importance. Economic power, in the sense described [here], and which rather naturally obsessed pre-war socialists when they were analysing capitalism, now poses fewer problems than other forms of power which have nothing to do with ownership or private industry as such, and indeed cut across the capitalist-socialist controversy.[3] These are first the power of the enlarged and bureaucratic state: secondly, the power of a small hierarchy of Court, Church, and influential newspapers, either to block reform or to impose its own social and moral standards on groups and individuals: and thirdly, the power of those who control the bureaucratic mass organization, whether public or private – the BBC, the Coal Board, and the Trade Unions quite as much as ICI or Unilever.

[...] I do not share all the current alarmism about the extreme menace which they present – what one might call respectively 'Crichel Down', 'Establishment', and 'managerial revolution' fears. Nevertheless I do believe that these aspects of power are of greater significance than the economic power to control production and distribution decisions, now that this is so much less concentrated and irresponsible than it was before the war.

Again, statements about the decline in the economic power of the capitalist class are not to be taken as statements about *social* class. They do not imply that social class is necessarily any less pervasive or significant in Britain than it was, or even that no 'upper-class', in some sense of social status and prestige, can now be said to exist. Economic power is only one aspect of social class; and other aspects may remain just as relevant even though this one has diminished in importance. It is quite consistent to say both that Britain remains to an exceptional degree a 'class society', and that no ruling class exists in the narrow Marxist or economic sense [...]

3. It is curious that the socialist, as opposed to the radical, tradition has comparatively little to say about any aspects of power other than the economic and political power of privately-owned industry.

References

LASKI, H. J. (1937), *Liberty in the Modern State*, Penguin.

LEWIS, R. and MAUDE, A. (1949), *The English Middle Classes*, Phoenix House.

MATTHEWS, H. L. (1947), *New York Times*, 25 November.

WHYTE, W. H. (1952), *Is Anybody Listening?*

WILKINSON, E. (1939), *The Town That was Murdered*, Gollancz.

Elitism and Pluralism

19 R. Presthus

Pluralism and Elitism

From 'Theoretical framework', in R. Presthus, *Men at the Top*, Oxford University Press, 1964, pp. 10–28.

Pluralism

There has been a curious reluctance on the part of scholars precisely to define 'pluralism'. Perhaps it is one of those terms one takes for granted. It is defined here as a sociopolitical system in which the power of the state is shared with a large number of private groups, interest organizations, and individuals represented by such organizations. The ultimate philosophical justification for pluralism lies in natural law, in the belief that the individual's right of free association emanates from God. In brief, pluralism is a system in which political power is fragmented among the branches of government; it is moreover shared between the state and a multitude of private groups and individuals. 'Elitism', which we may define as its antithesis, is a system in which disproportionate power rests in the hands of a minority of the community.[1] [. . .]

The origins of the pluralist rationale probably lie far back in history. Pluralism is inspired by the ancient fear of government, which results from impersonal, arbitrary rule, and by the reluctant conclusion that power corrupts in geometric progression as it grows. The possibility of curbing government's excessive demands by fragmenting its power was recognized as early as the

1. Technically, the antithesis of pluralism is 'monism', which from Aristotle to Bentham has meant that the state is the highest sovereign power, to which all its constituent associations are legally and ethically subordinate.

Greek city states. Aristotle, for example, believed that revolutions were caused by narrowing too much the circle of government; in effect, they followed when power and its prerequisites were limited to a single circle. He noted, too, that stability, the aim of every form of government, requires balance among its various parts (*Politics*, 1306–13).

This fearful conception of governmental power which underlies pluralism is clear in our own Constitution and in the American tendency to interpret it *negatively*, as a limitation upon government rather than as an instrument which grants great power to it. The founding fathers' pervasive fear of government is explicit in their efforts to limit its power. As a result, Madison, who was almost surely influenced by the *Vindiciae Contra Tyrannos*, set down a classic defence of pluralism in *The Federalist*, no 10. The institutionalization of this view is seen in our 'separation of powers' system and its checks-and-balances which doubly ensure that government can act expeditiously only in crises. Power is shared among the three great branches, each of which, in turn, exercises some portion of the specific power mainly allocated to the others.

Modern conceptions of pluralism, however, reflect the rise of industrial society, in which every other interest tends to be subordinate to *raisons d'état*. This rationale suggests that power is highly fragmented, that it is so amorphous, shifting, and tentative that few can be said to have more power than others over any period of time. Power is broadly shared among a congeries of competing public and private groups; those in high places may appear to have great power, but in reality they are only mediators among conflicting interests, for whose power and support they must continually bargain. Things get done by compromise; to get along, one goes along. Government and the bureaucracy may be viewed as disinterested umpires in the struggle among private groups for larger shares of desired values [. . .]

A critical assumption of pluralism is that it provides for the broadest possible representation of private interests *vis-à-vis* the state. But a problem arises in that such interests often achieve their ends at the expense of a broader, unorganized public, usually composed of individuals in their role as consumers. On any given social issue, the voice of this majority often goes unheard, while those with an immediate interest speak loudly. That the claims of the latter are usually rationalized in the 'public interest' is of tactical interest, but hardly changes the essential dilemma. This inequality of bargaining power, which reflects the reality of inequitable access and power disequilibria between organized interests and the unorganized majority, may be recognized; it does not, it seems, vitiate the normative appeal and assumed consequences of pluralism [. . .]

The pluralist case also rests on the argument that the essential thing is competition and participation among organized *groups*, not among individuals. That is, it may be argued that pluralism requires access and participation by *organizations*, which are necessarily directed by the few. One logical problem here is the organismic fallacy which imputes to organizations an existence apart from their members. Another assumption is that leaders do, indeed, represent their constituents and that merely by joining an organization, the individual makes his will felt [. . .]

An aspect of pluralism, which gives it a somewhat quaint character, is the changing popular attitude toward the modern state. On balance, and with many qualifications, what we have seen in the United States is the gradual erosion of the negative conception of the state, which is part of the classical pluralist view, in favour of a happier definition of its role. Today, the state is often seen as the only viable means of *ensuring* economic and civil liberty, as in the case of the Negro. This changing perspective may reflect a growing recognition that, among all social entities, the state alone possesses both ability to recognize and the resources to meet growing demands for security in industrial societies. As a result, many interests now look to the state for welfare bounties, subsidies, and the arbitration of competing group interests, rather than regarding it as a monolithic threat. In this normative sense, the pluralist conception of the state has been turned upside down.

Traditional conceptions of pluralism have changed in another way. Such reassessments may be based upon the changing nature of many groups which, instead of remaining *bona fide* instruments of pluralism, have become oligarchic and restrictive insofar as they monopolize access to governmental power and limit individual participation. As one observer notes, 'the voluntary organizations or associations which the early theorists of pluralism relied upon to sustain the individual against a unified omnipotent government, have themselves become oligarchically governed hierarchies' (Kariel, 1961). Such groups have so 'collectivized' the individual member that, although he remains vital to the extent of providing the numerical base upon which the group's power rests, he has little influence on its policies. Often using democratic forms, its leaders maintain oligarchic control of the organization's resources. They *are* the organization, representing it before other publics, personifying its major values. A not too subtle rationalization follows whereby rank-and-file members are defined as somehow not true representatives of the group. Their role and judgements remain 'unofficial'. The effects on participation are generally restrictive, since the rank and file often accepts such limitations.

Viewed as independent systems, then, the private groups that give meaning to pluralism are rarely pluralistic, in the sense of having competing power centres *within* them. Such groups no longer meet traditional pluralist assumptions, because of the great inequality of bargaining power that characterizes them. The pluralism that exists is too often restricted to the few powerful organizations that monopolize most social areas. Producer groups, linked fundamentally by an economic interest, dominate, and the less disciplined voluntary associations rarely compete successfully with them in the struggle for access and influence.

Such developments underlie the changed conditions and meaning of pluralism, which continues nevertheless to be defined and defended in traditional terms. An example of recent efforts to accommodate pluralism to its new environment is seen in the area of community power structure research. Its advocates now argue that pluralism exists if *no single elite* dominates decision making in every substantive area. In effect, if bargaining and opposition among three or four elite groups (who usually make up something less than 1 per cent of the community) persist, pluralism remains viable. The existence of competition among elites, so to speak, has become the essential criterion. This is obviously a realistic theory in an age of superorganization, but whether by itself it provides a valid measure of 'pluralism' remains questionable. Certainly this is a much more restricted definition than that traditionally associated with the concept.

Some conditions of pluralism

Such qualifications suggest that the concept of pluralism must be made more specific if it is to serve as a framework for systematic field research. Some necessary conditions of pluralism must be set down, against which research findings can be interpreted. Such conditions can provide empirically testable propositions which enable us to avoid a retreat into faith insofar as the documentation of the viability of pluralism is concerned. While the following propositions do not include every facet of pluralism, they do include several of its basic contemporary tenets:

1. *That competing centres and bases of power and influence exist within a political community.* To meet the pluralist standard, lively competition among several individuals, elites, or groups is required. Moreover, in a pluralistic community, the *bases* upon which power rests will be variable, i.e. money power would be challenged by other bases of power, including class, expertise, access, and the control of the media of communication. To some extent, such power bases overlap; in a capitalistic society, for example, personal wealth and the control of the means of production often enable their possessors to co-opt several of the others. But viable competition among many elites possessing *different* bases of power is a critical factor in the pluralist equation, and it is related to the notion of 'countervailing power', i.e. the assumption that a built-in stabilizer exists whereby the rise of highly organized centres of power inspires opposing centres which tend to bring the system into equilibrium.

2. *The opportunity for individual and organizational access into the political system.* Access is vital because it provides an instrument by which support and opposition toward a proposed measure may be expressed. Penetration of the formal political system must be possible if decisions are to be rational and

equitable, i.e. if they are to benefit from opposing points of view and to satisfy the demands of opposing interests. A panoply of constitutional and procedural guarantees makes such access possible. Yet, it remains necessary to determine empirically the extent of individual and group access by an analysis of specific decisions. It is important to note here that individual participation has been undercut by the complexity of issues and the growth of group representation as the typical means of political negotiation and influence.

3. *That individuals actively participate in and make their will felt through organizations of many kinds.* . . . The dichotomy between organizational leaders and their members is denied; unless groups are given some organic reality beyond that based upon their members, it seems that the group thesis must assume that individuals turn to collective action mainly to gain their individual desires. Certainly, voting, the most characteristic form of political participation, is in the last analysis an eminently individual behaviour. Not that the individual's political values and electoral preferences are not influenced by his group associations, but rather that the political parties must evoke his participation on an individual basis.

4. *That elections are a viable instrument of mass participation in political decisions, including those on specific issues.* Two facets of this proposition are important. Not only do elections presumably provide a meaningful method of generalized mass influence over political leaders, but the assumption is that most adult citizens do, in fact, *use* their electoral power when referenda are available on specific issues. This assumption is especially vital because the electoral instrument is more accessible than other media of influence and access, such as legislative hearings, officeholding, organizational leadership, etc. In this sense, it is the most practical weapon in the pluralist armoury.

5. *That a consensus exists on what may be called the 'democratic creed'.* The importance of this consensus lies in the motivation to participate inspired by the belief that the democratic creed of the community is, in fact, operational. That is, voting, organizational membership, and other political activity are activated by an acceptance of the validity of the normative

propositions underlying the social system. To some extent, these values provide the cement that holds society together. The absence of this consensus, which may culminate in alienation, seems to result either in a withdrawal from active participation or in somewhat indiscriminate efforts to defeat all community proposals.

Conditions of elitism

We can now consider the nature of elitism. We shall use this term to define the condition that exists when the propositions above are not operational. Elitism is a pattern of decision making characterized by limited mass participation in community issues, and their domination by small groups of specialized or general leaders. This term suits the main drift of the analysis in the sense that it seems to define the conditions sometimes found in community power structure research; for example, the tendency for decisions to be initiated and directed by one or a few leadership groups. 'Elitism' also enables us to speak of change, 'competition among the few', and differential bases of power according to the substantive character of a decision. Elitism, in sum, connotes rule by the few, and when it occurs, we may assume that the five conditions of pluralism outlined above are rarely met.[2]

In a community context, we assume that a decision-making continuum exists, ranging from a high degree of pluralism at one end to a low degree (i.e. elitism) at the other. Empirically, the position occupied by any given decision along this continuum will vary according to the combination of factors that characterize it, as well as according to the criteria used to define pluralism. This problem will be discussed below. For the moment, let us merely say that community decision making is viewed here as occurring along a *continuum,* and is characterized by varying degrees of rank-and-file participation in major decisions and competition among the elites who play a direct,

2. Here, it should be noted, we are specifically rejecting the revisionist notion that pluralism is adequately defined when competition or specialization exists among the elites participating in community decisions. Our definition, which we believe is more in keeping with the historical spirit and meaning of the concept, requires as necessary conditions some measure of 'rank and file' and organizational participation in such decisions.

initiating role in them. Elitism connotes domination of the decisional process by a single group or a few men, limited rank-and-file access, little or no opposition, and a failure on the part of most of the adult community to use their political resources to influence important decisions. It refers to the tendency of power, defined as the chances of a group to achieve its ends despite opposition, to rest in relatively few hands.

It is not assumed here that those who have power can achieve their ends all the time, or that they constitute a single, impenetrable, monolithic entity, or that the locus of power does not change historically, or that community power rests entirely upon the possession or control of economic resources. Such requirements, it seems, are a caricature of power relations, if not a mere straw man.

We do assume that a power elite, if found, will constitute a very small proportion of the community, and that it will not be representative in social terms of the larger community. It will be made up largely of middle- and upper-class people, who possess more of the skills and qualities required for leadership, and who tend to share certain values about politics, mobility, and requirements of leadership that differentiate them to some extent from others. However, the most critical basis of differentiation will probably be found in class status and leadership resources, rather than in attitudinal differences.

A corollary of these assumptions is that such elites are subject to relatively little influence from the rest of the community. Their power may rest upon expertise, class, status, or wealth, but its distinguishing feature is a decisive control of such resources. Elitism connotes limited numbers, limited consultation with affected groups, disproportionate control of scarce resources of money, skill, and information, and a certain continuity and commonality of interest. While political elites in Western society will typically operate through nominally 'democratic' forms, i.e. through public meetings, elections, referenda, and so on, these media are sometimes manipulated to achieve a democratic 'consensus' that has little substance. For example, when presidential primary elections are made the target of vast and unequal expenditures of funds, organized like advertising campaigns, and carefully selected to ensure certain desired consequences, there is some doubt that the essentials of democratic participation have been met, even though technically its procedures have been followed. Elitism, as a political instrument, often rests upon similar highly differentiated and unequal access to valued resources [. . .]

If one is to verify the proposition that decision making in a given community tends toward the 'low' (elitist) end of the continuum, it is presumably necessary to demonstrate by some generally acceptable indexes of participation that a single elite group has exercised determinative influence across several policy areas.[3] Some such criterion has been set by pluralists who have either made such studies, or have made critical judgements about the research of others.

This criterion, however, seems unduly demanding, and to some extent unfair, because it puts the burden of proof squarely on the researcher to demonstrate that 'elitism', so defined, exists. He must not only prove that a monolithic community power structure exists, but if he should find instead that, say, three or four distinct elite groups share power among different types of decisions, the case for pluralism presumably remains viable. I am not sure, however, that pluralism (any more than elitism) should be accepted as a given; it should be equally incumbent upon advocates of pluralism to demonstrate by equally careful research that the community political system is indeed pluralistic. Otherwise, the debate remains essentially normative, with the pluralist enjoying most of the advantages of tradition and normative preference. More important, there is little incentive for the pluralist to do additional field research, which might reinforce his claims [. . .]

3. A problem of criteria arises here. Any researcher must establish cutoff points to differentiate categories that are not always intrinsically quantitative. Such categories include not only 'elitism' and 'pluralism', but the distinction between 'decision makers', 'influentials', and the 'rank and file' members of the community whose participation has often been found to be mainly limited to referending decisions made by others.

Reference

KARIEL, H. S. (1961), *The Decline of American Pluralism*, Stanford University Press.

20 S. E. Finer

The Political Power of Private Capital

Excerpts from S. E. Finer, 'The political power of private capital, part 1', *Sociological Review*, vol. 3, 1955, pp. 279–94.

Many people have noticed that private economic enterprises take decisions that make or mar the happiness and the destinies of their employees and of many others who depend directly or indirectly upon them: the fate of the people of Jarrow is a case in point. Also, that such private economic decisions may conflict with the overt desires of a large section, even a majority of the population. On the strength of these and similar observations, it has been argued that such private decisions are incompatible with a democracy since 'it is not the electorate but the owners of industrial property who . . . determine the economic policies of the country' (Cripps, 1948).

This argument leads to the assertion that to be fully or more fully democratic, electorates must assume control of private economic enterprises or a major part of them. The argument with which we shall deal, however, is quite a different one. It says that a peaceful transition to this stage of affairs can or will be rendered difficult, nugatory, or even impossible by the 'political power' which private capital wields. The first argument provides a reason for harnessing or regulating formerly private decisions: the view with which we are dealing concerns the ways and means by which private capital defends itself from being harnessed and regulated.

[. . .] The best way to begin seems to be to establish on the most extended definition a list of all conceivable advantages which private businessmen might possess for influencing political action; and then, under each heading, all the uses to which they might feasibly put these advantages. In the abstract, then, the principal political advantages of private capital seem to be [under] five [headings: organization, riches, access, patronage and surrogateship].

Organization

In most industrialized countries today, private businessmen are highly concentrated, both industrially (by combination, holding company, and price-associations) and organizationally, in trade associations of all kinds. Furthermore, they operate behind closed doors so that their 'invisibility' is also a source of advantage.

1. The *concentration of ownership and/or control of business enterprise* is a familiar indictment. For example, it is reckoned that the profits of fifty large industrial concerns in Britain accounted in 1950 for about one-third of all industrial profits; of these fifty companies, thirty-three were connected, by directorships, with eight major banks.

2. Furthermore, *business enterprises form a vast nexus*. Producers consume each others' products. Both rely on distributors, and on the common services of banking and insurance houses, transport contractors, builders and the like. Contracting and sub-contracting carries this nexus through differing social strata, down to barrow-boy and owner-driver where it is hard to say where 'capital' and 'labour' end or begin.

This interconnectedness is a source of self-division as well as of solidarity. In Britain, for instance, throughout the inter-war period railways sought to suppress road transport, coastwise shipping to curtail rail competition, while tramp-owner fought tramp-owner and haulier haulier. And, throughout, the great transport users watched exactingly to prevent any combination or price-ring.

On the other hand in certain situations, e.g. the threat of nationalization, the inter-connectedness is a source of solidarity; for dislocation in one industry ramifies through the whole. All productive industry and all traders rallied to the road hauliers' defence when their nationalization was threatened. The Society of Motor Manufacturers and Traders feared disturbance to their market: the Chambers of Commerce, the NUM, the FBI, depended on hauliers' services to keep down the costs of railway transport.

Indeed the FBI, in its protest against the Labour Party's nationalization proposals laid its greatest stress on the disturbances they would create. The nationalization of iron and steel 'would gravely endanger the smooth and effective restoration of the steel-using industries'. Nationalization of road haulage would cramp the flexibility and efficiency of a service 'closely integrated with productive industry'. The acquisition of undertakings ancillary to the industries of coal, steel, railways and the like (e.g. railway docks, hotels, etc.) would create special difficulties in the twilight zones where private firms and government ones would compete.

3. *Businessmen are strongly organized in special interest groups.* In England, for instance, apart from some 2500 trade associations of which about one half are manufacturers' associations, there are the 'peak organizations' represented by the FBI, the NUM, and the Association of British Chambers of Commerce. It is impossible to say precisely how many firms are represented by these three bodies, as their membership overlaps considerably; but the FBI alone, through individual and association-membership, provides a forum for some four-fifths of all those manufacturing enterprises in Britain which employ more than eleven workmen. The ABCC, apart from its manufacturer members (who are mostly members of the NUM or FBI also), represents some 25,000 merchants, shippers and agents. It would be rare to find a large firm of any description, save for retailers (who have their own organizations) that is not represented by one or other of these three 'peak' associations. In the USA the Chamber of Commerce of the US, and the National Association of Manufacturers play a like role, and have a similar coverage.

Riches

Mobilized and concentrated in this way, business can dispose, immediately, of large sums of money. As a group it tends to be considerably wealthier than other interest groups; it can produce the money much more quickly than they can, and can spend it for a longer period.

Apart from the social esteem with which wealth invests its possessors, it appears to open to them the following political opportunities.

1. *To pay for propaganda*: for example, to own newspapers; to pay for articles, television and radio programmes; and to finance public campaigns. The Congressional Hearings, in 1934–5, on the Lobbying Activities of the Public Utilities, as well as the subsequent Select Committee on Lobbying Activities of 1950 provide pages of examples of money lavishly bestowed on this object in the USA.

2. *To subscribe funds to political parties*: as for instance the Ruhr industrialists at Goering's house in 1932 put up a purse for the Nazi Party, as Ruhr industrialists largely endow the FDP today, and as British businessmen subscribe, as individuals, to the Conservative Party.

3. *To bribe legislators and officials*: There are still countries and parts of countries where the mass purchase of legislative votes or official favour is a recognized mode of conducting business; as for example the Anaconda Copper Company's long domination of Montana politics, or United Fruit Company's control of Costa Rica and Honduras.

4. *To buy protection*: The pre-war US saw company agents sworn in as deputy policemen; firms which employed their own 'coal and iron police' against strikers; private detectives, strike-guards, 'missionaries' and the like, employed as private forces by employers. In a similar category falls the financing of political militias like the Italian *fasci di combattimenti* in 1922, and the French *ligues* in 1934–6.

Access

In most old-established industrial states, close connections exist between those in authority and private businessmen. Between them and legislators, civil servants, judges and often the officers of the armed forces, there are many ties of family, acquaintance-ship and interchange. This offers three political opportunities to businessmen.

1. *Access to governing circles*. Businessmen can be guided quickly to the centre of decision making: find it possible to put their case informally and *ad hominem*, which is often the most effective way; and since they are either personally known to, or 'vouched for' before the governing circles, tend to be trusted more than outsiders.

2. *This connection between ruling circles and businessmen* which may be very close indeed in some countries at certain times, also permits of businessmen bringing moral pressure to bear on their friends 'inside', whenever an unpopular policy is being followed. This could lead to situations like the Curragh 'mutiny', where officers resigned their commission rather than carry out the Government's policy.

3. *More important than both perhaps is that intangible but very real link, a common ideology:* common outlook, manners, conventions, pre-suppositions. There is a spiritual *rapport* even before contact is made on a particular issue. Unfortunately, researches have only begun to explore this field; but of its general importance in this context there can be no doubt.

Patronage

We call businessmen employers and managers without any longer realising what these words signify: the German equivalent *'arbeitgeber'* conveys more of the matter for it literally means the 'work-giver'. By virtue of giving work, the employer gives livelihood; and by the obverse, the withdrawal of 'work' he sanctions his right to manage. The present period of full employment in this country should not blind us to the fact that for centuries, the giving and withholding of 'work' has seised businessmen of a vast advantage over their employees who thereby have become largely their dependents and clients. Hence our expression *patronage* which is chosen to express the dependency of numerous families upon businessmen's private decisions. This patronage opens to them two great political possibilities:

1. *The intimidation of individual workpeople or their dependents* for expressing views which, freely permitted by the laws, nevertheless incur the displeasure of the patron. It must be remembered that in times of unemployment, to deprive a man of his job is to deprive him, his wife and his children of food and shelter. This is a fearsome penalty to exact. To blacklist him and deprive him of a livelihood *permanently,* surpasses nearly all the penalties which the State ever inflicts.

2. Similarly, *dominance in the conduct of the firm or industry,*

i.e., control over the pay, hours and conditions of work, which, in their turn determine the pattern and figure on which the work-people live out their lives. In the last resort this dominance is based on the employers' right to 'lock-out' his employees. Thus in 1926 the coal owners locked-out the miners. They proposed thereby to force these to accept reductions which, in South Wales would reduce wages from 78s. to 46s. a week, and in Durham by 18s. per week.

But the same end can also be achieved by private armies, propaganda and individual intimidation.

In *Matter of Remington Rand*, large numbers of professional strike-breakers and operatives, known as 'missionaries', 'nobles' and 'under-cover' men, were hired by the company . . . They jostled pickets and terrorized striking employees. In *Matter of Sunshine Mining Company* supervisors fostered the formation of two strike-breaking organizations, the 'Vigilantes' and the 'committee of 356'. . . . A mass demonstration was arranged by these organizations against the strikers and handbills were distributed saying – 'Vigilantes are ready to take care of any radical organizers . . . ropes are ready.' Confronted by this situation the pickets disbanded before the demonstration was held (National Labour Relations Board, 1938).

Surrogateship

Even in a highly regulated economy, like Great Britain's during the War, private business has a wide discretion in carrying out work which is in fact, all of it, 'affected with the public interest'. Nor is the economic health of the community much less 'affected with the public interest' in peacetime, when regulation is relaxed, and in some economies, minimal. The fact that the businessman's work, although conducted as his private enterprise is nevertheless something which affects all members of the community (it is in fact a very highly decentralized form of public administration) permits us to express its relationship to government as that of a surrogate, a deputy. Such surrogateship confers on private industry two important possibilities:

1. The thwarting of government's policy by deliberately slowing down activities government wants to foster, or speeding up processes government is trying to discourage, in order to discredit authority and create distress and unrest. This is to pursue

a *politique de pire*. Banks have often been offenders: thus the *Banque de France*, in 1935, refused to discount government bills; moreover, in May 1935, during the financial panic, it failed to raise bank rate: and by these means it effectively forced the premier, M. Flandin, to abandon his chosen policy and to return to one of deflation.

2. The thwarting of government policy by refusing the Government the expert, scientific and technical advice on which it relies, on which it tends to predicate its own administrative structure and practices and thereby its commercial and industrial policies.

Appraisal

This list adds up to something formidable. Imagine, first, the combined use of all these possibilities in an assault upon an unpopular government. The solidarity and staying power of capital is assured by its economic and organizational concentration; and it thereby conducts its operations in the dark. It instigates public campaigns against the government's 'mismanagement'; and through its newspapers and inspired articles it promotes scares, in banner headlines. It increases its financial support of the Opposition parties in anticipation of the election it proposes to force. It persuades its inside sympathisers to 'go slow' on government policy, and receives inside information from them. Meanwhile it precipitates the very conditions for which, through its propaganda, it blames the government: it locks out its workers, bringing production and distribution to a halt, it causes panics in the banks and money market, and suppresses the denunciations of government supporters by its strong-arm men and private militias.

Or, perhaps, slow siege is preferred to sudden storm. Here the attack is played out in slow motion. The picture that results from this is more prosaic and more credible than that of sudden assault. Newspapers, films, radio programmes, public meetings quietly, cunningly, and constantly create the atmosphere of disillusion, of apathy, of disappointment. The opposition parties use their now swollen political funds to improve their organization, and increase their propaganda. The government, while no industry openly defies it, finds its wishes met with procrastination; difficulties appear at every corner: industrial relations suffer, production and employment flags; and at last, both government and people are wearied out and weary of one another. At the election, it becomes clear that the citadel has been taken from within – the political parties supported by the businessmen find their victory almost unopposed.

The first picture, with its hysteria and storm troops and cataclysm looks like Weimar on the eve of Nazidom. The second is the picture of Britain 1946–51 as some left-wing and Communist publicists conceive it. But the similarity must not mislead us into concluding that because the composite picture of private capital's political potentialities looks like a real situation, it is therefore the explanation of how this real situation came about. At best it is only a hypothesis. To prove it we should have to have evidence that private capital did in fact use all these possibilities open to it: this is precisely what we shall have to examine in the instance of Britain.

And indeed there are *prima facie* reasons for rejecting this hypothesis right away. For one must notice how our list of advantages and attendant political possibilities has been established. We have, as we warned, taken the most imaginative and extended view of these possibilities: and we have therefore brought together, in one aggregate:

1. Possibilities, not probabilities.
2. The experience of a whole range of different countries, not one country.
3. The experience of different times and circumstances.

The list looks formidable because it has been *conflated*. It must therefore be re-examined.

Our purpose is to explore, in respect to contemporary Britain, in what the political power of private capital consists and by what means it is exercised. In short, which items on our list are used in this country, and to what extent are they effectual in the political process?

Now, first of all, our list merely records abstract possibilities. It does not record capital's *effective* capacity to act. And the two are not the same. It is possible, beyond doubt, for businessmen to pay bribes to legislators and officials. In this country people do not behave like that. It is possible to corrupt an elector; but the electorate is now so large that it is not worth the trouble and the risk involved. What may or can conceivably happen is not the same as something likely to happen. And in this way if we identify bare possibilities with effective capacity, we in effect assume the very thing we are trying to prove – that the power of government is ineffective to curtail or abrogate the political potentialities of private capital.

Nearly every heading in the list is supported by an example. It would have been very easy to have multiplied these. But these examples have been deliberately drawn from a variety of countries; had they been drawn solely from English experience, they would have been very restricted. Now the fact that a particular possibility has been used by businessmen in, say, the USA or Germany, merely proves that it is a real possibility for the purposes of our list. It by no means proves that it is an effective possibility for a British businessman. The seduction of civil servants and even legislators by bribes, gifts and favours is still common in the USA, so common as to lead to a proposal to establish a Commission on Ethics in Government. But in Britain while the Stanley Case showed the matter to be possible, the public reaction to this case, and the subsequent report of the Select Committee on Intermediaries showed it to be so highly unusual, and so shocking, that it can be ruled out as an effective possibility for British private capital. And so must the financing of private political militias, and bribery of electors, and so forth.

Our inquiry, it must be stressed again, is to try to find evidence for these possibilities having been utilized here in the last generation, and on that basis to assess the likelihood of their being used, given similar circumstances, in the near future. In such an inquiry foreign experiences are quite inadmissible: they presuppose that the counter-power of government is the same in all countries. This is ridiculous. To suppose that because, for instance, the US government has failed to stamp out the seduction and corruption of some of its servants by the emissaries of private capital the British government is *ipso facto* equally powerless to do so would be mockingly rejected by everybody.

Yet this is precisely to what the admission of foreign experience in this context would commit us. Suppose Panama is strong in preventing everything but bribery, Venezuela everything but private armies, Uruguay everything but bankers' pressure, etc., etc. Suppose this to be the case. It will not follow that, in all three countries, private capital is capable of bribery, private armies and financial pressure. Indeed, by the very terms of our statement, this is ruled out.

This fallacy of method is often used by writers on both the Left and the Right. Thus, a Labour Party pamphlet called *Monopoly* says 'Finally there is the political power that great monopolies wield. In the Fascist countries the alliance of monopoly capitalism with political reaction was notorious and open. In the democracies it is less blatant. But there can be no doubt that it is the Right Wing Parties which they support.' Similarly, a trade unionist can say that unless and until steel and iron were nationalized 'the Government is open to economic pressure and political blackmail by the iron and steel monopoly interests which have always been the hard core behind capitalist reaction. It was the steel monopoly of Germany that backed Hitler and placed the Nazis in power. The fall of the Labour Government in 1931 was largely brought about by the cooperation of British capitalist monopoly and Wall Street' (Gardner, 1947). Similarly, at chapter 13 of his *National Capitalism*, which is entitled 'Capitalist sabotage of Labour governments', Davies lists experiences in France, USA and New Zealand, before coming to 'sabotage possibilities facing the next Labour Government'. But this trick and failing is not confined to the Left. It was the method by which W. H. Lecky in his *Democracy and Liberty* sought to prove that the inevitable concomitants of democracy, as such, were public extravagance, electoral and administrative corruption, and the pillage of the rich. It is, in part, the method by which F. A. Hayek has persuaded tens of thousands that the growth of government regulation of industry in Britain corresponded to a similar phase in Germany which had led to Nazism, and that *therefore* this must be its inevitable consequence to Britain also.

Nor is this all. Two out of the five 'advantages' are exceedingly *mutable*. These [. . .] are [. . .] Patronage and Surrogateship. (It will be noticed that these are the ones that carry with them the possibility of bringing to bear on government indirect and invisible economic pressure as against the political and overt activities of Wealth. And the circumstances by which Patronage and Surrogateship may be altered are, respectively, the state of the employment market, and the degree of state regulation.

(a) The power to intimidate individual workpeople, and likewise an effective dictatorship over the management process, are not fixed and permanent conditions. They depend on labour's bargaining power. In the depressed twenties and thirties, the unions were weak, while in many industries, e.g. coal, the market was so poor that temporary stoppages of production caused little hardship to the owners. That condition has not existed in Britain for some fifteen years. The change in the employers' patronage power has been starkly brought home in recent strikes in BEAC and [in 1955] in Rolls Royce.

Full employment has similarly qualified the employers' dominance in the conduct of industry. This is recognized by responsible Trade Unionists. 'In the old days we had in many industries and occupations no strength at all. So different is the scene we survey today. We are stronger than ever. We are participants, on almost equal terms, in industry; we influence and initiate policy: we are consulted and respected by governments: we have access to all ministries, municipalities and national institutions' (O'Brien, 1953).

(b) Likewise does the surrogateship of private businessmen alter with altered conditions. Paradoxically, it alters with the very conditions which this surrogate power is supposed to be able to prevent: the restrictive and regulatory activities of government. The extent of business independence is not fixed. The assumption that it is so depends on a notion of private property which is tautologous: that 'private' property is unabridgeably private, for otherwise it ceases to be 'private property'. This view was thrown over by the very TUC itself as early as 1932. The report of its Economic Committee says:

According to traditional notions, control was automatically vested in the owners of property. Most people would say that a person owns property when he is able to do what he wishes with it, i.e. completely controls it. In this strict sense of the term, however, there is hardly such a thing as complete private control in industry at the present day. The owners of industrial capital have not for a very long time been able to do whatever they pleased with their own property. They have been limited in some respects by legislation such as Factory Acts, etc. and by all kinds of regulations made in the interests of the community (1932).

The war and the period of control that has followed it, and which largely continues, has still further circumscribed the surrogateship of private capital and the political potentialities which flow from it.

Finally, the list does not distinguish between constitutional and unconstitutional activities: nor, it may be said, do many of the theorists who urge the need to restrict the political power of private capital. Thus Laski could write in 1935:

In the choice between peaceful transformation and the maintenance of privilege at the cost of conflict, the owners of property now, as in an earlier day, are prepared *rather to fight for their legal privileges than to give way*. That attitude is shown not merely by the barbaric overthrow of democratic institutions in Fascist countries. It is shown even more clearly (sic) by *the resistance to social reform* in the United States and Great Britain.

Here the line between the perfectly constitutional (however reprehensible) actions of the British property owners and 'conflict' and 'fighting' is completely obliterated; while the author also succeeds in giving the impression (which he certainly did not mean) that in Britain the 'fighting' and 'conflict' was sharper even than in Nazi Germany.

This confusion between constitutional and non-constitutional behaviour is not entirely accidental. To someone who loathes private capital and all its works it may appear of little moment *how* it maintains its power: the loathesome thing is that it does so. It was on these grounds that Lenin and his whole line of followers have lumped into one category all 'bourgeois' countries whether they be democracies, or dictatorships, liberal or totalitarian. But the distinction between constitutional and non-constitutional practices does make a great deal of difference to the 'catastrophe' argument already cited, and to our entire conception of the nature of private capital's power. If it can be shown, for instance, that in Britain the means used to sustain its position in society have been exclusively constitutional, and that it has, constitutionally, accepted adverse and limiting decisions, the case for the catastrophe theory is seriously weakened. And similarly, our definition of private capital's political power will be significantly altered: for in the quotations cited above it is tacitly assumed that this consists, not only of constitutional means, but of invisible 'sabotage', 'resistance' and the like, which hits below the belt.

In fact, the failure to differentiate between constitutional and unconstitutional means, where this is deliberate and not simply confused, depends on two presuppositions. One, an ethical judgement, is open to the reader to adopt or reject as he pleases; the other itself depends on that same assumption about the powerlessness of government which we have already had occasion to notice and which assumes the very argument it tries to prove, viz. that opposed by capital the State is powerless.

The first presupposition is the ethical judgement that 'big business' is a vested interest, and a sectional interest, and so, *ex hypothesi,* in opposition to the public good. So indeed it may be, and so, in so far as it is a sectional interest, it is almost always likely to be. But our reaction to this view is part of our private understanding of democracy. It is possible to take the view that, since it is legally tolerated, it has as much right to put its views forward as any other section of the community. It is true, of course, that businessmen's associations do not preach the doctrines of social democracy. But neither do trade unions speak the language of private enterprise. The road hauliers have never pressed the claims of the railways to greater traffic, and the railways have never once agreed to abdicate to road haulage. What does one expect special interest groups to do but defend their members' special interests? What are they constituted for if not that? If they are permitted to form freely they have a right to express their views in a constitutional fashion: and the assumption is that they enjoy this right for the purpose of converting a majority to their side.

The second presupposition is in part an answer to this argument. 'These are wealthy people, with an advantage over us, poor as we are,' this argument runs. 'It is true that they are few but their wealth makes up for that, for they can, even by constitutional methods, get a majority on their side. So that' – and this is where the second presupposition begins – 'we are ruled by *a small minority who are self appointed and responsible to nobody but themselves*.' The answer to this set of pleas is, surely, clear enough. First the fact, if it is a fact, that this minority gets a majority on its side by constitutional means is a very poor reason for believing that it is impossible for them ever to lose it by constitutional means: and an even worse reason, many might think, for wishing to deny them their democratic rights. Secondly, while it is certainly true that they are, unlike the boards of nationalized industries, self appointed, it is not necessarily true that they are responsible to nobody but themselves. To say that they are is to assume, once again, that they cannot be controlled and regulated in the public interest by public bodies.

There is in short no political power of private capital as such. There is the political power of British businessmen, during a particular period and in particular circumstances: and likewise of American businessmen, German, French, Latin American and so forth. All we have been able to do so far is to see what the term may possibly imply, and then to show that in certain places, times and circumstances, it implies something less than the abstract possibilities. If we want to know what it has implied in Britain over the last thirty years, the only way to find out is to look.

References

CRIPPS, S. (1948), speaking on the Iron and Steel Bill, *Hansard*, 15 November.
ECONOMIC COMMITTEE (1932), *Report*, TUC.
GARDNER, J. (1947), *TU Congress Report*, Amalgamated Society of Foundry Workers.
LASKI, H. J. (1935), *The State in Theory and Practice*, Viking Press.
NATIONAL LABOUR RELATIONS BOARD (1938), Annual Report.
O'BRIEN, T. (1953), 'Address to T.U. Congress', National Labour Relations Board.

S. E. Finer 353

21 R. A. Dahl

A Critique of the Ruling Elite Model

R. A. Dahl, 'A critique of the ruling elite model', *American Political Science Review*, vol. 52, no. 2, 1958, pp. 463–9.

A great many people seem to believe that 'they' run things: the old families, the bankers, the City Hall machine, or the party boss behind the scene. This kind of view evidently has a powerful and many-sided appeal. It is simple, compelling, dramatic, 'realistic'. It gives one standing as an inside-dopester. For individuals with a strong strain of frustrated idealism, it has just the right touch of hard-boiled cynicism. Finally, the hypothesis has one very great advantage over many alternative explanations: It can be cast in a form that makes it virtually impossible to disprove.

Consider the last point for a moment. There is a type of quasi-metaphysical theory made up of what might be called an infinite regress of explanations. The ruling elite model *can* be interpreted in this way. If the overt leaders of a community do not appear to constitute a ruling elite, then the theory can be saved by arguing that behind the overt leaders there is a set of covert leaders who do. If subsequent evidence shows that this covert group does not make a ruling elite, then the theory can be saved by arguing that behind the first covert group there is another, and so on.

Now whatever else it may be, a theory that cannot even in principle be controverted by empirical evidence is not a scientific theory. The least that we can demand of any ruling elite theory that purports to be more than a metaphysical or polemical doctrine is, first, that the burden of proof be on the proponents of the theory and not on its critics; and, second, that there be clear criteria according to which the theory could be disproved.

With these points in mind, I shall proceed in two stages. First, I shall try to clarify the meaning of the concept 'ruling elite' by describing a very simple form of what I conceive to be a ruling elite system. Second, I shall indicate what would be required in principle as a simple but satisfactory test of any hypothesis asserting that a particular political system is, in fact, a ruling elite system. Finally, I shall deal with some objections.

A simple ruling elite system

If a ruling elite hypothesis says anything, surely it asserts that within some specific political system there exists a group of people who to some degree exercise power or influence over other actors in the system. I shall make the following assumptions about power (see Dahl, 1957):

1. In order to compare the relative influence of two actors (these may be individuals, groups, classes, parties, or what not), it is necessary to state the scope of the responses upon which the actors have an effect. The statement, 'A has more power than B', is so ambiguous as to verge on the meaningless, since it does not specify the scope.

2. One cannot compare the relative influence of two actors who always perform identical actions with respect to the group influenced. What this means as a practical matter is that ordinarily one can test for differences in influence only where there are cases of differences in initial preferences. At one extreme, the difference may mean that one group prefers alternative A and another group prefers B, A and B being mutually exclusive. At the other extreme, it may mean that one group prefers alternative A to other alternatives, and another group is indifferent. If a political system displayed complete consensus at all times, we should find it impossible to construct a satisfactory direct test of the hypothesis that it was a ruling elite system, although indirect and rather unsatisfactory tests might be devised.

Consequently, to know whether or not we have a ruling elite, we must have a political system in which there is a difference in preferences, from time to time, among the individual human beings in the system. Suppose, now, that among these individuals there is a set whose preferences regularly prevail in all cases of disagreement, or at least in all cases of disagreement over key political issues (a term I propose to leave undefined here). Let me call such a set of individuals a 'controlling group'. In a full-fledged democracy operating strictly according to majority rule, the majority would constitute a controlling group, even though the individual members of the majority might change from one issue to the next. But since our model is to represent a ruling elite system, we require that the set be *less than a majority in size*.

However, in any representative system with single member voting districts where more than two candidates receive votes, a candidate *could* win with less than a majority of votes; and it is possible, therefore, to imagine a truly sovereign legislature elected under the strictest 'democratic' rules that was nonetheless governed by a legislative majority representing the first preferences of a minority of voters. Yet I do not think we would want to call such a political system a ruling elite system. Because of this kind of difficulty, I propose that we exclude from our definition of a ruling elite any controlling group that is a product of rules that are actually followed (that is, 'real' rules) under which a majority of individuals could dominate if they took certain actions permissible under the 'real' rules. In short, to constitute a ruling elite a controlling group must not be *a pure artifact of democratic rules*.

A ruling elite, then, is a controlling group less than a majority in size that is not a pure artifact of democratic rules. It is a minority of individuals whose preferences regularly prevail in cases of differences in preference on key political issues. If we are to avoid an infinite regress of explanations, the composition of the ruling elite must be more or less definitely specified.

Some bad tests

The hypothesis we are dealing with would run along these lines: 'Such and such a political system (the US, the USSR, New Haven, or the like) is a ruling elite system in which the ruling elite has the following membership'. Membership would then be specified by name, position, socio-economic class, socio-economic roles, or what not.

Let me now turn to the problem of testing a hypothesis of this sort, and begin by indicating a few tests that are sometimes mistakenly taken as adequate.

The first improper test confuses a ruling elite with a group that has a *high potential for control*. Let me explain. Suppose a set of individuals in a political system has the following property: there is a very high probability that if they agree on a key political alternative, and if they all act in some specified way, then that alternative will be chosen. We may say of such a group that it has a *high potential for control*. In a large and complex society like ours, there may be many such groups. For example, the bureaucratic triumvirate of Professor Mills would appear to have a high potential for control (1956). In the City of New Haven, with which I have some acquaintance, I do not doubt that the leading business figures together with the leaders of both political parties have a high potential for control. But a potential for control is not, except in a peculiarly Hobbesian world, equivalent to actual control. If the military leaders of this country and their subordinates agreed that it was desirable, they could most assuredly establish a military dictatorship of the most overt sort; nor would they need the aid of leaders of business corporations or the executive branch of our government. But they have not set up such a dictatorship. For what is lacking are the premises I mentioned earlier, namely agreement on a key political alternative and some set of specific implementing actions. That is to say, a group may have a high potential for control and a *low potential for unity*. The actual *political effectiveness* of a group is a function of its potential for control *and* its potential for unity. Thus a group with a relatively low potential for control but a high potential for unity may be more politically effective than a group with a high potential for control but a low potential for unity.

The second improper test confuses a ruling elite with a group of individuals who have more influence than any others in the system. I take it for granted that in every human organization some individuals have more influence over key decisions than do others. Political equality may well be among the most Utopian of all human goals. But it is fallacious to assume that the absence of political equality proves the existence of a ruling elite.

The third improper test, which is closely related to the preceding one, is to generalize from a single scope of influence.

Neither logically nor empirically does it follow that a group with a high degree of influence over one scope will necessarily have a high degree of influence over another scope within the same system. This is a matter to be determined empirically. Any investigation that does not take into account the possibility that different elite groups have different scopes is suspect. By means of sloppy questions one could easily seem to discover that there exists a unified ruling elite in New Haven; for there is no doubt that small groups of people make many key decisions. It appears to be the case, however, that the small group that runs urban redevelopment is not the same as the small group that runs public education, and neither is quite the same as the two small groups that run the two parties. Moreover the small group that runs urban redevelopment with a high degree of unity would almost certainly disintegrate if its activities were extended to either education or the two political parties.

A proposed test

If tests like these are not valid, what can we properly require?

Let us take the simplest possible situation. Assume that there have been some number – I will not say how many – of cases where there has been disagreement within the political system on key political choices. Assume further that the hypothetical ruling elite prefers one alternative and other actors in the system prefer other alternatives. Then unless it is true that in all or very nearly all of these cases the alternative preferred by the ruling elite is actually adopted, the hypothesis (that the system is dominated by the specified ruling elite) is clearly false.

I do not want to pretend either that the research necessary to such a test is at all easy to carry out or that community life lends itself conveniently to strict interpretation according to the requirements of the test. But I do not see how anyone can suppose that he has established the dominance of a specific group in a community or a nation without basing his analysis on the careful examination of a series of concrete decisions. And these decisions must either constitute the universe or a fair sample from the universe of key political decisions taken in the political system.

Now it is a remarkable and indeed astounding fact that neither

Mills (1956) nor Hunter (1953) has seriously attempted to examine an array of specific cases to test his major hypothesis. Yet I suppose these two works more than any others in the social sciences of the last few years have sought to interpret complex political systems essentially as instances of a ruling elite.

To sum up: The hypothesis of the existence of a ruling elite can be strictly tested only if:

1. The hypothetical ruling elite is a well-defined group.

2. There is a fair sample of cases involving key political decisions in which the preferences of the hypothetical ruling elite run counter to those of any other likely group that might be suggested.

3. In such cases, the preferences of the elite regularly prevail.

Difficulties and objections

Several objections might be raised against the test I propose.

First, one might argue that the test is too weak. The argument would run as follows: If a ruling elite *doesn't* exist in a community, then the test is satisfactory; that is, if every hypothetical ruling elite is compared with alternative control groups, and in fact no ruling elite exists, then the test will indeed show that there is no minority whose preferences regularly prevail on key political alternatives. But – it might be said – suppose a ruling elite *does* exist. The test will not *necessarily* demonstrate its existence, since we may not have selected the right group as our hypothetical ruling elite. Now this objection is valid; but it suggests the point I made at the outset about the possibility of an infinite regress of explanations. Unless we use the test on every possible combination of individuals in the community, we cannot be certain that there is not some combination that constitutes a ruling elite. But since there is no more *a priori* reason to assume that a ruling elite does exist than to assume that one does not exist, the burden of proof does not rest upon the critic of the hypothesis, but upon its proponent. And a proponent must specify what group he has in mind as his ruling elite. Once the group is specified, then the test I have suggested is, at least in principle, valid.

Second, one could object that the test is too strong. For suppose that the members of the 'ruled' group are indifferent as to the outcome of various political alternatives. Surely (one could argue) if there is another group that regularly gets its way in the face of this indifference, it is in fact the ruling group in the society. Now my reasons for wishing to discriminate this case from the other involve more than a mere question of the propriety of using the term 'ruling elite', which is only a term of convenience. There is, I think, a difference of some theoretical significance between a system in which a small group dominates over another that is opposed to it, and one in which a group dominates over an indifferent mass. In the second case, the alternatives at stake can hardly be regarded as 'key political issues' if we assume the point of view of the indifferent mass; whereas in the first case it is reasonable to say that the alternatives involve a key political issue from the standpoint of both groups. Earlier I refrained from defining the concept 'key political issues'. If we were to do so at this point, it would seem reasonable to require as a necessary although possibly not a sufficient condition that the issue should involve actual disagreement in preferences among two or more groups. In short, the case of 'indifference versus preference' would be ruled out.

However, I do not mean to dispose of the problem simply by definition. The point is to make sure that the two systems are distinguished. The test for the second, weaker system of elite rule would then be merely a modification of a test proposed for the first and more stringent case. It would again require an examination of a series of cases showing uniformly that when 'the word' was authoritatively passed down from the designated elite, the hitherto indifferent majority fell into ready compliance with an alternative that had nothing else to recommend it intrinsically.

Third, one might argue that the test will not discriminate between a true ruling elite and a ruling elite together with its satellites. This objection is in one sense true and in one sense false. It is true that on a series of key political questions, an apparently unified group might prevail who would, according to our test, thereby constitute a ruling elite. Yet an inner core might actually make the decisions for the whole group.

However, one of two possibilities must be true. Either the

inner core and the front men always agree at all times in the decision process, or they do not. But if they always agree, then it follows from one of our two assumptions about influence that the distinction between an 'inner core' and 'front men' has no operational meaning; that is, there is no conceivable way to distinguish between them. And if they do not always agree, then the test simply requires a comparison at those points in time when they disagree. Here again, the advantages of concrete cases are palpable, for these enable one to discover who initiates or vetoes and who merely complies.

Fourth, it might be said that the test is either too demanding or else it is too arbitrary. If it requires that the hypothetical elite prevails in every single case, then it demands too much. But if it does not require this much, then at what point can a ruling elite be said to exist? When it prevails in seven cases out of ten? eight out of ten? nine out of ten? Or what? There are two answers to this objection. On the one hand, it would be quite reasonable to argue, I think, that since we are considering only key political choices and not trivial decisions, if the elite does not prevail in *every* case in which it disagrees with a contrary group, it cannot properly be called a ruling elite. But since I have not supplied an independent definition of the term 'key political choices', I must admit that this answer is not wholly satisfactory. On the other hand, I would be inclined to suggest that in this instance as in many others we ought not to assume that political reality will be as discrete and discontinuous as the concepts we find convenient to employ. We can say that a system approximates a true ruling elite system, to a greater or lesser degree, without insisting that it exemplify the extreme and limiting case.

Fifth, it might be objected that the test I have proposed would not work in the most obvious of all cases of ruling elites, namely in the totalitarian dictatorships. For the control of the elite over the expression of opinion is so great that overtly there is no disagreement; hence no cases on which to base a judgement arise. This objection is a fair one. But we are not concerned here with totalitarian systems. We are concerned with the application of the techniques of modern investigation to American communities, where, except in very rare cases, terror is not so pervasive that the investigator is barred from discovering the preferences of citizens. Even in Little Rock, for example, newspaper men seemed to have had little difficulty in finding diverse opinions; and a northern political scientist of my acquaintance has managed to complete a large number of productive interviews with White and Negro Southerners on the touchy subject of integration.

Finally one could argue that even in a society like ours a ruling elite might be so influential over ideas, attitudes, and opinions that a kind of false consensus will exist – not the phony consensus of a terroristic totalitarian dictatorship but the manipulated and superficially self-imposed adherence to the norms and goals of the elite by broad sections of a community. A good deal of Mills' argument can be interpreted in this way, although it is not clear to me whether this is what he means to rest his case on.

Even more than the others this objection points to the need to be circumspect in interpreting the evidence. Yet here, too, it seems to me that the hypothesis cannot be satisfactorily confirmed without something equivalent to the test I have proposed. For once again either the consensus is perpetual and unbreakable, in which case there is no conceivable way of determining who is ruler and who is ruled. Or it is not. But if it is not, then there is some point in the process of forming opinions at which the one group will be seen to initiate and veto, while the rest merely respond. And we can only discover these points *by an examination of a series of concrete cases where key decisions are made:* decisions on taxation and expenditures, subsidies, welfare programs, military policy, and so on.

It would be interesting to know, for example, whether the initiation and veto of alternatives having to do with our missile program would confirm Mills' hypothesis, or indeed any reasonable hypothesis about the existence of a ruling elite. To the superficial observer it would scarcely appear that the military itself is a homogeneous group, to say nothing of their supposed coalition with corporate and political executives. If the military alone or the coalition together is a ruling elite, it is either incredibly incompetent in administering its own fundamental affairs or else it is unconcerned with the success of its policies to a degree that I find astounding.

However I do not mean to examine the evidence here. For the whole point of this paper is that the evidence for a ruling elite, either in the United States or in any specific community, has not yet been properly examined so far as I know. And the evidence has not been properly examined, I have tried to argue, because the examination has not employed satisfactory criteria to determine what constitutes a fair test of the basic hypothesis.

References

DAHL, R. A. (1957), 'The concept of power', *Behavioral Science*, vol. 2, July, pp. 201–50.

HUNTER, F. (1953), *Community Power Structure*, University of North Carolina Press.

MILLS, C. W. (1956), *The Power Elite*, Oxford University Press.

22 J. Playford

The Myth of Pluralism

Excerpts from J. Playford, 'The myth of pluralism', *Arena*,
no. 15, 1968, pp. 34–47.

Pluralism is a widely accepted theory of the way Western industrial democracies work. It is believed to be particularly
applicable to the United States of America which is seen as a
complex interlocking of economic, regional, religious and ethnic
groups, whose members pursue their various interests through
private associations. These associations in turn are coordinated,
regulated, contained and encouraged by the government. It is
assumed that power in America is distributed in such a manner
as to guarantee that no one group can dominate any particular
segment of society. When an interest threatens to gain the upper
hand, opponents emerge to put it in its place. Pluralism is said
to stand for the guarantee of freedom, the preservation of
diversity, the limitation of power and protection against extrem-
ist mass movements. Its proponents put forward an harmonious
picture of American society composed of a multitude of self-
regulating interest groups, enjoying amicable relations with one
another and with the government. From de Tocqueville to Bell
and Lipset there has been no lack of apologists for pluralism,
which has become a term of praise in the academic political
vocabulary. As Kariel (1966) has observed: 'Virtually all the
academic studies of American politics undertaken today seem
to confirm this soothing vision of American politics as an inter-
minable process which gives every interest its due.'

It is the purpose of this [essay] to draw attention to the
weaknesses of pluralism which lie in the ideological consequences of its application to the reality of American society. A
number of radical social scientists have critically examined the
major premises of the pluralists to show that a liberal rhetoric
is used to uphold a most conservative ideology. In particular,

Wolff (1965) has brilliantly demonstrated that the application of the theory involves ideological distortion in three different ways. The first stems from the 'balance-of-power' interpretation of pluralism; the second arises from the application of the 'referee' version of the theory; and the third is inherent in the theory itself.[1]

The 'balance of power' theory

According to the balance-of-power theory of pluralism, the major groups in society compete through the electoral process for control over the actions of the government. The politicians are forced to accommodate themselves to a number of conflicting interests, among which a rough balance is maintained. The major groups said to comprise American society today are the big economic groups, representing labor, business, agriculture and the consumer, and the large ethnic and religious communities. There are also a number of well-established voluntary associations such as the American Medical Association and the veterans' organizations. It is essentially a static picture of American society. Changes in the patterns of social or economic groups tend to be unacknowledged because they deviate from the frozen picture depicted by the theorists of pluralism. Thus, the application of the theory always favors existing groups against those in process of formation.

The 'countervailing power' of supposedly co-equal units is stressed by the pluralists. Milbrath (1963) has described the equilibrium thus achieved as follows:

An important factor attenuating the impact of lobbying on governmental decisions is the fact that nearly every vigorous push in one direction stimulates an opponent or coalition of opponents to push in the opposite direction. This natural self-balancing factor comes into play so often that it almost amounts to a law.

1. See also the critical reviews of this work by liberals Spitz and Aiken in *Dissent* (New York) and the *New York Review of Books* respectively and the subsequent correspondence in both journals (*Dissent*, September–October 1966, November–December 1966, January–February 1967, May–June 1967; the *New York Review of Books*, 9 June 1966, 26 January 1967). I am particularly indebted to Wolff's essay for a number of the formulations used in this [essay].

An approximate equality is said to be maintained between business and labor, but the fact that labor constitutes the overwhelming majority of the population is not seen as a reason for allocating influence in proportion to relative numbers. Organized labor represents directly only about a quarter of the total American labor force and its share in decision making has never involved more than the tangential bargaining process of wages – hours – conditions – benefits for workers in its particular jurisdictions. Today, even this narrow bargaining priority is being assaulted by 'national interest' no-strike pressures in defence industries and in key industries such as railroads, steel and automobiles (see Burlage, 1965). As for the large corporative institutions, Hacker (1965) has shown that they are largely free to determine the level and distribution of the national income, to direct the allocation of resources, to decide the extent and rate of technological and economic development, to fix the level and conditions of employment, the structure of wage rates, and the terms and tempo of production. They are not effectively nullified by countervailing forces. Consumers in general have always been notoriously unorganized beyond the few cooperatives and magazines which cater to the middle class. McConnell (1966, p. 350) has said that 'the unstated assumption that the thesis of a given force will create its own antithesis is no more than the wishful metaphysics of countervailing power'. And Mills (1956, p. 246) has noted that 'to say that various interests are "balanced" is generally to evaluate the *status quo* as satisfactory or even good; the hopeful ideal of balance often masquerades as a description of fact'.[2] Mills goes on to point out that the theory of balance often rests upon the idea of a natural harmony of interests: 'So long as this doctrine prevails, any lower group that begins to struggle can be made to appear inharmonious, disturbing the common interest.' Or, as Carr (1949) expressed it: 'The doctrine of the harmony of interests thus serves as an ingenious moral device invoked, in perfect sincerity, by privileged groups in order to justify and maintain their dominant position.'

Another important way in which the established image of the

2. See also Loewenstein (1957); Rossiter (1964), especially ch. 5; Reagan (1963); Perlo (1963).

major economic groups in American society conservatively falsifies social reality is that the existence of an assumed approximate parity between business and labor overlooks or suppresses the fact that there are many non-unionized workers and small businessmen whose interests are ignored in the pluralist picture. The theory of pluralism does not promote the interests of the unionized against the non-unionized, or of large against small business. However, by presenting a picture of the American economy in which those disadvantaged elements simply do not appear, it perpetuates the inequality by ignoring rather than justifying it. The concrete application of pluralism supports inequality and injustice by ignoring the existence of certain legitimate social groups such as migrant workers, white-collar workers and small businessmen, not to mention Negroes, Puerto Ricans, Mexicans, the aged and the unemployed. As Perrow (1964) has observed: 'Political pluralism simply has not reflected the interests of those who probably need most representation.'[3] Thus, we may speak of the pseudo-pluralism or sham pluralism of contemporary American politics.

Referring to the exclusion of many individuals from any membership or effective participation in the pluralist system, McConnell (1966) has written:

Thus farm migrant workers, Negroes, and the urban poor have not been included in the system of 'pluralist' representation so celebrated in recent years. However much these groups may be regarded as 'potential interest groups', the important fact is that political organization for their protection within the pluralist framework can scarcely be said to exist.

Schattschneider (1960, p. 35) has brought forward impressive evidence to show that the pluralist system ignores the diffuse, the unorganized and the inarticulate. It has a very pronounced business or upper-class bias and is loaded and unbalanced in favor of a fraction of a minority of the American people: 'The flaw in the pluralist heaven is that the heavenly chorus sings with a strong upper-class accent. Probably about 90 per cent of the people cannot get into the system.' For example, only a minority of farmers belong to farm organizations and

3. See also Kirchheimer (1966).
4. See also Bachrach (1967, pp. 36–7).

those who do not participate are largely the poorer ones. It is the rural poor, moreover, among whom the major problems of the farm population are concentrated.

The theorists of pluralism ignore the unrepresentative nature of the leadership of many groups in the system. In large-scale oligarchical associations the individual is smothered very effectively. There are few checks or limitations upon the power of small groups of leaders. Even where Americans have joined an organization, they do not belong to anything genuinely theirs. As Kariel (1961, pp. 3–4) has observed: The organizations which the early theorists of pluralism relied upon to sustain the individual against a unified government have themselves become oligarchically governed hierarchies, and now place unjustifiable limits on constitutional democracy.[5]

Rothman (1960, p. 22) has also pointed out that there is little evidence that group members influence the conduct of their leaders. Members tend to be apathetic, attend few meetings and rarely participate in group deliberations. In fact, decisions are taken by self-perpetuating oligarchies. One could say that pluralism is not the politics of group conflict but the politics of group leadership conflict, with the leaders socialized into the dominant values of American society [. . .]

In pluralist politics, there is a very sharp distinction between legitimate and non-legitimate interests. A group or interest within the framework of acceptability, no matter how bizarre its policy, can be sure of securing some measure of what it seeks. No legitimate interest gets all of what it wants, but it is not completely frustrated in its efforts. In the words of one well-known celebrant of the American political system, 'all the active and legitimate groups in the population can make themselves heard at some crucial stage in the process of decision' (Dahl, 1956, p. 137). On the other hand, an interest outside the system, no matter how reasonable or right it may be, receives no attention whatsoever. Pluralism does not extend its tolerance for diversity to movements which are felt to threaten the perpetuation of the existing social order. A policy or principle lacking legitimate representation has no place in the society and its proponents are treated as 'dangerous extremists', 'irrational crackpots', or

5. See also McConnell (1966, p. 342).

'foreign agents'. According to Perrow (1964, p. 422), one of the major defects of pluralism is the view that 'conflict on the part of the less privileged is automatically deemed disruptive, while the harmony of interests exists for those who have interests worth harmonizing'. The very sharp line between acceptable and unacceptable alternatives has led Wolff to describe the territory of American politics as being 'like a plateau with steep cliffs on all sides rather than like a pyramid'. On the plateau are all the interest groups which are recognized as legitimate, while in the deep valley all around lie the extremists and the outsiders [. . .]

The balance-of-power version of pluralist theory tends to deny new groups or interests access to the political plateau. It does this by ignoring their existence in practice, not by denying their claim in theory. Of course, after a struggle some groups such as labor in the thirties manage to climb onto the plateau where they can count on some measure of what they seek. Thus, pluralism acts as a brake on institutionalized change or change within the system. It does not set up an absolute barrier to social change, but it certainly slows down the process of transformation.

The referee theory

Although some pluralists assume that 'countervailing power' emerges somehow naturally, others such as Galbraith realize that government intervention is necessary to help create it. According to the referee theory of pluralism, the role of the federal government is to supervise and regulate the competition among interest groups in the society so that none of the interests represented will abuse their power to gain unchecked mastery over some sector of social life. Out of the applications of this theory have come the anti-trust bills, pure food and drug acts, Taft-Hartley Law, as well as the complex system of quasi-judicial regulatory agencies in the executive branch of American government. Kariel (1961) has shown that this 'referee' function of government systematically favors the interests of the stronger against the weaker party in interest-group conflicts. By tending to solidify the power of those who already hold it, the government plays a conservative, rather than a neutral role in American society.

Kariel details the ways in which this discriminatory influence is exercised. For example, in the field of regulation of trade unions, the federal agencies deal with the established leadership of the unions. In such matters as the supervision of union elections or the settlement of jurisdictional disputes, it is the interests of those leaders rather than the competing interests of rank-and-file dissidents which are favored. Again, in the regulation of agriculture, the leaders of farmers' organizations draw up the guide-lines for control which are then adopted by the federal inspectors. In each case, the unwillingness of the government to impose its own standards or rules results not in a free play of competing groups, but in the enforcement of the preferences of the existing predominant interest.

Another massively documented review of the undemocratic character of the pluralist system is to be found in McConnell (1966). He demonstrates that many of the governmental agencies supposedly regulating the economy have become the hand-maidens of dominant group interests. Almost everywhere one turns, it is to find public subservience to the dominance of the reigning oligarchies of private groups, each of which tends to be a law unto itself within the sphere of its own domain.[6]

One of the unhappy consequences of government regulation is that interests which have been ignored, suppressed, or which have not yet succeeded in organizing themselves for effective action, will find their disadvantageous position perpetuated through the decisions of the government. The government, by simply enforcing the existing rules in the game, does not thereby remove injustices in pluralist politics. In fact, it may actually make matters worse, because if the disadvantaged groups band together and fight it out, the government will accuse them of breaking the rules and throw its weight against them. For example, the American Medical Association exercises a strangle-hold over medicine through its influence over the government's licensing regulations. Doctors who are opposed to the AMA's political positions, or even to its medical policies, do not merely have to buck the entrenched authority of the leaders of the organization. They must also risk the loss of hospital affiliations, speciality accreditation, and so forth, all of which powers have

6. See also Mills (1956).

been placed in the hands of the medical establishment by state and federal laws. These laws are written by the government in cooperation with the very same AMA leaders. Not surprisingly, the interests of dissenting doctors do not receive favorable attention [. . .]

The limits of pluralism

The monolithic reality behind the pluralist facade has been eloquently portrayed by a number of critics of American society, particularly the non-socialist Goodman and the socialist Marcuse. Goodman, in his recent Massey Lectures, points out that genuine pluralism would mean conflict and not harmony, increased class consciousness and faculty power in the universities. He then goes on to condemn pseudo-pluralism as follows:

For the genius of our centralized bureaucracies has been, as they interlock, to form a mutually accredited establishment of decision makers, with common interests and a common style that nullify the diversity of pluralism. Conflict becomes coalition, harmony becomes consensus, and the social machine runs with no check at all. For instance, our regulatory agencies are wonderfully in agreement with the corporations they regulate . . .

There is a metaphysical defect in our pluralism. The competing groups are all after the same values, the same money, the same standard of living and fringe benefits. . . . There can be fierce competition between groups for a bigger cut in the budget, but there is no moral or constitutional countervailing of interests (1967, pp. 127–9).

Marcuse (1964, pp. 50–51) argues even more strongly that the reality of pluralism extends rather than reduces manipulation and coordination in American society:

At the most advanced stage of capitalism, this society is a system of subdued pluralism in which the competing institutions concur in solidifying the power of the whole over the individual. . . . Advanced industrial society is indeed a system of countervailing powers. But these forces cancel each other out in a higher unification – in the common interest to defend and extend the established position, to combat the historical alternatives, to contain qualitative change.

For the administered individual, of course, pluralist administration is far better than total administration: 'One institution might protect him against the other; one organization might mitigate the impact of the other; possibilities of escape and redress can be calculated. The rule of law, no matter how restricted, is infinitely safer than rule above or without law.'[7]

The theory of pluralism in all its forms has the effect of discriminating not only against certain groups or interests, but against certain sorts of proposals for the solution of social problems. Wolff (1965), for example, argues that there are some social ills in America whose causes do not lie in a maldistribution of wealth, and which cannot be solved therefore by the techniques of pluralist politics. He takes as an example the fact that America is growing uglier, more dangerous, and less pleasant to live in, as its citizens grow richer. The reason is that natural beauty, public order, and the promotion of the arts, are not the special interest of any identifiable group. Accordingly, Wolff observes that

. . . evils and inadequacies in those areas cannot be remedied by shifting the distribution of wealth and power among existing social groups . . . fundamentally they are problems of the society as a whole, not of any particular group. That is to say, they concern the general good, not merely the aggregate of private goods. To deal with such problems, there must be some way of constituting the whole society a genuine group with a group purpose and a conception of the common good. Pluralism rules this out in theory by portraying society as an aggregate of human communities rather than as itself a human community; and it equally rules out a concern for the general good in practice by encouraging a politics of interest-group pressures in which there is no mechanism for the discovery and expression of the common good.

Pluralism does not acknowledge the possibility of wholesale reorganization of American society: 'By insisting on the group nature of society, it denies the existence of society-wide interests – save the purely procedural interest in preserving the system of group pressures – and the possibility of communal action in pursuit of the general good.' Pluralism is fatally blind to the evils which afflict the entire body politic. It obstructs consideration of the sort of largescale social reconstruction which is so needed to remedy those evils [. . .]

7. For Marcuse's impact on some of the most creative radical thinkers in the social sciences, see Wolff and Moore (1967).

Preoccupation with the stability of the social and political system characterizes the writings of the pluralists. A young historian, Rogin (1967, p. 293), has recently written that while their concern with stability is to safeguard individual freedom,

... their interest in the freedom of the nongroup member and in the problem of freedom within the group is minimal. Because the pluralists are so quick to see dangers to stability, their concern for liberty in practice can become secondary. Thus for the authors of *The New American Right*, the great danger of McCarthyism was its attack on social stability. The damage done to innocent individuals received much less notice.[8]

The pluralist vision, Rogin continued, is a distorted one. The concern for stability and the fear of radicalism have interfered with accurate perception:

Thanks to its allegiance to modern America, pluralism analyses efforts by masses to improve their conditions as threats to stability. It turns all threats to stability into threats to constitutional democracy. This is a profoundly conservative endeavour. Torn between its half-expressed fears and its desire to face reality, pluralist theory is a peculiar mixture of analysis and prescription, insight and illusion, special pleading and dispassionate inquiry. Perhaps pluralism may best be judged not as a product of science but as a liberal American venture into conservative theory (p. 282).

The same point was also made by Lowi (1967, p. 24), who noted that 'It is amazing and depressing how many 1930s left-wing liberals have become 1960s interest-group liberals out of a concern for instability.'

The pluralist stance has well served the widely proclaimed 'end of ideology' in the West.[9] The attribution of all virtue to the pluralist system has been accompanied by a revulsion against ideology (including any large goals in politics) and a cynicism about the meaning of the 'public interest'. While the Left insists that morality and politics are indivisible, the pluralists segregate ethics from politics. The *status quo* defended by Lipset and Bell is the already achieved good society. They have reduced

8. The contributors to *The New American Right*, included Lipset, Parsons, Riesman, Glazer and the editor, Bell.

9. The 'end of ideology' thesis is set forth in Bell (1962, pp. 393–407); Lipset (1963, pp. 403–17); Dahl and Lindblom (1953, pp. 3–18).

politics to a constellation of self-seeking pressure groups peaceably engaged in a power struggle to determine the allocation of privilege and particular advantage (see Rousseas and Farganis, 1965).[10]

10. For further sharp rebuttals to the 'end of ideology' thesis, see La Palombara (1966); Aiken (1964); Bell and Aiken (1964); Harrington (1967, pp. 103–112); Newman (1961, ch. 10). 'The Conservative Mood: Daniel Bell and the End of Ideology'.

References

AIKEN, H. D. (1964), 'The revolt against ideology', *Commentary*, April, pp. 29–39.

BACHRACH, P. (1967), *The Theory of Democratic Elitism: A Critique*, Little, Brown.

BELL, D. (ed.), (1955), *The New American Right*, Criterion Books.

BELL, D. (1962), *The End of Ideology*, Collier.

BELL, D., and AIKEN, H. D. (1964), 'Ideology – a debate', *Commentary*, October, pp. 69–76.

BURLAGE, R. (1965), 'The American planned economy', *New University Thought*, Summer.

CARR, E. H. (1949), *The Twenty Years Crisis*, Macmillan.

DAHL, R. A. and LINDBLOM, C. E. (1953), *Politics, Economics and Welfare*, Harper and Row.

DAHL, R. A. (1956), *A Preface to Democratic Theory*, University of Chicago Press.

GOODMAN, P. (1967), *Like a Conquered Province: The Moral Ambiguity of America*, Random House.

HACKER, A. (1965), 'Power to do what?' in I. L. Horowitz (ed.) *The New Sociology*, Oxford University Press, pp. 134–46.

HARRINGTON, M. (1967), *The Accidental Century*, Penguin.

KARIEL, H. S. (1961), *The Decline of American Pluralism*, Stanford University Press.

KARIEL, H. S. (1966), *The Promise of Politics*, Prentice-Hall.

KIRCHHEIMER, O. (1966), 'Private man and society', *Polit. Sci. Q.*, March, pp. 16–24.

LIPSET, S. M. (1963), *Political Man*, Mercury Books.

LOWENSTEIN, K. (1957), *Political Power and Governmental Process*, Chicago University Press.

LOWI, T. (1967), 'The public philosophy: interest-group liberalism', *Amer. Polit. Sci. Rev.*, March.

MARCUSE, H. (1964), *One-Dimensional Man*, Beacon Press.

MCCONNELL, G. (1966), *Private Power and American Democracy*, Knopf.

MILBRATH, L. W. (1963), *The Washington Lobbyists*, Rand McNally.

MILLS, C. W. (1956), *The Power Elite*, Oxford University Press.

NEWMAN, W. J. (1961), *The Futilitarian Society*, Braziller.

PERLO, V. (1963), *Militarism and Industry*, International Publishers.

PERROW, C. (1964), 'The sociological perspective of political pluralism', *Social Research*, Winter.

LA PALOMBARA, J. (1966), 'Decline of ideology: a dissent and an interpretation', *American Political Science Review*, March, pp. 5–16.

REAGAN, M. (1963), *The Managed Economy*, Oxford University Press, New York.

ROGIN, M. P. (1967), *The Intellectuals and McCarthy: The Radical Specter*, MIT Press.

ROSSITER, B. (1964), *The Mythmakers*, Houghton Mifflin.

ROTHMAN, S. (1960), 'Systematic political theory: observations on group approach', *Amer. polit. Sci. Rev.*, March.

ROUSSEAS, S. W., and FARGANIS, J. (1965), 'American politics and the end of ideology', in I. L. Horowitz (ed.), *The New Sociology*, Oxford University Press.

SCHATTSCHNEIDER, E. E. (1960), *The Semisovereign People*, Holt, Rinehart & Winston.

WOLFF, R. P. (1965), 'Beyond tolerance', in R. R. Wolff, B. Moore Jr. and H. Marcuse, *A Critique of Pure Tolerance*, Beacon Press.

WOLFF, K. H., and MOORE, B., JR (eds.) (1967), *The Critical Spirit: Essays in Honor of Herbert Marcuse*, Beacon Press.

23 P. Bachrach and M. S. Baratz

Two Faces of Power

P. Bachrach and M. S. Baratz, 'Two faces of power', *American Political Science Review*, vol. 56, 1962, pp. 947–52.

The concept of power remains elusive despite the recent and prolific outpourings of case studies on community power. Its elusiveness is dramatically demonstrated by the regularity of disagreement as to the locus of community power between the sociologists and the political scientists. Sociologically oriented researchers have consistently found that power is highly centralized, while scholars trained in political science have just as regularly concluded that in 'their' communities power is widely diffused.[1] Presumably, this explains why the latter group styles itself 'pluralist', its counterpart 'elitist'.

There seems no room for doubt that the sharply divergent findings of the two groups are the product, not of sheer coincidence, but of fundamental differences in both their underlying assumptions and research methodology. The political scientists have contended that these differences in findings can be explained by the faulty approach and presuppositions of the sociologists. We contend in this paper that the pluralists themselves have not grasped the whole truth of the matter; that while their criticisms of the elitists are sound, they, like the elitists, utilize an approach and assumptions which predetermine their conclusions. Our argument is cast within the frame of our central thesis: that there are two faces of power, neither of which the sociologists see and only one of which the political scientists see.

1. Compare, for example, the sociological studies of Hunter (1953), Pellegrini and Coates (1956) and Schulze (1958), with the political science studies of Sayre and Kaufman (1960), Dahl (1961), and Long and Belknap (1956). See also Polsby (1960).

Against the elitist approach to power several criticisms may be, and have been, levelled.[2] One has to do with its basic premise that in every human institution there is an ordered system of power, a 'power structure' which is an integral part and the mirror image of the organization's stratification. This postulate the pluralists emphatically – and, to our mind, correctly – reject, on the ground that

... nothing categorical can be assumed about power in any community.... If anything, there seems to be an unspoken notion among pluralist researchers that at bottom *nobody* dominates in a town, so that their first question is not likely to be, 'Who runs this community?', but rather, 'Does anyone at all run this community?' The first query is somewhat like, 'Have you stopped beating your wife?', in that virtually any response short of total unwillingness to answer will supply the researchers with a 'power elite' along the lines presupposed by the stratification theory.

Equally objectionable to the pluralists – and to us – is the sociologists' hypothesis that the power structure tends to be stable over time.

Pluralists hold that power may be tied to issues, and issues can be fleeting or persistent, provoking coalitions among interested groups and citizens, ranging in their duration from momentary to semipermanent.... To presume that the set of coalitions which exists in the community at any given time is a timelessly stable aspect of social structure is to introduce systematic inaccuracies into one's description of social reality.

A third criticism of the elitist model is that it wrongly equates reputed with actual power:

If a man's major life work is banking, the pluralist presumes he will spend his time at the bank, and not in manipulating community decisions. This presumption holds until the banker's activities and participations indicate otherwise.... If we presume that the banker is 'really' engaged in running the community, there is practically no way of disconfirming this notion, even if it is totally erroneous. On the other hand, it is easy to spot the banker who really *does* run community affairs when we presume he does not, because his activities will make this act apparent.

2. See especially Polsby (1960, p. 475–81).

P. Bachrach and M. S. Baratz 377

This is not an exhaustive bill of particulars; there are flaws other than these in the sociological model and methodology[3] – including some which the pluralists themselves have not noticed. But to go into this would not materially serve our current purposes. Suffice it simply to observe that whatever the merits of their own approach to power, the pluralists have effectively exposed the main weaknesses of the elitist model.

As the foregoing quotations make clear, the pluralists concentrate their attention, not upon the sources of power, but its exercise. Power to them means 'participation in decision making'[4] and can be analyzed only after 'careful examination of a series of concrete decisions' (Dahl, 1958). As a result, the pluralist researcher is uninterested in the reputedly powerful. His concerns instead are to

1. Select for study a number of 'key' as opposed to 'routine' political decisions.

2. Identify the people who took an active part in the decision-making process.

3. Obtain a full account of their actual behavior while the policy conflict was being resolved.

4. Determine and analyze the specific outcome of the conflict.

The advantages of this approach, relative to the elitist alternative, need no further exposition. The same may not be said, however, about its defects – two of which seem to us to be of fundamental importance. One is that the model takes no account of the fact that power may be, and often is, exercised by confining the scope of decision-making to relatively 'safe' issues. The other is that the model provides no *objective* criteria for distinguishing between 'important' and 'unimportant' issues arising in the political arena.

There is no gainsaying that an analysis grounded entirely upon what is specific and visible to the outside observer is more 'scientific' than one based upon pure speculation. To put it another way:

3. See especially Dahl (1958) and Herson (1961).
4. This definition originated with Lasswell and Kaplan (1950, p. 75).

If we can get our social life stated in terms of activity, and of nothing else, we have not indeed succeeded in measuring it, but we have at least reached a foundation upon which a coherent system of measurements can be built up. . . . We shall cease to be blocked by the intervention of unmeasurable elements, which claim to be themselves the real causes of all that is happening, and which by their spooklike arbitrariness make impossible any progress toward dependable knowledge (Bentley, 1908).

The question is, however, how can one be certain in any given situation that the 'unmeasurable elements' are inconsequential, are not of decisive importance? Cast in slightly different terms, can a sound concept of power be predicated on the assumption that power is totally embodied and fully reflected in 'concrete decisions' or in activity bearing directly upon their making?

We think not. Of course power is exercised when A participates in the making of decisions that affect B. But power is also exercised when A devotes his energies to creating or reinforcing social and political values and institutional practices that limit the scope of the political process to public consideration of only those issues which are comparatively innocuous to A. To the extent that A succeeds in doing this, B is prevented, for all practical purposes, from bringing to the fore any issues that might in their resolution be seriously detrimental to A's set of preferences.[5]

Situations of this kind are common. Consider, for example, the case – surely not unfamiliar to this audience – of the discontented faculty member in an academic institution headed by a tradition-bound executive. Aggrieved about a long-standing policy around which a strong vested interest has developed, the professor resolves in the privacy of his office to launch an attack

5. As is perhaps self-evident, there are similarities in both faces of power. In each, A participates in decisions and thereby adversely affects B. But there is an important difference between the two: in the one case, A openly participates; in the other, he participates only in the sense that he works to sustain those values and rules of procedure that help him keep certain issues out of the public domain. True enough, participation of the second kind may at times be overt; that is the case, for instance, in closure fights in the Congress. But the point is that it need not be. In fact, when the maneuver is most successfully executed, it neither involves nor can be identified with decisions arrived at on specific issues.

upon the policy at the next faculty meeting. But, when the moment of truth is at hand, he sits frozen in silence. Why? Among the many possible reasons, one or more of these could have been of crucial importance:

1. The professor was fearful that his intended action would be interpreted as an expression of his disloyalty to the institution.

2. He decided that, given the beliefs and attitudes of his colleagues on the faculty, he would almost certainly constitute on this issue a minority of one.

3. He concluded that, given the nature of the law-making process in the institution, his proposed remedies would be pigeonholed permanently. 'But whatever the case, the central point to be made is the same: to the extent that a person or group – consciously or unconsciously – creates or reinforces barriers to the public airing of policy conflicts, that person or group has power.' Or, as Schattschneider (1960, p. 71) has so admirably put it: 'All forms of political organization have a bias in favor of the exploitation of some kinds of conflict and the suppression of others because *organization is the mobilization of bias.* Some issues are organized into politics while others are organized out.'

Is such bias not relevant to the study of power? Should not the student be continuously alert to its possible existence in the human institution that he studies, and be ever prepared to examine the forces which brought it into being and sustain it? Can he safely ignore the possibility, for instance, that an individual or group in a community participates more vigorously in supporting the *nondecision-making* process than in participating in actual decisions within the process? Stated differently, can the researcher overlook the chance that some person or association could limit decision-making to relatively non-controversial matters, by influencing community values and political procedures and rituals, notwithstanding that there are in the community serious but latent power conflicts?[6] To do so is, in

6. Dahl *partially* concedes this point when he observes (1958) that 'one could argue that even in a society like ours a ruling elite might be so influential over ideas, attitudes, and opinions that a kind of false consensus will exist – not the phony consensus of a terroristic totalitarian dictatorship but the manipulated and superficially self-imposed adherence to the norms

our judgement, to overlook the less apparent, but nonetheless extremely important, face of power.

In his critique of the 'ruling-elite model', Dahl argues that

the hypothesis of the existence of a ruling elite can be strictly tested only if . . . [t]here is a fair sample of cases involving key political decisions in which the preferences of the hypothetical ruling elite run counter to those of any other likely group that might be suggested.

With this assertion we have two complaints. One we have already discussed, that is, in erroneously assuming that power is solely reflected in concrete decisions, Dahl thereby excludes the possibility that in the community in question there is a group capable of preventing contests from arising on issues of importance to it. Beyond that, however, by ignoring the less apparent face of power Dahl and those who accept his pluralist approach are unable adequately to differentiate between a 'key' and a 'routine' political decision.

Polsby, for example, proposes that 'by pre-selecting as issues for study those which are generally agreed to be significant, pluralist researchers can test stratification theory' (Polsby, 1960). He is silent, however, on how the researcher is to determine *what* issues are 'generally agreed to be significant', and on how the researcher is to appraise the reliability of the agreement. In fact, Polsby is guilty here of the same fault he himself has found with elitist methodology: by presupposing that in any community there are significant issues in the political arena, he takes for granted the very question which is in doubt. He accepts as issues what are reputed to be issues. As a result, his findings are fore-ordained. For even if there is no 'truly' significant issue in the community under study, there is every likelihood that Polsby (or any like-minded researcher) will find one or some

---

and goals of the elite by broad sections of a community . . . This objection points to the need to be circumspect in interpreting the evidence.' But that he largely misses our point is clear from the succeeding sentence: 'Yet here, too, it seems to me that the hypothesis cannot be satisfactorily confirmed without something equivalent to the test I have proposed', and that is 'by an examination of a series of concrete cases where key decisions are made . . .'.

and, after careful study, reach the appropriate pluralistic conclusions.[7]

Dahl's definition of 'key political issues' in his essay on the ruling-elite model is open to the same criticism. He states that it is 'a necessary although possibly not a sufficient condition that the [key] issue should involve actual disagreement in preferences among two or more groups' (1961, p. 467). In our view, this is an inadequate characterization of a 'key political issue', simply because groups can have disagreements in preferences on unimportant as well as on important issues. Elite preferences which border on the indifferent are certainly not significant in determining whether a monolithic or polylithic distribution of power prevails in a given community. Using Dahl's definition of 'key political issues', the researcher would have little difficulty in finding such in practically any community; and it would not be surprising then if he ultimately concluded that power in the community was widely diffused.

The distinction between important and unimportant issues, we believe, cannot be made intelligently in the absence of an analysis of the 'mobilization of bias' in the community; of the dominant values and the political myths, rituals, and institutions which tend to favor the vested interests of one or more groups, relative to others. Armed with this knowledge, one could conclude that any challenge to the predominant values or to the established 'rules of the game' would constitute an 'important' issue; all else, unimportant. To be sure, judgements of this kind cannot be entirely objective. But to avoid making them in a study of power is both to neglect a highly significant aspect of power and thereby to undermine the only sound basis for discriminating between 'key' and 'routine' decisions. In effect, we contend, the pluralists have made each of these mistakes; that is to say, they have done just that for which Kaufman and Jones (1954) so severely taxed Floyd Hunter: they have begun 'their structure at the mezzanine without showing us a lobby or foundation', i.e., they have begun by studying the issues rather than the values and biases that are built into the political system

7. As he points out, the expectations of the pluralist researchers 'have seldom been disappointed' (1960).

and that, for the student of power, give real meaning to those issues which do enter the political arena.

There is no better fulcrum for our critique of the pluralist model than Dahl's recent study of power in New Haven (1961).

At the outset it may be observed that Dahl does not attempt in this work to define his concept, 'key political decision'. In asking whether the 'notables' of New Haven are 'influential overtly or covertly in the making of government decisions', he simply states that he will examine 'three different "issue-areas" in which important public decisions are made: nominations by the two political parties, urban redevelopment, and public education'. These choices are justified on the grounds that 'nominations determine which persons will hold public office. The New Haven redevelopment program measured by its cost – present and potential – is the largest in the country. Public education, aside from its intrinsic importance, is the costliest item in the city's budget'. Therefore, Dahl concludes, 'It is reasonable to expect . . . that the relative influence over public officials wielded by the . . . Notables would be revealed by an examination of their participation in these three areas of activity' (p. 64).

The difficulty with this latter statement is that it is evident from Dahl's own account that the 'notables' are in fact uninterested in two of the three 'key' decisions he has chosen. In regard to the public school issue, for example, Dahl points out that many of the notables live in the suburbs and that those who do live in New Haven choose in the main to send their children to private schools. 'As a consequence,' he writes, 'their interest in the public schools is ordinarily rather slight' (p. 70). Nominations by the two political parties as an important 'issue-area', is somewhat analogous to the public schools, in that the apparent lack of interest among the notables in this issue is partially accounted for by their suburban residence – because of which they are disqualified from holding public office in New Haven. Indeed, Dahl himself concedes that with respect to both these issues the notables are largely indifferent: 'Business leaders might ignore the public schools or the political parties without any sharp awareness that their indifference would hurt their pocketbooks. . . .' He goes on, however, to say that the prospect of profound changes [as a result of the urban-redevelopment program] in ownership, physical layout, and usage of property in the downtown area and the effects of these changes on the commercial and industrial prosperity of New Haven were all related in an obvious way to the daily concerns of businessmen (p. 71).

Thus, if one believes – as Dahl did when he wrote his critique of the ruling-elite model – that an issue, to be considered as important, 'should involve actual disagreement in preferences among two or more groups' (p. 67), then clearly he has now for all practical purposes written off public education and party nomination as key 'issue-areas'. But this point aside, it appears somewhat dubious at best that 'the relative influence over public officials wielded by the social notables' can be revealed by an examination of their nonparticipation in areas in which they were not interested.

Furthermore, we would not rule out the possibility that even on those issues to which they appear indifferent, the notables may have a significant degree of *indirect* influence. We would suggest, for example, that although they send their children to private schools, the notables do recognize that public school expenditures have a direct bearing upon their own tax liabilities. This being so, and given their strong representation on the New Haven Board of Finance,[8] the expectation must be that it is in their direct interest to play an active role in fiscal policy-making, in the establishment of the educational budget in particular. But as to this, Dahl is silent: he inquires not at all into either the decisions made by the Board of Finance with respect

8. Dahl (1961, pp. 81–2) points out that 'the main policy thrust of the economic notables is to oppose tax increases; this leads them to oppose expenditures for anything more than minimal traditional city services. In this effort their two most effective weapons ordinarily are the mayor and the Board of Finance. The policies of the notables are most easily achieved under a strong mayor if his policies coincide with theirs or under a weak mayor if they have the support of the Board of Finance. . . . New Haven mayors have continued to find it expedient to create confidence in their financial policies among businessmen by appointing them to the Board.'

to education nor into their impact upon the public schools.[9] Let it be understood clearly that in making these points we are not attempting to refute Dahl's contention that the notables lack power in New Haven. What we *are* saying, however, is that this conclusion is not adequately supported by his analysis of the 'issue-areas' of public education and party nominations.

The same may not be said of redevelopment. This issue is by any reasonable standard important for purposes of determining whether New Haven is ruled by 'the hidden hand of an economic elite' (Dahl, 1961, p. 124). For the economic notables have taken an active interest in the program and, beyond that, the socio-economic implications of it are not necessarily in harmony with the basic interests and values of businesses and businessmen.

In an effort to assure that the redevelopment program would be acceptable to what he dubbed 'the biggest muscles' in New Haven, Mayor Lee created the Citizens Action Commission (CAC) and appointed to it primarily representatives of the economic elite. It was given the function of overseeing the work of the mayor and other officials involved in redevelopment, and, as well, the responsibility for organizing and encouraging citizens' participation in the program through an extensive committee system.

In order to weigh the relative influence of the mayor, other key officials, and the members of the CAC, Dahl reconstructs 'all the *important* decisions on redevelopment and renewal between 1950–58 . . . [to] determine which individuals most often initiated the proposals that were finally adopted or most often successfully vetoed the proposals of the others'.[10] The results of this test indicate that the mayor and his development administrator were by far the most influential, and that the 'muscles' on the Commission, excepting in a few trivial instances, 'never

9. Dahl does discuss in general terms (pp. 79–84) changes in the level of tax rates and assessments in past years, but not actual decisions of the Board of Finance or their effects on the public school system.

10. 'A rough test of a person's overt or covert influence,' Dahl states in the first section of the book, 'is the frequency with which he successfully initiates an important policy over the opposition of others, or vetoes policies initiated by others, or initiates a policy where no opposition appears' (p. 60).

directly initiated, opposed, vetoed or altered any proposal brought before them' (p. 131).

This finding is, in our view, unreliable, not so much because Dahl was compelled to make a subjective selection of what constituted *important* decisions within what he felt to be an *important* 'issue-area', as because the finding was based upon an excessively narrow test of influence. To measure relative influence solely in terms of the ability to initiate and veto proposals is to ignore the possible exercise of influence or power in limiting the scope of initiation. How, that is to say, can a judgement be made as to the relative influence of Mayor Lee and the CAC without knowing (through prior study of the political and social views of all concerned) the proposals that Lee did *not* make because he anticipated that they would provoke strenuous opposition and, perhaps, sanctions on the part of the CAC?[11]

In sum, since he does not recognize *both* faces of power, Dahl is in no position to evaluate the relative influence or power of the initiator and decision maker, on the one hand, and of those persons, on the other, who may have been indirectly instrumental in preventing potentially dangerous issues from being raised.[12]

11. Dahl is, of course, aware of the 'law of anticipated reactions'. In the case of the mayor's relationships with the CAC, Dahl notes that Lee was 'particularly skillful in estimating what the CAC could be expected to support or reject' (p. 137). However, Dahl was not interested in analyzing or appraising to what extent the CAC limited Lee's freedom of action. Because of his restricted concept of power, Dahl did not consider that the CAC might in this respect have exercised power. That the CAC did not initiate or veto actual proposals by the mayor was to Dahl evidence enough that the CAC was virtually powerless; it might as plausibly be evidence that the CAC was (in itself or in what it represented) so powerful that Lee ventured nothing it would find worth quarreling with.

12. The fact that the initiator of decisions also refrains – because he anticipates adverse reactions – from initiating other proposals does not obviously lessen the power of the agent who limited his initiative powers. Dahl missed this point: 'It is,' he writes, 'all the more improbable, then, that a secret cabal of notables dominates the public life of New Haven through means so clandestine that not one of the fifty prominent citizens interviewed in the course of this study – citizens who had participated extensively in various decisions – hinted at the existence of such a cabal' (p. 185).

In conceiving of elite domination exclusively in the form of a conscious cabal exercising the power of decision making and vetoing, he overlooks a

As a result he unduly emphasizes the importance of initiating, deciding, and vetoing, and in the process casts the pluralist conclusions of his study into serious doubt.

We have contended in this paper that a fresh approach to the study of power is called for, an approach based upon a recognition of the two faces of power. Under this approach the researcher would begin – not, as does the sociologist who asks, 'Who rules?' nor as does the pluralist who asks, 'Does anyone have power?' – but by investigating the particular 'mobilization of bias' in the institution under scrutiny. Then, having analyzed the dominant values, the myths and the established political procedures and rules of the game, he would make a careful inquiry into which persons or groups, if any, gain from the existing bias and which, if any, are handicapped by it. Next, he would investigate the dynamics of *nondecision-making;* that is, he would examine the extent to which and the manner in which the *status quo* oriented persons and groups influence those community values and those political institutions – as, e.g., the unanimity 'rule' of New York City's Board of Estimate[13] (see Sayre and Kaufman, 1960, p. 640) – which tend to limit the scope of actual decision making to 'safe' issues. Finally, using his knowledge of the restrictive face of power as a foundation for analysis and as a standard for distinguishing between 'key' and 'routine' political decisions, the researcher would, after the manner of the pluralists, analyze participation in decision-making of concrete issues.

We reject in advance as unimpressive the possible criticism that this approach to the study of power is likely to prove fruitless because it goes beyond an investigation of what is objectively measurable. In reacting against the subjective aspects of the sociological model of power, the pluralists have, we believe, made the mistake of discarding 'unmeasurable elements' as unreal. It is ironical that, by so doing, they have exposed

more subtle form of domination; one in which those who actually dominate are not conscious of it themselves, simply because their position of dominance has never seriously been challenged.

13. For perceptive study of the 'mobilization of bias' in a rural American community, see Vidich and Bensman (1958).

themselves to the same fundamental criticism they have so forcefully levelled against the elitists: their approach to and assumptions about power predetermine their findings and conclusions.

References

BENTLEY, A. (1908), *The Process of Government*, Harvard University Press.

DAHL, R. A. (1958), 'A critique of the ruling-elite model', *Amer. Polit. Sci. Rev.*, vol. 52, June, pp. 463–69.

DAHL, R. A. (1961), *Who Governs?* Yale University Press.

HERSON, L. J. R. (1961), 'In the footsteps of community power', *Amer. Polit. Sci. Rev.*, vol. 55, December, pp. 817–31.

HUNTER, F. (1953), *Community Power Structure*, University of North Carolina Press.

KAUFMAN, H., AND JONES, V. (1954), *The Mystery of Power*, *Public admin. Rev*, vol. 14.

LASSWELL, H. D., and KAPLAN, A. (1950), *Power and Society*, Yale University Press.

LONG, N. E., and BELKNAP, G. (1956), 'A Research Program on Leadership and Decision-Making in Metropolitan Areas', Governmental Affairs Institute.

PELLEGRINI, R., and COATES, C. H. (1956), 'Absentee-owned corporation and community power structure', *Amer. J. of Sociol.*, vol. 61, March, pp. 413–19.

POLSBY, N. (1960), 'How to study community power: the pluralist alternative', *J. of Politics*, vol. 22, August, pp. 174–84.

SAYRE, W. S., and KAUFMAN, H. (1960), *Governing New York City*, Russell Sage.

SCHATTSCHNEIDER, E. E. (1960), *The Semisovereign People*, Holt, Rinehart & Winston.

SCHULZE, R. (1958), 'Economic dominants and community power structure', *Amer. Sociol. Rev.*, vol. 23, February, pp. 3–9.

VIDICH, A., and BENSMAN, J. (1958), *Small Town in Mass Society*, Princeton University Press.

Egalitarian Democracy

24 T. B. Bottomore

Equality or Elites?

'Equality or elites?', in T. B. Bottomore, *Elites and Society*, Penguin, 1966, ch. 7, pp. 129–50.

Democracy, in one of its established meanings, implies that there should be a substantial degree of equality among men, both in the sense that all the adult members of a society ought to have, so far as is possible, an equal influence upon those decisions which affect important aspects of the life of the society, and in the sense that inequalities of wealth, of social rank, or of education and access to knowledge, should not be so considerable as to result in the permanent subordination of some groups of men to others in any of the various spheres of social life, or to create great inequalities in the actual exercise of political rights. The advocates of equality have never been concerned to claim anything so foolish as that individuals are exactly alike or equal in physique, intelligence, or character. They have based their case upon a variety of other considerations, among which there are three which have a particular importance. The first is that for all their individual idiosyncracies, human beings are remarkably alike in some fundamental respects: they have similar physical, emotional and intellectual needs. That is why there can be a science of nutrition, and in a less exact way, sciences of mental health and healing, and of the education of children. Furthermore, the range of variation in the qualities of individuals is relatively narrow, and there is a clustering about the middle of the range.

If this were not so – if there were truly differences of kind, rather than of degree, among men; if there were brute beasts at one extreme and angels or god-like beings at the other – then one of the factual supports of the egalitarian case would be removed.

The second point is that the individual differences among men and the social distinctions between them are two separate things. Long ago, Rousseau (1762) made this important distinction:

I conceive that there are two kinds of inequality among the human species; one, which I call natural or physical, because it is established by nature, and consists in a difference of age, health, bodily strength, and the qualities of the mind or of the soul: and another, which may be called moral or political inequality, because it depends upon a kind of convention, and is established, or at least authorized, by the consent of men. This latter consists of the different privileges, which some men enjoy to the prejudice of others; such as that of being more rich, more honoured, more powerful or even in a position to exact obedience.

We cannot tell with any certainty how far these two kinds of inequality have been in correspondence in most of the societies which have existed up to modern times. The theory of the circulation of elites was intended in part to suggest that they were; that the most able individuals in every society succeeded in entering the elite, or in forming a new elite which in due course became pre-eminent. But we have seen earlier that the historical evidence produced in support of this thesis is quite inconclusive, and that the more abundant evidence available in the case of modern societies (which are generally regarded as displaying an exceptional degree of social mobility) does not confirm it. The major inequalities in society are in the main social products, created and maintained by the institutions of property and inheritance, of political and military power, and supported by particular beliefs and doctrines, even though they are never entirely resistant to the ambitions of outstanding individuals.

These considerations lead on to the third point which I have to make about the character of the egalitarian arguments. If neither inequality nor equality is a natural phenomenon, which men have simply to accept, the advocacy of one or the other does not consist in the presentation of a scientific argument based wholly upon matters of fact, but in the formulation of a moral and social ideal. We can *opt* for equality, and although in so doing we have to pay attention to matters of fact which bear upon the practicability of the ideal and upon the means appropriate for attaining it, the ultimate justification for our option is not itself any matter of fact but a reasoned claim that the pursuit of equality is likely to create a more admirable society. In using the term 'we' I mean to refer specifically to men living in the societies of the twentieth century; for it was difficult in any earlier age to form a practical conception of a stable and durable egalitarian form of society, given the insecurity of economic life, the absence of effective means of communication, the inadequacy of education, and the lack of knowledge about social structure and individual character. The twentieth century is unique in offering to men for the first time the opportunity and the means to fashion social life according to their desires; and it is both hopeful and terrible for that reason.

It is not my purpose here to set out the moral case for equality,[1] but rather to consider the social and political problems which beset the pursuit of equality, and the criticisms, other than moral objections, which the elite theories bring against it. It will be convenient to begin by examining Marx's conception of a 'classless society', both because it presents the ideal of equality in a form which is more widely accepted than any other in the modern world, and because it was the principal source from which, by opposition, the elite theories themselves arose. Everyone knows that Marx did not write a blueprint for the socialist society which he envisaged and desired;[2] nevertheless, it is unmistakably clear from those of his writings which refer to the future socialist society, what he regarded, in broad outline, as its distinctive features. Marx's sketch of the classless

1. It is admirably expounded in Tawney (1952).
2. Surprisingly, this is often held against him, instead of being regarded as a mark of wisdom, and of profound faith in the creative capacities of men which were manifest even within the constraints of class societies and would be so much more easily made effective when those constraints were removed.

society incorporates moral, sociological and historical elements. The moral aspect is treated most fully in some of his early manuscripts, and particularly in the *Economic and Philosophical Manuscripts* of 1844 (see Bottomore, 1963), but it is by no means neglected in his later writings.[3] From this aspect a class-less society is defined as one in which men would exercise a much greater, and equal, control over their individual destinies; would be liberated from the tyranny of their own creations such as the state and bureaucracy, capital and technology; would be productive rather than acquisitive; would find pleasure and support in their social cooperation with other men rather than antagonism and bitterness in the competition with them. Marx did not always express himself with the same optimism about the possibility of attaining this condition of society,[4] but he never ceased to regard it as the ideal. His notion of what would constitute self-determination for the individual was expressed in a variety of ways. In the first place, the individual had to be freed from determination by his class or occupation; as Marx wrote in *The German Ideology*,

the communal relationship into which the individuals of a class entered, and which was determined by their common interests over against a third party, was always a community to which these individuals belonged only as average individuals, only in so far as they lived within the conditions of existence of their class. It was a relationship in which they participated not as individuals but as members of a class. But with the community of revolutionary proletarians, who establish their control over the conditions of existence of themselves and the other members of society, it is just the reverse; the individuals participate as individuals. It is just this combination of

3. See, for example, his discussion in *Capital* (1890), vol. 1, of the means to overcome the harmful effects of the division of labour, and in *Capital*, vol. 3, of the conditions of human freedom; his praise of the Paris Commune for its institution of genuinely democratic self-government, in *The Civil War in France*; and his comments upon the programme of the Socialist Workers' Party of Germany in *Critique of the Gotha Programme*.

4. For instance, in the passage on human freedom in *Capital*, vol. 3, Marx declares that the sphere of economic production is a realm of necessity 'under any possible mode of production'. 'The realm of freedom only begins, in fact, where that labour which is determined by need and external purpose, ceases; it is therefore, by its very nature, outside the sphere of material production proper.'

individuals (assuming, of course, the advanced level of modern productive forces) which brings the conditions for the free development and activity of individuals under their own control; conditions which were formerly abandoned to chance and which had acquired an independent existence over against the separate individuals.

Secondly, the individual had to be freed from domination by a remote, inaccessible and unaccountable government and administration, and to participate as fully as possible in deciding issues of general social importance. Marx held up as a practical instance of such participation the Paris Commune, in which the functions of government were undertaken by municipal councillors, chosen by universal suffrage, responsible and revocable at short term, and in which all public functions from those of the members of the Commune downwards were done at *workmen's* wages.

The sociological element in Marx's conception is to be found in his assertion that the principle of inequality is embodied in the institutions of social class – the division between owners of the means of production and non-owners – and more fundamentally in the division of labour in society, especially the division between manual and intellectual work. It follows that equality is to be attained by the abolition of classes, which will entail the suppression of the division of labour. Marx always insisted strongly upon this last condition. In *The German Ideology* he expressed it in a somewhat romantic form:

as soon as the division of labour begins, each man has a particular, exclusive sphere of activity, which is forced upon him and from which he cannot escape. He is a hunter, a fisherman, a shepherd, or a critical critic,[5] and must remain so if he does not want to lose his means of livelihood; whereas in communist society, where nobody has one exclusive sphere of activity but each can become accomplished in any branch he wishes, production as a whole is regulated by society, thus making it possible for me to do one thing today and another tomorrow, to hunt in the morning, fish in the afternoon, rear cattle in the evening, criticize after dinner, in accordance with my inclination, without ever becoming hunter, fisherman, shepherd or critic.

5. Marx refers here to the Young Hegelians who called their modified Hegelian philosophy 'critical criticism'.

Later, in the first volume of *Capital* (1890), he conveyed the same idea in more realistic terms:

the detail-worker of today, the limited individual, the mere bearer of a particular social function, will be replaced by the fully developed individual, for whom the different social functions he performs are but so many alternative modes of activity. One step already spontaneously taken towards effecting this revolution is the establishment of technical and agricultural schools, and of *écoles d'enseignement professionel*, in which the children of the working men receive some instruction in technology and in the practical handling of the various implements of labour. . . . There can be no doubt that when the working class comes into power . . . technical instruction, both theoretical and practical, will take its proper place in the working class schools.

Marx's argument, therefore, is directed just as much against the idea of functional elites – even elites recruited solely on the basis of merit – as against the idea of classes. The division of labour, and above all the division between those who think and plan and those who merely perform the necessary manual labour, continually recreates the class system; and it confines the individual within a sphere of life which he has not chosen for himself and in which he cannot acquire the means to develop all his faculties.

The historical element in this conception has two aspects. First, Marx presents a historical scheme, applicable mainly within the area of Western civilization, in which the forms of domination and servitude – master and slave, feudal lord and serf, industrial capitalist and worker – constitute a series which is distinguished by an increasing awareness of the contrast between man's qualities as an individual and his qualities as a member of a social category.

in the course of historical development . . . there emerges a distinction between the personal life of the individual and his life as it is determined by some branch of labour and the conditions pertaining to it . . . In a system of estates (and still more in the tribe) this is still concealed: for instance, a nobleman is always a nobleman, a commoner always a commoner, irrespective of his other relationships, a quality inseparable from his individuality. The distinction between the personal and the class individual, the accidental nature of conditions of life for the individual, appears only with the emergence of class, which itself is a product of the bourgeoisie. ... The contradiction between the personality of the individual proletarian and the condition of life imposed on him, his labour, becomes evident to himself, for he is sacrificed from his youth onwards and has no opportunity of achieving within his own class the conditions which would place him in another class (*The German Ideology*).

To this series Marx added a further term, the classless society of the future in which there would no longer be any sharp contrast between the personal qualities of the individual and the conditions of his social life, in which each individual would be able to develop his faculties to the fullest extent and would experience limitation only as a natural being, who is obliged to produce his material means of existence and who is mortal.

Secondly, Marx regards the classless society as a form of society which is only conceivable, and can only be achieved, at the historical moment when capitalism attains its fullest development, because the consummation of capitalism produces for the first time a subject class – the proletariat – which contains within itself no elements of further social differentiation. When the proletariat has been liberated by the expropriation of the capitalist owners of industry it will create new social institutions which will express its own homogeneity and solidarity and preclude the formation of new privileged groups in society.

Few modern advocates of equality would dissent from Marx's moral ideal of the classless society; but they would question some of the sociological and historical arguments with which Marx explained the manner of its advent and defined its characteristics. They would object still more to what used to be the orthodox Marxist interpretation (but it has been changing in recent years) of the classless society, which reduced the concept to little more than a technical expression describing a state of affairs in which there is no private ownership of industry. The major objection to Marx's own account must be that it portrays the attainment of a classless society – of genuine equality and liberty – as a once-for-all affair : at one moment men are living in the egoistic, acquisitive, conflict-ridden world of capitalism; at the next, pre-history has come to an end and men are engaged in creating the new institutions of a classless society. This is not quite fair to Marx inasmuch as he allows for a period of transition between capitalism and socialism – described by that phrase of ill-omen 'the dictatorship of the proletariat' – and for stages of development towards the 'higher phase of communist society' (*Critique of the Gotha Programme*). But it is fair in the sense that Marx never for a moment considers the possibility that under certain circumstances new social distinctions and a new ruling class might emerge in the society which succeeds capitalism; for example, from the dictatorship of the proletariat itself, which is so easily transformed into the tyranny of a party. This is a point of weakness in the Marxist doctrine which the elite theorists, and notably Michels,[6] attacked so successfully; and a new cogency has been given to their criticisms by the experiences of the USSR and the East European countries under Stalin's rule. Thus, Aron (1950, p. 131) is able to describe the classless society in these terms:

There is still, however, in such a society, a small number of men who in practice run the industrial undertakings, command the army, decide what proportion of the national resources should be allocated to saving and investment and fix scales of remuneration. This minority has infinitely more power than the political rulers in a democratic society, because both political and economic power are concentrated in their hands. . . . Politicians, trade union leaders, public officials, generals and managers all belong to one party and are part of an authoritarian organization. The unified elite has absolute and unbounded power. All intermediate bodies, all individual groupings, and particularly professional groups, are in fact controlled by delegates of the elite, or, if you prefer it, representatives of the State. . . . A classless society leaves the mass of the population without any possible means of defence against the elite.

Aron then considers an objection to this account, namely that the idea of a classless society is being confused with a more or less accurate picture of Soviet society, and he admits that

a different type of classless society is in theory possible. In present conditions, however, other types of classless society are extremely unlikely. In order to avoid a monopoly of power in the hands of the group of men in control of the state, it would be neces-

6. See especially, *Political Parties* (1949), part 6, ch. 2.

sary to restore a large number of centres of power; the various undertakings or trusts should become the property of those working in them, of local or trade union communities, instead of the centralized state. At the present time such decentralization is unlikely to come about, for psychological and technical reasons. . . . It is possible to conceive also that the elite power might not constitute a sort of religious and military sect and might be organized as a democratic party. There again, however, the idea which is possible in theory is extremely unlikely in practice. . . . Even more, the ideological monopoly preserved by the elite in power seems to me to correspond to an inherent requirement in such a regime. . . . In short, the unification of the elite is inseparable from the concentration of all economic and political power in its hands and that concentration is itself inseparable from the planning of an entirely collectivized economy.

Is it possible to meet these objections and to formulate in a more acceptable way the ideal of an egalitarian society? Let us note, first, some important resemblances between the classless society in the USSR as described by Aron, and the mass society which Mills portrays as developing in the USA. In a mass society, which Mills contrasts with a democratic 'society of publics':

(1) Far fewer people express opinions than receive them; for the community of publics becomes an abstract collection of individuals who receive impressions from the mass media. (2) The communications that prevail are so organized that it is difficult or impossible for the individual to answer back immediately or with any effect. (3) The realization of opinion in action is controlled by authorities who organize and control the channels of such action. (4) The mass has no autonomy from institutions; on the contrary, agents of authorized institutions penetrate this mass, reducing any autonomy it may have in the formation of opinion by discussion (1956, p. 304).

Among the most important structural characteristics of both the classless society and the mass society are the decline or disappearance of intermediate organizations – voluntary associations small enough for the individual to have an effective say in their activities – and the increasing distance between the leaders and the masses in all types of organization. It is obvious that these characteristics are very much more pronounced in the Soviet-type societies than in the Western countries, where there is no political or legal bar to the formation of associations, and where open as well as hidden competition for the allegiance of the citizens takes place between the large organizations; but there are also common features which have been produced by more general causes, among them the growth in the size of organizations brought about by technological advances (in production, communication, etc.), the increasing influence and control exercised by the state over economic production, irrespective of the type of economy, which is determined very largely by the massive production of war materials, and the international rivalry between nations organized on a semi-war footing, which is favourable to the growth of centralized and authoritarian political leadership.

Not all of these adverse influences can be combated effectively within the limits of a single society; they also call for changes in the relations between nations. Those problems which can be dealt with on a national level arise very largely from the size and complexity of organizations and, as Aron points out, from the authoritarian tendencies implicit in centralized economic planning, especially in a collectivized economy. The attempt to solve them has to proceed along several different lines, . . . the greatest possible decentralization of political authority by the transfer of responsibility for decisions, wherever feasible, to local and regional councils and to voluntary associations, and the extension of self-government to the economic field by the creation of appropriate new institutions, such as the workers' councils in present-day Yugoslavia. The danger that a new ruling class of political bosses and industrial managers will be formed in a collectivized economy can be met, not only by the introduction of self-government in the factory, but also by limiting the scope of collective ownership. It does not seem to me necessary to the attainment of an egalitarian society that all small-scale retail trading or farming, or semi-artisan production, should be absorbed into large collective enterprises. At the least, this should be treated as a practical question, and the propensity of such private economic activities to engender new social classes and new inequalities should be carefully studied in the light of experience. Similarly, the dangers of an intellectual dictatorship can be met by giving a large degree of autonomy to educational and cultural organizations.

In the intellectual sphere it is particularly important that there should be independent associations which compete with each other; not only in the case of sound and television broadcasting and the press, but also in book publishing and in scientific research. But this requirement is quite compatible with public ownership. The associations could well be owned or effectively controlled by their members, while being supported to a large extent by public funds and subject to general regulation by a national authority. This is already the situation of universities in most Western countries. The same principle can be applied also to the operation of industry and commerce. The individual enterprises may be owned and most of their policies decided upon by those who work in them, and they may compete with each other in respect of price and quality at least as effectively as privately owned enterprises now do, while being subject to controls of various kinds in the interests of a national economic plan. The achievements of a system of this kind, which combines public ownership with a form of market economy, in Yugoslavia, show that although there are many practical difficulties this is a viable form of economic organization and no longer simply a Utopian dream.[7] There does not seem to be any reason for supposing that in advanced industrial societies, which do not have to engage in the arduous business of primary capital accumulation, the control of the economy as a whole by a central planning authority need be any more rigorous or authoritarian under a system of public-ownership such as that which I have outlined than under a private enterprise system; for in both cases there will be very similar problems to be faced and similar techniques can be employed. In France, for example, the postwar economic planners have had very considerable powers and they have not been subject to any close control by the elected representatives of the people. In Britain the recently established National Economic Development Council, if its activities are to have any meaning, will be obliged to propose restraints and incentives, to be enforced by the central government, which will bring about the desired kind and rate of economic growth.

These considerations are sufficient, I think, to cast serious

7. For a brief account of the Yugoslav system, see Singleton and Topham (1963).

doubt upon Aron's assertion that it would be impossible to achieve, in a collectivized economy, a genuine decentralization of power, or to escape intellectual and cultural uniformity. It is true, of course, that even in a classless society which had carried decentralization very far, and in which numerous independent associations flourished, there would exist some fundamental agreement among the members of society upon the general features of its organization. But this must be the case in any society which is to endure, and as we have seen, those who regard democracy as being sustained by a plurality of competing elites still introduce the qualification that the competition must not be pushed to extremes and that there must be an underlying consensus of opinion. The hope of those who advocate equality is that the experience of living in a society which was drawing rapidly closer to this ideal would eventually persuade men of its value. If this occurred, there would remain all manner of intellectual disagreements and of choices as to a personal way of life, but there would be general agreement upon the desirability of social equality and opposition to those inequalities which produce and maintain lasting distinctions between whole categories of men.

Let me now return to another problem which is posed by Marx's conception of a classless society. According to Marx, the division of labour is not only in itself an impediment to the full development of each individual, a form of bondage, but is also the source from which arise the major social classes, which establish still more obdurate limitations of human freedom. The division of labour has, therefore, to be 'overcome': that is, abolished and transcended. But does it make sense to speak of 'abolishing' the division of labour in a modern industrial society? At first sight the problem seems more intractable now than in Marx's own day, for the specialization of occupations, including intellectual occupations, has proceeded rapidly, and in the sphere of industrial mass-production the subdivision of tasks has reached a point where the individual worker appears more and more as an adjunct to the machine, whose daily work is confined to the performance of a few simple, thoughtless and repetitive movements. Nevertheless, there have been other changes in work, and a new range of possibilities can now be seen, which make Marx's vision of the future a great deal more plausible. First, there have been changes in the nature of occupations, brought about especially by the development of automation. The effect of automation is to eliminate the worker on the assembly line and to replace him by a more educated and responsible individual whose function is to supervise very complicated chains of production which are controlled in detail by machines. At present these changes affect only a small part of industry, but they will become increasingly important. Secondly, the high productivity of modern industry has already made possible a reduction of working hours, and its accelerating rate of growth will bring within the capacity of all the advanced industrial countries, in the next decade or two, the establishment of a working week of some twenty-five or thirty hours. These countries are about to produce a new and revolutionary phenomenon; namely, a 'leisure class' which comprises the whole population. In the USA the first signs of such a condition of society can already be seen; in 1962, for example, the New York branch of the International Brotherhood of Electrical Workers gained for its members a basic five-hour day and twenty-five hour week.[8] Thirdly, if there were introduced in publicly owned industries the kind of self-management which I discussed earlier, and if this type of public ownership were established in all large enterprises, the range of the work activities of manual and clerical workers would be considerably extended. The individual worker would no longer be confined within his specialized task, but would also take part in the planning and management of production.

Together, these various changes in the organization of working life would modify profoundly the sense of the division of labour. The individual with abundant leisure would have the opportunity, as Marx believed, to devote himself to more than one activity, to express himself in diverse fields of endeavour, both physical and intellectual; and even as an economic producer he would find more occasion to develop all-round abilities

8. The division of labour and the growth of leisure are examined at length from a point of view which is very similar to my own in G. Friedmann (1962).

by participating in the work of management and by learning something of the science and technology upon which the operations of industry are based. The division of labour would become more evidently a technique which men have to use in producing their means of life, but which they must also control; it would no longer shape and constrict the whole of their lives, turning one man irrevocably into a worker on the assembly line, another into a clerk, and a third into a tycoon. Such changes imply, and they are already beginning to produce, a vast expansion of education in all its forms – an extension of the period of universal secondary education, higher education for a large proportion of those between the ages of eighteen and twenty-one, adult education on a large scale, with special facilities for those who decide at a mature age to prepare themselves for a new occupation – and the provision, on an immense scale, of equipment for sport and recreation. Perhaps I may conclude this discussion, and at the same time illustrate how slowly new and radical ideas make their way in the world, by quoting from one of the most eminent of British economists, whose vision of the role of labour in a future society was very close to that of Marx. Marshall, in an essay on 'The Future of the Working Classes' which was published in 1873, wrote:

That men do habitually sustain hard corporeal work for eight, ten or twelve hours a day, is a fact so familiar to us that we scarcely realize the extent to which it governs the moral and mental history of the world; we scarcely realize how subtle, all-pervading and powerful may be the effect of the work of man's body in dwarfing the growth of the man. . . . Work, in its best sense, the healthy energetic exercise of faculties, is the aim of life, is life itself; and in this sense every one [in the ideal society which Marshall conceives] would be a worker more completely than now. But men would have ceased to carry on mere physical work to such an extent as to dull their higher energies. In the bad sense, in which work crushes a man's life, it would be regarded as wrong. The active vigour of the people would continually increase; and in each successive generation it would be more completely true that every man was by occupation a gentleman . . . that condition which we have pictured . . . a condition in which every man's energies and abilities will be fully developed – a condition in which men will work not less than they do now but more; only, to use a good old phrase, most of their work will be a work of love; it will be a work which, whether conducted for payment or not, will exercise and nurture their faculties. Manual work, carried to such an excess that it leaves little opportunity for the free growth of his higher nature, that alone will be absent; but that *will* be absent. In so far as the working classes are men who have such excessive work to do, in so far will the working classes have been abolished.

So far I have considered mainly those objections to the idea of a classless, egalitarian society which take as their main theme the dangers of intellectual tyranny and political dictatorship. There is, however, another important line of criticism which brings to light a different aspect of the problem of elites. It has often been maintained, in one form or another, that the advancement of civilization has depended, and does always depend, upon the activities of small minorities of exceptionally gifted people. Ortega y Gasset (1930) says it in *The Revolt of the Masses*:

As one advances in life, one realizes more and more that the majority of men – and of women – are incapable of any other effort than that strictly imposed on them as a reaction to external compulsion. And for that reason, the few individuals we have come across who are capable of a spontaneous and joyous effort stand out isolated, monumentalized, so to speak, in our experience. These are the select men, the nobles, the only ones who are active and not merely reactive, for whom life is a perpetual striving, an incessant course of training.

In a similar manner, Bell (1928) argues that a civilized society is characterized by reasonableness and a sense of values, and that these qualities can only be produced, implanted and sustained by an elite. Now some part of what is asserted by these writers is undoubtedly true; namely, that civilization has been greatly advanced by the work of exceptional men. (It has also been greatly retarded by the activities of other exceptional men.) But this is not to say that such men, with their associates or followers, form a social elite, still less that they are in the majority of cases a *ruling* elite. They may have little social prestige, or be treated with active disdain by the rulers of society; they may be dependent financially upon the patronage of an upper class, without forming part of it. Their contribution to society is of an individual kind, not ordinarily dependent upon the formation of a distinctive social group; very often it is more strongly affected by the support and enthusiasm which their work calls forth in a whole population (as in fifth-century Athens) or in a whole class (as in Renaissance Italy or in eighteenth-century France). Exceptional men might perhaps be regarded as forming an elite in the first of the senses which Pareto gave to the term – namely, the category of those who have the highest ability in their branch of activity – except that in this sense many activities which have little or nothing to do with the advance of civilization would be included, and that the elites so defined would be made up of talented individuals rather than of those who have exceptional creative powers. It would really be better to use some other term; for example, the term 'creative minority', which Toynbee seemed to be using in his *Study of History* to refer, not to an elite group, but to a simple plurality of individuals. Thus he says that 'In all acts of social creation the creators are either creative individuals or, at most, creative minorities . . .'[9]

Those who seek to defend the elite doctrines by referring to the importance of intellectual and artistic creativity commit two errors: first, they neglect the vital interplay between creative individuals and the society in which they live – which is perhaps most evident in the case of scientific work, but is also to be traced in the history of painting or architecture, in literature, in religious movements and in moral reforms – and secondly, they assume that such individuals associate together as an elite or elites which can only exist in a hierarchically ordered society, and which can exist best in a society divided into stable and enduring classes. In this last conception, as it is expressed, for example, by Eliot (1948, p. 49), the subject of discussion is apt to change from the creation of culture to the transmission of culture. In Eliot's view there are, in every complex society, a number of levels of culture; it is important for the health of

9. Vol. 3, p. 239. However, in his concluding volume, in which he reconsiders his work, Toynbee approaches more closely the elite theories, in saying: 'By a creative minority I mean a ruling minority in which the creative faculty in human nature finds opportunities for expressing itself in effective action for the benefit of all participants in the society. . . . By a dominant minority I mean a ruling minority that rules less by attraction and more by force' (vol. 12, *Reconsiderations*, p. 305).

society that these different levels should be related to each other, but also that they should remain distinct, and that the manners and taste of society as a whole should be influenced by the highest culture. This can only happen, since culture is transmitted primarily through the family, if there exists an upper class composed of families which are able to maintain over several generations a settled way of life. Eliot admits that the existence of an upper class does not guarantee a high culture: '. . . the "conditions of culture" which I set forth do not necessarily produce the higher civilization: I assert only that when they are absent, the higher civilization is unlikely to be found.' Nevertheless, it *may* be found. We have as yet no direct experience of the way of life of an egalitarian society, and we can do no more than estimate the probability of its being able to create and preserve a high level of culture. Creation is an individual act, but it is facilitated by a general enthusiasm and liveliness in society at large, and we may reasonably expect that an egalitarian society, in which leisure was widespread and individuals were encouraged to develop their talents, would be at least as creative as those which accomplished great things in earlier periods when the economic conditions and the class structure of society were being rapidly transformed. As to the conservation and transmission of a high culture, we may well dissent from the view that it has been, and must be, primarily the work of the family. In the past, many other social groups – religious associations, philosophical schools, academies – have been at least as important as the family in transmitting culture; the family, i.e. the families of the upper class in society, have usually passed on, if they have passed on at all, something that has been conserved and kept alive elsewhere, by associations which enjoyed no great stability of membership from generation to generation. In a classless society the distance between high culture and lower types of culture would be less great, and regional and local diversity might become more pronounced; and the cultural heritage would be handed on, even more than in the past, by educational institutions and voluntary associations of every kind, and less than formerly by particular families. It is possible, too, that the conservation of culture, which is bound up inextricably in present-day societies with the maintenance of class privileges, would be less strongly emphasized – or at least change its aspect – and come to be taken much more for granted; while the power to create new forms of culture, to make new discoveries in the arts and sciences, would be more highly regarded and encouraged.

The theorists of elites defend, by these various means, the legacy from the inegalitarian societies of the past, while making concessions to the spirit of equality. They insist strongly upon an absolute distinction between rulers and ruled, which they present as a scientific law, but they reconcile democracy with this state of affairs by defining it as competition between elites. They accept and justify the division of society into classes, but endeavour to make this division more palatable by describing the upper classes as elites, and by suggesting that the elites are composed of the most able individuals, regardless of their social origins. Their case depends, to a large extent, upon substituting for the idea of equality the idea of equality of opportunity. But this latter notion, besides having quite a different moral significance, is actually self-contradictory. Equality of opportunity, as the expression is habitually used, presupposes inequality, since 'opportunity' means 'the opportunity to rise to a higher level in a stratified society'. At the same time, it presupposes equality, for it implies that the inequalities embedded in this stratified society have to be counteracted in every generation so that individuals can really develop their personal abilities; and every investigation of the conditions for equality of opportunity, for example in the sphere of education, has shown how strong and pervasive is the influence upon individual life-chances of the entrenched distinctions of social class. Equality of opportunity would only become a reality in a society without classes or elites, and the notion itself would then be otiose, for the equal life-chances of individuals in each new generation would be matters of fact, and the idea of opportunity would signify, not the struggle to rise into a higher social class, but the possibility for each individual to develop fully those qualities of intellect and sensibility which he has as a person, in an unconstrained association with other men.

References

ARON, R. (1950), 'Social structure and the ruling class', *Brit. J. Sociol.*, vol. 1, no. 2, pp. 126–43.

BELL, C. (1928), *Civilization, An Essay*, Chatto & Windus.

BOTTOMORE, T. B. (ed.) (1963), *Karl Marx: Early Writings*, Watts.

ELIOT, T. S. (1948), *Notes Towards the Definition of Culture*, Faber.

FRIEDMANN, G. (1962), *The Anatomy of Work*, Heinemann.

MARSHALL, A. (1873), 'The future of the working classes', in A. C. Pigou (ed.) *Memorials of Alfred Marshall*, Macmillan, pp. 101–18.

MARX, K. (1846), *German Ideology*, edited by R. Pascal, 1938.

MARX, K. (1890), *Capital*, translated E. Untermann, 1906, Kerr.

MICHELS, R. (1949), *Political Parties*, Free Press.

MILLS, C. R. (1956), *The Power Elite*, Oxford University Press.

ORTEGA Y GASSET (1930), *The Revolt of the Masses*, translated 1961, Allen & Unwin.

ROUSSEAU, J. J. (1762), *A Dissertation on the Origin and Foundation of the Equality of Mankind*, Everyman edition of *The Social Contract and Discourses*, 1913.

SINGLETON, F., and TOPHAM, A. (1963), 'Yugoslav workers' control: the latest phase', *New Left Review*, no. 18, pp. 73–84.

TAWNEY, R. H. (1952), *Equality*, 4th edn, Allen & Unwin.

Acknowledgements

Permission to reproduce the Readings in this volume is acknowledged from the following sources:

1 Richard D. Irwin Inc.
2 Prentice-Hall Inc.
3 Harvard University Press
4 H. G. Simon and the American Economic Association
5 R. J. Audley and BBC Publications
6 RAND Corporation and Little, Brown & Company
7 ABP International
9 W. A. Gamson
10 Harvard University Press
11 George Allen and Unwin Ltd and Stanford University Press
12 *Parliamentary Affairs*
13 Princeton University Press
14 Clarendon Press, Oxford
15 Longman
16 George Weidenfeld & Nicolson Ltd and Basic Books, Inc.
17 Monthly Review Press
18 Jonathan Cape Ltd and Macmillan & Company
19 Oxford University Press, Inc.
20 *Sociological Review*
21 American Political Science Association
23 American Political Science Association
24 C. A. Watts & Company Ltd

Author Index

Subject Index